G000276005

The THOMAS the TANK ENGINE MAN

Brian Sibley

The Story of the Reverend W. Awdry and his Really Useful Engines

HEINEMANN LONDON

In Memory of two people without whom
The Railway Series would not have been
what it is (and might not have existed at all)

Margaret Emily Awdry (1912 - 1989)

and

George Edward Vere Awdry (1916 - l994)

First published in Great Britain in 1995
by William Heinemann Ltd, an imprint of Reed International Books Ltd
Michelin House, 81 Fulham Road, London SW3 6RB

ISBN 0 434 96909 5

Printed in Spain

Contents List

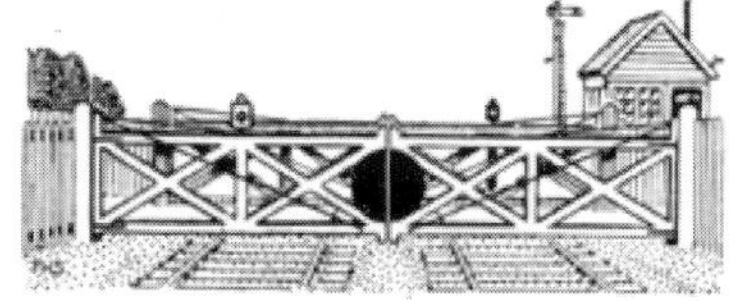

Point of Departure

It began with a telephone call: 'Do you know anything about the Thomas the Tank Engine Man?' It was John Forrest, then a radio producer with the B.B.C.'s Religious Broadcasting Department. I had worked with John on several religious programmes, and was known to have an obsessive fascination with children's books and their writers, having already made radio features about A. A. Milne, Lewis Carroll and J. M. Barrie.

However, I knew very little about the creator of *Thomas the Tank Engine*, other than the fact that he was the Reverend W. V. Awdry, a Church of England clergyman – hence, I deduced, the interest from Religious Broadcasting. But the question awoke my curiosity, and, by the end of our conversation, I had agreed to research, write and present a programme about Mr Awdry and his famous little engines.

I must confess to having felt a little apprehensive. For one thing, whilst I had read *The Three Railway Engines*, *Thomas the Tank Engine* and a few of the other early books, I was certainly not familiar with all the titles in the Railway Series. Also, and this I hesitate to confess, I was in no sense a railway buff. When I was small, it was my father – a lover (then and now) of everything to do with railways – who played with my clockwork Hornby 00 gauge train set, while I, to his great irritation, preferred making up stories about the people who worked in the station and playing with the farm animals that lived alongside the line. When I grew older, my feelings towards engines tended to be governed by where they took you – to the country or, even better, to the seaside.

However, having agreed to interview W. V. Awdry, I read the entire Railway Series and, by the time my producer and I set off to meet the author, I was not only steeped in the stories, I was bursting with questions. Happily, interviewer and interviewee hit it off on their first meeting and the result was an excellent programme, warmly received by the critics.

The work done, I found myself wondering whether the research I had started might not have another use – possibly a book about Mr Awdry and his engines. Two years of discussions with various publishers were followed by five years of silence; then, in 1993, Rosemary Debnam of Reed Children's Books decided that, with the approaching fiftieth anniversary of the Railway Series, the time, at last, had come – which is how I found myself sitting next to Wilbert Awdry at his 82nd birthday lunch. To my great delight, our conversation virtually picked up where it had left off seven years before.

That then is how this book came into being. It could not, however, have been written without a great deal of help and co-operation from others, and I record here my appreciation to them.

My greatest debt of gratitude goes to the Awdry family. To begin with, I drew on the interviews, recorded in 1986 for the radio broadcast, with Wilbert; his late wife, Margaret (who greatly impressed me with her warmth, hospitality and strength of character); and his son, Christopher. Later, I spent a great many hours in conversation with Wilbert Awdry, in person and in numerous (and usually *long*!) telephone calls.

Wilbert Awdry unhesitatingly gave me access to his meticulously-kept files of manuscripts and correspondence; to early drafts for an autobiography; to Awdry family papers and photographs; railway holiday journals recorded by Wilbert and his brother, George; and diaries kept by himself and by his mother, who recorded her son's day-to-day life from his birth until his marriage in 1938.

Subsequently, Wilbert Awdry read the typescript for this book and – assisted by his secretary Kathy Vickers – pointed out several errors, made numerous helpful suggestions, offered much additional information but never once asked for anything to be censored.

George Awdry, who died during the writing of this book, gave me several interviews during which he talked about many things, from memories of his and Wilbert's childhood to their later 'discovery' of the Island of Sodor. A former librarian, he well understood the needs of the researcher and made available to me several important documents and papers.

Christopher Awdry – for whom the stories were first told and who is now their storyteller – gave me a long interview and much valued assistance: identifying photographs, supplying railway information and reading the book in typescript. And whenever Christopher was off on one of his many jaunts in connection with the Railway Series, his wife Diana was always supremely helpful.

Wilbert Awdry's daughters, Veronica and Hilary – together with their respective husbands, Richard Chambers and Alfred Fortnam – gave me every assistance by sharing remembrances of their father and thoughts about his work as well as offering unhesitating encouragement when it was most needed.

His Royal Highness The Prince of Wales most generously made known to me his childhood feelings about the early books in the Railway Series which he received, as a first birthday present, from their author.

Eric Marriott – former Assistant Managing Director of Kaye & Ward, and editor of Wilbert Awdry's books from the third to the last, and twenty-sixth, title – took tremendous interest in this project and gave it his unstinting support by recalling the publishing history of the Railway Series; by allowing me access to invaluable archives; and by reading and commenting on parts of the typescript. What began as an act of co-operation, happily ended as one of friendship.

This book has also immeasurably benefited from conversations and correspondence with many other Really Useful People:

Mary Cadogan, an authority on so many aspects of children's literature; Brian Doyle, author of *The Who's Who of Children's Literature*; Miles Kington, writer and broadcaster; Professor Jeffrey Richards of the History Department at the University of Lancaster; and Michael Rosen, children's writer and broadcaster; all of whom generously contributed their critical opinions.

John Welch, former Sales Manager with Edmund Ward, for writing of his memories of selling the Railway Series.

Mrs Kate Holland, daughter of the late C. Reginald Dalby, for ferreting out information about her father and his career, and for permission to quote from his unpublished autobiography *Me: The Odyssey of a Nobody*.

Mrs Peggy Kenney, widow of the late John T. Kenney, for providing details of her husband's life and work.

Peter and Gunvor Edwards for their recollections of illustrating the last nine titles in the Railway Series to be written by Wilbert Awdry.

Clive Spong for talking about his work illustrating the titles written by Christopher Awdry.

Sir John Gielgud, Johnny Morris, William Rushton and Ringo Starr for memories of recording stories from the Railway Series.

Mrs Margaret Houlbrooke and Leonard Miall for information about Michael Barsley, the man who got *The Three Railway Engines* started on the right track.

Britt Allcroft and Angus Wright, of Britt Allcroft (Thomas) Ltd, for telling me how the *Thomas the Tank Engine and Friends* television series came into being.

Fiona Anderson for help in locating various archive recordings; Joan Bond, Librarian of the Catholic Central Library for providing information about Christian pacifism; the Reverend J. A. Coombs, Vicar of Emneth, for a copy of W. V. Awdry's *Notes for Visitors*; Lily Dean, College Secretary at St.

Peter's College (formerly St. Peter's Hall), Oxford, for access to files and a memorable guided tour; Ray Millard for lending items of correspondence with Wilbert Awdry; Philip Nokes, General Secretary of the Old Daunstseians Association, for background information on Dauntsey School; Corin Smith, Librarian of Wycliffe Hall, Oxford, for assistance with research and arranging for her colleague, John Gordon, to show me round the Hall; and the unknown historian of Ampfield whose notes on Vere Awdry's incumbency at St Marks provided vital information for the early chapters of the book.

Anthony Billett and Ralph Percival, whose respective theses (*Anglican Theological Colleges: Origins and Influences* and *Has Success Spoiled Thomas the Tank Engine?*) provided valuable information.

Denis Crutch, Richard Holliss, Michael Grosvenor Myer, Iona Opie and Edward Wakeling for their help with several literary puzzles.

Nicholas Jones and Charlotte Scott of Quanta who (as this book was nearing completion) began researching a television documentary about Mr Awdry for B.B.C. television's 'Bookmark' series, for so generously making available transcripts of interviews with the programme's contributors.

Sarah Devine, Assistant to Sir Andrew Lloyd Webber at The Really Useful Group Limited, for courteously replying to my request for information about Sir Andrew's aborted project to bring the Railway Series to television: 'As I am sure you can appreciate, Sir Andrew receives so many requests of this nature that it would be unfair for him to accept some and not others. It will not therefore be possible for him to contribute to your book.'

Ann Mills, for her homely hospitality during my visits to Gloucestershire; and Susan Price, Maureen Shakeshaft and Melanie White who, while looking after Mr Awdry, were always kind enough to look after me as well!

My friends at Reed Children's Books for their unflagging encouragement and unwavering patience during the long time in which it took for me to reach my destination: Penny Morris, Publisher, Properties and Licensed Characters Department; Rosemary Debnam, long-time associate of the Railway Series and latterly its editor and mine, who provided books, memories and much-needed items of research; Louise Cassell for checking and proof-reading the typescript; and Margaret Clark-Jones who did a vast amount of work in gathering and selecting illustrations and acting as designer and picture editor for the book.

Final thanks go to my father for giving me a very real sense of the romance of railways; to my mother for awakening in me passion for reading; and to my partner, David Weeks, for his intelligent – but affectionate – criticism of my work and, as always, for keeping me on the rails!

Oh, yes, and last (but by no means least) a special acknowledgement to John Forrest who started this whole business when he telephoned me and asked: 'Do you know anything about the Thomas the Tank Engine Man?'

Brian Sibley

The publishers also wish to thank the following for supplying additional picture material for this book: Packhams of Stroud, for copies of the Awdry family photographs (Plates I-III); Miss Valerie Petts, for permission to reproduce her painting of St Peter's College, Oxford (Plate IV); Britt Allcroft (Thomas) Ltd (Plate XXXII).

PROLOGUE

The Station Master's Office

'WELL, now,' says Wilbert Awdry in response to another of my interminable questions, 'if you want the answer to that, you'll have to go into the office and fetch me a folder: it's a green ring-binder file and you'll find it, under a pile of papers, on the third shelf down next to the filing cabinet.'

So, off I go. The sign on the door reads 'STATION MASTER', and inside the Station Master's office an agreeable clutter abounds: railway books, journals, magazines, maps and timetables; tottering piles of newspaper cuttings and clippings; and filing cabinets crammed with correspondence, much of it from young readers of the Railway Series.

It was here, in 1986, that I had my first conversations with Wilbert Awdry. I remember him then as a lean, slightly hunched figure, with a mane of silver hair and beetling brows that loured upon his spectacles, behind which twinkled sharp, blue-grey eyes. Puffing – engine-like – on a battered pipe, he had theorised about the personality of the steam engine. 'He's an extrovert,' he explained. 'Unless he is standing in a siding with his fire drawn, he has always got something to say. He likes people to know how he's getting on. For example, there's the goods engine who's always complaining of being badly treated.'

Giving a self-mocking chuckle – lest I should take him *too* seriously – he stoked his pipe with fresh tobacco, got up a new head of steam and was off once more: 'Then there's the express engine, bustling about saying, "Come on! Come on!", followed by a train of calm, unflappable coaches, saying, like dutiful wives, "Yes, dear, of *course*! Yes, dear, of *course*!", while all along you know they're thinking about much more important things, like when they're going to get a new coat of paint!'

Such views have occasionally got Wilbert Awdry into hot water, raising the hackles of those on the look-out for political incorrectness, and have even resulted in his books being banned from certain libraries. Other critical voices have vehemently condemned the Railway Series for being dull, predictable and repetitious; while admirers of the little books see them as inventive, imaginative and (with one or two exceptions, permissible in such a long series) written with wit, charm and energy.

On whatever side you come down, one thing is certain: nothing is going to change now; for although Wilbert's son, Christopher Awdry, continues to add new books to the series, the 'onlie begetter' of Thomas the Tank Engine and the others hasn't written about his famous engines for many years.

Although, at the age of 84, his mind is razor sharp, his physical health no longer allows him to be as active as he was: his beloved model railway gathers dust, he seldom gets into the office these days – hence my mission in search of the green folder – and he rarely puffs on one of his old pipes. He still smokes cigarettes, however, particularly when settling down with 'a good book' (by which he means, among others, P. G. Wodehouse, Agatha Christie, Hammond Innes, Georgette Heyer and Ellis Peters) or to talk about those engine characters that played such an important part in his life and which have guaranteed him some kind of immortality.

Despite almost weekly articles in the press, speculating on how much he earns from the sale of his books and all the subsidiary paraphernalia, Wilbert has a modest lifestyle: his only luxuries – apart from the cigarettes and fresh supplies of thick historical novels – are a video recorder which he uses to tape any good thrillers and Westerns that may get televised; a chair lift (originally installed for his late wife, Margaret) and the services of a live-in carer. His house, in Stroud, says much about his character: it is one of those sensible, four square, red-brick houses, such as a stationmaster might once have lived in – if only the railway line had been nearer.

Wilbert Awdry has spent over half his life being labelled an eccentric. His eccentricity, such as it is, is an abiding affection for the lost age of steam locomotion: an age that he has celebrated – and, in a very real sense, kept alive – by creating the characters in his children's books, which now sell all over the world.

And the children who read them still write to tell the author which of these little engine characters is their favourite – boastful Gordon, grumpy Henry, hard-working Edward, cheerful Percy or, most famous of all, mischievous Thomas the Tank Engine. They sometimes write to tell the author that they have spotted inconsistencies in the illustrations but, most of all, they write to ask questions. Thirty years ago, such questions tended to be along the lines of 'Can you tell where Toby keeps his coal?'; today, they're more likely to be: 'Does Thomas have a girlfriend?', 'Has Thomas ever become sick?', 'How old is Thomas?' or 'Does Thomas have summer holidays?'

Thomas and his friends are very much in evidence in the Station Master's office – and, indeed in the rest of his house: their smiling smoke-box faces are to be found on wastepaper bins, lampshades, clocks, trays, cushion covers, cups and saucers as well as on embroidered pictures worked by Margaret Awdry.

The things which Mr Awdry has around him are but a tiny fraction of a phenomenal merchandising enterprise of the kind usually associated with such characters as Mickey Mouse or Snoopy. There are currently over 800 products available, including Thomas lunch-boxes (as carried by Prince William on his first day at school), notebooks and stationery, bedside lights, duvet covers (with matching pillowslips), money-boxes, toothbrushes, nursery cutlery, 'mug and egg cup sets' and a Thomas plate on which to serve a meal of Thomas spaghetti shapes (signals, tracks, guards, Fat Controllers and Thomases) in tomato sauce.

There are also various three-dimensional steam train models. Some, improbably, are 'cuddly engines' made of soft fabrics; more authentically, there are engines to push along, pull along or wind up, and others ironically powered by electricity. The demand for Thomas merchandise is seemingly limitless: one company, Ertl, who manufacture die-cast metal toys based on the Railway Series, put three million character engines into the market during 1994 alone. And the earning power of such products is substantial; Ertl, who have been marketing Thomas toys for twelve years, estimate their annual turnover at around four and a half million pounds.

This vast industry is largely a spin-off from the highly successful film series – 100 episodes and more to come – produced by the company Britt Allcroft (Thomas) Ltd, first shown on television and now available on twelve videos with worldwide sales running into millions. Yet, for all the ingenuity with which these films are produced (and the skill with which they have been marketed) their success is founded on twenty-six little books whose author is described on their title-pages as 'The Rev. W. Awdry'.

So what is the reason for the success of these books? Is it their text: sharp and tightly written with sly little jokes and rhythmic sounds but, nevertheless, always true to railway lore? Or is it the illustrations: capturing the hustle and bustle of station and shed and those trackside scenes – embankments of spring flowers, rolling meadows of summer lushness, whirling autumn leaves, brooding clouds of winter rain and frosted Christmas-card landscapes – depicted in vivid, iridescent colours?

Perhaps the reason children first come to love the books is rather more prosaic. For Brian Doyle, writer on children's literature, it is all a matter of size – or, rather, lack of it: 'They can be slipped into small pockets without any trouble at all, to be taken out at convenient (or, indeed, inconvenient) moments during the day to be read or looked at or chuckled over.' Adults may refer to them as 'little books' but, to a child, the Railway Series – like the books of Beatrix Potter – are essentially child-sized.

Sales of Wilbert Awdry's books, in their familiar oblong format with brightly-coloured illustrations, total some twenty-five million copies; and, in addition, the stories now appear in many other versions – at the last count there were over 200 titles – including board books, bath books, lift-the-flap books, pop-up books, peep-through books, press-out model books, easy-to-read books, early learning books, sticker-books and, most recently a 'noisy book' with six buttons which the young reader can press in order to hear various sounds from the railway – including the voice of the Fat Controller himself saying 'Really Useful Engine'. Wilbert Awdry's characters – appearing in all this diversity of shapes and sizes – have now reached total worldwide sales of fifty million copies, making him the most successful children's writer of the century.

The original stories were written to be read aloud and a few years after they were published a record was produced of the author doing just that. Since then the stories have been recorded on disc by Johnny Morris and William Rushton, on radio by Sir John Gielgud, and on the soundtrack of the television series by former Beatle, Ringo Starr. Most of all, of course, they have been read aloud by many millions of parents.

In reading these stories to their children, parents have come to know the characters and their various exploits every bit as well as their offspring. Some years ago, Mrs Pat Powell (a mother of three) wrote a charming letter of mock complaint to the author:

> Have you ever tried to explain to elderly neighbours that when your children are yelling 'Rubbish' or 'Dirty Objects' at each other, they are not being rude, but merely indulging in literary quotations? Have you ever had to undergo the funny looks of passers-by as you choo-choo-choo your way up a hill with a twin push-chair with son No. 3 standing on the back letting go with violently piercing whistles? Have you ever had a child refuse to do as he is bade, replying 'It's bad for my swerves'? Well, I have and it's all your fault.

What is, perhaps, surprising about the continued success of the Railway Series – and it certainly surprises its creator – is that few of today's youngsters who know the books by heart have ever seen a steam train, let alone travelled in one; in fact, neither have most of the parents who buy the books for their children. To children, the Island of Sodor (home of the Fat Controller's railway) is a Never-Never Land. Like other such places – one thinks of Wonderland, Narnia, Oz and Middle-earth – it is both fantastic and, at the same time, absolutely real. To adults, the stories have about them an atmosphere of yearning romance, a wistful glimpse back in time to a less complicated age.

'In common with other skilled story-spinners,' writes Mary Cadogan, authority on children's literature, 'Awdry has created a microcosmic world in which his engaging cast of headstrong or shy, boastful or understanding engine "characters" have flourished and become archetypal. We continue to enjoy their cosy but exhilarating exploits which transport us, through the excitements of steam-train journeys, into a nostalgically serene era that Awdry has contrived to keep alive in the here and now.'

Apart from which, they may also hint at a desire to know that we are on the right track, travelling along the straight and narrow-gauge; which may be why so many clergymen seem to have a passion for steam railways. 'Some deep sense of affinity,' wrote George Hill, 'seems to draw parsons to firebox and footplate. It must be something to do with a correspondence between steam as a driving force and the spirit which bloweth where it listeth, or with the symbolism of rails guiding the soul to its predestined terminus.'

As for stations, Jeffrey Richards and John M. MacKenzie, writing in their book, *The Railway Station: A Social History*, describe these buildings, whether large or small, as being essentially ecclesiastical:

> *If the station is seen as a cathedral or chapel, it can also be seen to possess in its heyday a Bible every bit as imposing and sometimes even as impenetrable as the Authorized Version* (Bradshaw), *incense (steam), and liturgical chanting ('The train now standing at platform 3 is . . .', 'Close the doors and stand clear', 'All change').*

'Railways and the Church,' Wilbert Awdry once remarked, 'both had their heyday in the mid-nineteenth century; both own a great deal of Gothic-style architecture which is expensive to maintain; both are regularly assailed by critics; and both are firmly convinced that they are the best means of getting man to his ultimate destination!'

Part of this almost religious mystique about railways comes, perhaps, from the observation of ritual, a sense of regularity and order, which is both satisfying and reassuring. The fact that timetables must be followed, lines kept to and signals obeyed, has its own appeal for young readers who, as Jeffrey Richards observes, 'love ritual and repetition – especially repeated readings of the same stories'.

If true, then the analogy might reasonably be extended to suggest that engines are like human beings. The late Reverend Teddy Boston, a long-time friend of Wilbert Awdry (who appears in the Railway Series as the Fat Clergyman) once said: 'The steam engine is the nearest thing to a living being made by man'; and certainly Thomas and friends succeed, and survive, because of their strongly drawn human personalities. Readers – young and old – identify with the engines, sharing in their happiness and their sadness; seeing in the struggles, triumphs and failures of the railway engines a reflection of their own hopes, fears, ambitions and frustrations.

The stories of those engines are now famous throughout the world, and this book – the result of many visits to the Station Master's office – tells how they came to be written and of the man who wrote them.

CHAPTER ONE

"Eyes full of twinkles"

'HE is not a pretty baby.' A somewhat uncomplimentary remark, particularly since it was written by the baby's mother, but there were, apparently, compensations: he was 'healthy looking' and had 'a quantity of soft brown hair'. Most significantly, he was described as having 'bright blue-grey eyes that are full of twinkles'.

These notes appear in a stocky manuscript-book, on the inside page of which appear (in strong block capitals) the words: 'WILBERT VERE AWDRY. RECORD BOOK.' In over one hundred and sixty pages, Wilbert's mother, Lucy Awdry, lovingly noted just about everything that happened to 'Baby' during the first two years of his life, together with press cuttings and dozens of photographs, often framed with decorations delicately painted in watercolours.

One of the first of these, within a border of stylised flowers and foliage, shows Wilbert with a half smile and a bright, focused look that suggests a mix of curiosity and concentration; qualities which, like the twinkling eyes, Wilbert Awdry still possesses.

He arrived at 5.22 on the afternoon of 15th June, 1911, at Ampfield Vicarage in Romsey, Hampshire. Lucy Awdry described her newborn son as a short ('but very perfectly formed') baby who had 'long fingers and toes', a 'mouse-face' (with the 'Awdry chin and ears') and 'a loud and persistent voice'. Loud enough to inspire his father, the Reverend Vere Awdry, to pen a little verse in Wilbert's *Record Book*:

Who's dat squalling on Daddy's bed?
Little fat baby with face very red.
Fill his little mouth with a little boiled water,
Dat's de bes' cure for a little cross snorter.

Vere Awdry also made a list of 'Sounds which at sundry times have led Wilbert's deluded relations to rush to his assistance', including: 'Cockerel "A"; Cockerel "B"; Cockerel "C" (since deceased); a Traction Engine; a Concertina; Mary the Ass; Sundry Motor Cars; Romsey Town Brass Band; Cows in the Field Opposite; the Scullery Pump; an Owl and the Saw-Mill.'

Although this light-hearted catalogue is indicative of Vere Awdry's youthful personality, Wilbert's father was fifty-seven years old when his son was born. Vere was himself a late child of his own father, John Wither Awdry, who was fifty-nine when his ninth son and thirteenth child (of an eventual family of fifteen) was born in 1854.

John Wither Awdry (Wilbert's grandfather) was the eldest son of John Jeremiah Awdry and Jane Bigg-Wither, a family of landed gentry living in a grand country house at Notton, a hamlet within the parish of Lacock, about three miles from Chippenham in Wiltshire. John Wither Awdry had been educated at Winchester and Christ Church, Oxford, where, in 1816, he obtained a Bachelor of Arts degree. Four years later he became a Master of Arts and a Fellow of Oriel College, and in 1822 was called to the Bar. It was the beginning of a distinguished legal career which led to his appointment, in 1830, as a Puisne Judge in Bombay, a position which carried with it a knighthood. Before leaving for India, Sir John married a cousin, Sarah Maria Awdry, the daughter of the Reverend Jeremiah Awdry, absentee Vicar of the Essex parish of Felstead.

In the first half of the nineteenth century, India was controlled by the East India Company (the British government did not assume rule until 1858, the year after the Indian Mutiny) and it was in the Company's courts in Bombay that Sir John – as British judges had done since 1781 – sought to administer 'justice, equity and good conscience'. Sir John clearly discharged his duties well since, after nine years service on the bench, he was appointed Chief Justice of the Supreme Court in Bombay.

1839, the year in which Sir John received his promotion, saw the death of his wife, Sarah, who had borne her husband two boys and a girl: John (who died within a year of his birth), John Jeremiah and Jane. As was customary at the time, Sir John – being a professional man with a young family to care for – quickly remarried, taking for his bride Frances Ellen Carr, the daughter of the then Bishop of Bombay. A year after their marriage, Sir John's new wife gave him a son, Thomas, who was the first of what was to be a large second family. Another son, William, was born in 1842, the year in which Sir John – learning that his father, John Jeremiah Awdry, was ill – returned to England and the family home at Notton. Two years later, at the age of 78, the elder John Awdry died and his son inherited Notton House and the family estate.

Notton House was an imposing three-storey building, flanked on each side by two-storey wings with long elegant windows. The plain facade was relieved by balustraded balconies outside the second-storey windows and above the pillared entrance, while the rigid formality of the building was softened by an extensive growth of Virginia creeper.

Sir John resumed his legal career in 1848, when he was made Chairman of the Wiltshire Quarter Sessions, an appointment he held for the next eighteen years. During that time, Sir John also served as a Commissioner under the Oxford University Reform Act of 1854, and was sent to report on various aspects of the law of Jersey.

The Awdry family continued to grow with a new birth almost every year: Sarah, Ambrose, Frances, Charles, James, Elizabeth, Herbert and, in 1854, Wilbert Awdry's father, Vere. Two more daughters – Mary and Priscilla – completed the family of twelve children, all born within nineteen years of marriage.

A picture of everyday life at Notton House, in 1873, is found in a diary kept by a cousin, Margaret Jane Awdry, who – due to the illness of her father, the Reverend Walter Herbert Awdry – lived for a time with her aunts and uncles at Notton. Margaret (known as Daisy) described a social life that was clearly very different from that which she experienced at her father's terraced house on the Isle of Man. There were French lessons and innumerable church services, but there were also dinners and dances ('We had great fun. We danced Quadrilles, Lancers, Waltzes etc.') and games of Whist and Bezique. Outdoor activities included blackberrying and nut-gathering expeditions as well as such garden entertainments as battledore and shuttlecock and one of Victorian England's universal diversions: 'We played croquet all the afternoon and I am so tired I have not a leg to stand up on!'

There was also a potentially more dangerous pastime: 'I had my first try at archery today. I only got two arrows in the whole time . . . a blue and a white . . . but Uncle John makes me frightened; he goes so near the target that with my bad shots I am very afraid of shooting him . . .'

Life at Notton House was not always harmonious and young Daisy recounts tedious evenings when a silence settled on the inhabitants as well as various moments of awkwardness that left her feeling 'dull and gloomy':

> I put my foot in it today at Notton. I marched into the drawing room and to my dismay found about a dozen people in the room, and a heap of strangers to whom I had to be severally introduced. It was fearful. I wished myself anywhere at that moment; but all I could do was get very red.

In one of the earliest entries in her diary, Daisy refers to her uncle as 'the great Sir John', and photographs of him show a daunting figure with a high forehead, a firm-set jaw, steely eyes and long, white side-whiskers; while Lady Awdry, a substantial woman dressed in black, with a white lace cap on her centrally-parted hair, is the epitome of Victorian matronhood. These photographs of Sir John and Lady Awdry with various members of their large family outside Notton House are believed to have been taken by the pioneering photographer, William Henry Fox Talbot, who lived at nearby Lacock Abbey.

Sir John Awdry's children had grown into a tribe of highly individual characters. John Jeremiah Awdry, the eldest son by the first marriage was a gifted carpenter, but chose instead a career in the army, serving as a Lieutenant with the 3rd Foot Regiment (known as The Buffs). In 1862, at the age of 28, he contracted Malta fever and died. John Jeremiah's carpentry tools were inherited by his young half-brother, Vere, who shared his manual dexterity. Years later, those same tools passed to Wilbert, who used them for, among other things, the building of his various model railway layouts.

Thomas Awdry, the first child of Sir John's second marriage (and, on the death of John Jeremiah, the family heir) married a cousin, Mary Olivier Awdry and went to New Zealand, later returning to settle in Salisbury. Another son, Ambrose, joined the Royal Engineers, rose to the rank of Major and was serving in India, as A.D.C. to the Governor of Madras, when he was killed in a riding accident.

Charles Awdry, three years Ambrose's junior, was destined to become the financial success of the family. On the strict orders of his father, Charles read for – and was called to – the Bar. However, he found that Briefs were very slow in coming, and Charles began looking for other career prospects. He had become friendly with a young Mr Smith, later the 'Son' of the stationers, W. H. Smith & Son, and accepted his suggestion to join the family firm. Charles Awdry was shown no favouritism and was expected to work his way up in the company from the bottom. Through ability and hard work, however, Charles eventually became a partner and, following the death of his parents, had the financial means with which to save Notton House and the estate.

The seventh of Sir John's children was James Awdry, whom Daisy Awdry described in her diary as 'very jolly' and 'not in the least like his brothers and sisters'. In November 1873, James, who was twenty-five and an officer in the Merchant Service, fell in love with the Awdrys' governess, Kate Chittendon, and scandalised the family by declaring his intention to marry her. Sir John and Lady Awdry, considering Miss Chittendon to be their son's inferior, opposed the union. Daisy – without knowing what she was reporting – recorded the occasion in her diary:

> Worked this afternoon in the school-room as all the rest were gone to Bath. Miss Chittendon lets me, she teaches so well; I wonder if I shall ever teach like her.
> There is something up with Jim tonight; but I heard naught about it. He had no dinner and has not appeared all evening – neither has Miss Chittendon, and there have been mysterious 'talks' and 'wants to speaks', and the others have been very silent – more so even than usual. I'm glad I don't live here.

James left Notton House the next day followed, at a later date, by Kate. Married in 1876, the couple emigrated to New Zealand.

The young Vere Awdry had a strong affection for two of his brothers: William, twelve years his senior, and Herbert, who was just three years older than him. 'They were,' says Wilbert, 'the kindest to him who, as the youngest boy in a large family, was of not much account.' It was by combining the names of William and Herbert that Vere got the name 'Wilbert' with which he later christened his son.

Photographs of William Awdry show a young man with a solemn expression and a fine set of mutton-chop whiskers. The high forehead and the determined line of the jaw, common features among the Awdrys, suggest a man of single-mindedness and ambition. At Balliol College, Oxford, he achieved academic and athletic success, receiving a First in Greats and becoming a Rowing Blue. In 1866, William Awdry became a Fellow of Queens College and, two years later, was appointed Second Master at Winchester public school.

At the surprisingly early age of thirty, William was made Headmaster of Hurstpierpoint School in West Sussex, a position he held for seven years until appointed Principal of Chichester Theological College. From 1886, for the next thirteen years, William was Vicar of Amport in Hampshire, after which he was consecrated Bishop Suffragan of Southampton.

In 1896, William Awdry went to Japan as the Anglican Bishop of Osaka and a year later became Bishop of South Tokyo where he remained until 1908 when ill-health caused him to resign. Aged only sixty-eight, but after a lifetime crowded with activity and Christian service, William Awdry died at Winchester in 1910.

Many years later, Wilbert Awdry had an opportunity to read his Uncle William's missionary papers and diaries which showed that, ecumenically, the Bishop was far in advance of his time. In the late 1800s and early 1900s, the Church of England, the Roman Catholic Church and the Free Churches not only kept themselves to themselves, but openly competed with each another by stressing the differences between the denominations. Such was the situation encountered by Bishop William in Japan where, due to denominational differences, converts moving from one area to another did not always find the Christian welcome for which they had hoped.

After much thought and prayer, Bishop William decided that the only way forward was for each denomination to cease operating in isolation and begin placing emphasis on their basic unity in Christian belief. He urged clergy to meet for united worship and for the discussion of mutual problems, hoping that through friendship and the furtherance of common aims, sectarian distrust might be allayed and the way paved for the formation of a Church in Japan which would combine the best elements of each denomination. 'He was,' says Wilbert, 'broadminded enough to see and urge that Unity did not necessarily mean uniformity – of worship for instance – a great advance for those somewhat rigid times.'

When a breakdown in the Bishop's health resulted in his having to return from Japan, the movement – the first of its kind – was abandoned, although William's hopes for ecumenism were eventually to be revived by other church organisations in the world, such as the United Church of South India.

When, in 1965, Wilbert Awdry retired as a parish priest and undertook 'freelance duties', he too discovered the extent to which Christians of different denominations hold matters of faith and belief in common. Like his uncle before him, however, Wilbert also came to realise that differences in the form of worship remain a not inconsiderable obstacle to unity. On arriving at a church, Wilbert recalls, he would invariably be greeted by one of the wardens who would say: 'We just have an ordinary service, Vicar.' Wilbert would then give them what he considered to be 'an ordinary service', only to be told, when it was over: 'Our Vicar doesn't do it quite like you did,' or 'Our Vicar normally leaves out that bit, and puts another bit in there!' Nevertheless, Wilbert's delight in the differences between denominations, and within his own, show him as sharing the religious tolerance of Bishop William.

Vere Awdry's other favourite brother, Herbert (or Bert) was the nearest to him in age and had a personality that it was impossible not to like. When, for example, Daisy Awdry met the 22-year-old Bert in 1873, he made quite an impression on his young cousin. 'I wish I had a big brother like him,' she confided to her diary, 'I think he is so nice and really good, and not like other young men who hate their homes and go elsewhere.' A photograph of him, taken when he was in his mid-twenties, shows a clean-cut youth with a sharp, slightly up-tilted nose and arched eyebrows giving him a pleasingly quizzical expression.

Herbert was eventually to become Classics Master at Wellington College, Crowthorne, a post which he held for upwards of thirty years. He was a regular lecturer on the annual Hellenic Society Tours of Greece, and amassed a fascinating collection of walking sticks and shepherd's crooks.

Never marrying, Herbert eventually acquired a reputation for being something of an eccentric. For example, he would often arrive at his local railway station in a great rush, only to find that he had no money with which to buy a train ticket. The Booking-clerk, becoming used to this situation, would issue a ticket and take Herbert's silver half-hunter watch as a pledge that the debt would eventually be paid.

In the days of penny-farthing bicycles, Herbert was a familiar sight pounding along the Berkshire lanes at great speed, having barely allowed himself sufficient time to keep an appointment. 'On one such occasion,' recalls Wilbert Awdry, 'Uncle Bert hit a stone or pothole and landed on the roadside. He was undamaged physically, a bush having broken his fall, but he had torn his trousers in an embarrassing place. As he was due to take the chair at a meeting, this was disastrous. Fortunately, the next passer-by happened to be wearing a long overcoat and Uncle Bert persuaded the man to lend it to him. Afterwards, he returned the coat with a letter of thanks and a sovereign in the pocket to compensate for the inconvenience caused. Uncle Bert was highly amused to receive, a few days later, a somewhat stiff note of acknowledgement together with a tract advocating temperance!'

Of the Awdry girls, the youngest was Priscilla, or Prilly. Described by her nephew, Wilbert, as 'romantic and impractical and devoted to cats', she never married but kept house for her brother Bert. Two of the sisters, Sarah and Mary (known in the family as Polly) married clergymen, although Sarah's husband, the Reverend Luke Walford, died within a year of marriage and Polly's marriage to the egotistical Reverend Frederic Daustini Cremer was far from happy. Polly, who was Vere Awdry's favourite sister was a keen, 'green-fingered' gardener, a gifted sketch-artist and a woman of character, originality and humour: all of which qualities were ignored by Frederic Cremer. Family legend has it that the reason Polly made such a poor match was that Frances insisted on playing 'gooseberry' whenever a likely young man visited Notton and paid attentions to her sisters; Mr Cremer proving the only potential suitor with enough self-assurance to withstand Frances' mischief-making. Interference from Frances was also blamed for the fact that her other sister, Prilly, remained a spinster.

Frances (or, as the family called her, Fanny) was the fifth child of Sir John's second marriage. Wilbert describes his aunt as having been 'a somewhat peculiar and temperamental girl'; however, she had a gift for storytelling and wrote books with intensely moral themes, one of which Daisy

Awdry mentions in her diary: 'We have been reading Fanny's story on "Indian Children in the Snow and Ice". I like it so much, I only wish I could write something as good.'

Fanny Awdry had several literary friends including one of the most successful writers in the school of didactic Christian literature, Charlotte M. Yonge. Miss Yonge, who was associated with the Oxford Movement, was the author of *The Daisy Chain*, *The Chaplet of Pearls* and more than 150 other improving titles. Believing in self-denial and the inferiority of women, Charlotte Yonge never married. Neither did Fanny Awdry, although she was wooed by Reverend William Archibald Spooner, a friend of her brother, William. Dr Spooner, who later became Warden of New College, Oxford, had a nervous habit of transposing the initial letters or syllables of words with unintentionally amusing results, as when he told a student: 'You have deliberately tasted two worms and you can leave Oxford by the town drain.' Such entertaining infelicities of speech made Dr Spooner famous and came to be known as spoonerisms. Despite – or, maybe, because of – Spooner's celebrity, Fanny Awdry, the meddler in other people's marital chances, declined his suit.

This was the colourful group of personalities amongst whom Wilbert Awdry's father grew up. The young Vere Awdry's ambition was to go into the army, but commissions had to be bought and Sir John, having already done that for his sons John and Ambrose (both of whom had died while serving with the army), argued that he could not afford a third commission. Just as Sir John had earlier tried to force Vere's brother, Charles, to make the law his profession, so he now insisted that Vere become a solicitor. In the event, Sir John's wishes were again to be frustrated. After Vere had been admitted to the profession, his father bought him a partnership in a firm of solicitors in Marlow, Buckinghamshire. 'Having no enthusiasm for the job,' says Wilbert, 'Father's chief interests at the time were rowing, bell-ringing and the local Corps of Volunteers.'

Family memory has it that, after a few years, the senior partner decamped, as a result of which the firm had to be wound up and a number of creditors paid off. Sir John was obliged to help Vere clear the company debts, which involved him in considerable expense – more, in fact, than it would have cost to have bought an army commission. Shortly afterwards, in 1878, Sir John Awdry died at the age of seventy-three. Vere, then twenty-four, was determined to quit the legal profession, but was unsure what career to follow. One of his two favourite brothers, William Awdry, who, in 1879, had become Principal of Chichester

Theological College, suggested that Vere join him there for a few months, 'with no strings attached', in order to think through his future.

Vere eventually decided to remain at Chichester and prepare for Ordination. In 1887, Vere Awdry was ordained Deacon and appointed to the curacy of the parish of North Bradley with Southwick, near Trowbridge in Wiltshire. In August of that year, Vere was married to his 'beloved Margaret' – Margaret Emily Mann, a young woman he had met and fallen in love with when he was working at Marlow. Their happiness was short-lived as, the following year, Margaret died in childbirth. It was the first of many tragedies that were to afflict Vere Awdry over the years. The baby, a girl, survived and was christened Hildred Margaret Vere. One of the child's godmothers was Vere's widowed sister, Sarah Walford, who, since the untimely death of her husband, had become 'a universal aunt' and who now came to keep house for her brother.

Sarah accompanied Vere when, in 1891, he became Vicar of Broad Hinton, near Swindon, in Wiltshire, a move overshadowed by sadness. That June, the two year old Hildred died of convulsions. Four months later, Vere remarried; he took for his bride, Mary Louisa Mann, Hildred's other godmother and a cousin of his first wife, Margaret.

A year later, in November 1892, Mary bore her husband a daughter, Bridget Hildred Vere and, two years later, a son, Carol Edward Vere. In 1895, the family left Broad Hinton for Hampshire. Vere Awdry had been offered the parish of Ampfield, near Romsey, a living that was in the gift of the Dowager Lady Heathcote of Hursley Park whose husband, Sir William, had been a cousin and a great friend of Sir John Awdry.

Vere Awdry was a popular incumbent. A paramount concern – and one which doubtless endeared him to the local population – was the welfare of the children of the parish. Shortly before his arrival, the village school had been declared unfit and Vere embarked on a scheme to build a new school. Although the land was donated, the building costs had to be raised and, as the Parish Council minutes record, this was only achieved as a result of the 'indefatigable efforts' of the Vicar. Vere also introduced a twice-monthly children's service in church – an innovation which, doubtless, helped inspire Wilbert's later devotion to work with children.

Various little parish traditions were begun during Vere's time as Vicar: one such being the decoration of the church for Easter Sunday. Every spring, a corner of the vicarage field was filled with daffodils which the children were allowed to pick and bring into church; they were also encouraged to make up little bunches of primroses and, on Palm Sunday, were given lengths of coloured wool with which to tie up their posies for Easter Day.

Even though he had scarcely turned forty, parishioners were soon referring to Vere Awdry as being 'like a father', and Ampfield Vicarage was seen as a repository of advice, wisdom and practical help. The villagers knew, for example, that Mr and Mrs Awdry always kept a supply of simple medicinal remedies and they would go to the Vicarage for the treatment of minor ailments – always being careful to call at the *back* door!

Whilst making one or two modernisations at Ampfield (such as the introduction of church lamps instead of candles), Vere Awdry was in many ways conservative and certainly lacked his brother William's open attitude towards the Free Churches. While Sir William Heathcote had been alive, all tenants on the estate had to be 'of good character and members of the Church of England'; in fact, it was the landlord's proud boast that, in his village, there were 'no dissenters'. However, following Sir William's death, in 1881, this rigidly observed rule was relaxed and, within twenty years, there were sufficient followers of Methodism for a Primitive Methodist chapel to be built in Ampfield.

Vere Awdry – who had to walk past the chapel each day on his way to St Marks – did not welcome the presence of Nonconformists in the village and speaking from his pulpit, and in a letter to the local paper, he accused the chapel's minister of bringing schism into a previously united parish. The Methodist minister responded that he was simply providing a place of worship for those with Nonconformist convictions as well as offering Christian charity to anyone of any denomination.

When, in 1899, the Bishop of Winchester visited the parish of Ampfield, Vere Awdry was obliged to complete a confidential questionnaire in which he was asked: 'What places of worship are there in your parish not in connexion with the Church of England?' and 'What information can you give as to the numbers attending?' Vere noted the opening, during the previous year, of the Methodist chapel, adding: 'I cannot give accurate information as people are shy of acknowledging their defection, and can name only 6 or 7 families who make a practice of *regular* attendance there, having entirely ceased to attend church.'

Chapel-goers might, perhaps, have been forgiven for being 'shy' since they earned the contempt of employees on the Heathcote estate (who remained true to the church) and they experienced all kinds of minor humiliation, as when non-chapel children used to take gorse-branches and beat an old donkey living in the field next to the chapel, so that its agonised braying would disrupt the chapel sermons. Despite such annoyances, the chapel survived and was noted for its enthusiastic singing and for the excellence of the annual hot-cross bun tea, served on Good Friday, which also attracted a number of children from the church-going congregation. Completing the Bishop's questionnaire, Vere Awdry wrote: 'I have fancied a greater amount of indifference since the opening of the chapel owing no doubt partly to the influence of free teas and the other usual means employed to attract.'

At the time of the Bishop's visitation, Vere Awdry gave figures for church attendance as averaging 'about 50 to 60' on Sunday Morning and 'about 70 to 80' on Sunday Evening, plus 'about 45' schoolchildren. As to the 'moral condition of the district', Vere reported: '[It] is I think on the whole good, there being an almost entire absence of illegitimacy. Drinking is small and notably less since the change of Landlord (about 2 years ago) of our Village Inn.'

Although a serious man, Vere Awdry was no sobersides; he organised concert-parties and entertainments and participated in a pageant in Romsey in which he played the part of William of Wykeham, the fourteenth-century bishop of Winchester and Chancellor of England, who was hounded from power by John of Gaunt, but later pardoned and reinstated by Richard II. Wykeham was also the founder of New College, Oxford, and England's first public school, Winchester College. Wilbert Awdry has a photograph of his father splendidly attired in bishop's cope and mitre and looking every inch the prelate and statesman.

In April 1900, there was once more sadness in the Awdry household when the eight-year old Bridget died of appendicitis. The parishioners raised the sum of £3.18.1½ 'in memoriam B. H. V. A.'; while, in the vicarage drawing-room, photographs and mementoes of the dead child resided on what was referred to as the 'Bridget table'.

For a time following Bridget's death, Vere Awdry ceased making his regular visits to the local school, perhaps finding the presence of the children too painful a reminder of his loss. At home, Vere drew increasingly close to his sole surviving child, the six-year-old, Carol. When the parish fountain, standing just below the Vicarage, was rebuilt in 1900, it was young Carol who assisted his father by placing the keystone in the new arch.

A major interest which united father and son, and which was to have far-reaching effects on members of the family as yet unborn, began a few years later. As Vere Awdry noted in a hand-written account of 'The "A. M. R." : Ampfield (or Awdry) Model Railway': 'In 1906 or thereabouts, my boy aged 12 acquired a Model Steam Locomotive and 2 coaches, passenger and guard's-van, No 3 [2½"] gauge, and a certain amount of tin-plate rail.'

The locomotive was powered by steam and was, as Wilbert Awdry describes it, 'a passable representation of a Stirling (Great Northern Railway) Single'; the rolling-stock, however, was rather less authentic:

> The coaches were not of any particular pattern nor very like real ones, but they did for a while for want of better. Later I built two 4 wheeled coaches, turning the wheels for the same on my small lathe out of birch wood. These coaches were better though still easily capable of improvements; but, with the others, they made a train of decent length . . .

Carpentry was one of Vere Awdry's particular skills, inherited along with a number of woodworking tools from his half-brother, John Jeremiah Awdry. He had a workshop on the upper floor of an outhouse and for many years examples of his carpentry survived within the parish, such as the wooden sills for flower arrangements in each of the church windows. One Christmas, years later Vere would make his son, Wilbert, a scaled-down carpenter's bench and a set of tools: 'It was,' says the recipient, 'the best Christmas present I ever had.'

Various changes and developments took place within the church, including the removal of doors from the pews; and the abandonment of the totally enclosed pews (once used by the local gentry) in order to make way for choir stalls. Writing in her diary, more than fifty years earlier, Selina, Lady Heathcote had described these privileged seating arrangements as seen through the eyes of her five-year-old son, Charlie, who had asked his mother on returning from his first visit to church: 'What was the thing we went into, like a carriage with cushions in it, but it wasn't a carriage because it had no wheels?' The changes made in 1904 were not totally democratising, however, since the gentry still had reserved seating in the front rows.

A further tragedy hit the Awdry family in 1908 when Mary Louisa Awdry died of cancer. Grief-stricken once more, Vere again withdrew from some of his parish activities and, for a time, ceased visiting the school. Although Carol, now fourteen years of age, was attending school at Marlborough, the convention of the day made it essential for Vere to have someone keep house for him. Accordingly, Vere's niece, Edith Simeon, who was on the staff of Winchester High School and who had often cycled over to see her relatives at Ampfield, gave up her job and became his housekeeper.

Edith's closest friend on the staff at the High School was Lucy Louisa Bury who had often accompanied Edith on the cycle trip to visit Vere and Mary Awdry. When Edith became housekeeper at Ampfield Vicarage, Lucy – who was the daughter of a Darjeeling tea-planter – continued her visits. She got on well with Vere and it wasn't long before he asked her to marry him. At the time of her death in 1972, Lucy Awdry was in her nineties, which suggests that she must have been in her mid- to late twenties (and at least twenty-five years Vere's junior) at the time of their marriage in July 1909.

For the second time in a little over twenty years, Vere Awdry had married within a year of his previous wife's death. Despite their big difference in age, the couple were happily married and Vere once again picked up the threads of his life. Vere resumed visits to the village school, lending the glebe field for 'organised games', providing a piano, slates, sand-trays, books, balls and cartridges and targets for the older boys to practice rifle-shooting.

A new lightness of heart can be detected in pieces of humorous doggerel written out in a book which would later contain entries by his son, Wilbert, and his grandson, Christopher. One charming set of verses, part of which follows, is entitled 'Spring Cleaning (by a victim)':

Of all the horrors known to man
Please to imagine if you can
Anything more frightful than
That terrible Spring Cleaning.
It takes your appetite away
At breakfast when your wife doth say
'My dear we must begin today
The Annual Spring Cleaning.'

In vain a respite do you plead
Your wife and girls are all agreed
That the whole house at once doth need
A regular Spring Cleaning.
You feel such suddenness not fair
But those grim dragons do not care
For you, you may go anywhere
But shan't prevent Spring Cleaning.

The long-suffering husband discovers 'his hat is gone from off its hook'; he 'can't find an important book'; his 'study table is upset' and his shoes 'impossible to get' (since 'the floors are slippery and wet, and sloppy from Spring Cleaning'). Even after the victim is 'hunted out from room to room, choked by the dust raised by the broom', the catalogue of woes goes on:

As to your room you try to pass
You tread upon some picture glass
And someone bellows out: 'You ass
Have you forgot Spring Cleaning?'
Forgot! You've badly cut your toe
And while you try to staunch the flow
You feel you could say more than 'Oh!
Bother this vile Spring Cleaning.'

Colds come from windows opened wide
And though you sneeze out your inside
Those cruel Tyrants but deride
Your horror of Spring Cleaning.
And when tired out and in despair
You sink exhausted in a chair
A soapy swab drops on your hair
As if *you* need Spring Cleaning.

You jump up quickly in your wrath
And pitch head first into a bath
Put by the girls right in your path
With water for Spring Cleaning.
They laugh to see the plight you're in
Although you've badly barked your shin
And are soaked thro: right to the skin
They revel in Spring Cleaning.

There's not a carpet on the floor
You dare not open any door
Your heart's quite broke. How you abhor
This merciless Spring Cleaning.
And when its done and all your pain
Is over – well, you feel it's vain
For next year will return again
The horrors of Spring Cleaning.

The new Mrs Awdry also demonstrated a talent for versifying. On one of her visits to Ampfield, in the autumn of 1908, she had written:

Ampfield Oaks and Ampfield Beeches
Gleam and glow with autumn fires.
Cloistered in dark shiny leafage
Ampfield Church to Heaven retires.

Ampfield dogs are long and friendly
Ampfield children dear and round
Ampfield has the nicest Vicarage
For quite forty miles around.

Three years later, following the birth of her baby boy on 15th June, 1911, Lucy added two more verses:

Ampfield Roads are hot and dusty
Ampfield Pond has dried away.
In the Ampfield Vicarage garden
Only plantains hold their sway.

Ampfield dogs are white and lively
Ampfield mokes make strident sound
Ampfield holds the dearest Baby
In the whole world to be found.

Ampfield Vicarage was surrounded by trees and fields, in one of which lived a docile donkey named Polly (one of the 'Ampfield mokes'), who was occasionally harnessed to a local form of transportation known as the Polly-cart.

The Vicarage itself was a long, awkwardly shaped building with one wing, oddly placed windows, and a porch rather too grand for the facade. Wilbert's memories of the Vicarage, being those of a small boy, are of a large building: 'The sort of house that I imagine when I read P. G. Wodehouse's stories of Lord Emsworth.' The ground floor was taken up with a drawing-room, dining-room, his father's study and a broad staircase leading to the upper storey where the morning-room served as Wilbert's nursery.

As he grew up, the young Wilbert would have the freedom of the house, allowed even beyond the green baize door that led to the domestic quarters: a butler's pantry, a lamp-room (where the oil-lamps were cleaned, filled and had their wicks trimmed) and the kitchen with its huge kitchen-range. These were signs of an earlier, more prosperous incumbency; but Vere Awdry could not afford a butler or an extensive domestic staff. The house was managed by

Bessie Page, 'a cook and maid-of-all-work', with assistance from a local girl, Annie King. The large garden was tended by John Pack.

A week after Baby's arrival saw the celebrations to mark the Coronation of King George V and Queen Mary. June 22nd proved to be a day of heavy rain so many of the planned outdoor sporting events had to be postponed. According to the *Hampshire Chronicle,* impromptu indoor games – including stilt races, egg-and-spoon races and hoop races – were held in the local corn stores, 'affording great amusement'. There were also various tugs-of-war between various opposing factions: Married v. Single Men and Married v. Single Women ('in both of which matrimony triumphed over single blessedness'). There were teas and dancing and, when the rain finally abated, a fireworks display, 'obtained from Messrs. Brock, of Crystal Palace fame', which was set off 'without hitch or accident' and, as the *Chronicle* reported: 'In spite of the damp atmosphere, everything did exactly what it was intended to.'

There was a special church service which, Lucy Awdry noted in her *Record Book*, 'Baby was allowed to attend'. He wore his Coronation medal and 'behaved beautifully, only making one very mild remark before the National Anthem'. Carol Awdry was home from Marlborough for the Coronation celebrations and to meet his half-brother for the first time. Despite the vast age difference between them, Carol formed a deep attachment to the little newcomer.

Over the next few weeks, the entries in Lucy Awdry's diary reflect the common joys and anxieties of any mother: signs of growth and developing awareness ('He blinks his eyes at the approach of a finger'), hostility towards vaccination ('There were many yells of indignation') and the various difficulties experienced by the baby's mother and nanny, Nurse Heaton, in getting their charge to accept certain domestic arrangements: 'My first attempt to bath Baby. It took nearly $^{3}/_{4}$ hour. Baby most indignant. Nurse and I very much agitated and exhausted.'

The baby's Christening took place, on 30th July, when he was seven weeks old. His godparents were his half-brother, Carol; his mother's sister, Katherine Bury and her best friend, Edith Simeon, as well as a friend of Vere's, Radclyffe Sidebottom, who was a curate at Romsey. The service was conducted by the baby's father who named him Wilbert (after his brothers William and Herbert) Vere. Lucy Awdry recorded that her son 'behaved well, but this was due more to his Nanny's tact than his own inclinations and he certainly disapproved of the cold water with which his Father christened him . . . [He] was made a great deal too much of during the rest of the afternoon with the result that he gave his mother a good deal of trouble at night.'

The Christening cake was decorated with a tiny cot 'made by his Father and trimmed by Nanny' and Christening presents included a silver mug and napkin ring, 'a sweet little pair of red kid shoes' and, from Carol, a "Jacko" (a mischievous-looking toy monkey) all of which were depicted in one of the delicate watercolour decorations to Lucy Awdry's *Record Book*. The following page shows a rather different collection of objects: one half-chewed slipper and the sole of another, a piece of basket and the head of a broom (all ravaged by teeth-marks), a ball and a lead. These were the proud possessions of Sprack:

> Any account of Baby's earliest days would be incomplete which did not tell of the charming way in which our seven-month-old fox terrier puppy has taken Wilbert under his charge.
>
> At first we were afraid he might be jealous and he was not admitted into the room where Baby slept. But he was most good and quiet, and haunted the passage upstairs on the chance of being let in, so that one day Nurse took him to see Wilbert sleeping in his cot. He was much excited and of course wanted to lick him, but he made no sound and very soon learnt that it was not permissible to touch Baby's face.
>
> Next day, when Baby was awake, his Father laid him on the ground beside Sprack who immediately rolled over on his back and wriggled near enough in that position to lick the tiny fingers. Since then whenever Wilbert is left out of doors alone, either in his basket or his pram, Sprack is generally on guard: usually lying in a 'couchant' position within three or four yards of it, sometimes reaching up to see that all is well; sometimes abolishing birds from the adjacent bushes. He is much worried and very restless when baby cries, and walks gravely beside the pram if it is pushed up and down the lawn.

In a later entry, Lucy Awdry recorded that Sprack had 'stopped a most exciting chase to come and "mind Baby" in the churchyard at my request whilst I filled my jug at the fountain'. She also noted numerous delightful anecdotes about Wilbert and his father: 'This morning, Vere began to lather his face for shaving whilst talking to Baby. His face puckered and he gave a cry but he was soon brought to understand that Daddy remained essentially the same.'

Vere's love for his young son can be seen from a verse which he inscribed on a page interleaved between his wife's accounts of Wilbert's day-to-day activities. The poem, a parody of Isaac Watt's piece of moral versification, 'The Voice of the Sluggard' (subsequently re-written by Lewis Carroll as 'The Voice of the Lobster') is entitled '12.30 Noon':

'Tis the voice of the Infant, I heard him complain:
'You have left me too long, I must call out again.
I'm a really good Baby, as all the world knows,
So while waiting for Mummy I'll play with my toes.'

I stood in the passage and heard, through the door,
'Um Mum' and 'Dad Dad' and some Baby words more.
I opened it gently, and as I peeped through
The young rascal saw me and chortled 'a-goooo'.

Not where Mummy had put him; he'd wriggled quite free
Of the bedclothes; and spluttered and bubbled with glee.
And he danced and he kicked when he saw me come in,
And held out his arms with a shout and a grin.

How could a good Daddy expect to resist,
When his face is well smeared with a chubby wet fist?
Well I couldn't; and didn't and great was his joy
When I picked up that big dancing bright Baby Boy.

A few weeks later, Lucy observed that Wilbert was 'beginning to apply "Mum-mum" and "Dad-dad" much more decidedly to the right persons' and had begun practising a new selection of words including "Goo' bwoy" of himself and " 'Ack, 'Ack" in order to summon the long-suffering Sprack.

Again and again, Lucy commented on her son's gentle, good-humoured nature and 'his wistful half-smile' which would often burst out 'into delighted chuckles'. Elsewhere, she noted: 'he is full of fun and loves to pretend to be going to do what I have forbidden – chuckling when he is prevented.' Rarely crying or grumbling and 'very seldom noisy', Wilbert was often found singing 'soft songs to himself'.

Nevertheless, an early indication of stubbornness (one of Wilbert Awdry's particular character traits) was noted during his thirtieth week of life: 'He now knows much more definitely what he wants to do and how to do it.' It wasn't long, however, before Wilbert's determination was getting him into trouble:

> A coldness has arisen between me and my son today: He is a *very* obstinate little person and on occasions nothing will induce him to drink his bottle. He much prefers rusks and orange juice or gravy and hopes he may be allowed

> these if he holds out long enough. Today, he has steadily refused to drink from his bottle for 15 hours so at last I wrapped his protesting limbs up in a blanket, held his head firmly in my arm, opened his mouth like a dentist and poured it down his throat. He was speechless with amazement and indignation and most of it got down! He was very cross over it, so when I brought him down to his high chair during our dinner, I told Vere and Carol he was in disgrace. We therefore took no notice of him and he appeared thoroughly to understand the situation. He lolled back in his chair with a corner of rusk, trolling a little song in a most unconcerned manner – till at length he made a determined bid for attention by putting his feet on the table cloth. This was allowed to pass so he attempted to follow his feet and got so entangled with his tray that we had to 'solemnly' set him to rights. Towards the end of dinner he made some approach to repentant sounds so that his family gladly received him into its arms once more. The whole proceeding shows a more advanced state of intelligence than I was aware of and shows also that many battles will probably have to be fought in the near future.

Wilbert also showed great curiosity in the world around him, being fascinated by snowfall, intrigued by the method used by Sprack to work his jaws and suitably mystified on finding 'another baby' in a mirror.

By his first birthday – which he celebrated with 'a very small bit of chocolate sponge-cake' (a life-long favourite of Wilbert's) – his mother described him as 'a tall, wiry child – very strong hands and tough knees and toes – a merry face and a healthy colour, fair towsley hair much inclined to curl – blue changeably-coloured eyes.' Pastimes were listed as talking to his reflection in the looking-glass and a tendency 'to sit immediately under his Daddy when he is either washing or shaving and hammer his defenceless toes with the nearest toy'.

There are few observations in Lucy Awdry's *Record Book* about anyone other than Baby, but in July 1912, she noted: 'Wilbert's father has not been at all well so that Dr Livingstone said that he must take a good holiday as soon as possible and that I must go with him, but *not* the little boy.' Such a holiday, however, appeared to be out of the question for financial reasons – an indication that the probably limited wealth of Sir John Awdry had not found its way down to his twelfth child.

Help came from Aunt Maggie, the wife of Vere's brother, Charles. Having risen to a partnership in the firm W. H. Smith, Charles Awdry had acquired a personal fortune with which he had purchased Lavington Manor in Wiltshire, a grand house with gabled roofs, tall chimneys and a clock-tower. As the Manor was some way from Lavington Station and Charles was an important passenger of the railway, a special platform had been erected for him at which trains stopped 'on request'. One day, earlier in 1912, Charles had alighted from a train, missed the platform and taken a severe fall from which he subsequently died.

Margaret Awdry – whom Wilbert later recalled as being, thereafter, in permanent mourning for her husband, 'like Queen Victoria for Prince Albert' – not only undertook to look after Wilbert but sent her brother and sister-in-law the money for their holiday.

For Wilbert the four weeks at Lavington Manor was a mixed experience: accompanied by the Awdry's maid, Annie, he was at first devastated at being separated from his mother and refused to let Annie out of his sight. Gradually, he permitted the attentions of members of the family and staff who showed him the pictures that hung on the walls of the corridors and staircases and introduced him to the stuffed animals that lurked on landings and in the maze of passageways.

Wilbert developed a particular affection for one of the young footmen, Walter, and for the butler, Archer, who entertained the child by stationing himself by the light-switch (Lavington had electricity provided by its own generator) so that Wilbert could 'blow out' the electric lights – an experiment which had to be repeated over and over, for at least ten minutes at a time! 'They gave me,' says Wilbert, 'a right, royal time!'

On returning from holiday, Lucy Awdry recorded various of Wilbert's exploits at Lavington in her *Record Book* concluding:

> These incidents show with what great kindness and affection our small boy was treated and when we went away, I could not get at him to take him downstairs for the crowd who were saying goodbye to him. When the motor took us from the front door, the top landing windows were gay with waving handkerchiefs.

Writing of her son at age two years and two months, Lucy Awdry described him as 'still a thin and tall child' and made a passing reference to 'the bend in his foot' being 'now much better'. Wilbert had been found to have a weakness in left leg. The Awdry's had taken their young son to see a London consultant, Dr Jackson Clarke, who had prescribed the wearing of heavy and uncomfortable leg-irons. Later accounts of Wilbert running about 'untiringly' and making 'absurd attempts at jumping', suggest that the problem was fairly minor and, as much as anything, reflected an over-anxiousness on the part of his mother.

One of Wilbert's favourite pastimes was taking bicycle rides with Carol who was now at Sandhurst military academy, fulfilling his father's frustrated ambitions. Carol bought a wicker carrier which fitted onto the front of his bicycle and in which, to his 'huge delight', Wilbert was allowed to travel. A photograph of this form of locomotion appears in Lucy Awdry's diary together with the observation that, 'Wilbert has not had the slightest fear of it from the first. I think Sprack was the most anxious of us all.'

As Wilbert began toddling and then walking, he was able to share another interest with his step-brother and father – 'The Ampfield Model Railway'. Occasional issues of a hand-written publication, the 'Vickridge Gazette', named the A. M. R.'s Traffic Manager and Locomotive Superintendent as 'Mr E. V. Carroll', the Superintendent of the Line as 'Mr W. Ilbert, and the General Manager as 'Mr A. Dadd', otherwise identified as Vere Awdry, who wrote of the line:

> At first we only ran the train indoors, but the frequent laying and taking-up of the road in time damaged the rails so that derailments were frequent. We felt we must have something better.
>
> After much prospecting, we selected a route in the garden for a permanent outdoor railway and cut the first sod in May 1910. Rails, chairs etc. were procured from Messrs Bassett Lowke [the first British company to manufacture railway models], and in the summer of that year, we laid about 10 yards of rail and made a platform of what is now Littleoak Station [near to the site where an oak tree had been felled]. Each holidays we did a little bit more, until we now have a single line, about 40 yards long with double road through Littleoak Station, with a platform each side, a proper station on the 'Down' side and a shelter station on the 'Up'. The line extends about 4 yds beyond Littleoak at one end and Bush Down Tunnel at the other, in each case running round the curve in a deep cutting so that the train can disappear from sight. Further extension is unfortunately impossible in either direction owing to the nature of the ground.
>
> The Station buildings, Station Master's house, fencing, bridges, stairs, signal-box and levers, telegraph-poles, signals, platform lamps and all accessories we made ourselves. The bogies and wheels for the coaches were bought from Messrs Bassett Lowke, but the coaches were built by us.

Wilbert's first experience of a real railway had been a journey to Salisbury in February 1912, of which his mother had written: 'He took very kindly to the train and did not object to the tunnel.' Among a list of Wilbert's first words

(such as 'Moo', 'Baa' and 'Gee-gee') can be found the phrase 'Puff-puff', and he was soon lending his assistance with the running of the A. M. R.

'As a reward,' says Wilbert, 'for being a good boy (with a capital 'G' and a capital 'B'), I was allowed to have what was called "Coach-run", taking one of the coaches, setting it on the line and just pushing it along.' Photographs show Wilbert, dressed in a smock with a frilly collar, carrying one of the coaches, giving it a little push along the line and sitting expectantly by the mouth of what was known as the Bushdown tunnel. 'Needless to say,' recalls Wilbert, 'when Father and Carol had a steaming session, I was allowed to watch, but *kept firmly under control*!'

Remembering those 'Coach-runs', Wilbert describes how he would give it a push, 'sending it running for some distance' while listening for 'the characteristically smooth clickety-click of the wheels as they passed over the rail joints – a sound which has given me pleasure all my life.' Those carefree summer days in the garden at Ampfield Vicarage were the foundation of a life-long love-affair with railways and the genesis of all those stories about Edward, Gordon, Thomas and the other engines of Sodor.

The A. M. R. often received visitors: there were children from the parish who, years later, recalled having gone to see the trains and to hear the Vicar give 'a very interesting and instructive talk'; there were also 'professional visitors', local plate-layers and railwaymen who were members of Vere's congregation and who were invited to attend 'steaming days'. 'They enjoyed themselves thoroughly,' recalls Wilbert, 'not only playing trains but also taking any chance they could get of "putting the parson railwayman right"!' However, Vere Awdry's knowledge of railway matters meant that such opportunities were few and far between.

There were, from time to time, disasters on the line. On one occasion, the 'Vickridge Gazette' was obliged to report that traffic had been halted 'on the Lane End and Mokesfield section of the A. M. R'. (Mokesfield being named after the field where Polly the donkey lived). This hiatus was due to 'the falling in of the roof of Bushdown tunnel', about which the 'Gazette' observed: 'It would be ungenerous on our part to recapitulate the cause of the calamity, but it may be well to say that it was from a preventable cause for which the company is in no way responsible.'

The 'preventable cause' was Lucy Awdry. 'Instead of using the proper means of access to the sidings behind the tunnel,' recalls Wilbert, 'Mother trod on the earth roof of the tunnel itself before it had properly set. Her foot went right through and she had to be rescued!' The 'Vickridge Gazette' report continued:

> The energy and promptitude displayed in the necessary repairs will be realised when it is stated that the roof of nearly one third of the tunnel had to be rebuilt entirely, and the immense amount of debris to be removed from the permanent way rendered the work a matter of time, and that traffic has been able to be resumed in little more than a week reflects the greatest credit on all concerned. It is satisfactory to be able to state that only the Person responsible for the accident sustained any injury from it; and, as we learn that she is in a fair way to recovery all may be regarded as well.

On another occasion, Carol started up the train when the track wasn't clear and a twig or an acorn on the line caused a spectacular derailment. Vere Awdry photographed the scene of the crash, developed the picture and took it to a photographic firm in Romsey in order to obtain an enlargement. As an account by Vere reveals, it wasn't long before this innocent event became a *cause célèbre*:

> By the request of the photographer who did the enlargement, [it] was exhibited one morning in his window at Romsey. The result was both astonishing and amusing. It was stated (with perfect truth) that it had happened within 5 miles of Romsey. The newspaper offices were besieged for papers to see all about it, and by 10 a.m. there was not a paper to be got in Romsey for love or money. The photographer was also besieged, and at last promised to reveal the locality at 5 p.m. Great was the amusement of some and the indignation of others when the announcement appeared that it had occurred on my *Model* Railway!
>
> But the photographer, who was just starting business in the town, got a really good advertisement, for, being market-day, all the neighbourhood came to see it.

The closing pages of Lucy Awdry's *Record Book* contain a series of photographs of 'The Men of the Family'. Taken in July 1913, they show Wilbert wearing a woolly jumper, trousers and beret, standing on a chair; Vere Awdry, tall and gaunt, in black suit and clerical collar, his eyes shadowed by his wide-brimmed hat; and Carol with an upright stance which betrays his military training and a determinedly serious expression. They are accompanied in some of the pictures by the beloved Sprack.

These were to be the last pictures taken of a happy family before fate turned their world upside down. On 28th June, 1914, in the Bosnian capital, Sarajevo, the Austrian Archduke Francis Ferdinand and his wife were assassinated by a Bosnian Serb. It was the falling pebble that would, within a few months, become the avalanche known as the Great War. On 1st August, Germany ordered general mobilisation and declared war against Russia; two days later they were also at war with France; then, during the night of 3rd-4th August, German forces invaded Belgium. Great Britain, who had no concern with Serbia and was under no obligation to fight on behalf of either Russia or France was, however, committed to defend Belgium and so, on 4th August, declared war on Germany.

Carol Awdry, who was twenty years old and who had passed out of Sandhurst as a 2nd Lieutenant earlier in 1914, was with the Royal Munster Fusiliers when they set out for France as part of the first Expeditionary Force. Just thirteen days later, on 27th August, Carol was killed in action, during the retreat from Mons.

Vere Awdry received the tragic news in a letter from the senior surviving officer of Carol's regiment:

> 'C' company, to which your son belonged, was chosen to watch the right rear of our battalion when the army was retiring from Mons. Capt. Rawlinson selected your son to take his platoon to an exposed position on the far edge of a village named Fesmy, through which our line of retreat lay. He performed the duty in a most able manner, and though harassed by a nasty fire, he held on while the battalion withdrew and then rejoined with his little force intact. It was commendable performance, worthy of one of far greater age and experience than your son. At Oisy, the company was detailed to act as a rearguard. Again they were sharply engaged by largely increased forces, but they gallantly held their own, your son again holding a detached position at an important crossroads, and again the battalion could withdraw in safety. Your boy's party was the last to come in, and although he lost some men, he saved many more. By six o'clock, it was discovered that we were cut off from the main body. The battalion shook out of the attack in an attempt to break through, every officer doing good work, your son no less than the others. With sword drawn, he led his men in support of the attack which was in progress in front, and as he advanced, fell, shot through the lungs. His death was painless and practically instantaneous. By his death we have lost a cheery companion, an honourable gentleman, and an officer of distinct promise, such as we can ill-afford to lose. He is buried with 8 brother officers near the railway station at Etreux.

The Officer in Charge at Sandhurst added: 'Your son was quite one of the best boys I've ever had in my company – an example to everyone. I knew his end was bound to be glorious and honourable. He died, as he lived, a gallant English gentleman.'

The loss of his third child devastated Vere Awdry. 'It was,' says Wilbert, 'the supreme tragedy in my father's life.' On receiving the news, Vere went to Hove, to stay with Thomas J. Bullick, a friend from his days at Chichester Theological College, who was now Headmaster of Marlborough House preparatory school, where Carol had been a pupil. It was from here that Vere was to write to his parishioners of his grief:

> We are inclined perhaps to ask why the splendid young fellow in the prime of life and with all his future – as we call it – before him, should be so suddenly cut off while older and possibly feebler ones are left. 'The Lord has need of him'. That is the answer. He needed him in particular for some good purpose of His own which we here cannot and shall not know in this world. Nothing is done by God by mere chance . . . Death has come, but a death to be proud of, not that probably others have not died equally brave and noble deaths – we know many have – but he was our boy, our own lad. He has lived his whole life amongst us at Ampfield, and we can be proud of that Ampfield lad, who had proved himself trustworthy and faithful even unto death.

For Wilbert, too young to take in the news, there was a sense of having lost – despite many years difference between them – an understanding companion who had doted on his young half-brother. Only a few months before Carol's death, Lucy Awdry had noted that one of Wilbert's names for himself – along with Daddy's Pet, Mummy's Darling and Nanny's Sweetheart – was Brother's Twopence. Although he could not know it at the time, however, the ghost of that brother would haunt Wilbert for many years as he strove to measure up to the idealised hero-figure, so cruelly cut down in the prime of life.

CHAPTER TWO

"I am working very hard"

'WILBERT loves dancing with his shadow when going to bed,' wrote Lucy Awdry who, having filled all the pages in her *Record Book*, continued her observations on her son's development in conventional diaries, which she then entered up into a large manuscript book that had belonged to Carol Awdry during his days at Sandhurst. The inside cover and first page have been stamped with a rubber-stamp: 'C. E. V. Awdry, R. M. F. [Royal Munster Fusiliers] Feb, 26 1914', and a note in Carol's handwriting reads: '*Jottings* on mistakes made in the field and the lessons to be learnt therefrom. C. E. V. A.' Sadly, he did not live long enough to either make mistakes or to learn from them.

In taking over the *Jottings* book, Lucy Awdry pasted in a picture postcard by the celebrated comic artist, Donald McGill. Depicting a little boy engaged in various activities, it carries the rhyme: 'Working, playing, eating, drinking, All day long of you I'm thinking. An' when I've nothing else to do, I just sit down an' think of you!'

The little boy whose day-by-day doings and sayings were recorded by Lucy Awdry was demonstrating a lively interest in the world around him. Describing her son as 'a regular little parrot at catching up words in other people's conversation', Wilbert's mother noted: 'He is fond of listening to nursery rhymes and has a special name for each. "Blackbird" is "Sing a Song of Sixpence", "Johnny Green" is "Ding Dong Bell", "Tree Top" is "Rock-a-bye Baby".'

Lucy Awdry also read and told stories to Wilbert, among them the fairy-tales of 'Goldilocks and the Three Bears' and, an especial favourite, 'Chicken-Licken' with its much-repeated pronouncement, 'The sky is falling!', and its roll-call of farmyard characters with funny names such as Henny-Penny, Cocky-Locky and Turkey-Lurky. Literary stories included Lewis Carroll's *Alice's Adventures in Wonderland* and *Through the Looking Glass* with their punning dialogue and nonsense rhymes and the more recently published *Just So Stories* by Rudyard Kipling, which included 'The Elephant's Child' – memorable for repetitious onomatopoeic phrases like 'the banks of the great grey-green, greasy Limpopo River, all set about with fever-trees'. Years later the use of rhymes, rhythms and repetitions would play an important part in the creation of Wilbert Awdry's own stories.

There were also books by Beatrix Potter, who was still writing and illustrating children's stories. A Potter book which quickly became one of Wilbert's favourites was her 1909 publication, *The Tale of The Flopsy Bunnies*, which begins: 'It is said that the effect of eating too much lettuce is "soporific". *I* have never felt sleepy after eating lettuces; but then *I* am not a rabbit. They certainly had a very soporific effect upon the Flopsy Bunnies!' It was daring of Beatrix Potter to use such a rarefied word (even if she did explain what it meant) but, as Wilbert observes 'children love the magic of high-sounding words', and Potter knew that. The young Wilbert was no exception: 'I drove my mother crackers: "Soporific! Soporific! Soporific!" I loved that word and I kept repeating it!'

Lucy Awdry recorded the fact that Wilbert liked 'having little stories made up for him' and she followed Beatrix Potter's example by writing out her stories in small, black-covered note-books containing a page of text (printed, in order to help Wilbert learn to read) with a facing illustration. The stories were based on domestic happenings such as the story of 'Gertie and the Frog'. Gertrude – or Gertie – Whatmore was an Ampfield girl in her late teens who came to work at the Vicarage as 'garden boy' when, in 1916, the gardener, John Pack, was called up to fight in the Great War, and who remained with the Awdry family for the rest of her life.

The story, as Wilbert recalls it, began with Gertie's foot about to descend on a large frog: 'Gertie trod on the Frog. Did she kill it? No. Fetch a dust-pan and brush and sweep it up.' There is no doubt that as Lucy Awdry invented her little stories and made them into child-sized books, she was sowing in Wilbert's fertile young imagination the seeds of a storytelling tradition.

Wilbert learned quickly: on 4th March, 1914, Lucy Awdry noted: 'Wilbert taught himself all his capital letters in three days'; and, two weeks later, he taught himself 'all his small letters' in just *one* day. He demonstrated a literary precocity when he described stars fading in the morning light as 'sinking into heaven'. Wilbert also coined at least one expression that would have been worthy of one of his railway engine characters when, aged five, he remarked: 'I am working very *hard*; you can't expect me to be working at *full* speed!'

In addition to the influence of his mother, there was also his father's rhyming and versifying, some of which was composed specifically for Wilbert's amusement; such as a little verse-story about Sprack, the dog – 'written for Wilbert's benefit' – and which parodies a folk song about 'The Little Crawfish':

There was a little Pussy Cat with black and silky fur
And Wilbert called her 'Zeppelin' so loudly did she purr.
With a hi jingle jingle and a ho jingle jingle
And a hi jingle jingle jingle ha

And she purred and she purred as she squirmed about one's heel
And not far off was 'Spracky Dog' a-cadging for a meal.
With a hi jingle jingle etc etc

'O Zeppelin, O Zeppelin, O Zeppelin,' said he
'Have you got a little breakfast that you can give to me?'
With a hi jingle jingle etc etc

She gave him what she didn't want, he thought it very nice
He wasn't long about it and he ate it in a trice.
With a hi jingle jingle etc etc

And while he was eating it, she sat and washed her face
She was not a bit afraid of him but kept him in his place.
With a hi jingle jingle etc etc

Sprack's plate was by the table a-waiting for him there,
But when Zeppelin went near it, he jumped down off his chair.
With a hi jingle jingle etc etc

And he snarled and he growled just as angry as could be
And then ran after Zeppelin and chased her up a tree.
With a hi jingle jingle etc etc

But very soon she had revenge upon the selfish Sprack
For when he wasn't looking, she just jumped upon his back!
With a hi jingle jingle etc etc

Despite Vere Awdry's light-hearted wit – and the weekly presence in Ampfield Vicarage of the humorous magazine, *Punch* – Lucy Awdry was 'very particular' about what Wilbert read and never allowed him to have any of the popular children's comics of the day. Such publications were, therefore, forbidden fruit, and one of the most desirable of its kind was a paper called *Rainbow*.

Bessie Page, the Awdrys' cook, sometimes took Wilbert with her on visits to her parents who lived in Wickham, Hampshire. Such trips were always a big adventure, leaving early in the morning on the milk cart and not returning until mid-evening. Bessie's father, who ran a newsagents, always gave Wilbert a copy of *Rainbow*, which the boy would smuggle back into the Vicarage to be read in secret. Wilbert was particularly taken with the front-page antics of the Bruin Boys under the mischievous leadership of Tiger Tim: 'I loved them, but my mother had a theory that reading about the Bruin Boys' unruly escapades made *me* naughty!' If ever Lucy Awdry discovered her son in possession of a copy of *Rainbow*, the offending object was immediately confiscated and destroyed. Wilbert, however, remained unrepentant about his allegiance to the Bruin Boys, which may go some way towards explaining why his own fictional characters are so often allowed to indulge in pranks and capers.

A publication which Wilbert *was* permitted to read was *The Railway Magazine*, of which his father had a run of bound copies (dating from around 1904). 'They were,' says Wilbert 'my favourite picture-books as a child! Of course, I couldn't read the articles but I pored over the pictures and photographs and read the captions, which were usually printed in capital letters. I was soon able to tell from the picture of a particular locomotive to which railway it was likely to belong.' *The Railway Magazine* became food and drink to young Wilbert and, many years later, would become an important resource for the writer in search of out-of-the-way plots for his railway stories.

Lucy Awdry's *Jottings* book is full of glimpses of a happy childhood: snowy February days with 'Wilbert very busy all morning, digging a path to the front gate'; and sunny June afternoons in the vicarage garden: 'Wilbert very good and trustworthy at helping pick strawberries, [he] gets the fattest one as wage when they are all spread out in a dish.' There were all kinds outings: to Winchester, with his mother, where they saw Lord Kitchener and the King ('Very grave and stern. Wilbert disappointed that the King had no crown on.'); to the seaside at Brighton, Broadstairs and Swanage; and an unsuccessful visit to the pantomime, *Sinbad*, by which 'he was much bored and begged not to stop till end'.

In Ampfield, Wilbert was taken to see a local farmer hand-sowing wheat by the traditional broadcast method and to watch lambs being dipped in Pond-field. He attended various church events: from solemn occasions such as a service of dedication for a pair of stained-glass windows in memory of Carol (held two days after what would have been the dead boy's twenty-first birthday), to a New Year Parish Tea at which his father performed 'The Inky Boys'. This was a popular sketch based on one of the moral poems in the

English translation of Heinrich Hoffmann's *Der Struwwelpeter*, in which three naughty boys who mock a 'woolly-headed black-a-moor', receive summary justice when they are seized by 'tall Agrippa', a sinister character who dunks them in his 'mighty inkstand' until they are 'black as black can be'.

There were occasional dramas as when Wilbert was attacked and knelt on by Polly the donkey: 'He was very sick in the night and 4 times next day'; or the less serious mishap which occurred on a day when he was out sailing a 'celluloid frog' with his father and fell head-first into a stream: 'A great joke,' wrote Lucy Awdry. 'Daddy changed his clothes for him while I was taking [a] Mothers' meeting and knew nothing about it!'

Nor was this, in Wilbert's memory, an isolated occurrence. The stream ran beside a lane down which Vere would take the young Wilbert for his daily walk on afternoons when Lucy was engaged at the Vicarage, presiding over Mothers' Union meetings:

> It was a sizeable stream fed by the over-flow from a horse-trough in a nearby field, which was itself fed by a spring which never seemed to fail. The lane-side stream was fast and turbulent, and the exciting thing about it was not only the rate at which it flowed, but also that as the lane twisted so it changed its course from one side to the other by means of tunnels under the road. It was great fun to launch paper boats, of which father usually had a supply, and scamper along beside them, nudging them free from obstacles with a stick, watching them dive into the tunnels and waiting anxiously at the other end for them to emerge.
>
> In the end we decided that bits of stick were preferable for this game than paper boats which soon became waterlogged during their rough passage and all too often sank. Bits of stick on the other hand, when carefully chosen, were less likely to get entangled, and slipped more easily through the tunnels. Father used to roll up my sleeves and hanging on to me as best he could, would help me chase my 'boats' along. Inevitably, from time to time, disaster struck and I would fall into the stream! That, of course, was the end of the walk, but father made it into fun too. He would whisk me home and get me changed and clean and dry before we told my mother anything about it!

'Boating' expeditions which did not end in disaster served a useful purpose, since they permitted the cleansing of dirty hands that would most certainly not have found favour with Wilbert's mother. The cause of dirtiness was invariably a visit to the local blacksmith's shop, one of the delights of a walk along the Romsey Road which 'never seemed to pall'. Wilbert would watch 'with awestruck wonder' as the iron, heated until it was white hot in the roaring forge, was hammered – 'with practised, effortless skill' – into a horseshoe and then quenched in a bucket of water with a whoosing noise and a great cloud of steam.

Wilbert admits that he can 'remember nothing' of the walks he took with his mother ('I probably found them dull,') whilst those on which he was accompanied by his father have remained vividly alive for him – particularly 'a delight which only father could provide':

> If he had information from railwaymen friends that something interesting was happening – it might be a new engine, built at nearby Eastleigh running trials; or a Special Train for royalty or some visiting V.I.P.; or even if the local plate-layers gang were working on the Baddesley stretch – we would ignore the blacksmith and the stream and follow the lane until it dived under a railway bridge. A gate on the right hand side of the road opened into a field through which the railway ran on an embankment. Once through the gate, we would scramble up the embankment and walk along the track-side ballast to where the right-of-way widened and we could stand right back and wait, well clear, for the engine or train to come along. A thrilling experience for a small boy to feel, at close hand, the pleasurable excitement and vibration of its passing. If any of the plate-layers were there, we would watch them at their work. If it came on to rain we would adjourn to their nearby line-side hut, built of old sleepers. Here they made us very welcome.
>
> I thought the hut marvellous; mother would have thought it dirty, smelly, untidy and smoky, redolent of strong tobacco which, for me, gave it an atmosphere almost of a fairy-tale quality. I would sit looking at all the odd things and tools which seemed to collect there, wondering what they were for, storing up questions to ask father afterwards. Questions to which he nearly always knew the answers.
>
> I would listen, too, to father and the men talking usually about their railway, and what shone through was their pride in both. At the age of five or six, I cannot have understood much of it; but young as I was I must have absorbed something of the atmosphere of those days which has stayed with me for the rest of my life.

On a practical level, railways were for the Awdry family – as for most other people – the only way of travelling; Wilbert's imagination, however, was undoubtedly caught by the romanticism of steam locomotion. Perhaps he also sensed that such expeditions as he was now making with his father would once have been shared with Carol and that it was emotionally important for his father that his surviving son should share his passion for railways.

On 21st July, 1916, Gertie took Wilbert to stay with his maternal grandmother in Salisbury where they remained for almost a month. This exile was brought about by the imminent birth of another child. The child, a boy, was born on 10th August, making his entrance (as his mother noted in her *Jottings* book) 'to the sound of guns – possibly bomb practice'. The fact that Vere Awdry was sixty-two and that it had been five years since Wilbert's birth, suggests that but for the death of Carol, a new baby might never have been conceived.

Indeed, Carol's death had been a double-edged sword. The boy's mother, Mary Louisa, had had a private income and had left him £500 per annum in her Will. Before going to war, Carol had himself made a Will in which he bequeathed this legacy to his father. As a result of Carol's death, Vere inherited an annual sum that was twice the value of his living as parish priest. Had it not been for this money it is doubtful how long he would have been able to maintain a large vicarage with even a modest domestic staff, let alone contemplate extending his family.

The Awdrys decided that their new son would be named George Edward Vere. Lucy Awdry described him as being 'a very well dispositioned baby' with a 'sweet smile'. There is a common belief that any baby, however plain, is beautiful to a mother's eyes. If so, then Lucy Awdry was either particularly clear-sighted or remarkably cold in describing George – as she had done with his elder brother – as 'not good looking'.

A little over a week after George's birth, Gertie Whatmore brought Wilbert home to Ampfield. Having spent much time with Wilbert and shown herself capable of managing children, Gertie was asked to became George's nurse – a move which necessarily changed her relationship with Wilbert. Lucy Awdry noted that Wilbert, whom she hadn't seen for four weeks, was 'looking big and bonny and quite fat', and was 'very happy at seeing George'. Wilbert has rather different memories: 'They told me I had a young brother to play with, but I was rather disgusted to find that he was just a baby and that I hadn't got a hope of playing with him! I wanted some one my own age, but, of course, he was *always* five years younger than me!' A random entry in his mother's diary, eight months later, records one instance of what, to the young Wilbert, must have been deeply frustrating: 'Bessie and Wilbert [built] a big snowman by drawing room window. G[eorge] and G[ertie] watched from inside.'

In later life – despite Wilbert's conviction that George was intellectually his superior – the Awdry brothers would become close, sharing an interest in railways and railway modelling, taking holidays together and collaborating on the creation of the fictional Island of Sodor; but as children Wilbert did not, he confesses, 'get on' with his brother. Wilbert was, therefore, trapped between his father's two other sons: the dead hero and the new-born replacement. Although he was too young to know why he felt the way he did, Wilbert resented his younger brother.

The problem was compounded by the fact that, from his earliest days, George was a sickly child. Both boys succumbed to various chills, colds and a virulent bout of influenza; but, whilst Wilbert always bounced back, George seemed to take longer to recover or, worse, developed complications. George's tendency towards sickliness distanced him even further from his brother and made Lucy Awdry concentrate so much attention on her younger son that he would never succeed in cutting the apron strings.

Despite the birth of his new son, Vere Awdry continued to grieve for Carol, and since life at Ampfield seemed to hold so many memories and reminders of his dead boy, he decided to retire. He wanted to return to his native Wiltshire and he asked his cousin, Eddy Awdry, who was a solicitor in Chippenham, to find him a house in the village of Box.

Vere remained at Ampfield until a new incumbent could be appointed, the move finally being made in August 1917. The Ampfield Model Railway – of which the 'Vickridge Gazette' had once said: 'The popularity of the line is so well established owing to the scrupulous care taken by the Directors to study the convenience of their patrons' – was taken up, never to be re-laid. There would be other model railways, but the A. M. R., with which were associated so many memories of Carol, would run no more.

Ties with Ampfield were not totally severed: Bessie Page left the family because the move would have taken her too far away from her family, but Gertie, now an indispensable part of the household, accompanied the Awdrys. Vere also kept in touch with several of his parishioners, including the family of his former gardener, John Pack. Vere was godfather to John's son, Wilfred, and had given the child Carol Awdry's Bible as a Christening present. Then, when John Pack was called up to fight, Vere had taken over responsibility for the rent on the family's cottage, an undertaking he maintained for the duration of the war.

Box's chief claims to fame were the remains of a Roman pavement, the burial place of Mrs Bowdler, mother of the editor of the (Bowdlerized) *Family*

Shakespeare and the site of the Box Tunnel, constructed in 1841 by Isambard Kingdom Brunel for the Great Western Railway. Measuring one mile and seven furlongs, it was, at the time, the longest railway tunnel in Britain.

The house in Box – it was to be the first of three different homes over the next few years – was called The Wilderness. From Vere's dressing-room it was possible to see the Great Western main line from Paddington to Bristol and, with the aid of a telescope, to make out the engines which pulled the trains. Father and son enjoyed their long-range train-spotting: 'We had note books and soon got to know the times when trains came through. If Father could read the name on the engine and if I was in the room at the time, we could both put the name down in our books; but if I wasn't in the room when the train was "spotted" then I was not allowed to list it!'

Lucy Awdry's diary notes a number of railway journeys taken by Wilbert – on one of which, to his grandmother in Salisbury, the guard (having been tipped to keep an a eye on the young traveller) allowed Wilbert to ride in the guard's van. George was also introduced to train travel and, like his brother, enjoyed the experience. On beginning to talk, George numbered among his first words (as his brother had done) 'Puff-puff'.

The picture of Lucy Awdry which emerges from her *Jottings* book is of a woman enjoying the experiences of family life and reporting even the mishaps with a sense of amused resignation:

> Wilbert went with Daddy and me to tea at Mrs Erskine's. We found he was to have his in the nursery and he made a fearful scene. Meanwhile at home, George had managed to bolt himself into the drawing-room whilst Gertie was shutting up the rest of the house and she was obliged at last to break a pane of glass in the window and pull him through the opening. Wilbert was pushed in through the same hole to undo the bolt on our return. So there was great agitation all round.

Between the lines, however, one sees an accomplished organiser of others, a former teacher always determined to interest her children – often regardless of their wishes – in some activity or other which might broaden their minds. Wilbert, for example, was taken to see his first lantern-slide lecture which, judging from its being titled 'Interned in E. Africa', was more instructive than entertaining; and even the curious diversion of an 'open-air cinema' (shown in a local paddock) turned out to be a film about war-helpers.

True, there was a visit to Bristol to see the suspension bridge, the cliff railway and the zoo, but on such outings it was Lucy who determined what the children saw and how long they could spend on any one activity before moving on to see or do something else. Without realising it, Lucy Awdry was creating a controlled, possessive environment from which her sons would eventually wish to escape. Only one of them, Wilbert, would do so.

On 7th November, 1918, Lucy Awdry recorded one of the final stages of the Great War: 'Daddy was at Corsham Hospital as night orderly and Wilbert was in Daddy's bed. There was a false "alarm" of peace and the bells jangled on and off from 10.40 - 11. I went out and others. George trotted about the next day saying: "I heard the bells of peace". Anyhow, the Germans were retreating rapidly and the Allied fleets sailed through the Dardanelles.' Four days later, the Armistice was signed and there were services of thanksgiving and a bonfire on the cricket field. For Vere Awdry, who 'took short prayers and a hymn', it must have been a day of mixed emotions: relief that the war was finally at an end but, at the same time, one of overwhelming grief that his beloved Carol would not be among those soon returning from the front.

The following February, the Awdrys moved to Townend, their second house in Box where, in July 1919, Peace Celebrations were held in torrential rain. The following year they moved again, to Lorne Villa (renamed Journey's End) which was some 200 yards from the western end of Box Tunnel. At that point, the Great Western main line climbs for some two miles at a gradient of 1 in 100 and a tank engine was kept in the shed not only to marshal the wagons in what was then a busy goods yard, but also to assist heavy freight trains up the incline:

> These trains usually ran at night. Lying in bed as a child I would hear a heavy goods train coming in and stopping at Box station, then the three whistles, crowing for a banker, a 0-6-0 pannier tank-engine, which would come out of his little shed to help the goods train up the gradient. There was no doubt in my mind that steam engines all had definite personalities. I would hear them snorting up the grade and little imagination was needed to hear in the puffings and pantings of the two engines the conversation they were having with one another: 'I can't do it! I can't do it! I can't do it!' 'Yes, you can! Yes, you can! Yes, you can!'

Clearly, here was the inspiration for the story about Edward helping Gordon get up the hill which, twenty-five years later, Wilbert was to tell his son, Christopher:

> *'I can't do it, I can't do it, I can't do it,' puffed Gordon.*
> *'I will do it, I will do it, I will do it,' puffed Edward.*

'I can't do it, I will do it, I can't do it, I will do it, I can't do it, I will do it,' they puffed together.

There were two tunnels at Box: one was the short, 200 yard Middle Hill tunnel, the other, about 1/2 mile uphill, was the long one. Wilbert and his father used to walk along the path running just below the Middle Hill tunnel for a mid-day outing which they called 'Going down to see The Great Bear and St Bartholomew':

> We used to have lunch about one o'clock. At about 12.40, if they were running to time, two trains – one going down the hill towards Bath and Bristol, the other coming up – would pass each other by the London side of the Middle Hill tunnel. The train coming down from Paddington would be hauled by 'St Bartholomew', while the one heading for Paddington would be hauled by 'The Great Bear'.

Following the success of the two-cylinder, 4-6-0 locomotives belonging to the Saint Class, G. J. Churchward had designed a Class of four-cylinder, 4-6-0 locomotives which became known as the Star Class, being named after various constellations. These locomotives proved themselves capable of handling, with ease, any traffic load given to them. However, the directors of the Great Western Railway, hearing rumours that other companies were planning larger and more powerful locomotives that would eclipse their engines, persuaded Churchward (against his better judgement) to design and build a four-cylinder, 4-6-2 Super Star, the first of which was The Great Bear:

> Father had low opinion of 'The Great Bear'. The first 'Pacific' type locomotive, it was the largest engine to have been built in Britain and was designed simply to show what the Great Western could do. Faults quickly emerged and it was never really satisfactory – in fact, it was eventually rebuilt as a four-cylinder, 4-6-0.
>
> In contrast, Father was very fond of the free-running 'Saint Class' which was utterly reliable. If we failed to see the two trains pass, it was invariably because 'St Bartholemew' was on time and 'The Great Bear' was running late!

By the time the family was living at Journey's End, a new chapter had opened in Wilbert's life. In September 1919, Lucy Awdry took Wilbert on another of her jaunts to London, taking the motor bus to St Paul's and a tram along the Embankment to Westminster; all of which, however, was a prelude to taking the train to Sussex to stay with Aunt Polly and her husband, the Reverend Daustini Cremer, at Seaford Vicarage. After three days of playing on the beach at Seaford, Lucy took Wilbert to his ultimate destination – Marlborough House School.

The Headmaster of what was the preparatory school for Marlborough House was the Reverend Thomas J. Bullick, a friend from Vere Awdry's days at Chichester Theological College. The school had between fifty and sixty pupils, taught in three classrooms: the first of which, for Juniors, was divided into two teaching areas by a blackboard. Thomas Bullick was assisted by his wife and his sister-in-law, Gertrude White, as well as by a Miss Pitcher and two male assistant teachers.

Unlike a lot of boarders, Wilbert did not suffer from home-sickness, being happy to be away from what he was already identifying as the stifling atmosphere created by his mother. However, he was not happy at Marlborough House, partly because Carol had preceded him at the school and Wilbert felt that he was being constantly – and unfavourably – compared with his dead half-brother: 'I simply didn't live up to the standard set by Carol. They were always expecting me to, but I never did.'

Not only did Wilbert feel that he was falling far short of expectations, he found it difficult to get on with one of his teachers. Gertrude White, Mrs Bullick's sister, had a particularly unsettling manner: 'You could never be sure of her,' recalls Wilbert. 'One day everything would be all right for you, the next everything would be all wrong, and you never knew why.' What made the situation impossible, was that Wilbert could not discuss his concerns at home since the Bullicks were family friends. Indeed, Wilbert had visited the school several times with his parents before becoming a pupil and, on one occasion, insisting that the same Miss White have an overnight loan of his much loved toy monkey, Jacko.

Another blight on Wilbert's days at Marlborough House was the new Matron, Miss Wotton. Her predecessor, Miss Acton, was 'a plump, cheerful, motherly sort' who got on well with the boys and even permitted a little high spirits in the dormitory. Miss Wotton, however, was 'an entirely different pair of shoes', and ruled with a will of iron. Wilbert learnt one valuable lesson at Marlborough House which would undoubtedly shape his attitudes, as an adult, towards his own and other people's children: 'I realised that to a young boy, all grown-ups are queer and a law unto themselves!'

There were days out in Brighton with his mother, going on the Palace Pier and riding along the promenade on Britain's first electric railway. There were the usual improving expeditions – a trip to Bristol to hear the writer Lowell Thomas give a lecture on 'Allenby in Palestine' (about which Wilbert recalls nothing); but there were also more enjoyable weekend visits to London, during which an exhausting sight-seeing itinerary – the Houses of Parliament, Westminster Abbey and Cathedral, the Natural History and Science Museums, the Tower of London, 'a travel talk on Burma at the Philharmonic Hall' and an evening service at the Chelsea Hospital – was mercifully interspersed with such delights as Maskelyne and Devant's magic show at the Egyptian Hall, a trip to London Zoo and outings to the cinema (still silent in those days) to see Douglas Fairbanks swashbuckling his way through *Robin Hood* and *The Mark of Zorro*.

Sandwiched between all these activities were the things that *Wilbert* wanted to do, such as visits to the stations at Waterloo, Euston, St Pancras and King's Cross, all of which were, in turn, endured rather than enjoyed by his mother: 'Those were the rare occasions when I got my own way. For the most part the trips were of her organising and not always the things I wanted to do. Whenever I decided to do something, she would always produce what *she* thought was a better plan.'

The summer holiday of 1922 saw Wilbert taking a trip to Scotland (Glasgow, Oban, Iona, and Edinburgh) with his mother and grandmother which involved a lot more museums, monuments, castles and cathedrals, but which Wilbert enjoyed because they travelled by boat and train, saw the Forth Bridge and were able to go inside Fingall's Cave. More satisfying by far were those activities which he shared with his father and which were usually a combination of train journey and bicycle-ride to such places as Stonehenge and the huge White Horse carved on the hillside at Uffington in Berkshire.

At Easter 1924, both parents and both children (together with Gertie who was now considered part of the family) took the first of several holidays in the West Country visiting such beauty spots as Mousehole, Madron, Kynance Cove and Land's End. On their return to Box, Vere and the boys formally cut the first sod of a new garden railway, but it was a vain attempt to recreate one of the joys of an era that could never return.

Nevertheless, railways figured in an expedition made in June that year, when the family visited the British Empire Exhibition at Wembley. Lucy Awdry recorded that they had 'wasted a long time waiting to see the Queen's Doll's House and then had to hurry past it', and noted that they had 'managed to lose each other in The Palace of Engineering'. Wilbert's memory suggests that this may not have been entirely accidental since he was keen to visit the locomotives on display and remembers seeing two magnificent engines, Caerphilly Castle and Flying Scotsman ranged side by side.

The visit to Wembley marked, for Wilbert, a realisation that his father was far from robust: 'I persuaded him to take me on the "Switch-back" ride and when we came to the end he had been so shaken up by the experience that he had difficulty in getting out.' The fact was, his father was old. As a child Wilbert had dreaded visits to his aunts Fanny, Prilly and Lily: 'They seemed to me so incredibly old and dull. It never occurred to me that they were of comparable age with Father, because he was rarely inactive and never dull.' It was only when Wilbert had gone to Marlborough House School that he had realised just how old his father was: 'I saw my father alongside other parents and had long and heated arguments with boys who insisted that he must be my grandfather.' Vere Awdry was, indeed, old enough to have been Wilbert's grandfather; the extraordinary thing is that his actual grandfather had been born in 1795. 'I was born,' says Wilbert, 'out of my generation.'

At the end of every holiday there loomed the return to Marlborough House: 'Looking back on the place, after so many years, I'm tempted to be too kind to it. The truth is that for at least ten days before going back to school, the most terrible feeling of dread would settle upon me.'

Whilst still conscious of being overshadowed by the seven-years dead Carol, Wilbert made headway, being moved up into the top class for English and French – a subject hedged about with problems: 'Miss White insisted that "a" be pronounced as in "have", but if you used that pronunciation in Mrs Bullick's class you got into terrible trouble!' He also started learning Latin, which he enjoyed, discovering more about English grammar from Thomas Bullick's Latin lessons than he had learned in any of his English lessons.

Despite the problems he had experienced in babyhood with a weakness in his left leg, Wilbert successfully participated in school sports: coming second in the 100 yards race, and winning a cricket ball as a long jump prize – achievements that were to be repeated in his senior school and university careers.

Escape came on 18th December, 1924 when, clutching 'a beautiful Shakespeare as a leaving present', Wilbert left Marlborough House School for the last time. Only a few days earlier, his parents had received a telegram to say that he had gained a scholarship to Dauntsey School, in West Lavington, near Devizes, Wiltshire.

The school had been founded in 1542 under the Will of William Dauntsey, a local man who had become a wealthy London merchant. Dauntsey gave certain properties to the Mercers' Company – of which he had been a prominent member – so that the revenue might be used to establish a school in West Lavington. 'For the next four hundred years,' writes Philip Nokes, General Secretary of the Old Dauntseians Association, 'this endowed charity school led an obscure and humble existence, providing fairly basic education for children from West Lavington and neighbouring villages.'

Change came in 1895, when the charity was re-established on a very different footing, as a result of which a new site was acquired and buildings were erected. Called Dauntsey Agricultural School, its aim was to provide an agricultural education as well as some academic teaching. To begin with, Dauntsey's did not do well. Some of the scholars were rough and ready and bad language was not uncommon. Certainly it was considered an unsuitable establishment by the staff at Marlborough House School. 'It was,' says Wilbert, 'not on Gertrude White's list of approved public schools!'

At the time Wilbert joined the school – 'a great, long, T-shaped building with the Headmaster's block at one end' – it was educating 120 boys, a number of whom were the sons of farmers. By the fourth form, pupils had to decide whether to study for the Cambridge School Certificate examination or go into agricultural training, which took place in a number of farm buildings on the site.

Dauntsey School (as its name was changed to in 1930) had recently come under new management with the appointment of George W. Olive, M.A., as Headmaster. Far from being an agriculturalist, George Olive was a former Second Master of Oundle School in Northamptonshire, with an interest in developing the curriculum towards a more general education. Olive raised the standard of Dauntsey's by securing a staff with excellent qualifications. One such was the science master, E. R. B. Reynolds, who had fought in the 1914-18 war, during which he had been badly shot up. On demobilisation, Reynolds had gone to Durham University where he got a First Class Degree. Other characters on the staff included F. N. S. Creek, a Cambridge Association Football Blue, who used to play for the Corinthians and R. S. Barron, an especially tall teacher who was nicknamed 'Georgie Giraffe'. 'I'm afraid,' says Wilbert, 'we ragged Georgie rather a lot – but the extraordinary thing was, he stuck it!'

The atmosphere at Dauntsey's was very different to the tight-laced mood which had prevailed at Marlborough House School. It was not that there were less rules, for there were plenty, listed and pinned to the underside of desk lids. One such injunction ran: 'Tuck is a luxury and not a necessity, for the food supplied is good in quality and ample in quantity. These regulations are to prevent greediness and the bad habit of eating between meals.' What was refreshing was that, every now and again, the boys at Dauntsey's made a spirited attempt at breaking some of these rules!

Wilbert enjoyed the fact that Dauntseians engaged in the usual schoolboy japes such as a prank regularly played with the lighting that was worthy of the mischievous Bruin Boys. There being, at the time, no electricity, the school was lit by acetylene, fuelled by a gas plant in the workshop. Before prep, a boy would slip outside and blow down the gas pipe so that the lamplight faded away, making prep impossible until the master in charge of mechanics, E. L. ('Levi') Batten, restored the lights!

Wilbert was 'altogether much happier' at Dauntsey's and threw himself into school life joining the Debating, Dramatic and Science Societies; membership of the latter resulting in the following entry for December 1925 in Lucy Awdry's diary: 'Wilbert got damaged in a slight explosion before the Conversazione of the Science Society. I went by the 1.55 bus [and] brought him home with me next day.' Members of the society had been giving a demonstration of various chemical operations, one of which was the manufacture of oxygen. Wilbert's partner in the experiment, a boy named Hedges, was very short sighted and mistook black powdered carbon for the real catalyst, manganese dioxide, which is also black. The effect, as Wilbert recalls, was devastating: 'BANG! Hedges escaped unscathed while my face was spattered by bits of glass and red hot debris. It was fortunate that – very unwillingly – I had put on my spectacles which prevented anything from getting into my eyes.'

Wilbert also joined the Camera Club, which confirmed his fascination (inherited from his father) with photography. In later life, Wilbert was to use his considerable skills with a camera not just for the ubiquitous family 'snaps' but to compile valuable photographic records of his railway travels and discoveries.

The Camera Club darkroom was also home to the Radio Club, of which Wilbert (an early enthusiast of radio) was in charge. If, however, the darkroom was ever left in a mess, George Olive would lock it up, making it impossible for the Club to get at the radio. On one such occasion, at the request of the boys in the school rest room, Wilbert had levered open a window, climbed into the darkroom and switched on the radio set:

> The next day in assembly, Olive stood up and said: 'When I lock a room I expect it to stay locked. One of you boys has been into that darkroom. I know the boy who did this and that boy knows I know!' Thinking the game was up,

> I decided to confess, but he didn't really know it was me because I had my hand up for some time and he was so busy staring at the younger boys, whom he obviously suspected, that he didn't notice! In fact, I had to call out and say: 'It was me!' As a result of which, I got six of the best!

This was a rare misdemeanour and, as a leaving report from George Olive shows, Wilbert had 'throughout shown a very good character'. Indeed, Wilbert became a school prefect – 'an appointment,' his headmaster later wrote, 'which I never make unless I am quite sure of the character of the boy'.

The question began to be addressed: what should Wilbert do when he completes his schooling? Initially, there seems to have been no thought of Wilbert going on to higher education, partly because family income would not allow it and partly because his mother did not see him as particularly promising academic material. A curious entry in Lucy Awdry's diary for 1926, notes: 'There was talk of Wilbert taking up building and contracting and I had several interviews in Bath about it.' 'This,' says Wilbert, 'was another of mother's schemes.'

At one point, Lucy Awdry looked into the possibility of Wilbert going to work in Canada, where her brother, Arthur, lived. She discussed this idea when she visited her brother in 1927 and lined up an interview in London for Wilbert with a Mr Busfield, who was one of Uncle Arthur's Canadian business friends. Mr Busfield took Wilbert to the theatre to see *The Importance of Being Earnest*, gave him tea and talked to him about various career opportunities in Canada. 'Mother,' says Wilbert, 'didn't think I had enough push – so she tried to get behind me and do a bit of pushing – but it didn't work!' The analogy to those contrary coaches and troublesome trucks attempting to push around the engines in the Railway Series is irresistible. The only thing to come of the Canadian discussions was the recommendation that Wilbert first acquire a degree.

Wilbert found it increasingly hard to cope with time spent at home. His father was often out deputising for priests who were sick or on holiday; and his mother, when not attempting to organise Wilbert, was devoting an increasing amount of her time and attention to worrying about the sickly George. To add insult to injury, George rapidly outgrew Wilbert (despite being five years his junior) and reached a height of 6' 5", as a result of which the elder brother was expected to wear the younger brother's cast-offs.

Wilbert admits that, as a youngster, he resented George's recurrent bouts of illness which he suspected were as much as anything due to his mother's overpowering anxiety for her younger son. Whatever the reason, it prevented the boys from sharing many activities. As a baby, George had been too young for Wilbert to play with; now that they were older and might have shared interests and activities George always seemed unwell.

The brothers did begin a model railway layout together at Journey's End. Electric models were available but, says Wilbert, 'beyond our touch'; so they made do with a clockwork 00 gauge railway purchased at pocket-money prices ('an engine costing two shillings and sixpence, coaches at nine pence, trucks at sixpence and lengths of tin-plate rail for three pence') laid out in a garden shed sold to them 'at a knock-down price' by a neighbour who was moving.

Wilbert and George also shared a passion for the wireless and particularly enjoyed the popular 1920's B.B.C. comedy programme featuring an eccentric family called *The Buggins Family*, whose comic exchanges they committed to memory and often re-ran (even fifty years later):

MR BUGGINS: Don't switch the wireless off, Grandma, you've spoilt the first decent bit of humour I've had for a fortnight!

GRANDMA: You ain't got no humour to speak of and if you had it wouldn't be decent!

Back at school, Wilbert continued his studies, passing his School Certificate with credits in English, History, French, Latin and Chemistry. Being, as he puts it, 'interested in electrics of all sorts', Wilbert decided to study for his Higher Certificate (the equivalent of today's 'A' Levels) in Physics, Chemistry and French.

Wilbert was also attending Confirmation classes led by the school chaplain, a local vicar named Percival Sexty, who was to play a key role in his later career. Wilbert was confirmed in the faith of the Church of England on 26th November, 1926 at West Lavington church by the Bishop of Salisbury: 'I think I shared the experience of a lot of Confirmation candidates in that the service didn't live up to what I had been told to expect of it. I waited for something to happen – to feel "different" after the Bishop had laid hands on me – but all I felt at first was an acute sense of disappointment.'

Wilbert may have entertained doubts about whether he should have gone forward for Confirmation for when, following the service, he was confined to the school sick-room with 'water on the knee', he was relieved that this excused him from having to attend his first Communion at Percival Sexty's church. What Wilbert saw as 'a blessing in disguise' meant that he was able to receive the sacrament from his own father on Christmas Day 1926.

The following year, the family had what was to be their last holiday together on the Channel Island, Jersey, which Vere had visited as a small child and was anxious to see again. Holidays, as Wilbert recalls them, were invariably 'geared down for George' who, on this occasion, was confined to a wheel chair.

As far as Wilbert's parents were concerned, the holiday on Jersey was a success: 'We had a very happy time indeed there,' wrote Lucy Awdry, 'Daddy especially was intensely happy and well and he pushed George about in his chair with great vigour.' However, Vere Awdry was seventy-three and had experienced several years of indifferent health. Nevertheless, he had continued to work, preaching and officiating at different churches on virtually every Sunday, duties which often involved considerable travelling. During a train strike in 1924, when he was then seventy, Vere made a twenty mile journey home on foot in torrential rain, an ordeal which badly affected his health.

His age and his unrelenting commitment to his work took their toll. On 1st January, 1928, Lucy Awdry recorded that 'Daddy was not feeling at all well'; and, a month later his doctor was describing him as being in 'a very serious state of health'.

Wilbert who was at Dauntsey School for his seventeenth birthday on 15th June, received a postcard from his father:

Dear old Boy
Just a line to wish you many happy returns of your birthday tomorrow. I am on my back now as no doubt Mother has told you but hope to be on my hind legs again long before you get home. Mother and I are sending you a knife which I hope will please you.
No time for more.
Your aff.
Dad

Two weeks later, Vere appeared to be getting better and by 4th July was able to take a short walk with his wife: 'It was,' wrote Lucy Awdry, 'such a joyful and hopeful thing.' On 12th July, a postcard arrived from George, who was now a day boy at Dauntsey's and living with Gertie Whatmore in a cottage near the school. George had recently had his bicycle stolen:

My dear Mother,
Today I am going into Devizes about my bike as the police have caught the

chap and I have to go to the police court about it.
George

Lucy Awdry took the card up to Vere's bedroom with his breakfast tray and later wrote in her diary that he was 'most amused about it'. The diary entry continues: 'An hour later, Daddy fell in his room (I was downstairs). He never recovered consciousness.'

At Dauntsey's, George Olive sent for Wilbert and told him that a car was waiting to take him home: 'Nobody told me what had happened. I knew something was wrong with father, but, until I arrived home, I didn't know what it was.'

Over the years, Wilbert had got used to his father being away for several days at a time and the fact that he was not around did not, at first, seem particularly strange. Besides, there was little time for thinking: George was staying with relatives and there was only Wilbert to help his mother: 'I do not know what I should have done without Wilbert,' wrote Lucy Awdry, 'he was ready to do everything that was wanted.'

Then came the funeral on 16th July. John Pack, who had been the Awdry's gardener at Ampfield, travelled to Box to act as one of the pall-bearers. For Wilbert, the service was cathartic: 'It was only then that it hit me. I felt, suddenly, as if everything in life had changed for ever and I broke down in the pew and wept.'

Among the letters of condolence received by Lucy Awdry was one from Archdeacon Talbot that testifies to the affection and esteem in which her husband was held:

My dear Mrs Awdry,
I am so grieved for you and your family in the passing of your dear husband.
He was so remarkable a man that I shall never forget him. His dignity, his piety, his zeal made an impression wherever he went.
He will be greatly missed in our churches, and how much more in your own family circle – I do tender you my most sincere sympathy.
May God help and comfort you and show you the way in this dark hour.
Ever yours sincerely,
R. T. Talbot

Some months later, a carved panel was put up in one of the many places of worship where Vere Awdry had served as priest: 'Here for a space Vere Awdry prayed and taught and made plain to all who heard him the glory of the word.'

Of Lucy Awdry's reaction, it is difficult to speak with any certainty. She was grieved by the death of her husband, but theirs was an unusual relationship. Were they in love? 'I don't think they were,' says Wilbert, 'at least, it was not the first fond careless rapture because my father was too old. The real love of his life was his beloved Maggie, his first wife. And, in a way, his second wife, Mary, because she too had known and been fond of Maggie.'

Wilbert recalls his mother telling him that Vere so often talked about what 'his Mary' and 'his Maggie' had done that, in self-defence, she 'invented a Charles and a Henry' whom she would talk about whenever Vere began discussing his former wives.

It took Wilbert some time to come to terms with his father's death: 'He'd always been in the background; and although he didn't particularly say anything or make his influence felt in a disciplinary way, he was always there and the house ran round him.'

After a week, Wilbert returned to Dauntsey's. 'I remember,' he says, 'standing in the common room, trying to pick up the pieces, to connect things up. The other boys were generally shouting about but there was one chap, G. A. [later Sir Gordon] Ransome, with whom I had never been particularly friendly, but whom I happened to know was, so to speak, an orphan like me. Ransome came up to me and, without specially saying anything, shook me by the hand. I knew that he understood what I was going through and that helped me begin to get back into the swim of life again.'

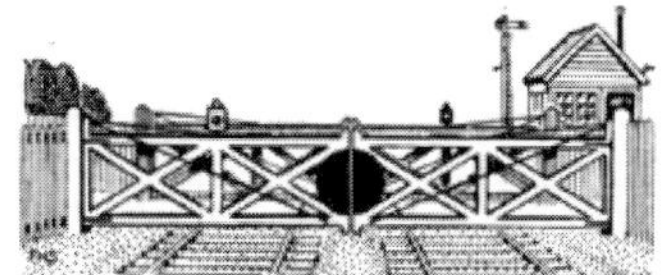

CHAPTER THREE

"A very charming fellow indeed"

RECALLING family life, after the death of his father, Wilbert describes his mother as being 'lumbered' with George and himself: 'Certainly she felt she was doing her duty by us, but with it she was increasingly possessive and she did make it extremely uncomfortable for George and I if we didn't agree to do the things of which she approved.'

In August 1928, a notice appeared in the property columns of the local newspaper: 'LADY Wants to SELL Convenient HOME. Six miles from Bath, good trains and bus. Three Sitting, Five Bedrooms, Bathroom; Gas and Water; small Garden, Greenhouse; good cupboards and storage room; Immediate Vacant Possession.'

Having sold Journey's End, Lucy Awdry and Gertie Whatmore moved to Great Cheverell, so as to be close to Dauntsey School. It was now possible for the boys to live at home, but whilst George was a day boy, Wilbert clung to his independence and remained a boarder until he left school.

The new house had 'quite a number of useful out-buildings', and Wilbert and George were soon collaborating on a new model railway layout. An old stable became a carpentry shop with shelving all round the wall on which the trains would eventually run. With 'great daring and at considerable risk', the brothers fitted up an electric cable running from the house along the garden, on a series of posts, and through a hole in the stable wall to where they fixed a socket for an electric soldering iron. 'It would have made an electrician's hair stand on end,' says Wilbert, 'but somehow we managed to survive!'

The boys decided to make their own rails, getting a garage in Devizes to cut tin-plate sheet into strips for sleepers and buying square buzz-bar wire, used for wiring-up radio sets, which they soldered onto the sleepers : 'It made very good track – and it was *amazingly* cheap!'

Wilbert took another step in his quest for independence when he received his first lessons in driving from James Browning, the local taxi-man. Now eighteen years old, Wilbert had begun to spread his wings. 'We saw much of George and his friends,' observed Lucy Awdry in her diary, 'Wilbert came occasionally, but he had more to do!' The exclamation-mark makes clear her feelings.

The question of Wilbert's career was an on-going bone of contention. It was eventually agreed that Wilbert should try for a degree and the most obvious subject to choose, in view of Wilbert's interest in things mechanical and electronic, was engineering. Three months before Vere Awdry's death, Lucy had taken Wilbert to Bristol to see the university there. As with several of his 'mother's schemes', Wilbert managed to deflect the Bristol proposal: 'Soon after this,' his mother noted, 'Wilbert had a thought of studying Analytical Chemistry.' Although this was something he had read about in a careers brochure, it probably represented little more than a desire to try and determine his own future.

Wilbert's school days were drawing to a close. He had done well at Dauntsey's, entering into all aspects of school life with enthusiasm and a strong sense of responsibility. He had played for the school First XI cricket team and, in December 1928, took part in the end of term dramatic presentation of Shakespeare's *Henry IV, Part I*. Sixty-seven years on, Wilbert can still rattle off the speeches of the offended Thomas Percy, Earl of Worcester: 'Our house, my sovereign liege, little deserves the scourge of greatness to be us'd on it – and that same greatness too which our own hands have holp to make so portly.'

Lucy Awdry attended the production at which she spoke with her son's French master, Mr Ault, who was 'very enthusiastic about Wilbert's French'. A month later, Ault visited Mrs Awdry and urged her to let Wilbert pursue French instead of Physics and Chemistry, but the die was cast. 'It proved to be a big mistake,' recalls Wilbert, 'because I passed in electronics but not in the other branches of Physics!'

Despite this setback, there was now talk of Wilbert trying for one of the Oxbridge colleges. Cambridge was favoured because there was no requirement to pass an entry examination for the University, whereas Oxford required prospective students to sit what is called the Oxford Responsions. However, it was to Oxford that Wilbert wanted to go. He had first visited what Keats described as 'the finest city in the world', in April 1923, when he was still at Marlborough House School. The purpose of the trip was, ostensibly, to consider whether Wilbert might go on to Magdalen College School, but – since it was his mother who accompanied him – the trip also involved the usual quota of sightseeing.

Lucy Awdry and her son visited Christ Church crossing Tom Quad where, within living memory, the Reverend Charles Lutwidge Dodgson had studied, tutored and (under the pen-name Lewis Carroll) written *Alice's Adventures in Wonderland*; they also visited Magdalen College, where, within a couple of years, C. S. Lewis – another academic to achieve fame as a writer for children – would take up residence. They attended a service in the Cathedral, went on the river and, on 23rd April (Shakespeare's birthday), visited the Bodleian Library to see the First Folio of the Bard's plays, that was exhibited only on that one day in the year.

Support for Wilbert's ambition to go to Oxford came in a letter from Dora Vernon, a friend of Lucy Awdry who was a courtesy aunt to Wilbert. Married to Philip Vernon, an Oxford don, 'Aunt Dora' had been asked for her advice; her reply, wrote Lucy Awdry in her diary, 'directed our thoughts to Oxford'. New colleges were being established, one of which offered opportunities to boys, such as Wilbert, who came from low-income families.

St Peter's Hall (now St Peter's College) began as a dream of Bishop Francis James Chavasse, former Bishop of Liverpool. Retiring in 1923, Chavasse had gone to live in New Inn Hall Street, Oxford. Close by was the church of St Peter-le-Bailey, of which, twenty-five years earlier, he had been rector. During Chavasse's time at St Peter-le-Bailey, a wind of change had begun to blow through Oxford. In 1871, the University of Oxford had recognised Keble College as a New Foundation. Keble had been conceived, financed and built in order to 'make all the academical and other privileges of Oxford life accessible to men of limited means and also maintain the traditional association of university education with the Church of England'.

Whilst Bishop Chavasse had always acknowledged that Keble College was 'a proof of what can be done by the exercise of faith, foresight, courage and self-sacrifice', as an Evangelical Christian he viewed the ethos of Keble College as distinctly 'High Church'. He began to shape a scheme for creating a new college that would follow the example set by Keble, but with allegiance to the Evangelical, rather than the Anglo-Catholic, wing of the church.

Since, in 1923, the Rector of St Peter-le-Bailey was not living in the Rectory, Bishop Chavasse rented and moved into the handsome Georgian building in New Inn Hall Street. Next door stood the church, built to accommodate a congregation of 500 but serving an increasingly dwindling parish. It was in 1926, as an early account explains, that Bishop Chavasse framed his vision: 'As he moved among the gardens and buildings of St Peter-le-Bailey his sagacious eye perceived how they might be rescued from their obscurity and transformed into a rich opportunity.'

Money was raised and, whilst Bishop Chavasse did not live to see the fruit of his labours, St Peter's Hall opened in October 1929 with the Bishop's son, Christopher Chavasse as its first Master.

It was discovered that, in order to get into St Peter's, Wilbert didn't have to re-sit his Higher School Certificate, since he was able to offer his School

Herbert ('Bert') Awdry (1851-1909). One of Vere Awdry's favourite brothers who, with William, provided the name 'Wilbert' given to Vere's second son.

Sir John Wither Awdry (1795-1878), Wilbert's grandfather, from a portrait made when he was around fifty years old.

William Awdry (1842-1910). Vere's other favourite brother, later Bishop of Osaka and South Tokyo, Japan.

ABOVE Sir John and Lady Awdry and members of their family photographed, possibly by William Henry Fox Talbot, outside Notton House, Wiltshire, in October 1867.

LEFT Vere Awdry (1854-1928), Wilbert's father.

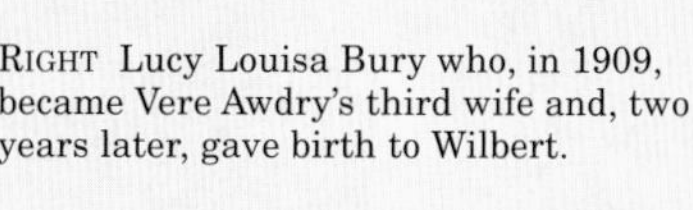

RIGHT Lucy Louisa Bury who, in 1909, became Vere Awdry's third wife and, two years later, gave birth to Wilbert.

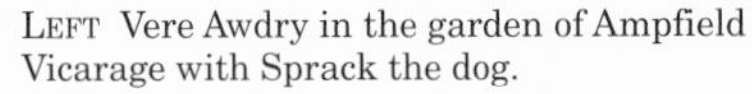

LEFT Vere Awdry in the garden of Ampfield Vicarage with Sprack the dog.

RIGHT Lucy Awdry, Wilbert's mother, whose decorated *Record Book* charts her son's first year of life.

BELOW CENTRE Pages from Lucy's diary showing photographs of the Ampfield Model Railway which ran in the vicarage garden.

INSERT Wilbert having a 'coach-run' with one of the coaches on the A.M.R.

Carol and Bridget Awdry playing in the garden of Ampfield Vicarage; photographed sometime before Bridget's death in 1900.

'He had a quantity of fluffy hair, almost black, and a loud and persistent voice...' Wilbert Vere Awdry, photographed in 1911.

Wilbert Awdry riding in a wicker carrier on his half-brother Carol's bicycle – an event from which young Wilbert always derived 'huge delight'.

Carol Edward Vere Awdry in his uniform as 2nd Lieutenant with the Royal Munster Fusiliers, with whom he was serving when he was killed during the retreat from Mons in August 1914.

RIGHT Gertie Whatmore who came to work at Ampfield Vicarage in 1916 and remained as a companion to Lucy Awdry until her death.

Vere, Carol and Lucy Awdry, photographed in July 1913, the year before war broke out and Carol Awdry went to his death.

Vere Awdry taking part in Romsey pageant as William of Wykeham, the fourteenth century Bishop of Winchester and Chancellor of England.

'The Men of the Family': Vere, Wilbert and Carol Awdry (with Sprack the dog) photographed in July 1913.

Wilbert Awdry, now a school boy, with his younger brother, George.

Dauntsey School (formerly Dauntsey Agricultural School) where Wilbert was a pupil from1924-1929. His uncles, Charles Awdry and Colonel R. W. Awdry both served as chairman of the school governors.

Wilbert Awdry (goalkeeper) pictured at the centre of a school XI in the 1920s. Wilbert had a love for most sports, particularly cricket and rowing at which he excelled during his college days.

Part of St Peter's Hall (now St Peter's College), Oxford.

The brothers Wilbert and George Awdry, photographed in the 1920s.

'I hung on for dear life and hoped for the best ...' Wilbert astride a camel in Palestine.

'Pharaoh's Treasury' at Petra, 'the rose-red city – "Half as old as Time".' It was here that Wilbert Awdry proposed marriage to Margaret Wale.

Wilbert and companion *en route* by train for Damascus.

Wilbert's photograph of Jerusalem, taken during his three-year period as a teacher at St George's School. Wilbert visited many of the places of pilgrimage within and around the city, an experience which gave a new dimension to his Christian faith.

ABOVE St George's School, Jerusalem where Wilbert taught for three years from 1933.

LEFT The Jericho Road, on the way down to Allenby Bridge; Margaret Wale (left) and Miss Wilson by a sign showing sea level.

The Church of All Saints, Odiham, Hampshire, where Wilbert Awdry was appointed curate in 1936.

Wilbert and his fiancée Margaret Wale, back from the Holy Land for a brief holiday in England, pictured with Wilbert's Aunt Polly in 1937.

Tuesday
August 30 1938 Wilbert's & Mea's Wedding.
At eight in the morning a lovely day & a beautifully tranquil service with Holy Communion. The Vicar Mr. McClagan has known them all many years. (his wife was there too.)
Mr & Mrs Wale Mr & Mrs Penny, Doris Pethord & a certain 'Brenda' were the only ones there besides ourselves.
We all went back to the Wales to breakfast which was beautifully organized.
They went off by train to Ambleside at 12.34. after lunch Mr. Wale & a friend of his met us & took us round the Cathedral – we then went back to help send off the cards & cake
on 31st we went over the China Factory & Commandery & in the afternoon met Mrs Wale & Mrs Penny for a motor coach trip to the Malverns & Tewkesbury
Sept 1st we returned home.

ABOVE Lucy Awdry's diary entry for the day of Wilbert's and Margaret's marriage. The photograph shows the happy couple outside the house of Margaret's parents in Worcester and a scrap of the material from which Margaret's dress was made is pinned to the page.

Margaret Emily Wale, to whom Wilbert became engaged at Easter 1936.

RIGHT Walnut Tree Cottage at Odiham, Wilbert and Margaret Awdry's first married home.

Wilbert and Margaret Awdry with their new-born son, Christopher, July 1940.

St Nicholas Church, King's Norton, where Wilbert served his third curacy.

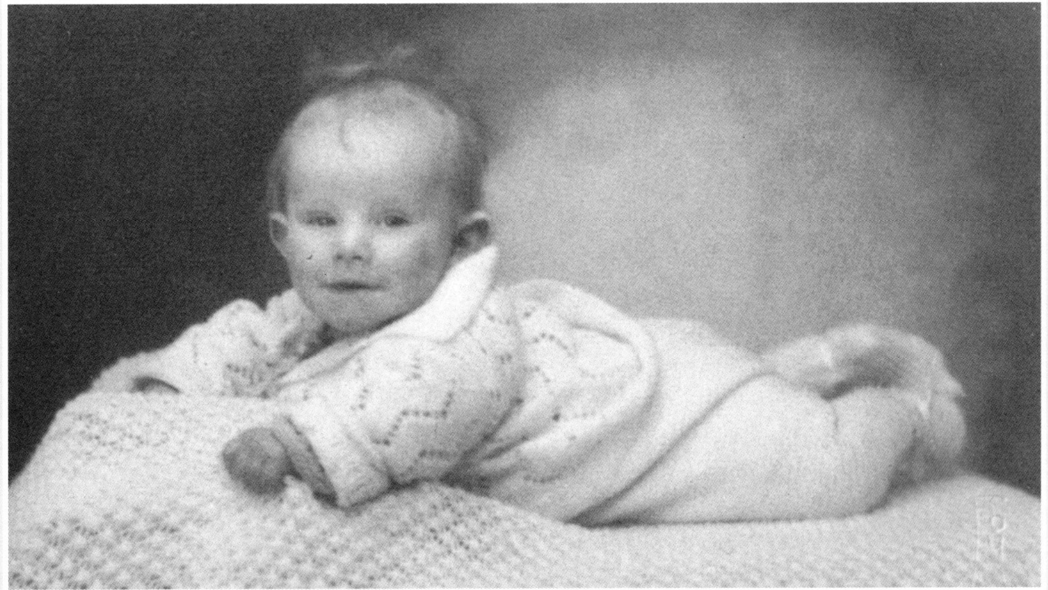

Christopher Vere Awdry, the little boy who would eventually provide the inspiration for the telling of what became the first volume of the Railway Series.

Christopher Awdry at two years old with his mother and maternal grandmother.

Wilbert and Margaret Awdry's two daughters, Hilary and Veronica.

The Church of the Holy Trinity at Elsworth, Cambridgeshire, where Wilbert Awdry became rector in 1946.

Margaret Awdry (far right with Hilary) and the team of church-cleaners at Elsworth.

Chilly bathers! Hilary, Christopher and Veronica Awdry during a family holiday at St Anne's-on-Sea, August 1950.

Christopher, Veronica and Hilary Awdry together with a young friend have fun on a merry-go-round at a Church Fete at Elsworth. Wilbert Awdry turns the handle in the background.

ABOVE Beside the sea-side: Wilbert and his children during a holiday in the 1950s.

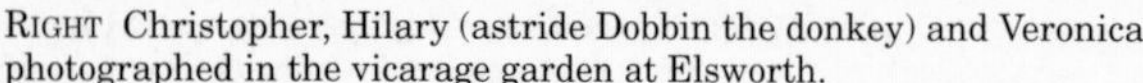

RIGHT Christopher, Hilary (astride Dobbin the donkey) and Veronica photographed in the vicarage garden at Elsworth.

Certificate together with an extra subject, Maths, which he passed with credit.

Wilbert received fine letters of commendation from the staff at Dauntsey School; the Headmaster, George Olive, describing him as 'a strong-charactered boy in whom I should put every trust'. His form master, E. R. B. Reynolds, wrote:

> I have always found him perfectly reliable and trustworthy; he bears an exemplary character. He is a boy of very good ability in science and mathematics, to my personal knowledge, and he applies himself to problems in science, particularly, in a very intelligent manner. I am sure he would prove a worthy member of any college and I recommend him for St Peters with every confidence.

On 30th April, Christopher Chavasse wrote to 'W. V. Awdry Esq.': 'I am very glad to be able to accept you for St Peter's for the Michaelmas term 1929. And I am sure you will do all in your power to help me build up the right traditions at the Hall.'

Leaving Dauntsey's, Wilbert passed the summer in company with Pierre Adeleine, a young Frenchman from Beaune who came to Britain on a cultural exchange: five weeks with the Awdrys – including two weeks in Oxford on what was presumably a familiarisation exercise for Wilbert, involving what Lucy Awdry described as 'a good deal of college sight-seeing' – followed by five weeks in France. Leaving for what was Wilbert's first overseas visit (beyond the Channel Islands) the two young men stopped off for a day in Paris with some of Pierre's student friends and, as Lucy Awdry notes in her diary – with perhaps a hint of disapproval – did not arrive in Beaune until four o'clock the following morning!

Wilbert returned home from France on 3rd October and, one week later, left Great Cheverell for Oxford as one of St Peter's first Collegiate members following the official recognition of the college. Looking back on 1929 in her diary, Lucy Awdry rightly described it as having been 'Wilbert's Year'.

Wilbert Awdry first entered St Peter's Hall, as visitors still do, through the front door of Linton House, a fine three-storey building in honey-coloured stone built in 1797; latterly the Rectory of St Peter-le-Bailey, now the college Library. Today, Linton House has a portico; then it had only the crest of the crossed keys of St Peter which Bishop Chavasse had put up above the doorway.

Behind Linton House and the Chapel (formerly the church of St Peter-le-Bailey) ran a long building which contained three Residential Staircases, overlooking a garden bounded by part of the old City Wall and a distant view of Oxford Castle. The garden made a picturesque corner with a lawn, a magnificent mulberry tree and the fourth Residential Staircase, built on a right-angle. An ornate doorway lead to four floors of student rooms, the topmost being in the sharply roofed attic beneath tall chimney-stacks. It was in one of these rooms that Wilbert had a double study which he shared with another undergraduate, H. G. ('Snoop') Wood.

Having 'come a complete cropper' over his Higher School Certificate, Wilbert wasn't, at first, sure what to read. He 'stalled' for a year by reading for the preliminary examination, Pass Moderations – comprising Latin, French, Economics and English – which, once passed, would allow him to read French, English or History: 'I wasn't going to read Science *at all*!' However, at his first sitting, in the Hilary term of 1930, Wilbert failed his Pass Mods. He re-sat the exam in the Trinity term, passed and chose the subject for his degree: 'I plumped for a subject that was reasonably simple and straightforward – Modern History.'

Life at Oxford was not all study and Wilbert actively involved himself in the sporting life of the college. Since there were only some fifty men at St Peter's Hall, each had a chance to represent the college in at least one sport: 'As well as being in the College Cricket XI, they tried me at hockey and even at athletics – I must have been a very keen chap! – in which I damaged myself considerably trying to run a hurdle race!' What he really enjoyed, however, was rowing, and he became a member of the 1931 St Peter's Hall 'Eight'. Wilbert rowed 'bow', No. 1, in the front of boat and, as was later reported in a testimonial from the college, became 'famous for pulling an oar far beyond what might be expected from his weight'.

In his second year, Wilbert would enjoy a remarkably successful rowing season and, for the rest of his life, would keep his oars – inscribed with the crew's names and their victories – mounted on the walls of his various rectories and vicarages. Eventually, when Wilbert retired to a much smaller house in Stroud, where wall space was at a premium, the oars had to be cut down to their blades, although they were still given pride of place in the hall where they hang to this day.

While Wilbert was at Oxford he began, for really the first time, to consider his attitude towards the Christian faith: 'Until then, I suppose, I had taken those things for granted. Although I had been brought up in a completely Christian home, religion was never forced on us. We were not allowed to play games with cards or dice, but otherwise there were few, if any, restrictions and, unlike many children, we were not expected to read "special" books on a Sunday. Provided we went to church once, the rest of the day was free. Since there was no real compulsion about it, there was nothing to rebel against and I grew up taking that tolerant attitude for granted.'

At Oxford, matters of faith and belief were challenged and debated and whilst Wilbert avoided 'getting tied up to any particular "ism" ', there were a number of men at St Peter's Hall who were Christian, among them his friend David Mercier (whose father was Vicar of Huyton, near Liverpool) with whom he shared bicycle rides and a vacation in Belgium. Wilbert also came 'under the influence' of various undergraduate religious societies such as the Oxford Inter-Collegiate Christian Union. Gradually, the faith he had subscribed to as a matter of course since his childhood began to have a personal meaning for him.

After two years' study Wilbert got a degree. 'It was,' he remarks, 'only a Third Class – but a *brilliant* Third Class: "Gamma + +" !' The decision as to what he would do next had already been reached. 'I finally decided,' he says, 'that the job for me was that of a parson.' As simple as that? Perhaps not. Pressed as to whether, at this point in his life, he believed he had a vocation for the priesthood, Wilbert admits that it was, to a certain extent, the best option available to him. It was a profession about which, as a clergyman's son, he knew a great deal; Wilbert would be following not just in his father's footsteps but also in those of his uncle, Bishop William Awdry. The decision taken, it was necessary for Wilbert to find a place at a theological college.

The concept of the theological college, where men trained for the ministry, had only emerged at the end of the nineteenth century. Hitherto, someone could enter Holy Orders simply on the strength of an Oxbridge degree in classics or logic and after having had a few months 'work experience' with an ordained clergyman. Invariably, ordained men returned to work in the area where they had lived before going to University and where their social standing was already established. As the historian G. M. Trevelyan has expressed it, the clergy were, for the most part, 'a rather more learned branch of the squireachy'; indeed, a church dictate of 1864 expressed the view that 'a man of refined taste and good social position carries more influence with the lower classes than one destitute of these qualifications'.

Even after the establishment of theological colleges – such as the one at Chichester of which William Awdry had been principal – the class system continued operating so that even sons of wealthy tradesmen were often unable to get parishes, being passed over in favour of those from the higher echelons of society.

Of the theological colleges which came into being, some were founded by Diocesan Bishops, while others grew out of movements within the church, such as the Oxford Movement and the Evangelical Revival. In 1877, one such group of Evangelicals – partly hoping to prevent young clergymen from 'dabbling in ritualistic practices' – founded two colleges: Ridley Hall in Cambridge (named after the sixteenth century Protestant martyr, Nicholas Ridley) and Wycliffe Hall in Oxford (dedicated to the memory of John Wycliffe, the fourteenth century theologian and philosopher). Ridley and Wycliffe were designed to be 'finishing schools' for Oxbridge graduates of an Evangelical persuasion.

The first Principal of Wycliffe was the Reverend R. Baker-Girdlestone, considered 'a great Bible-student, a man of real learning and wisdom, of humility and patience'. He was in need of the latter qualities, since, in its first year, Wycliffe Hall had only *one* student – who left with poor health after the Lent term! It was to be five more years before the number of students reached double figures.

In 1889, Wycliffe acquired a new principal, Dr Francis Chavasse, Rector of St Peter-le-Bailey (where he would later found St Peter's Hall). Chavasse was a man of considerable charisma and his association with Wycliffe brought many new students to the college. During the eleven years before Chavasse left to become Bishop of Liverpool, he trained many students – no less than six of whom went on to become bishops.

By the time Wilbert Awdry went to Wycliffe Hall, there was no longer any opposition within the church towards theological colleges. In fact, in 1906, the House of Canterbury had expressed the desire that 'after a good degree at some university, men in training for Holy Orders should spend one year in a theological college'. Fourteen years later, the Church of England instituted a General Ordination Examination.

Wycliffe Hall – or 'Wickers' as students called it – occupied a grand four-storey red-brick house on the Banbury Road, backing onto the University Parks which ran down to the River Cherwell. Wilbert was interviewed by the then Principal, Dr (later Bishop) George Francis Graham-Brown to see if he was, as Wilbert puts it, 'proper material'. The General Ordination Examination was a two year course, but a student with a degree could take a one year course in order to sit for his Diploma in Theology. Since Wilbert's degree results were as yet unknown – enquiries were made of Christopher Chavasse at St Peter's.

A letter from Chavasse, supporting Wilbert's candidature, suggests that even if Wilbert may have still entertained doubts about his 'calling', they were not shared by others:

> I can recommend Mr W. V. Awdry with all my heart as a suitable candidate for ordination . . . I cannot speak too highly of his character or his behaviour. He possesses average ability and is developing in intellectual capacity . . .

> I have always hoped he would see his way to take Holy Orders, especially as he has been one of the leaders in everything of a religious character in the Hall. His moral character is beyond reproach, and he is a very charming fellow indeed.

Wilbert went to Wycliffe Hall in 1932, and, in July of the following year, sat and passed the examination for his Diploma in Theology. Wilbert's tutor (later a Master of St Peter's Hall) was the Reverend Julian Thornton-Duesbury who, during Wilbert's year, was appointed to the headship of St George's School, Jerusalem. 'Thornton-Duesbury,' says Wilbert, 'was firmly of the opinion that anyone wanting to be ordained should first show that they could hold down a secular job, so he offered me a three year contract as a schoolmaster.'

A multi-racial boy's school, St George's was run as a missionary endeavour which meant that Jewish and Moslem parents wanting their children to be educated had to accept that they would also receive teaching in the Christian faith. The school had some two hundred pupils, of whom a little less than half were boarders. Locating pupils within the right class was not always easy since there was no system of birth registration and staff could rarely be sure of a boy's age. The youngest pupils were taught by Arab mistresses, after which they were taught in English by Arab masters and then in English by the English staff members. Wilbert was required to teach everything – English, Mathematics, History and Geography – but the experience would be invaluable and there was the not inconsiderable bonus for a student of Theology planning to enter the Christian ministry of being in the Holy Land and having an opportunity to walk 'in the steps of the Master'.

Wilbert was twenty-two years old when he arrived in Jerusalem on 26th September, 1933. The son of his mother, he immediately began recording his experiences in letters home which she later transcribed into a diary:

> 1st day in Jerusalem – Saw official reception of Empress of Abyssinia, all the Abyssinian Priests in their gorgeous robes swinging incense about. We got to the place just inside the Jaffa Gate about 9.15 and waited till she arrived. There was a most tremendous crowd, as more and more people came we were pushed farther back till we were right in front of a very smelly butcher's shop and I was made to lean heavily against a large piece of meat or it may have been the butcher himself, I couldn't turn round to see.

Wilbert's three years in Palestine were to have a powerful effect on his life:

at St George's, he learnt to get along with many different types, classes and races; he developed, in the classroom, invaluable skills in communication; he continued the process of liberating himself from the overpowering influence of his mother (his letters home were 'selective' in what they reported); and his faith acquired a new vividness from visiting the sites – genuine or reputed – of many of the events related in the Bible.

At the excavated site of the 'Gabbatha' (the 'Pavement' in what was once the Fort of Antonia) Wilbert was deeply moved by the realisation that this was where the palace of Pontius Pilate had stood and where Jesus would have been brought for trial: 'These very stones must have been the ones on which Jesus walked when he started off to Calvary carrying His Cross.'

Wilbert was able to visit many of the places referred to in both the Old and New Testaments, at first as a marvelling tourist, later as a guide for students on a visit from 'Wickers'. Within Jerusalem itself Wilbert walked along what the Crusaders called 'The Street of Bad Cooking' where food was still sold and, he noted, 'still smells very bad indeed'; he saw the Pool of Bethesda, where Jesus told the paralyzed man to take up his bed and walk; the prison within the House of Caiaphas the High Priest, where Jesus was held prisoner; and the quarries where, centuries before even those events, stone had been cut for the building of Solomon's Temple.

Wilbert visited the villages of Capernaum, where Jesus healed the servant of the Roman Centurion; Bethany, where he raised Lazarus from the dead; Ain Karim, 'a lovely village built on two sides of a valley', traditionally believed to be the birthplace of John the Baptist; and Cana, where Wilbert attended a wedding of Amin Saffoureh, who was one of the masters at St George's: 'It was a holiday for the whole village. The young men danced queer dances . . . and, at about 11.15, all the men in our party, the friends of the bridegroom, went up to fetch the bride. We went into the house and all sat round the sides of the room and had some coffee given to us and waited till the bride was ready.' It was in this village, almost two thousand years earlier, that Christ himself had attended a marriage feast and performed his first miracle by turning water into wine.

In Bethlehem, Wilbert was much moved by his visit to the Church of the Nativity. The church's West door having been bricked-up, probably during the Turkish persecution, Wilbert entered, as do all visitors, through 'a very tiny door about 3ft 6 high,' which ensured 'that anyone going into the place of our Lord's birth should have to bow his head.' It was an experience which Wilbert was never to forget and, in later years, would often refer to in talks at his children's church services.

Describing the interior of the Church of the Nativity, Wilbert wrote: 'The high altar is shut off from the main part of the church by a magnificent screen. Just before you get to it, you turn down some steps to your left into a very dark cave-place which is the traditional site of the stable. On your right as you go down there is a big brass slab on the floor marking the site of the birth of our Lord and on the left is the Manger. It is beautifully decorated and with a lot of candles burning.' Wilbert went several times to the Church of the Nativity, on one occasion for a Christmas Carol service, and was always aware of feeling 'the most wonderful atmosphere of centuries of devotion'.

Wilbert journeyed to Damascus – 'the oldest city in the world they claim' – where St Paul was taken after being blinded by his conversion experience:

> We went down the Street Called Straight, which our guide, an old flat-nosed gentleman with 'Amayyed Hotel Interpreter' in gold letters on his front insisted on calling the 'straight called street', but which is not really straight at all . . . We went out through the gate by which St Paul was probably brought in, and went along outside the city wall to the place where he was supposed to have been let down in a basket.

Wilbert was impressed by his first sight of the Sea of Galilee: 'It was bright moonlight, no wind at all, perfectly calm and still, just gentle little waves, the moon making a silver path through the water, the mountains rising darkly out of the lake with the lights of Tiberias twinkling away on our right hand about 15 miles away.' He did not, however, enjoy a visit to the Dead Sea:

> We bathed, but once is enough for me. The water tastes vile, sea water is a pleasant drink compared to it. It gets in your eyes and you can't see. I was trying to get out but the wind was blowing the water in my eyes and I had to swim with my eyes shut. When I opened them again, I found I was swimming right out to sea again. There was an off-shore wind which made things more difficult – added to which one can't swim properly in that water because your legs come out of it at every stroke. I really began to get the wind up. I thought I was never going to get back to the shore. However, I did eventually and found myself covered with a greasy layer of salt which had to be washed off . . . The water's only merit is that it is warm and you can stay in it for hours without catching cold, those as want to, mind you!

On the banks of the River Jordan – 'the water was very muddy and low' – Wilbert recalled the Old Testament story of Naaman, the commander-in-chief of the King of Damascus who, despite being 'a great man' and 'mighty in valour', was afflicted with leprosy. Naaman sought the help of the prophet Elisha and was insulted when told to bathe in the Jordan seven times. It was not easy for Naaman to overcome his pride and seek his cure in such a humiliating way. 'Imagine Naaman's feelings,' wrote Wilbert, 'when told to go and wash in a muddy river! I sympathised with him very much.'

One of the most powerful experiences of his time in Palestine was being in Jerusalem during Holy Week, the time when Christians recollect the great drama that unfolded on the first Easter. On Palm Sunday 1934, Wilbert followed what is believed to be the route of Christ's triumphal entry into Jerusalem. This was the first of several such devotional walks which he took: 'On Maundy Thursday evening we walked in the moonlight from where the Upper Room is supposed to have been, round the outside of the Walls to Gethsemane.' The following morning, Good Friday, Wilbert walked along the Via Dolorosa – the Way of the Cross – from the Church of the Scourging to the Church of the Holy Sepulchre. Then, on Easter Day itself, Wilbert and one of his colleagues, Roy Harris, took the two and a half hour walk to the village of Emmaus (Kebebeh), on the road along which the two disciples were walking when they encountered the risen Christ.

Wilbert went by railway to Cairo: 'The sand blows in through the windows, even though they are shut and everything in the train seems covered with it.' He visited, and went inside, the pyramids ('nothing much to see, sloping, slippery passages and very hot') and took a camel ride:

> It was the first animal I had ever ridden in my life and I was rather nervous, particularly as he seemed to want to bolt and charged straight into a donkey which was standing nearby. I don't know what happened to the donkey, I hung on for dear life and hoped for the best. It was all right when the camel walked because then you could just sway backwards and forwards with it; but, when it trotted, there was a jerk every time it put a foot down and that meant four for each step it took. When it was going fairly fast that was all right because one could rise in one's stirrups as on a horse, but its usual method of progress was a slow trot where one couldn't, and I got shaken up like a pea in a bucket, and was so sore and stiff that when after we got to Sakhara a man came along with a cart and offered to take us to Memphis in it, we accepted with joy.

At Sakhara, Wilbert saw the Tomb of the Bulls where the twenty-four sacred bulls of Egypt, being 'one at a time the incarnation of the God' were mummified and entombed: 'There are long, dark corridors containing nothing but the granite coffins of the bulls.'

Wilbert's mother was doubtless pleased to read her son's accounts of such sight-seeing expeditions. He recounted his visit to the Temple of Karnak with its 'avenue of alabaster sphinxes', and to the tomb of Tutankhamen: 'Long low passages ending in square pillared rooms and leading endlessly into other rooms, the walls covered with hieroglyphics, [and] finally coming to an empty granite coffin.' Later, in Cairo Museum, Wilbert saw the treasures ('simply amazing workmanship') that had been removed from the tomb. With a visit to Cairo Zoo, it might easily have been an expedition organised by Lucy Awdry; however, the fact that Wilbert was not being 'organised' into enjoying these outings probably accounts for the pleasure which he clearly derived from them.

There were less pleasant aspects to life in Palestine: the unwanted attentions of mosquitoes ('Palestine flies are very impertinent and self assertive!'); the scourge of the Sirocco, 'an East, warm, dusty wind which dries up anything that is not already dried up and gets into your mouth, nose and throat, and makes everybody very irritable and snappish'; and the rains, coming in sudden, torrential floods that turned the streets of the old city into rivers – although, this did at least ensure that the thoroughfares 'were washed for once'. There were also transportation problems:

> We had hired a bus to take the party back to Jerusalem on Sunday evening at 9.30. We got down there and found the bus deserted and a lot of noise coming from a house opposite. The door opened and the driver came out. We had arrived, we said, and wanted to start. 'Oh,' he said, 'we can't start yet, we have a puncture and I have not yet mended it. You will have to wait.' He begins to think for the first time how he is to mend the puncture. He calls his friends in the house to his help – they leave the door open so he can have light on the wheel which he proceeds to examine. His friends are interested and gather round, and block out the light from the door. He curses them, and they disperse only to become interested again, and again gather round. The process is repeated.
>
> At length he realises that the tyre is definitely punctured – all possibility of its having been imagination is shattered because he has actually felt the tyre and found it soft. Then he decides to take the tyre off – but to do this he must lift the wheel off the ground. He has a most dilapidated screwjack which he places under the bus and starts turning amid advice from his friends. He lifts the bus a little way but it slips and comes down again. After a few efforts

he gives that up and readjusts the jack.
Meanwhile he makes the others do some work: they are to lift the bus up while he puts the jack underneath. This idea is not popular: but he has a compelling eye and tongue, also a spanner, so they do it under protest. We suggest that we should get home much quicker if they carried us there bodily in the bus – but our plan is not received with any great enthusiasm!
At length, having lifted the bus and put it onto the jack he is just unscrewing a nut (the first) when the bus comes down with a bang. This process is repeated three or four times till somebody thinks of using a pile of stones instead, and then we are well away. The tyre is put on, the bus is lifted off the stones, our luggage is put in and we start off with my legs dangling out at the back because there's no room for them on the luggage-covered floor.

There are several entertaining anecdotes of this kind in Wilbert's Palestine diary that demonstrate a gift for storytelling. One such is 'The Adventure of the Byzantine Cistern':

March 16, 1934. On Saturday Dr Petrie, Miss Bennett and Miss Senior and Miss Cowan and I went for a sort of picnic . . . Now I was the only person wise enough to have brought a Thermos . . . We came to Abu Ghosh, where there is a fine Crusader church in charge of the Benedictines. A very nice old Father took us round and refreshed us with wine and biscuits, we then told him that it was our intention to go on to Kebebeh . . . He told us it was 1 ½ hours walk and lay beyond a rather steep and rocky hill. He came with us halfway up the hill and then left us. We went on up the hill and it was hot, a little further and it was still hot – Kebebeh did not seem at all attractive – so we spent the afternoon sitting on the side of the hill in what shade we could find.
When tea time came we were all very thirsty. My Thermos was just enough to go round once. We had been told that on the top of the hill were cisterns carved out by the Byzantines. I lifted off the lid of one of these and then we had the idea of trying the cup of the Thermos onto a piece of string which was made longer by adding to it belts and scarves and handkerchiefs. We eventually made it long enough and so we lowered it gently down into the depths and began filling the Thermos with it. It was a long process because the cup was not tied on straight and could therefore only hold about half its right amount of water and then sometimes if we weren't careful it would bang against the side and spill. Just as we had got the Thermos half full, Dr Petrie and I both thought the other had the string and so it disappeared into the depths!

> Well, we weren't going to leave it at that, so we decided to fish for it, particularly as my handkerchief had not sunk yet and showed up very well. So, we got hold of bent pin, weighted it with a stone and put more belts, scarves, string and handkerchiefs on and set to work to fish; one of us being the anchor. I was the anchor first and then I took a turn at fishing. I was getting well down to it, it is very difficult to aim a small stone on the end of a string in a dark cistern. I had got it ready, when I, having aimed it, let go my end of the string with a plop. But the anchor dropped his end as well and so we were stringless, hankerchiefless, beltless and scarfless and cupless. However, there was one of the Fathers working near the top of the hill, and we explained to him in a mixture of French and English that we had dropped all these things down into the Byzantine Cistern. Was there a way in? I am sure he thought us absolutely raving mad. But he smiled and humoured us and said he would get hold of a ladder and send one of his Arab boys down . . .
> We got our things back the next morning. The Father was so honest that he returned not only the scarves, handkerchiefs and belts, but the string and the bent pin and the stone with which we weighted the contraption. Perhaps he thought we might want to go fishing again!!

The most far-reaching adventure happened in the more domesticated surroundings of a Christmas party in Jerusalem in December 1935. The party was for young English people living and working in the country, and in order to encourage the sexes to mix, the boys were invited to choose a partner. The process of selection, however, was to be determined by chance. A large sheet was hung up at one end of the room behind which were huddled the girls. There was a slit in the sheet through which the girls were obliged to thrust their arms whereupon each boy took hold of an outstretched hand, the person attached to which would be their partner for the evening!

If this sounds fun and romantic it wasn't particularly so for Wilbert. He was shy and awkward with girls and had never relished finding himself in situations where he had to be an entertaining partner. His timidity towards the opposite sex was deep-seated: 'Mother used to try and persuade me to go to family parties and dances, dressed up in best bib and tucker, but I didn't like it at all. I hated having to ask girls to dance and wondering what on earth to talk to them about!'

It is unlikely that Lucy Awdry would have welcomed a serious relationship had Wilbert embarked on one. When the family were living at Cheverell, there had been one girl to whom Wilbert had paid attentions: 'Her name was Lotte Werner and I thought I might get attached to her.' One midsummer night, they had cycled to Stonehenge to watch the sunrise but nothing romantic came of their occasional meetings.

At Oxford, Wilbert had 'found it easier' but, whilst meeting girls from time to time at lectures, he was still far from comfortable with the opposite sex. 'I only began to relax in Jerusalem where we met members of the female staff at the girl's college in the city and had parties at Christmas and Easter. But it was really all very mild!'

Wilbert's partner in Jerusalem was a dark-haired, bright-eyed young lady named Margaret Emily Wale. Having read English at the University of London and taken the Certificate in Education, Margaret was teaching girls at the English High School in Haifa.

Recalling the party where fate threw him and Margaret together, Wilbert says: 'She was a very striking young lady, but it was nothing special – at least, it was nothing special *at first*.' From time to time, however, they 'bumped into one another' and the friendship began to grow: 'During the school holidays, I used to spend time guiding people round Jerusalem and somehow or other Margaret usually managed to join the party!' Asked if Margaret set her cap at him, Wilbert thinks a moment and replies, with a chuckle: 'Well, she might have!'

When, in April 1936, Wilbert arranged a six-day trip to the mysterious and abandoned Nabatean city of Petra, in the desert of what was then Transjordan, 'Margaret took care to come along!'

Immortalised in the Reverend John William Burgon's lines as 'a rose-red city – "Half as old as Time"!', Petra takes its name from the Greek word for 'rock' and the city is, as Wilbert recalls, 'literally hewn out of the rock which has a delicate pink tinge in the last rays of the setting sun'. The journey there was long, dusty and dangerous:

> Miles and miles of sometimes basalt stony country sometimes sandy, sometimes shingly with purple hills looming in the distances, here and there a Bedouin encampment. On and on for miles and miles, dust blowing into the car in spite of closed windows – mirages coming up and disappearing, and the hot air seeming to move in endless waves along the horizon . . .

Eventually the travellers reached the Wadi Musa (the Valley of Moses) allegedly the site where Moses struck the rock and produced water for the thirsty Israelites. Here Wilbert and his party met their guides and had to continue their journey on foot:

> The Bedouin tribe who live at Petra were formerly a plundering crowd, but now the police have got these bandits under control and make them responsible for your safety. There has to be one armed guard to every three visitors, and we had two ruffians, one who was armed with an ancient percussion cap musket which I think would explode if fired, but the other had a German mauser rifle dated 1916 with a nickel steel barrel and quite efficient. These men were bound to bring us back safely . . .
>
> It was a walk of an hour and a half. The sun was setting behind the hills of Petra as we were walking down the twisty course of a dry river bed. After 3/4 hour, we came to a place where the valley narrowed to a mere slit in the rock perhaps three yards wide and the walls rose above us about 60 - 80 feet. This was the Sik, a narrow passage about a mile long which was the only entrance to the town and made the place impregnable.
>
> As we went further, the rock face on either side got higher and higher till it reached in places quite 100 ft above the path. The light got dimmer and dimmer and it was very eerie. Then, suddenly, when you were least expecting it, you came out from the narrowest part of the Sik into a wider and lighter space and in front of you you see one of the best of the buildings in the whole of Petra – 'Pharaoh's Treasury'.

Over the next few days, the party scrambled among the wild and rugged landscape or clambered up steps cut into the side of the sheer cliff face in order to explore the tombs and temples, their doors, windows, columns, porticoes and pediments carved with architectural precision from the brilliant rock: 'No description can give any idea of the glorious colours of the rocks at Petra – the general effect is rose-red, but all the colours of the rainbow are there in the most amazing patterns.'

The diary entry containing that description, notes: 'That was our last walk in Petra.' What it does not reveal is what happened on that walk, for that evening, Wilbert Awdry asked Margaret Wale to marry him.

Although Wilbert's letters (from which his mother constructed the 'diary') recorded many details of the trip, they made no reference to Margaret. Nevertheless, the couple had grown closer and Wilbert had begun working himself up towards making a proposal. For several days he had been trying to find the opportunity to 'pop the question'. The party comprised six people and when they travelled by car there were three passengers in the back so that, even when he was able to engineer sitting next to Margaret, they were never alone. That last night in Petra they slipped away from the others – 'although

really we shouldn't have been unchaperoned!' – and took a stroll in the half-light of early evening.

For Wilbert, it was now or never; do or die. Perhaps it was only here in the unreal roseate timelessness of Petra that such a scheme seemed possible. There was, of course, a dim anxiety in Wilbert's mind: 'What about Mother?' Thinking back to his childhood, Wilbert recalled innumerable attempts at 'beating mother', trying to do what he wanted and yet avoid her displeasure: 'If you weren't following on the dotted line, you felt an almost overwhelming miasma of disapproval. She was never really satisfied – she always thought there were ways in which you could do better. Wrong was wrong and right was never good enough.'

Wilbert's time in Palestine had begun to work a change in him and he started standing up to his mother's disapproving attitudes. Although he avoided mentioning it to Margaret, of one thing he was certain – his mother would not approve of his getting engaged. Nevertheless, that night in Petra, Wilbert found the courage to reach out for happiness.

Did he wonder if Margaret would accept his proposal? 'Yes, I did and it was a great relief when she said "Yes"! It was quite an extraordinary experience!'

On their first night back in Jerusalem, Wilbert and Margaret wandered around the old city so wrapped up in one another's company that, whilst they were surprised to find that the streets that normally bustled with life were quiet and deserted, they were oblivious to any sense of danger. Only when they got back to St George's did they discover that there had been riots in the city and they were lucky not to have encountered problems.

A few days later, Wilbert bought his fiancée an engagement ring in Jerusalem and wrote to tell his mother the news. The entry in Lucy Awdry's diary for 28th April, 1936, simply reads: 'A letter from Wilbert about Margaret.'

Before all this, Wilbert had discovered that the then Bishop of Winchester, Dr Garbett, would be in Jerusalem for Easter, and had made an appointment to see him in order to ask if he might be ordained in Winchester. The Bishop arranged for Wilbert to spend one more term at Wycliffe Hall, Oxford, in order to take his Deacon's examination. Providing he passed, the Bishop would then ordain Wilbert at Winchester in Advent 1936.

During what was Wilbert's last Easter in Jerusalem, he and Margaret received permission from the Patriarch of the Greek Orthodox Church to attend the Holy Fire service at the Church of the Holy Sepulchre, built on the reputed site of Christ's Tomb. They were given the best possible places, just in front of the Sepulchre itself and, like everyone in the church, they were handed unlit candles:

> The crowds got thicker and thicker till we were almost like sardines. It would have been impossible to fall and it was very difficult to move one's arms.
>
> All the lights in the church are put out. There is no attempt at silence, all the people are very excited and shout and ululate. Then the Orthodox Guardian of the Tomb puts a special lamp in there and the Tomb is closed and sealed. Then the Orthodox Patriarch processes round the Tomb three times and is joined by an Armenian Priest and two deacons. Then when he has got to the doors of the Tomb, the Patriarch has his cope and mitre taken off and goes in accompanied by the Armenian Priest. After he has prayed, the Greek Patriarch hands out the Fire.
>
> As the Holy Fire [representing the light of the Resurrection] appears, the bells in the tower and all the others in the church break out into the most amazing noise. The excitement is enormous: shouts and cries come from everybody and the light spreads all over the church from candle to candle. The people in the galleries let down candles which are lit and drawn up again.

Reflecting on this service, many years later, Wilbert says: 'It was absolutely remarkable! The service is an enactment of something which, miraculously, might once have happened. And, in a sense, there is something still miraculous about the way in which, within a surprisingly short space of time, the darkened church becomes ablaze with light and heat and yet, somehow, is not set on fire!'

After Easter, Margaret returned to Haifa. The young lovers hated being parted so soon after their engagement, but Wilbert managed to visit Margaret most weekends and they would take long walks together on Mount Carmel. Soon, however, they were to experience longer periods of separation, when Wilbert's teaching contract came to an end while Margaret's had still two years to run.

Wilbert returned to England in the July of 1936, accompanied by Margaret who was on leave. They visited Lucy Awdry who, with Gertie Whatmore as her companion, had moved to a house in Franconia Road, Clapham. George had followed Wilbert to St Peter's Hall from where he would go on to study librarianship. When not away at college, George continued to live with his mother. Although George had occasional girlfriends, something – or someone – always prevented any such relationships from developing and he was to spend the rest of his life living with his mother and Gertie until their deaths and, afterwards, alone.

Wilbert, however, had escaped; although his mother did her best to prevent the engagement reaching marriage: 'She kept on hinting that it was all too sudden, suggesting we should take more time.' It is doubtful whether Lucy Awdry would have thought any girl right for her son, but she considered Margaret particularly unsuitable: 'Mother was a bit of a snob, and when she found that Mr Wale was employed by the Post Office she decided that Margaret and her family were simply not good enough. Then she discovered that Margaret's father had been in a TB hospital and came up with the ploy that there might be a family susceptibility to tuberculosis and that, for that reason, we should abandon plans to marry.' However, the young couple refused to be intimidated: 'It was tough, but we dug our heels in, put our ears back and refused to be stampeded.'

Lucy Awdry quickly came to realise that Margaret would prove a strong adversary if she were to pursue her opposition to their marriage and so eventually decided to tolerate – even be friendly – towards her prospective daughter-in-law. Margaret's family had always nicknamed her 'Mew' partly from her initials and partly from the fact that, being plump rather than skinny like her brother and sister, she was sometimes called 'Fat Cat'. Now, with her name destined to change to Margaret Emily Awdry, Wilbert's mother gave her the new nickname, 'Mea'.

Margaret sailed for Palestine, while Wilbert – 'Now a retired missionary!' – returned to Wycliffe Hall to complete his preparation for ordination. The Principal of Wycliffe made various enquiries in order to find a vicar who would be prepared to take Wilbert as a deacon, and a meeting followed with Canon Jolly of Southampton who was looking for a curate. Deciding, however, that he would rather work in a country parish than in a town, Wilbert eventually accepted a post at Odiham in Hampshire.

In September, Christopher Chavasse, Master of St Peter's Hall, wrote a reference for Wilbert to the Bishop of Winchester:

> Mr W. V. Awdry was member of St Peter's Hall from 1929-32, when he took his degree and passed to Wycliffe Hall. I was very glad when, during his time at St Peter's, he told me that he was desirous of seeking Holy Orders. I am sure he has the root of the matter in him, and also that he has a real vocation for the Ministry. During his time at St Peter's he was well-behaved, industrious, and took his full share in the life of the Hall. He was popular, and displayed gifts of leadership; and his whole influence was towards what was right. I have seen very little of him since he left St Peter's, but from all that I hear, my impression of him has only been confirmed.

Wilbert took his M. A. in October 1936 and on 17th December went to Winchester where, three days later, he was to be ordained as a deacon in the Church of England.

CHAPTER FOUR

On The Right Lines

THE newspapers listed nine men ordained deacon in Winchester Cathedral on 20th December, 1936, and the first name on that alphabetical list was: 'W. V. Awdry, St Peter's Hall, Oxf., M.A., and Wycliffe Hall, Oxf.' Attending the solemn service in the great Cathedral, which has the distinction of being the longest in England, Wilbert's mother and brother heard the Bishop address the ordinands with the question: 'Do you think that you are truly called, according to the will of our Lord Jesus Christ, and the due order of this Realm, to the Ministry of the Church?'

Presented with a copy of the New Testament and charged with authority to preach the Gospel, Wilbert went on to attend Evensong at All Saints, Odiham, the parish where, two days before Christmas, he began his ministry.

Situated in Hampshire, about half-way between London and Southampton, Odiham is an ancient town. According to a 1907 guide-book, *Odiham and its Surroundings:* 'The early history of the town is lost in obscurity'; however, the Kings of Wessex had a villa there and it seems probably that the name began as 'Woodi-ham', meaning 'a clearing among the forest'.

The same publication contained a summary of Odiham's principal sights penned by 'a local "poet" ' for an issue of the *Parish Magazine:*

He who to Odiham comes must see the 'C's –
The Church, the Chalkpit, and the Clump of Trees;
And thence descending to the vale below,
The ancient Castle at North Warnborough.
Hard by remains a fifth 'C' to be seen –
The Basingstoke Canal, with banks so green.
Pursue the towing-path with roses sweet,
And cross the swing-bridge back to Odiham street.
Go, traveller, go the round and see the 'C's,
If not delighted you'll be hard to please!

The first of those 'C's, the Church of All Saints, contains evidence of such a variety of building styles it was once described as 'an illustrated history of English architecture'. It was in the twelfth century that Henry II gave the

Rectory of Odiham to the Canons of Salisbury Cathedral with whom it remained for seven hundred years until 1857, when it passed to the patronage of the Bishop of Winchester.

With its four-square tower and its unusual feature of having three aisles with roofs of the same height (the central one is usually higher), it has a solid, dependable, change-enduring appearance that acknowledges the history it has witnessed. As that early guide-book's author fancifully expressed it: 'Beneath our feet may be the dust of fair ladies who yearned for their warriors' return and beguiled the long hours in depicting their doughty deeds upon dreary yards of tapestry; spearmen and archers and sturdy yeomen, whose life was spent in tilling the Hampshire soil.'

At the time of the Domesday Book, the population of Odiham numbered 247; but by 1936 when Wilbert Awdry arrived as curate to the Reverend Lancelot Cole, it was a largish country town of almost fifteen times as many people. To begin with, Wilbert took lodgings in the village, but things got off to an uneasy start, largely because he was, as he puts it, 'young, naive and rather enthusiastic'.

In Palestine, Wilbert had become an active member (and, eventually, Branch Secretary) of the voluntary organisation, Toc H, which, among many activities, ran social groups with a Christian bias. Founded in 1915, the initials were derived from Talbot House ('Toc' being the old army signallers' designation for the letter 'T'), the name of the first chapel and club, established in memory of Gilbert Talbot, who was killed in the Great War.

The Toc H branch in Jerusalem was particularly active and provided rooms where British servicemen who were stationed in the city could rest and relax. Members visited hospitals and gave guided tours to places of pilgrimage. It was quite natural, therefore, that when Wilbert arrived in Odiham and discovered that there was a new R.A.F. aerodrome on the outskirts of the parish, he should have sought his vicar's approval to form a Toc H group with the aim of integrating the R.A.F. personnel into the life of the village.

Soon, aircraftmen were visiting Wilbert at his lodgings for tea and conversation. However, his landlady did not share Wilbert's youthful zeal for Christian hospitality and, although all 'refreshments' were charged to Wilbert's account, she had no hesitation in telling her lodger she considered his visitors to be little more than 'riffraff'.

The landlady was also annoyed by persistent attempts on Wilbert's part to get her and her husband to attend church. With maturity, Wilbert was to learn that such efforts are rarely successful and, in later parishes, he had excellent friendships with people who seldom if ever entered his church. But for his landlady in Odiham, it all proved too much and, in March 1937, she gave him notice.

Wilbert heard that a tenancy was available on a local property and decided to take it. His mother noted in her diary that she had received 'an S.O.S. from Wilbert to come and see Walnut Tree Cottage' and she and George were soon helping him to establish his new home.

One day, George arrived carrying a black cat that he and his mother's companion, Gertie Whatmore, had chosen from the Battersea Dogs' Home. The cat had a tendency to wander off, so Wilbert named her 'Emmeline', after the child in one of A. A. Milne's *When We Were Very Young* verses, who, on being told that her hands weren't clean, 'slipped between the two tall trees at the end of the green' and wasn't seen again for more than a week! Since there was a sign on the gate of Walnut Tree Cottage reading 'Beware of the Dog', Emmeline – when she did appear – was designated 'Honorary Dog'!

The move proved to be good for Wilbert, giving him both independence and an opportunity to learn a few everyday living skills. Mrs Cole, the vicar's wife, arranged for a local lady to tidy up and cook lunch, while the rest of the time and at weekends Wilbert looked after himself. This gave him the freedom to invite whoever he liked into his home. His guests included several airmen from Canada and New Zealand who had nowhere to go during their weekend leave. Wilbert would invite them to stay at Walnut Tree Cottage on the understanding that on Sundays, when he had Parish duties, the guests would be responsible for preparing the meals. The hospitality was basic but was clearly appreciated, since Wilbert received a number of grateful letters from airmen's mothers overseas.

Wilbert was twenty-five and as keen as mustard, but despite that – or maybe because of it – Wilbert's relationship with the vicar was decidedly formal. He was the first deacon for whom Lancelot Cole had been responsible and apart from the usual restrictions applying to deacons (no authority to officiate at weddings, baptisms or Holy Communion), it seemed to Wilbert that the vicar was somewhat reluctant to give him any responsibility.

'I didn't get much training,' Wilbert recalls, 'and so, more or less, ended up mainly as a signpost to the vicarage front-door.' Although Lancelot Cole taught him little, he did do one thing for which Wilbert has always remained grateful: 'He insisted that I cycle into Basingstoke one afternoon a week to take elocution lessons, for which he paid. I have since had no trouble over audibility when taking services or preaching and, in fact, abominate preaching with a microphone!'

Lancelot Cole was many years Wilbert's senior, and his wife was a pleasant but rather prim lady who did not possess much sense of humour. 'I am afraid,' says Wilbert, 'that I must have shocked her quite a lot with my undergraduate humour!' There was an occasion when Cole, who suffered with arthritis, was preparing for his annual holiday to the Worcestershire spa town of Droitwich, where he went to take the waters. 'Before you go,' said Wilbert, without thinking, 'I hope you'll give me your Last Will and Testament!' Mrs Cole, overhearing the jest, was decidedly not amused!

In the summer of 1937, Margaret returned to England on a visit, during which she went to stay at Walnut Tree Cottage – accompanied by her mother, as Wilbert puts it, 'to make everything proper'. Their time together was all too brief and Margaret returned to Haifa for a further year. However, the couple kept up a regular correspondence and at least Margaret could now envisage Wilbert in his Hampshire surroundings, just as he was able to picture her life in Palestine. Looking back on this period of separation from his fiancée, he says: 'It was a testing time for both of us, but it did give us a chance to find out if our feelings were still the same for one another.'

A year all but one day from becoming a deacon, Wilbert was once again in Winchester Cathedral, this time for his ordination to the Priesthood. Wilbert's mother was unable to attend the service on 19th December, 1937, being ill in bed – the result, she wrote in her diary, of 'too much parishing' – but his godmother, Edith Simeon, was present to take communion alongside him and see the Bishop lay his hands on Wilbert and pray that he might 'Receive the Holy Ghost for the Office and Work of a Priest, in the Church of God, now committed unto thee by the Imposition of our hands'.

By the time of his ordination as a priest, Wilbert had begun to feel a sense of direction to his life: 'As a deacon meeting other clergy, I felt as if I was the lowest form of ecclesiastical life! There were so many irritating restrictions, but once I was ordained priest I felt I really had got somewhere.' Saying this, Wilbert laughs, adding: 'But I still had a very great deal to learn!'

Although a fully fledged clergyman, Wilbert was still Lancelot Cole's curate and was expected, in the words of the Prayer Book, to 'reverently obey' the minister to whose 'charge and government' he was committed. But even if things were sometimes an uphill struggle, there was much now to look forward to – including his marriage to Margaret. The date for the wedding had been set for the end of August and, as the day drew near, the family helped turn Wilbert's bachelor accommodation at Walnut Tree Cottage into a home where a married couple might start life. His mother noted in her diary, at the beginning of August, that George and Wilbert 'resprung the sofa and began doing "improvements" ', while Gertie Whatmore visited Odiham 'to help with distemper and staining'.

Most of the redecoration was undertaken by a local builder and decorator, Mr Crocker, who, says Wilbert, 'took me on as his unskilled assistant and through whom I learned all sorts of tricks of the trade which have stood me in good stead ever since.'

Despite Wilbert's belief that a number of the Odiham parishioners had reservations about their young deacon, 114 of them subscribed to give the engaged couple a signed autograph book and wedding gift of £30.

A photograph of Wilbert and Margaret on their wedding day shows the groom looking rather serious (or maybe just conscious of the solemnity of the event), while his bride, in a smart two-piece suit and a nattily-angled hat, is wreathed in smiles.

The service was held in St George's Church, Worcester, and Wilbert's brother George assumed the duties of best man. Writing in her diary for Tuesday 30th August, 1938, Mrs Awdry recorded: 'Wilbert and Mea's Wedding. At eight in the morning, a lovely day, a beautiful tranquil service with Holy Communion.' Pinned to the facing page is a scrap of the material used for Margaret's wedding outfit.

Wilbert believes that his mother had come to accept Margaret because she had no choice in the matter; however, the fact that, over the years, they were to become 'pretty good friends' was undoubtedly due to Margaret's great strength of character. If Wilbert's mother was an indomitable character, she met her match in her daughter-in-law, who seems to have been determined to win acceptance while, at the same time, remain true to herself.

Richard Chambers, who was later to marry Wilbert and Margaret's first daughter, Veronica, recalls receiving a hostile reception from the elder Mrs Awdry who did not consider him quite the sort of suitor she had in mind for her granddaughter. He also recalls Margaret's sympathetic and supportive response, indicating that she herself had gone through a similar experience.

Whatever her reservations about Wilbert's marriage, Mrs Awdry seems to have been uncritical of events on the wedding day itself. After the ceremony, the family went to the home of Margaret's parents for a breakfast which, she wrote, was 'beautifully organised'. Then, while Mrs Awdry and Mr and Mrs Wale packed up and sent off wedding-cake, the newly-weds left Worcester by train for the Lake District and their honeymoon near Ambleside.

They stayed at Langdale Estate, a holiday centre near Ambleside, in what had once been a gunpowder factory. There were a number of little huts (a precaution against major damage in the event of an explosion) which had been converted into individual sleeping quarters, while meals were served in a central hall.

The weather, often unpredictable in the Lakes, was kind to the young couple and they took long walks. Both Wilbert and Margaret had developed a literary interest in the area from reading Hugh Walpole's 'Herries Chronicle', a quartet of novels set in Lakeland, which had begun publication, in 1930, with *Rogue Herries.*

They also saw Bridge House, perched precariously atop a bridge over Stock Ghyll in Ambleside, as well as visiting William Wordsworth's birthplace at Cockermouth and his later home, 'Dove Cottage', at Grasmere, which Thomas De Quincey had described as 'gleaming from the midst of the trees with a vast and seemingly never-ending series of ascents rising above it to the height of more than three thousand feet'.

The success of the Awdrys' marriage, from the beginning, was as much due to their individual interests as to the things they had in common. They also shared a good sense of humour. 'We laughed at a lot of the same things,' says Wilbert, 'which made a great and valuable difference.'

After their honeymoon – in that 'fair country' praised by Coleridge for 'the majesty of its beauties' and 'the beauty of its majesty' – the new Mr and Mrs Awdry returned to Odiham and Walnut Tree Cottage. Wilbert, however, was looking for a change and an opportunity seemed to present itself when he received a letter from Percival Sexty, who, as chaplain of Dauntsey's School, had prepared him for Confirmation. Sexty was still vicar of the Wiltshire village of Little Cheverell, but he was now additionally responsible for the parish of Great Cheverell and needed the assistance of a curate. He asked Wilbert if he could be interested in the position.

Since Wilbert's cousin, Robert, lived at Little Cheverell and he himself, with his mother and brother, had lived at Great Cheverell, the area held strong associations for Wilbert and he didn't hesitate to accept the offer: 'I had been with Lancelot Cole for two years and felt that I hadn't gained a great deal, so I thought I'd see what a change would do for me.'

The Awdrys moved at the beginning of 1939, but if Wilbert thought his second curacy was going to be easier than his first, he was seriously mistaken. Many of the people he had known when he was a boy were still living there and, although they accepted him as a priest, it wasn't, as he puts it, quite on the same neighbourly terms. A priest, like a prophet, is not without honour, save in his own country.

Compared with life at Odiham, Wilbert found that he had considerably more running about to do in his new parish and so learnt to drive a car, which was an essential skill in such a wide-spread rural area. But although Wilbert was given a measure of responsibility by Percival Sexty, he found him a rather autocratic figure; and when Wilbert made inevitable mistakes, Sexty simply 'pulled in his horns' and became rather aloof. The problem was partly that Percival Sexty had known Wilbert as a schoolboy; it was also due to a sharp difference in political views about the war clouds which, in 1938, began gathering upon the horizon.

In March, Germany began its invasion of Austria and Adolf Hitler was soon levelling his sights on Czechoslovakia. British Premier, Neville Chamberlain repeatedly flew to meetings with Hitler to hear the Fuehrer's demands that Britain and France agree to his being given the German-speaking areas of Czechoslovakia.

At home, the country was gripped in a paranoid fear that war was imminent: Air Raid Precautions came into force, barrage balloons were sent up all over London, mass evacuations were planned, gas masks were issued and, in town and city parks, trenches were dug for air-raid shelters. 'How horrible, fantastic, incredible, it is,' said Chamberlain in a speech, 'that we should be digging trenches and trying on gas masks here because of a quarrel in a far away country between people of whom we know nothing.'

Chamberlain's view was one for which there was considerable national support. However heroically the events of the First World War had been presented, the terrible carnage (of which Wilbert's half-brother, Carol, had been but one victim) had bred a determination to try and keep the peace so recently and so dearly won, and it was in this hope that the League of Nations had been established.

Pacifism found many eloquent spokesmen among Britain's men of letters, including Bertrand Russell, Siegfried Sassoon and A. A. Milne; while churchmen of all denominations began preaching a pacifist gospel. Some clergy felt that they had no alternative but to leave the Church; others preferred to remain and argue their position from within, such as Methodist minister, Donald (now Lord) Soper, who wrote: 'Pacifism contains a spiritual force strong enough to repel any invader.'

In 1933, while Wilbert was at Wycliffe Hall, the Oxford Union had debated and passed a resolution that it would 'under no circumstances fight for its King and Country'; and three years later, Canon Dick Sheppard had started the Peace Pledge Union which enlisted some 136,000 members. The voice of Christian pacifism was increasingly raised: 'In war, hatred becomes a duty, love ridiculous,' wrote John Graham, Quaker chairman of the Friends' Peace Committee. 'The fellowship of mankind, the brotherhood of man under the fatherhood of God, is earnestly denied in word and deed.' In 1937, Percy Harthill, Archdeacon of Stoke-on-Trent, founded the Anglican Pacifist Fellowship, and Wilbert Awdry became a member – to the considerable annoyance of Percival Sexty, who had strongly-held militarist views.

September 1938 saw Chamberlain return from his famous Munich encounter with Hitler, brandishing a piece of paper and declaring that it signified 'peace for our time'. But, by the following spring, this was seen to be a vain hope. Watching the last remnants of Czechoslovakia fall to the German Reich, Britain promised to support Poland if, as was expected, they were to become Hitler's next target.

A German-Italian military alliance – popularly known as 'The Pact of Steel' – was signed in Berlin in May 1939; and three months later, in Moscow, Germany signed a non-aggression pact with Russia. Then, on 31st August, Hitler gave orders to open hostilities against Poland and, early the next day, the assault began. It was six in the morning when bombs started falling on Warsaw.

For the people of Britain, Saturday 2nd September, 1939, saw life going on much the same as usual: a packet of twenty Player's Navy Cut cigarettes cost one shilling and a halfpenny and a bottle of Guinness was seven pence; Arsenal football team (then top of the First Division) beat Sunderland five goals to two and rain stopped tennis at Budleigh Salterton.

At 11.15 the following morning, people tuned into their wireless sets to hear Neville Chamberlain address the nation: 'I am speaking to you from the Cabinet Room at 10, Downing Street. This morning the British Ambassador in Berlin handed the German Government a final note stating that unless we heard from them by eleven o'clock that they were prepared to withdraw their troops from Poland, a state of war would exist between us . . . I have to tell you that no such undertaking has been received and that consequently this country is at war with Germany.'

Air-raid sirens wailed for the first time, beginning five-and-a-half years of uncertainty and anxiety, ration books, call-up letters, buildings burning in the blitz, tearful farewells on station platforms, iron railings being cut down (allegedly to make munitions) and hordes of unhappy young evacuees being herded onto trains wearing tie-on labels bearing their names.

Wilbert Awdry's response to the news of war was one shared by many others: 'At first I felt that the world had come to an end. But gradually, one got accustomed to the situation and simply tried to make the best of things.' What he was not prepared to consider, however, was what Percival Sexty expected of him.

Sexty said that it was Wilbert's duty to volunteer as an army chaplain. The young priest's conscience, however, did not lead him to such a view: 'Every soldier has got a soul and if he joins up in a belief that what he is doing is right, then that may, indeed, be the right thing for him. I simply couldn't be sure that it was the right thing for me.'

In addition to the friction between curate and vicar, Wilbert's general standing in Great Cheverell took something of a nose dive when, shortly after the outbreak of war, the evacuation of London's children began and he was made billeting-officer.

The process of billeting the often ragged and frequently frightened youngsters varied from place to place. In some villages there were scenes described as being 'reminiscent of a cross between an early Roman slave market and Selfridges' bargain basement'; a free-for-all in which farmers and householders vied with one another to pick those evacuees they thought looked the cleanest, fittest or the most likely to provide free labour. Elsewhere, as in Great Cheverell, someone was appointed to allocate the children to homes, which meant that almost everybody was dissatisfied and, as Wilbert puts it, his personal popularity was 'down with the wines and spirits'!

Wilbert and Margaret's own experiences with evacuees were typical of many families throughout Britain who took into their homes youngsters who were often unfamiliar with even rudimentary principles of hygiene and who were fearful of the alien country environment and distressed at being separated from their families. Like hundreds of other evacuees, the children from London's East End whom the billeting-officer allocated to himself were chronic bed-wetters and, never having had a pet, were permanently afraid of the Awdrys' little puppy dog, Toby.

In 1939 came long-awaited news: Margaret was to have a baby. Born in Devizes Hospital on 2nd July, 1940, he was christened Christopher Vere Awdry: Christopher because it was a name which Wilbert liked and Vere after both the baby's father and grandfather.

On 18th August, the day before he christened his son, Wilbert wrote to his old college tutor, Julian Thornton-Duesbery who, a year earlier, had been appointed Master of St Peter's Hall: 'The baby is doing well . . . and so is Margaret now – but she had to be in hospital for some time and we have only had her back about a fortnight.' The next paragraph reveals Wilbert's real reason for writing: 'Unfortunately we have to leave here by Sept 14th and haven't anywhere at the moment fixed up to go. We are having to leave because we are Pacifists – I have been one since 1937.'

The continuing tension between Wilbert and his vicar came to a head when Percival Sexty suggested that his curate might be happier under another vicar; in fact, he gave Wilbert a date by which he had to leave the parish. Wilbert's search for another curacy took him to a church in Salisbury, but just when it seemed that he had secured the job, he learned that the Bishop had refused to license him because of his pacifism.

Wilbert's desperation is clearly seen in his letter to Thornton-Duesbery: 'Sorry to bother you with my troubles, but I just don't know where to turn at the moment.' It seemed that he might have to find an alternative form of employment – perhaps working in the rescue services. 'Do you happen to know,' Wilbert wrote, 'of anything going that I could do? It looks at the moment almost as if I shall have to give up hope of a curacy, and try and find a job as a layman for the duration – but I hope it won't come to that.'

It *didn't* come to that. Thornton-Duesbery was delayed in his return from Jerusalem and it was almost three months before Wilbert received a reply. 'I do not entirely agree with your convictions on this subject,' wrote Thornton-Duesbery, 'but I have the utmost respect for them and for the courage of those who hold them at a time when they are unpopular.'

Wilbert's resolution to stand by his beliefs is an indication of his great strength of character and recalls a line by one of his favourite writers, Hugh Walpole, who wrote in *Fortitude*: ' 'Tisn't life that matters! 'Tis the courage you bring to it.' As the Second World War went on, Wilbert came to view the conflict as an evil which, like it or not, had to be lived with at the time. He remained, however, firm in his conviction that mankind ought always to view war as an unacceptable option.

Thornton-Duesbery concluded his letter by expressing the hope that, during the intervening period, Wilbert's future had 'become clearer' and fortunately it had. Wilbert's situation somehow had come to the attention of the pacifist Bishop of Birmingham, Dr Barnes. As a result, he received a letter, in September 1940, from Canon Thomas Sheldon Dunn, Vicar of King's Norton, Birmingham. The letter suggested the possibility of a curacy and came, says Wilbert, 'out of the blue, when I was rather down in the dumps and unsure what to do'. The first thing he did was to travel to King's Norton to meet Canon Dunn, whom he instantly liked.

After consulting Margaret, Wilbert wrote accepting the new post – although he still had to work out his last fortnight at West Lavington. Percival Sexty suspected all pacifists of being cowards, but since Birmingham was a dangerous area during the war, he could hardly accuse his curate of cowardice.

Nevertheless, Sexty was so afraid that Wilbert would 'let loose' and make his feelings known to the parishioners, that he would not allow him to take services on his last two Sundays. Wilbert, who out of loyalty to Sexty would have said nothing to embarrass him, looks back philosophically on what was a difficult time: 'At the time, I felt as if the bottom had dropped out of my world; but on reflection, I think it probably did both of us good when I went to Birmingham.'

The move might have offered Wilbert an escape from a strained professional relationship, but one thing was certain: life at King's Norton was going to be demanding. St Nicholas was a huge parish of some 50,000 people and had two daughter churches at nearby West Heath and Longbridge.

By the time Wilbert and Margaret and baby Christopher arrived in Britain's second city, the war was a year old. Although Birmingham was subject to a number of heavy enemy air raids, King's Norton was relatively safe, simply because the parish church of St Nicholas had a spire which served as a landmark for the German pilots.

Despite a belief that the church was probably too important to enemy air navigation ever to be bombed, the people of King's Norton still waited nightly for a raid. Wilbert remembers, while on 'Fire Watch' duty, listening to the German bombers coming up the Severn river valley, their engines making an ominous, deep-droning 'pom-pom-pom-pom'. At King's Norton the aircraft would divide, some going east to the factories around King's Heath; some west to the Austin motor-works and other industrial sites around Longbridge where many of the parishioners worked.

Like so many churches, St Nicholas is an amalgam of diverse periods and architectural styles. Its oldest part – two small round arches – dates back 900 years, but most of the building is from about 500 to 650 years old. One of the roofs was built around 1645, during the English Civil War, and legend has it that the original lead roofing was stripped for the making of bullets.

Canon Thomas Dunn was greatly loved – to Wilbert he was 'a wonderful old boy who was marvellous to work for' – but he was, nevertheless, very much 'The Vicar'. There was also another curate, Goronwy Davies, whose father was a Presbyterian minister, but who 'had side-stepped to the Church of England'. Goronwy Davies lived in West Heath and was responsible for the church there and at Longbridge, but Canon Dunn's years of experience had taught him to keep his curates on the move between parishes so as to discourage followers or favourites. 'Just because you had taken a service in a church one week,' recalls Wilbert, 'was no guarantee that you'd do so *next* week!'

At 9 o'clock every Monday morning, Canon Dunn and his two curates held what they called their 'Smoking Concert', when all three puffed on their pipes and the curates were given their jobs – such as Cemetery and Wedding Duties – for the week ahead. Not long after Wilbert arrived, the vicar gave him a particular responsibility of his own, putting him in charge of a slum-clearance area: 'He told me, "They are rough people who will present you with many problems. Don't bother me about details, I want you to work out solutions on your own. Of course, you'll make mistakes – hundreds of them – but, whatever mistakes you make, and however much I may have to disagree with you in private, I will always back you up in public." All of which meant that I was thrown in at the deep end and, as a result, learned a tremendous amount!'

The Awdrys enjoyed life at 65 Westhill Road, King's Norton. They had help in the home from 'a delightfully cheerful girl', named Alice, who lived in a local institution, the Moneyhull Colony, of which Wilbert was chaplain. Writing recently to Wilbert, Alice said that she looked back on her days with the Awdrys 'as the happiest time of her life'.

There was a lot of work to be done; as well as the slum-clearance area and the Moneyhull Colony, the parish was responsible for a large public cemetery at Brandwood End, King's Heath, and an isolation hospital for tuberculosis sufferers. Wilbert's duties entailed a lot of driving, but Canon Dunn always somehow managed to ensure that the authorities gave Wilbert the necessary extra petrol coupons.

When Goronwy Davies left, in 1943, another curate, John Skinner, joined the staff and Canon Dunn offered Wilbert the opportunity to take on responsibility for West Heath and Longbridge; it was the beginning of what Wilbert now looks back on as the time he most enjoyed.

Besides parish visiting and 'Hospital Duty', there were the Sunday morning children's services at the church of the Epiphany, Longbridge, which comprised 'two army type wooden huts' dating back to the 1914 War. This service was in addition to the afternoon Evensong and the services of Holy Communion and was often attended by adults. Among the grown-ups in the congregation was a Miss Leach who was 'Chief "rounder-upper" of the children', and whom Wilbert recalls as 'a rather formidable middle-aged lady'. Although the young curate had been warned by his colleagues that Miss Leach could be 'a tartar' if anyone got on the wrong side of her, she and Wilbert were 'fortunately always on good terms'!

Despite the very real problems of living in wartime, it seemed to Wilbert that, for his family, the quality of daily life had improved: 'As far as meals and so on were concerned, we had ration books and were entitled to certain things – meat, fish, tea and sugar – whereas during peacetime we lived on twopence-halfpenny a year and felt guilty if we spent anything on extras.'

When enemy bombers droned their way towards King's Norton, the couple took refuge in a Morrison shelter. Named after the Home Secretary and Minister of Home Security, Herbert Morrison, it was, as Wilbert describes it, 'a large, table-sized thing, covered in steel sheets'. They had first become available to householders in 1941 and, four years later, over a million of them were in daily use. By day, it served as Wilbert's study table, and when night-time air-raid warnings sounded, he and Margaret slept under it while Christopher was stowed in his pram in the safest part of the house – under the stairs.

Christopher was a good and, by and large, healthy baby – apart from a bout of pneumonia, shortly after they arrived in Birmingham, which resulted in his having to be treated with hot linseed poultices.

Wilbert much enjoyed fatherhood, and one of the fringe pleasures of parenthood was baby Christopher's usefulness as a source of literary inspiration! This first demonstrated itself, in a modest way, at Christmas 1942, when Christopher was almost two-and-a-half years old.

It was wartime, money was scarce and Christmas presents had to be simple and strictly utilitarian. Wilbert wanted to give Margaret a present from Christopher, so he purchased a small yellow tape-measure for a few pennies, from Woolworth's store in King's Norton and wrote a little rhyme – as if by Christopher – to accompany the gift:

> One day when I upset my Mummy's work-basket,
> I found something in there all tattered and torn,
> She takes it to measure my jerseys and trousers,
> But it can't measure right, cos it's terrible worn.
> So, one day when my Daddy went out to take funerals,
> I whispered to him, 'Get my Mummy a s'prise;
> A lovely tape-measure bright yellow and splendid,
> And then when she makes things, they'll be the right size!'

Two years later, at Christmas 1944, Margaret received another present from Christopher together, with another piece of doggerel from his father:

> My Mummy dear, some years ago,
> I gave you a tape measure;
> It shone with a bright yellow glow,

You thought it quite a treasure,
I liked it too, and then you see, to show appreciation,
I sucked it well, a joy to me, but bad for mensuration.
So, Mummy, here's another one,
This time it's pink and splendid,
With best love from your little son,
Who wants his trousers mended!'

But, between these two Christmas gifts, Wilbert and Christopher had unknowingly embarked on an altogether more ambitious form of literary collaboration.

CHAPTER FIVE

"A Little Engine Called Edward"

'IT all began,' says Wilbert, 'when Christopher caught measles . . . ' Like so many of the best books written for children – *Alice's Adventures in Wonderland, The Tale of Peter Rabbit, The Wind in the Willows* – the first book in the Railway Series, *The Three Railway Engines*, began, not with any idea of publication, but as a story told to please one particular child.

Christopher was two and not at all well. The doctor had said that he was to be kept in a darkened room and was not to use his eyes too much. So there he lay, with the curtains drawn, in the small bedroom over the front door at 65 Westhill Road, King's Norton. It was bad enough having the measles, which made him feel miserable, but he was also getting very bored with having nothing to do.

Wilbert and Margaret did their best to keep Christopher amused, but were rapidly exhausting the entertainment value of most of the stories and nursery rhymes they knew. One particular little verse, however, never seemed to lose its appeal for the young patient. It began:

Early in the morning,
Down at the station,
All the little engines
Standing in a row.
Along comes the driver,
Pulls the little lever,
Puff, puff! Chuff, chuff!
Off we go!

'The last lines,' recalls Wilbert, 'always resulted in a delighted chorus which had to be repeated over and over again!'

This rhyme is one of the mysteries in the world of verse. Although enormously popular, nobody knows who wrote it, or quite how old it is. It certainly dates back before the Great War, because it is mentioned in a book called *Songs and Slang of the British Soldier 1914-18*, since when it has passed all around the world and now exists in many different versions. Sometimes it begins 'Early in the morning . . .'; sometimes 'Down at the station . . .'; while, in America, it opens with the words 'Down at the *depot*'!

Wilbert illustrated the rhyme for Christopher by drawing a picture of some engines, just as they are described in the rhyme, standing in a row. 'I'm not much good at drawing,' he confesses, 'so I drew them the easiest way – head on!' This left a series of round blank spaces on the front of the smoke-boxes; so, just for fun, he drew in some little faces: one smiling, another looking stern, this one cross, that one sad . . .

It was the sad-faced engine that immediately appealed to Christopher, probably because he, too, felt rather sad. As Wilbert remembers it, the conversation between father and son went something like this:

'Why is he sad, Daddy?'
'Because he's old and hasn't been out for a long time.'
'What's his name, Daddy?'
'Edward!'

It was the first name that came into Wilbert's head. And so, by question and answer, he invented the Cinderella-type story of 'Edward's Day Out': how the little engine was given the chance to take out a train and was then kept waiting at a station by the guard who turned up late for work, 'running down the hill with his flags in one hand and a sandwich in the other'.

There was nothing new about using anthropomorphism in story-telling. To begin with the subjects were usually animals: from the fables of Aesop to countless books for children, including those of Lewis Carroll, Rudyard Kipling, Beatrix Potter, Kenneth Grahame and A. A. Milne. Later, artists and writers began imposing human characteristics on inanimate objects; among them, the train – that mechanical invention so often referred to, in its earliest days, as the 'Iron Horse'.

'They lent themselves to anthropomorphism by their appearance,' writes Professor Jeffrey Richards of Lancaster University, 'hurtling along at night, emitting smoke and flame, they might be mistaken for dragons.' This very idea was employed by American fantasy writer, Ray Bradbury, for a short story, 'The Dragon', in which – through a quirk of time – two medieval knights encounter something huge and unimaginable, wailing and shrieking, alight with 'a pink, yellow, orange sun-fire' and wreathed with 'great soft plumes of blinding smoke'. To them, the locomotive (for that is what it is) appears as terrifying as would a dragon to us:

> The midnight wilderness was split by a monstrous gushing and the dragon roared nearer, nearer: its flashing yellow glare spurted above a hill and then,

> fold on fold of dark body, distantly seen, therefore indistinct, flowed over that hill and plunged into a valley . . .

Such creatures, observes Jeffrey Richards, have to be tamed: 'As an integral part of the urban, industrial world, trains are given approachable, human scale and purged of their threatening and alien potential by anthropomorphism.' This, albeit unconsciously, is what Wilbert Awdry was doing when he told his son a story beginning with the words: 'Once upon a time there was a little engine called Edward . . . '

'For children,' continues Richards, 'trains tended to be associated with holidays, trips and suchlike pleasurable experiences, therefore Awdry had a head start in making them human.' Certainly, Christopher liked the story of 'Edward's Day Out', so Wilbert told him another.

The new story was about Edward and another engine, called Gordon. Named after a rather bossy little boy who lived down the road, Gordon 'was very big and very proud' and usually pulled the express; however, pride going before a fall, he has to take out a goods train (' "A goods train! a goods train! a goods train!" he grumbled. "The shame of it, the shame of it, the shame of it!" ') and then, worse indignity, gets stuck half way up a hill. It is little Edward who is called upon to save the day:

> *'I can't do it, I can't do it, I can't do it,' puffed Gordon.*
> *'I will do it, I will do it, I will do it,' puffed Edward.*
> *'I can't do it, I will do it, I can't do it, I will do it, I can't do it, I will do it,' they puffed together.*

The idea of an anthropomorphic engine with mechanical speech rhythms was not, in itself, a new one. In 1934, the British stage and revue actor Reginald Gardiner (later to appear in such Hollywood films as *The Man Who Came to Dinner*), made a gramophone recording of a humorous monologue entitled 'Trains'.

Reginald Gardiner's engines, unlike those created by Wilbert Awdry, are 'livid, furious beasts who loath humanity' and have 'colossal arguments' with their rails, which Gardiner reproduced in an extraordinary series of vocal sounds. Gardiner also presented a number of interesting theories, such as the true purpose of sidings 'on which a quite inexplicable thing called shunting takes place':

> This, of course, is just an excuse on the part of the railway company to provide homes for old engines. You see there comes a time with an engine when it

ceases to be virile and hearty and it just becomes long-funnelled and tiresome; so it's put on one of these sidings and given a lot of trucks to play with . . .

This notion, perhaps, recalls another engine: 'Edward liked shunting. It was fun playing with trucks. He would come up quietly and give them a pull . . .'

There was also *The Little Engine That Could*, created by American writer, Watty Piper. Although only a small engine, this plucky little character agrees to pull a train load of presents over a difficult mountain pass, motivating itself with rhythmic dialogue: 'I *think* I can! I – *think* – I – can! I — *think* — I — can!', getting slower and slower, as it struggles up the hill; and: 'I *thought* I could, I *thought* I could, I *thought* I could!', as it rushes joyfully down the other side.

This character inspired stories of other equally courageous American engines, including Doris Garn's *The Pony Engine*, and Casey Jnr – the little animated engine who first chugged onto cinema screens in the 1941 Walt Disney film *The Reluctant Dragon*, and reappeared, later the same year, pulling the circus train in Disney's *Dumbo*.

Wilbert has no recollection of these earlier engine characters, but the proliferation of so many similar ideas – often independently arrived at – suggests that the notion of engines with personalities is one which people, young and old, have always been willing to accept. As for Christopher Awdry, when he demanded a further railway story, Wilbert duly obliged, drawing his inspiration from another rhyme of which his son was fond:

Once, an engine attached to a train
Was afraid of a few drops of rain
It went into a tunnel,
And squeaked through its funnel
And never came out again.

The source of this verse was shrouded in mystery until Wilbert received a letter telling him that a similar ditty had appeared in a book of children's rhymes, published in 1902:

Once an engine when fixed to a train
Was alarmed at a few drops of rain,
So went 'puff' from its funnel,
Then fled to a tunnel,
And would not come out again.

Wilbert thinks it is possible that his half-brother, Carol, may have had a copy of this book. If so, then Wilbert may well have seen it and recalled the substance of it when, many years later, something was needed to amuse his son. Christopher's response to the rhyme was, once again, to ask questions:

> 'Why didn't he like the rain, Daddy?'
>
> 'Because he thought the rain would spoil his green paint with red stripes.'
>
> 'What was his name, Daddy?'

And, as with Edward, the storyteller seized on the first name that entered his head: 'Henry'.

These stories of Edward, Gordon and Henry were soon firm favourites with Christopher – and remained so, long after the measles had departed. 'We had to tell them over and over and over again,' says Wilbert, 'and as you had to tell the story in the same way, using the same words, I wrote them down on the back of old circulars – to my mind the best use for circulars!'

'I gather,' says Christopher, 'that I got to know the stories so well, that I began to correct father when he went "wrong". So he wrote them down as a form of self-defence, so he could get the words right next time!'

The stories were only intended, however, for family use; until, that is, Christopher's mother started comparing them with other stories then being published for children. 'I had seen books in shops which I didn't think very much of,' Margaret recalled in 1986, 'and I went home and said to Wilbert: "I think yours are quite as good – why don't you do something about it?" "Well," he said, "*What*? You tell me!" '

It is only possible to speculate about which books Margaret might have looked at, but there were certainly several children's stories about railways currently in the book shops. For example, there was *The Story of Casey Jnr*, a picture book based on the character in Walt Disney's *Dumbo*, who was described as having 'an old-fashioned smokestack and was just about as far from being a streamlined locomotive as anything could be'. Despite feeling 'as strong as ever', Casey looked terribly out of date and 'stood sadly in the yard behind the engine house, year after year, with a "For Sale" sign hanging from his nose. Until someone DID buy him . . .', which is how Casey Jnr became a circus train.

Another picture book was Mary Emett's *Anthony and Antimacassar*. Written in 1943, this charmingly whimsical story recounted the fantastical exploits of a little china pig and a Very Sorry Engine, and was illustrated by the author's husband, Rowland Emett, whose eccentric railway engines were a popular feature of the humorous magazine, *Punch*.

The following year saw the British publication of Virginia Lee Burton's book *Choo Choo: The Story of a Little Engine Who Ran Away*. Originally published in America in 1937, the book concerns a naughty engine who goes off on a wild adventure which results in its having to be rescued.

There was also Diana Ross' recently published story, *The Little Red Engine Gets a Name*, about a railway engine with headlamp eyes who is simply known as number 394. It yearns to follow the 'Pride of the North' and the 'Beauty of the South' onto the main lines and away to the city. When it eventually gets an opportunity to pull a royal train for the King, 394 is promoted to a Main Line Engine and given the name 'Royal Red'. That book appeared in 1942 and was followed by *The Story of the Little Red Engine* and eight more titles during the next thirty years.

Despite what others might have viewed as competition, Margaret Awdry persisted with her idea that Wilbert should do something about his stories. Although she had no knowledge of how anybody went about getting a book published, she wouldn't give up and mentioned the stories in a letter to Wilbert's mother. Mrs Awdry senior replied to say that a niece was married to someone whom she thought was connected with a firm of literary agents. If Wilbert cared to send the stories, she would forward them.

'In the manner of wives,' as Wilbert puts it, 'Margaret stuck pins into me to do something about it!' Remembering these events some forty years later, Margaret said: 'I did rather push it, I think, because I did feel they were good – and, of course, unusual.' There was no time to write out fair copies of the stories, so Wilbert sent off what he refers to as 'these dirty scraps of paper'. It was this somewhat unlikely manuscript that eventually came to the attention of Michael Barsley.

Wilbert's mother was wrong in thinking that Michael Barsley was an agent, but he was a published writer. Barsley, who was later to become a distinguished figure in British broadcasting (editing the television current-affairs programmes *Panorama* and *Roving Report*), was associated with a publishing company, Pilot Press, and was the author of a humorous book, *The Ultimate Papers of Colonel Bogus*, and two volumes of Lewis Carroll parodies, *Grabberwocky* and *Alice in Wunderground*.

In later life, Michael Barsley would often remark that he had a hand in getting the Railway Engines started on the right rails, and he was a lucky choice as a recipient of Wilbert's stories, since he would have undoubtedly appreciated their wit, charm and lightness of touch.

Pilot Press, however, did not publish children's titles, so Barsley offered them first to Puffin Books and then to a publisher called Transatlantic Arts, but failed to interest either of them in publication. Then, on 3rd May, he wrote to Wilbert's mother, saying that he had decided to show the stories to Edith Ray Gregorson, one of the directors of his own literary agents, World Press Features Ltd. Miss Gregorson read and liked the books and offered to try to place them with a publisher. 'I hope this is all right,' wrote Michael Barsley. 'It's a very reputable firm.'

Three days later, this reputable firm (not apparently having Wilbert's address) wrote a letter to Mrs Awdry to say that: 'the three little books written by your son: "The sad story of Henry", "Edward's day out" and one without a title, which we have called "Edward and Gordon", are most original and delightful.' Miss Gregorson added: 'For the first of these reasons, they will not prove easy to dispose of, especially to those firms which publish for the parents of young children, a most conservative type of purchaser.' It is interesting that, fifty years on, when children's publishing is far more adventurous, and when the Railway Series itself might now be seen as somewhat conservative, the stories of Henry, Edward and Gordon remain as popular as ever.

However, as Edith Gregorson predicted, it was not easy to find a publisher for the stories. They were offered first to Chatto and Windus who turned them down, as did Faber and Faber. Things looked a little more hopeful when Mr Desmond Tuck of Raphael Tuck expressed a keen interest in them, but, eventually, he too returned the manuscripts. 'He has been considering ways and means of using paper,' the agent explained, 'and is afraid that he cannot, under wartime conditions, take on your books. He is extremely sorry to have to make this decision, as he liked them very much.'

Paper shortages were affecting all forms of publishing, and children's books were particularly badly hit; indeed, Edith Gregorson believed that, had it not been for the war, there was little doubt that Wilbert's books would, by that stage, have been with the printer. 'If the war ends within a reasonable time,' she wrote, 'and the paper situation improves, we feel sure Mr Tuck would reconsider his decision.' World Press Features asked if they could retain the books 'in the hope of interesting another publisher in them', but it did not look promising.

Life went on for the Awdrys: Margaret was expecting another child and Wilbert didn't have time to give much thought to what was happening to Henry and company. Then, in September 1943, six months after the original hand-written manuscripts were passed to Michael Barsley, Edith Gregorson wrote with some good news. The stories had been sent to Edmund Ward, a printer in Leicester, who was keen to publish them 'in a good class style at a future date'.

Franklyn Edmund Ward had begun his career in print in 1920, when he joined Raithby Lawrence & Company Ltd (otherwise known as the De Montfort Press) as a sales representative. Franklyn Ward – known to friends as 'Lyn' and to colleagues as 'F.E.W.' – helped Raithby Lawrence & Co. develop their skills as the country's first colour printers and eventually became one of its directors.

F.E.W. later decided to set up a publishing company, in order to provide some book-printing for the De Montfort Press. This he did – trading under the name Edmund Ward – at 16 New Street, opposite Leicester Cathedral. There was a wartime dearth of children's books and Ward, with a view to redressing this state of affairs, placed an advertisement in *The Times*, in 1941, asking for manuscripts from new children's authors. His first publication, in 1943, was a book with colour illustrations, entitled *Rhymes for Young Nature-Lovers,* and thirteen other titles were added to the list before he received the manuscript of Wilbert's first three railway stories.

At last, Wilbert Awdry had a publisher interested in his work, but if he had ever seriously entertained any ideas of making a living from writing, he would have been sorely disappointed by Edmund Ward's offer.

As was then customary with many publishers of children's books, Ward purchased the copyright in his titles for an outright fee, rather than paying an advance and royalties. Despite the fact that Wilbert was represented by an agent, Edmund Ward undoubtedly realised, from the way in which the manuscript was offered to him, that he was dealing with an amateur who was unlikely to drive a hard bargain; as a result, he offered a payment of twenty-five pounds.

Measured against the present purchasing power of such a sum – and knowing, with hindsight, how successful this little book turned out to be – such a fee seems ludicrous. However, bearing in mind that Wilbert had yet to establish himself as an author (and that, the following year, Ward paid only £100 outright fee for a full-scale literary biography of Andrew Lang), £25 was quite generous – especially since, as Ward explained: 'It must be understood that we should have to have all the illustrations re-drawn by our own artist as the present ones are not good enough for the book we have in mind.'

The least satisfactory aspect to the offer – especially since, at the time, Wilbert didn't have any ambitions beyond the possibility of seeing his stories in print – was Ward's unwillingness to commit himself to a publication date, beyond saying that he 'thought we might do something with them when conditions become easier'.

Edith Gregorson's view was that 'while it is true that this offer is indefinite in the matter of publication date, it is also true that the MSS are in rough condition, not wholly calculated to appeal to every publisher in these very difficult times'.

It seems curious that Miss Gregorson hadn't previously pointed this out; in any event, she concluded her letter by expressing the opinion 'that you would probably be wise to instruct us to accept Edmund Ward's offer', adding that any subsequent books 'could be tried elsewhere with the advantage that earlier work by you would have been published by a high-class firm'.

Wilbert was genuinely surprised that anyone should be eager to purchase his stories: 'I didn't really think of them as being books at all, I simply thought of them as stories made up to keep my young son amused!' He decided, therefore, to accept Edmund Ward's offer. Maybe he was just a little disappointed at the somewhat brutal way in which his illustrations were dismissed; certainly he instructed the agents to ask Ward for the return of his pictures as soon as possible, which prompted Edith Gregorson to tactfully remark:

> There is no doubt that from the commercial point of view your stories are stronger than your illustrations, though the illustrations are very amusing. If you are contemplating further literary work, perhaps you would care to come and see us so we could discuss the implications of this state of affairs. We might, for example, interest a professional illustrator in embellishing a story by you. By seeing us, you might be saved some (commercially) misapplied labour.

On 14th October, World Press Features forwarded to Wilbert a cheque for twenty-one pounds and five shillings, being the fee, less their 15% commission. Edmund Ward agreed to return the illustrations as soon as he was able, but again pointed out that 'owing to the short supply of paper it is not at all certain when we shall be able to publish this book'.

Commenting on what she called 'this indefiniteness about the date of publication', Edith Gregorson remarked that, with the restrictions currently afflicting publishers, 'to achieve publication at all of a first book for children is no small feat; and you deserve every congratulation!'

Wilbert had to return a receipt for the fee and, in so doing, took the opportunity to express the hope that any artist chosen to illustrate his books 'should have a proper respect for accuracy of railway detail'. He could scarcely have known that this was but the prelude to what would eventually become a long-running battle to have his characters depicted in the way he wished.

At the time of his letter, however, it seemed unlikely that anyone would be illustrating anything for some while. Then, only two weeks later, Edith Gregorson wrote with the startling news that Wilbert might see his stories in print 'sooner than was anticipated'. Apparently, Edmund Ward had written to say that he was considering issuing them not as separate books but 'together in one book entitled *The Three Railway Engines*'.

Whilst this news was pleasing, it brought with it a problem: in order to produce the book in the way Ward wanted, another story was required, together with illustrations. 'It occurs to us,' wrote Ward, 'that a suitable fourth story might well be about Edward, Henry and Gordon. We should require eight illustrations, oblong in shape, with appropriate text matter of about 80-90 words for each of the drawings.'

Although it was emphasised that these drawings needed only to be 'in a "rough" state', a subsequent letter asked the agent 'to emphasise that the Rev. W. Awdry should arrange the illustrations evenly, so that we get approximately the same amount of copy opposite each picture'. Wilbert must have been irritated, to say the least, to find that although his illustrations were not considered good enough to publish, he was nevertheless expected to exercise artistic judgement in preparing them.

More importantly, there was the question of what to write about for the fourth story. The third story had ended with the disobedient Henry being bricked up in the tunnel where he had gone to hide from the rain:

> *Now Henry can't get out, and he watches the trains rushing through the new tunnel. He is very sad because no one will ever see his lovely green paint with red stripes again.*
>
> *But I think he deserved it, don't you?*

That was quite definitely the end of the story. When, in 1968, a young correspondent wrote to ask whether an engine was ever really shut up in a tunnel, like Henry, Wilbert replied: 'Yes. I think it was in America . . . As far as I recollect it wasn't because the engine was silly and afraid of the rain like Henry, but because he had stuck or come off the rails or something like that. Anyway, they got the driver, fireman and all the passengers out safely, but the tunnel was too narrow to get in and use cranes and things to put the engine right, and they found it easier to make another tunnel which was bigger and brick the old, small, awkward tunnel up.'

Wilbert had never envisaged having to write Henry out of trouble, which he would certainly have to do, if there was to be a story entitled 'Edward, Gordon and Henry'. To complicate matters further, Wilbert hadn't intended Henry to work the same line as Edward and Gordon. Miss Gregorson tried to make some helpful suggestions:

> Possibly the difficulty of the locomotives belonging to different railways could be overcome by making the action of the new story take place at a junction. This might in itself give rise to a good plot. But if the extrication of Henry from the tunnel proves artistically or ethically unsuitable, probably Messrs Edmund Ward would not insist upon his reappearance.
>
> Perhaps we could have a story with Gordon as hero. On the other hand, a story including Henry before repainting, and, possibly, of unreliable character, might be suitable for insertion at the beginning of the book.

This unexpected task did carry some compensation, in that World Press Features were proposing 'to ask Twelve Guineas for the new story'. Responding to the challenge, Wilbert decided that he would, after all, liberate the unfortunate Henry, and he was soon hard at work on the new story:

> *Edward and Gordon often went through the tunnel where Henry was shut up. Edward would say, 'Peep, peep —- hullo!' and Gordon would say, 'Poop, poop, poop! Serves you right!'*
>
> *Poor Henry had no steam to answer, his fire had gone out; soot and dirt from the tunnel roof had spoilt his lovely green paint and red stripes. He was cold and unhappy, and wanted to come out and pull trains too . . .*

Wilbert wrote to tell Edith Gregorson that he had started writing, only to be told that the publishers 'quite appreciate the difficulty of resurrecting Henry' and 'don't really mind which of the engines the story is about'. By that time, however, Henry was out and back on the rails again – although it was far from being the end of his problems.

As well as consolidating the personalities of what have proved to be three of the most popular engine characters, the story introduced someone who was to become the most important human in the Railway Series: later he became Sir Topham Hatt, the Fat Controller, but in the story of 'Edward, Gordon and Henry' he was simply known as 'the fat director'. He was originally intended as a rather pompous figure of fun, as when he explains why he cannot assist in trying to pull and push Henry out of his tunnel: 'My doctor has forbidden me to pull . . . My doctor has forbidden me to push.'

In subsequent books, this portly gentleman gradually developed into a firm, yet kindly character who – for the engines under his control – has an awesome, god-like status with powers to punish and reward. Indeed, since everyone knows that the author of the Railway Series is a clergyman, it is hardly surprising that Wilbert has received many letters, over the years, asking whether the Fat Controller represents God. It's an idea he is willing to go along with if, as he hopes, it will give his young readers 'an idea of there being someone who is in control of the world'.

By the end of November 1943, Wilbert had completed his story and sent it to his agents with a request that the publisher be asked to increase the number of repetitions used when the engines talk – something which Edith Gregorson agreed was 'an artistic advisability'.

These repetitions – 'A goods train! a goods train! a goods train! The shame of it, the shame of it, the shame of it!' – are, indeed, an important part of the stories' appeal, springing from a very old tradition that includes rhymed stories such as 'The House that Jack Built' and 'There Was an Old Woman Who Swallowed a Fly'. From Christopher's response to these rhythmic passages, Wilbert knew that other children would also enjoy, quickly memorise and soon be repeating the repetitious complaints of trucks and carriages or the struggles of the engines:

'Pull hard; pull hard; pull hard,' puffed Edward.
'We'll do it; we'll do it; we'll do it,' puffed Henry.

Edmund Ward wrote to say that they agreed that 'the engine noises should be repeated three or four times' and added that 'the new story rounds off the set very nicely and that an attractive little book can now be produced'.

Enclosed with the letter was a cheque for £10 14s. 2d.; a welcome addition to the family income since, two weeks later, a new member joined it. On 18th December, Margaret gave birth to a baby daughter whom, in order to keep alive the family name of 'Vere', they named Veronica. 'On the day of her birth,' Wilbert recalls with a laugh, 'she sent a remarkable telegram to her grandmother, giving nothing away – ARRIVED SAFELY STOP MOTHER WELL STOP VERONICA – which was very clever of her!' Obviously, Veronica's father had lent a helping hand.

With regard to the forthcoming book, Edmund Ward had been curiously silent on one particular issue. Edith Gregorson had once again reiterated the concern that: 'Mr Awdry's engineering detail will be carefully followed when the illustrations are prepared for publication. This is very important.' However, Ward did not reply to this point and Edith Gregorson told Wilbert that 'in writing to Messrs Ward, we have again called their attention to the desirability of ensuring in the illustrations reasonable accuracy of engineering detail'.

Wilbert's anxieties proved well founded, although it was a while before this became evident. The whole of 1944 passed without *The Three Railway Engines* being published; and, in February 1945, Edmund Ward explained that the delay was due to problems in obtaining paper. Printing, however, had now begun and finished copies were promised by April. In the event, they arrived on 12th May, just days after the Second World War ended with Germany's surrender. On 8th May, 1945, Britain had gone wild. Newspaper headlines had trumpeted the tidings: 'Good Morning! This is VE-Day'; 'It's All Over'; 'Complete and Crushing Victory'; 'The BRITISH Isles Again'.

The immediate euphoria gave way to other emotions; looking back on the ending of what had been five years, eight months and four days of war, Wilbert says: 'Most of the people were too exhausted to feel anything much more than a thankfulness that all the extra effort was over and you could relax a little.'

There was also, for Wilbert and his family, the pleasure of having a properly published copy of a book with the title *The Three Railways Engines* boldly on the cover. 'You will appreciate,' wrote the publishers, 'how difficult it is to maintain really good quality with the limited wartime resources available, but we hope the author will like his little book.' The print run was for 22,500 copies and the 'little book' cost Edmund Ward a total of £1569 to produce.

To young Christopher, there wasn't anything very remarkable about seeing the stories his father had told him written down in a book; as Wilbert observes: 'When you are five, books aren't made, they *happen*!' As for Wilbert, apart from the obvious pleasure at seeing the stories in print – and in a small, oblong format so agreeably suited to a child's hands and pockets – Wilbert was terribly disappointed by the illustrations. These pictures, which had been re-drawn because his own were not considered good enough, turned out to be uninspired and inaccurate.

Although no illustrator was credited on the title page of *The Three Railway Engines*, the pictures were by a lithographic artist named William Middleton, whom Edmund Ward knew through his printing connections. Middleton drew his pictures onto stone for which he was paid a fee of £62. Unfortunately, Middleton – who was inexperienced as an illustrator – had little sense of scale and not much idea about how to draw people. As for the engines, each had a flat disc (looking suspiciously as if it had been traced round a coin), stuck on the front of the smoke-box, on which faces had then been clumsily drawn. He also started what was to prove a long-running problem with Henry.

'Although the pictures I drew were crude,' admits Wilbert, 'with "stick men" and very elementary scenery, I was careful with the three engines. Each had a different wheel arrangement and shape so that Christopher could tell them apart easily.' Wilbert's sketches for the original manuscript showed Henry as a 4-4-2 engine (four bogey wheels, four driving wheels and two trailing wheels under the cab), but Middleton drew him, like Gordon, as a 4-6-2 engine.

The book's final illustration depicted Henry having his coat changed from green to blue, after which he became almost indistinguishable from Gordon. This state of affairs remained until *Henry the Green Engine*, in which Henry has an accident and is sent to Crewe to be given 'a new shape'.

'That very first artist,' says Wilbert Awdry, 'has got a lot to answer for!' As indeed he has. For example, in the episode in *The Three Railway Engines* where Henry refuses to come out of the tunnel, the text is quite clear about what happened: 'They took up the old rails, built a wall in front of him, and cut a new tunnel.'

Wilbert's original sketches clearly showed Henry stuck in the one tunnel, and this is why his being there presents the Fat Director with a problem. For reasons of labour and expense, many tunnels were built using a method called 'gauntletting': that is a single line on which trains can travel in either direction, one at a time. In his final picture, Wilbert showed *two* tunnels. The illustrator, William Middleton, however, showed two tunnels from the very beginning of the story, thereby making complete nonsense of the text.

Describing this location – later named the Ballahoo Tunnels – in his book *The Island of Sodor*, Wilbert explained this discrepancy by revealing that while work was in progress on the tunnel 'a section midway collapsed leaving two tunnels; something which frequently happened in the U.S.A., when rival railway companies were cutting through hills.

'Following "the Henry incident",' Wilbert writes, 'a second bore was cut to provide a double line,' adding, as a postscript: 'Tunnel scenes in *The Three Railway Engines* were incorrectly interpreted by the artist.' When, a few years after the book first appeared, the then illustrator of the series, C. Reginald Dalby, was commissioned to make new pictures for the book, he unfortunately re-drew the error when he might easily have dug Henry out of his confusion.

Writing to Wilbert on the publication of *The Three Railway Engines,* Edith Gregorson adopted a positive tone, although she clearly shared something of the author's disappointment:

> They seem to have made a very good job of it: with the very regrettable reservation that some of the railway detail deviates from accuracy. We repeatedly emphasised that the drawings must be accurate. Unfortunately, however, it is impossible to enforce conditions of this kind with publishers of children's books.
> Also, of course, the importance of accuracy would, in the case of a children's book, impress only those with a real love of railways, such as you (and, I may add, we) have! I am sure your book will be effective in giving many children a new interest in railways.

In suggesting that children wouldn't notice inaccuracies, Miss Gregorson couldn't have been more wrong. Over the years, Wilbert was to receive vast quantities of correspondence from young readers pointing out mistakes and inconsistencies in the illustrations; and since he knew that no child was going to be satisfied with the reply: 'The artist got it wrong', he tried, instead, to offer feasible explanations for the mistakes.

For example, in 1963, almost twenty years after the first publication of *The Three Railway Engines*, a young reader from New Zealand, named Ross, wrote to point out that the illustration on page 10 showed Edward backing onto a coach which had no coupling with which to be pulled. Wilbert's reply not only explained this discrepancy, but provided some additional detail about what happened on the next page of the story:

> One of the other engines has pulled so hard and so roughly that the couplings on the poor coach have come right off. They pushed the coach back into the shed, but forgot to mend her. Then, the next morning when Edward wanted them, they couldn't couple up until they'd fixed a new chain and hook. This took some while and the guard got tired of waiting and went off home for his 'elevenses'. His wife was busy when he got home and wouldn't make his sandwiches at once, so that was why, when Edward got to the station, he had to wait for the guard . . .

The same correspondent raised another interesting question: the book's first illustration showed Edward in the shed with five other engines; three of these he identified as Gordon, Henry and (from the third book in the series) James. But Ross wanted to know what the names of the *other* engines were, and whether there were any books about them? Giving an explanation that, in 1945, he could never have imagined inventing, Wilbert replied: 'The two other blue engines haven't got names at all, only numbers – one was 87546, and the other was 98462. They were engines that had been sent to the Fat Director (as we called him then) to try. But they were horrid engines and were very spiteful and mean to poor Edward and Gordon and James and Henry, so the Fat Director sent them away again and that is why there are no stories about them.'

Problems over the illustrations aside, Wilbert Awdry's first book was a success and showed him to be a gifted storyteller. Writing of the Railway Series in 1975, the critic Margery Fisher said: 'By ingeniously combining ordinary speech with onomatopoeic words (chuff, peep, agh, shooh and so on) and exact terminology, settings and action, this clever writer gives his engines "voices" and behaviour which sharply denote character.'

And it was those characters – and, in particular, their 'humanity' – which gave Wilbert's stories an originality that was apparent from his very first book. By the time *The Three Railway Engines* was published, Wilbert was already at work on another book which was to introduce a character who would eventually become the most popular engine in the entire Railway Series – Thomas the Tank Engine.

CHAPTER SIX

"A Cheeky Little Engine"

THOMAS the Tank Engine is painted sky blue with red stripes and has a beaming smile on his smoke-box. Of all the characters which Wilbert Awdry was to create, Thomas is the one for whom readers seem to have the greatest affection – perhaps because, although mischievous, he has such a happy-go-lucky personality:

> *He was a cheeky little engine . . . He thought no engine worked as hard as he did. So he used to play tricks on them. He liked best of all to come quietly beside a big engine dozing on a siding and make him jump.*
> *'Peep, peep, peep, pip, peep! Wake up, lazibones!' he would whistle, 'why don't you work hard like me?'*

Unlike Edward, Gordon and Henry, Thomas was inspired by a *real* engine – or, rather, by a real *toy* engine!

Having written the first book of stories, Wilbert decided to make Christopher a push-along model of Edward, with coaches and wagons, using odd bits of wood. This proved quite easy, especially since Wilbert had inherited some of his father's skill at woodworking. The boiler was a length of broomstick and the wheels were 'slices of broomstick and dowel'.

Christopher also wanted a model of Gordon, but as this was rather too difficult, Wilbert made, instead, a model of a little 0-6-0 tank engine. 'The natural name,' he says, 'was Thomas – Thomas the Tank Engine.'

The design of the model was dictated by the available materials, so the boiler was, once again, made from a piece of broomstick, the chimney was a tube of metal, the dome was a two-pronged metal paper-fastener with a rounded head, and the wheels were made from the flattened-out heads of drugget pins (normally used in carpet-laying) fastened on with screws.

On Thomas' side were the letters N.W.R. Later, when Wilbert chronicled the history of the railways of Sodor, 'N.W.R.' represented 'North West Region'; originally, however, the first two letters simply stood for '*N*o *W*here'! Thomas also carried a bright yellow number '1' on the side. 'As an inexperienced painter,' says Wilbert, 'I picked the easiest number I could; I certainly couldn't have managed a two!'

Later in the series – from *Henry the Green Engine* onwards – all the engines were given numbers (Edward: 2; Henry: 3; Gordon: 4; James: 5; Percy: 6 and so on) which helped confused readers to identify the different engines. However, it was appropriate that Thomas, the most famous engine of them all, should have been, right from the outset, Number One!

'The tank engine,' Wilbert recalls, 'was received with delight and we had to have stories about him, too!' Those stories were soon being told:

> *Thomas was a tank engine who lived at a Big Station. He had six wheels, a short stumpy funnel, a short stumpy boiler, and a short stumpy dome.*
> *He was a fussy little engine, always pulling coaches about. He pulled them to the station ready for the big engines to take out on long journeys; and when trains came in, and the people had got out, he would pull the empty coaches away, so that the big engines could go and rest.*

Wilbert wrote these new stories whenever he had a few moments to spare: he remembers writing most of one particular adventure during a half hour or so between the end of a Confirmation class at Longbridge and the beginning of a Church Council meeting. Not that writing was exactly effortless: 'It was only on the rarest occasions,' he says, 'that a story came easily and flowed so well that it seemed to be writing itself.'

Wilbert followed certain principles that were to govern the writing of all the books in the Railway Series. Allowing for the fiction, which railwaymen accept – that a steam engine has personality and can express it – the stories had to be accurate and consistent. They also had to be written with brevity, fluency and a careful choice of words. From the beginning, the engines and their exploits had to be 'drawn from life'; that is, based on real engines and real railway events. Unlike other authors who wrote stories about anthropomorphic trains, Wilbert was determined that his stories should remain true to authentic engine behaviour.

'Like all the best and most successful writers for children,' says John Welch, former Sales Manager at Edmund Ward, 'he didn't condescend to children. He wrote about a subject that he absolutely delighted in and knew a lot about, which was railways. The engines lived for him and that came across to children.'

Although less apparent in the first few books – because Wilbert did not yet see them as part of a continuing series – it became a characteristic feature of the books that each story followed neatly on from the one before. A book would also frequently contain references to a preceding volume: so we read, for example, of Thomas going up 'the hill where Gordon had stuck'.

'The stories,' writes Brian Doyle, authority on children's literature, 'are competent, cheerful and easy to understand; though the very occasional slang-word or colloquialism does tend to stand out like a rusty sleeper on an otherwise smooth and clear track!'

True, the Railway Series does contain a handful of words and phrases like 'Cor!', 'What a swiz!', 'Sez you!' and 'Scrag him!'; but, for the most part, Wilbert chose his words with care, to ensure that meaning was conveyed clearly and succinctly. At the same time, the text had to hold the interest of both the youngster who listened to the story and the grown-up who was reading it aloud.

Wilbert achieved this through the use of a vocabulary that was varied enough to satisfy adults, not to mention amusing them, with phrases such as 'All steam and connecting rods'. At the same time, Wilbert – who had never forgotten his own childish delight in the word 'soporific' after his mother had read him Beatrix Potter's *The Tale of The Flopsy Bunnies* – introduced new words to the child listener.

For example, the stories in what was to become *Thomas the Tank Engine* contain – in addition to railway terms like 'stationmaster', 'signalman', 'turntable' and 'coupling' – such words as 'dawdling', 'impatient', 'importantly', 'nuisance', 'swerved' and 'anxiously'. There are delightful touches, such as the description of Thomas speaking 'in a sad, groany, creaky, sort of voice', and a lot of pace and energy in the telling of the tale:

> *'Poop, poop,' he whistled. 'Get in quickly, please.' So the people got in quickly, the signal went down, the clock struck the hour, the guard waved his green flag, and Gordon was ready to start.*

In May 1945, Wilbert wrote to Edith Gregorson to tell her that he was working on a new book. 'We look forward to meeting Thomas,' the agent replied, and then immediately addressed the problem of who would illustrate such a book:

> The dilemma seems to be this. While your drawings are not quite sufficiently 'finished' (as they like to express it) for a publisher of children's books (a very unenterprising race in such matters), the ordinary draughtsman lacks not only the modicum of technical information required to deal with the subject satisfactorily, but also that serious interest in the subject necessary to success as a caricaturist of the subject.

If Edmund Ward liked the stories, Miss Gregorson proposed to 'tackle them again upon the question of that small amount of accuracy which so greatly enhances the effect'. She also suggested, in her quaint style, that they might be able to 'insert an artist of our own selection between you and Messrs Ward'. Lest all this give Wilbert too much hope, however, she concluded with the warning that it was 'always possible that Messrs Ward, a restless firm, may have lost interest in railways'.

Although the agents had told Wilbert that children's books often went quickly out of print, this did not happen with *The Three Railway Engines*; in fact, the book proved so popular that two further impressions were issued within a few months – one of 17,000 copies and another of 16,000 – and Wilbert recalls Edmund Ward writing to him: 'The book is selling so fast it frightens me!'

This comment may well have been tongue-in-cheek; certainly Eric Marriott, who, shortly afterwards, joined the company as editor, finds it hard to imagine Ward, a supreme salesman, being frightened by the success of a book. 'The thought foremost in his mind,' explains Marriott, 'was to keep the colour printing machines going with books which he could simply continue to reprint.' Ward's first colour book, *Rhymes for Young Nature-Lovers* was, for example, reprinted five times in six years. 'Capital costs in new material,' says Marriott, 'had to be restricted. *Re*printing was the password.'

What is surprising about the favourable public response to *The Three Railway Engines* is that it owed little or nothing to the pictures, which were dull, poorly coloured and lacking subtlety of line. Whilst the redrawn illustrations for the first book, and those in subsequent volumes, contributed significantly to the popularity of the series, the initial success was almost certainly due largely to the quality of writing – and to the stories' optimistic tone, which was so in tune with the public's mood in those immediate post-war years.

In June 1945, however, when Wilbert sent off the completed manuscript for *Thomas the Tank Engine*, assurances of success were still to come. The agents forwarded the stories to Edmund Ward without delay, although they probably had even fewer expectations than the author of it being accepted.

The new stories told of Thomas' modest ambition to lead a more exciting life than the one he had so far spent in the yard, pulling coaches about for the big engines. The book began, however, with Thomas getting himself into terrible trouble. Gordon, trying to pay off Thomas for his cheekiness, starts off from the station before anyone has a chance to uncouple the tank engine from behind. Thomas finds himself hurtling along until he is soon puffing and panting:

Poor Thomas was going faster than he had ever gone before. He was out of breath, and his wheels hurt him, but he had to go on.
'I shall never be the same again,' he thought sadly, 'My wheels will be quite worn out.'

In the next episode it looks as if things are going to go rather better for Thomas. Henry is ill, and the tank engine is given a chance to pull Henry's passenger train; this time, however, Thomas starts before the crew can couple Thomas onto the train. Dashing off without the coaches makes the passengers angry and gets Thomas into trouble with the Fat Director.

The third story has Thomas yearning to 'see the world', and the kindly Edward allowing the tank engine to take some trucks home for him. Unfortunately, Thomas has still to learn just how silly, noisy and troublesome trucks can be:

'We're stopping, we're stopping,' called Thomas.
'No! No! No! No!' answered the trucks, and bumped into each other. 'Go – on! – go – on!' and before his driver could stop them, they had pushed Thomas down the hill and were rattling and laughing behind him.
'Stop pushing, stop pushing,' he hissed, but the trucks would not stop.
'Go – on! – go – on!' they giggled in their silly way.

Thomas once again finds himself in trouble with the Fat Director, who tells him that when he has learnt about trucks, and how to keep them in their place, he will be 'a Really Useful Engine'. And that is exactly what Thomas shows himself to be in the book's final story.

'Thomas and the Breakdown Train' recounts how the tank engine comes to the aid of a new engine, called James, who has an accident when his wooden brake blocks catch fire. As a reward, Thomas is given a Branch Line all to himself; and the book ends with Thomas 'as happy as can be' as he 'puffs proudly backwards and forwards with two coaches all day'.

'I think the new stories are delightful,' Edith Gregorson told Wilbert, 'and certainly as good as the earlier ones.' She had, however, one reservation:

> Each story is really a variant on the same idea; Thomas, discontented with confinement, seeking escape, and the upshot. This should, I consider, be dealt with by making it clear throughout that this is, in fact, the theme of the book: Thomas' desire for greater freedom; three more or less abortive attempts to do this, and then his allocation to the Branch Line (as much success as this world offers!)

Despite Miss Gregorson's complaint that the book comprised 'four repetitions of the same basic idea', Wilbert firmly defended his stories. The notes which he kept of his reply show that, whilst conceding that the stories were about one engine, he did not accept that they all had the same theme:

> In my view, Thomas is quite happy in the yard till he finds he can't play tricks with impunity. Then the next two stories show him trying to escape – his first attempt fails; he succeeds in his second, but it is only touch and go. The fourth story shows him taking life seriously and he has grown up and is rewarded by a 'modest independence'.
> I agree that this development of Thomas' character would not strike anyone who has not lived with Thomas as long as I have – but is a study of his 'psychology' necessary in a children's book?

Two days later, the agent was writing to say that Edmund Ward would be pleased to read the new stories, but that this time the manuscript had to be typed if they were to consider it. Wilbert arranged for this to be done and, in an attempt at explaining the book's theme, offered Miss Gregorson a short introduction, that was also a form of dedication to the person who had inspired the stories:

> Dear Christopher,
> Here is your friend Thomas, the Tank Engine. He wanted to come out of the station-yard and see the world. These stories tell you how he did it.
> I hope you like them because you helped me make them.
> Your Loving Daddy

Edith Gregorson, who was not a person to give up so easily, replied that, in her view, 'the difficulty is by no means that your new stories are "all about the same engine"; that may even be an advantage. The difficulty is that they all show the engine doing basically the same thing.'

Having corresponded with Wilbert for over a year, Miss Gregorson really ought by then to have realised that it was virtually impossible to make him change his mind once it was made up. Nevertheless, she kept trying:

> I am interested in your explanation of the intended development of Thomas' character and life; but do not think that what you intend is really made clear in the stories. The introductory letter you propose goes some way towards the modification I originally suggested (by showing Thomas' predominant characteristic is the desire for liberty or change); and would, I dare say, suffice. If, however, you wish to convey the more elaborate development

> described in your letter, some alteration in and addition to the stories themselves is, I think, necessary.

Continuing in this slightly frosty tone, the agent closed her letter by saying that her real concern was, 'that we do not give the impression of failing powers of invention, an impression likely to be left with a publisher if he thinks that the same story has been told four times with variations without the *author being aware of it*!'

It is tempting to speculate quite what difference it would have made to Thomas' fame if Wilbert had embarked on a major rewrite, but it seems unlikely that Miss Gregorson's suggestions could have been incorporated without risk of the book becoming unbearably didactic. As it was, the publishers settled the matter once and for all.

The typed manuscript was sent to them in July; Edmund Ward was on holiday, but his general manager replied at once that he thought the new stories 'just as attractive as the ones we have recently published' and that he would show them to the Mr Ward as soon as he returned. Two months later, *Thomas the Tank Engine* was accepted for publication as a companion to *The Three Railway Engines*.

The incidents in the new book had been based on true-life incidents told to Wilbert by railwaymen. For example, James' accident caused by the wooden brakes was based on something which happened to Mr Willanbruch, a local L.M.S. guard living in Longbridge, who had been involved with a 'run-away' goods train on the nearby Lickey Incline. Because the stories had this strong thread of authenticity, Wilbert was once again concerned about the need to find the right illustrator for the book.

Since William Middleton, the illustrator of *The Three Railway Engines*, was clearly not acceptable, and since Wilbert's agents obviously had no confidence in Edmund Ward finding a more suitable artist, they decided to find one themselves. The publishers agreed to this, providing they were shown specimen drawings, and a fee of £75 was settled on 'for the full rights in the manuscript and drawings' – although Wilbert was still expected to provide rough drawings as a guide for the illustrator.

A month later, in October 1945, Edith Gregorson wrote to say that Edmund Ward was hoping to produce *Thomas the Tank Engine* 'sooner than one had expected'. As a result, she asked Wilbert 'to send as many of your drawings for this book as you can spare? It seems desirable that the other artist start work as soon as possible, without necessarily waiting for the whole set.'

It did not prove easy to find this 'other artist' who required 'a capacity for colour work and humorous draughtsmanship as well a rudimentary knowledge of railways'; but a month later, the agents wrote to say that they had decided to use an Admiralty artist named Reginald Payne.

At Ward's request, Payne had produced two specimen drawings ('a vast improvement on the drawings for *The Three Railway Engines*') and the agent happily reported that these 'meet the requirements in every way, being accurate and amusing'. In the event, Ward did not get text and drawings for £75; they paid Wilbert £45 (an improvement on the total fee of £37 12s. paid for the first book) and Reginald Payne received £94 10s. for the illustrations. There was, however, one problem:

> Mr Payne finds himself unable to make a satisfactory job of the work unless he has the same amount of original material to proceed from in each drawing. You will perceive that unless the measure of creative work contributed to each drawing by him is the same, the effect in the book will be inconsistent. Moreover, he is, in fact, unable to proceed at all without clear originals. Will you, therefore, be so good as to complete the missing drawings up to the level of those we have had from you in the past?

Easier said than done. Family life and work kept Wilbert busy. Soon it was December (a notoriously busy month for a clergyman); so it was not until January 1946, that Wilbert sent the agents another four drawings.

Edith Gregorson acknowledged these, remarking: 'You seem to us to be embarked upon a quite considerable literary career' and expressing the view that there was every chance of further railway books by Wilbert being published 'regularly and with increasing success'. This was actually a disarming preamble to a fairly severe reprimand. Wilbert's success, said the agent, put him in an 'enviable state of affairs' at a time when few authors found themselves being pressed for work and when most publishers were 'stalling off' their authors:

> You will, I am sure, do what you can not to jeopardise the excellent prospect opening before you . . . I think some quite special measures on your part would be warranted to complete the work. I think it is quite fortunate that we have succeeded in maintaining Messrs Ward's interest in the project as long as this . . . Should they fail to publish the book on account of late delivery, we shall still have to pay the artist. We should be remiss did we not point out your overwhelming interest in early completion.

This was too much for Wilbert, especially following the agent's attempts to get him to change the text of his stories. On receiving this extraordinary letter, he immediately drafted a reply in which he was scarcely able to suppress his anger:

> The situation is absurd – there am I, who cannot draw, being harried by cajolings and threats of financial loss, to draw pictures which are not fit for publication anyway . . . while we are employing (after having great difficulty in securing him) an artist at a substantial fee. It is the function of an artist to draw – that is what I have always been led to believe they are paid for.

Just how annoyed he was can be judged from the fact that he went on to say that, in the event of his producing any more books of a similar kind, 'there won't be any more drawings out of me – a rough sketch perhaps to give the general idea, but no more – I've had enough.' Subsequently, he crossed out this sentence and wrote, in a slightly more tempered – but just as unequivocal – style: 'I shall most certainly not produce illustrations of any kind. If a second person is to be employed to do illustrations, then that person must be solely responsible for them.'

Wilbert – who probably had no idea that the illustrator was being paid twice as much as he was getting – concluded by asking, quite reasonably, 'how such a matter is arranged when the writer is quite unable to produce any sort of illustration, however amateur?' Miss Gregorson at once conceded that Wilbert's comments were 'perfectly justified' and that the current arrangements were 'absurd'.

She went on to point out, however, that, as a new author, and with all the difficulties caused by the war and by paper shortages, he had little alternative but to put up with 'these rather absurd arrangements'. She was also probably right in saying that Edmund Ward was unlikely to be worried about *how* the illustrations were produced:

> Messrs Ward would be only too pleased for the illustrations to be left entirely to some hack of theirs, who would produce drawings inaccurate and inartistic.

Raising the spectre of more badly-drawn illustrations was, of course, calculated to win Wilbert's co-operation, as were Miss Gregorson's fulsome comments on the author's illustrations:

> Your own illustrations do not suggest that (in your words) you 'cannot draw'. On the contrary, it has been the view of my husband and myself and of

> various other people to whom we have shown your drawings that it would be much better if these drawings had been used from the outset, more or less unchanged. The truth is not that they are bad drawings, but that they have too much character for the commercial gentlemen who publish children's books. Like so much nowadays they are in a way too good rather than too bad.

This, of course, cut no ice with Wilbert who was only too well aware of his artistic limitations; but, irritating though it was, he had no alternative but to soldier on with this bizarre procedure of making sketches for the guidance of a professional illustrator.

'Time was short,' recalls Wilbert, 'and I made tracings (done with grease-proof paper from the kitchen) to produce the drawings of Thomas. I used the same designs several times, sometimes inverting them for variety.' Indeed, one of these pictures survives – a fascinating scrap of paper, later annotated by the 'artist': 'W.A.'s original design for Thomas based on model he made for Christopher. N.B. Designed so that both sides (directions) can be used.'

Reginald Payne slavishly followed Wilbert's sketches, and there are several pictures of Thomas which, apart from his facial expressions, are identical in the angle from which the engine is drawn – although, in fairness, the number of angles from which the engines can be drawn is severely limited by the need to see faces which cannot be depicted in profile.

A good example of the repeated use of an image is the picture (on page 17) showing Thomas frantically steaming off down the line attached to the rear of Gordon's train, which is identical to the one (on page 29) of Thomas blissfully steaming off down the line, unaware that he has left his train in the station! Yet another identical Thomas appears (on page 55) rushing off, with the breakdown train, to rescue James. And a reversed version was used for the illustration (on page 19) showing Thomas passing through a station where Gordon is chuckling over the fact that the Tank Engine now knows the meaning of hard work.

Towards the end of January 1946, Edith Gregorson wrote, forwarding Wilbert a letter from a reader of *The Three Railway Engines* who, whilst expressing the opinion that the author looked set to embark on a successful career ('a confidence,' added Miss Gregorson, 'which, as you know, we have always shared'), pointed out that the illustrations had not shown any signals.

'Perhaps,' wrote the agent, 'you would kindly insert signals into the remaining drawings; and we shall endeavour to persuade Mr Payne to put them into those already completed.' The use of the words 'endeavour to persuade', suggests that maybe all was not going quite as smoothly as might have been hoped. Certainly Wilbert heard nothing more for some time and eventually wrote to enquire whether the project had been derailed. Edith Gregorson replied:

> No, Thomas is still on the rails, but he has been delayed at our end by our artist having fallen a victim to London 'flu. A fair proportion of the drawings have been delivered to Mr Ward, but the final drawings have not yet been completed. I am making every effort to induce our invalid artist to complete his part of the work.

The following month, in April 1946, the agent was able to send Wilbert a cheque for thirty-eight pounds and five shillings, being his fee less commission. 'The drawings,' Miss Gregorson enthused, 'are both accurate and very handsome. They should, in our opinion, put the book into a considerably higher category than *The Three Railway Engines*.'

A small hitch arose a few days later, when Edmund Ward decided to shorten the book by two pages, and asked Wilbert to make a few cuts. It was an irritating task: trimming a text as economic as that in *Thomas the Tank Engine* was far from easy. Nor could it have been more inconsiderately timed, since it coincided with the birth of the Awdry's third child: a little girl born on 12th April and named Hilary (after the university term during which she made her entrance).

As for *Thomas the Tank Engine*, he didn't make his debut until the following December. That the book's eponymous hero was destined to become a household name would have surprised Wilbert and his publishers, but it was already clear that Thomas was an inspired creation.

Perhaps the secret of Thomas' success is that of all the railway engine characters his personality is closest to that of a child. As a result, we sympathise with him in his failings and delight in his belated success and the happy ending to which it leads:

> *He is never lonely, because there is always someone to talk to at the junction. Edward and Henry stop quite often, and tell him the news. Gordon is always in a hurry and does not stop; but he never forgets to say 'Poop, poop' to little Thomas, and Thomas always whistles 'Peep, peep' in return.*

Writing of *Thomas the Tank Engine*, many years later, the critic Margery Fisher said that the four stories 'are fair examples of artless-artful technique that has kept the Railway Series in the best seller lists'; and another commentator, John Churcher, claimed that this and the other early Awdry books 'put their author almost on a par with Beatrix Potter and A. A. Milne'.

Those judgments, of course, have been made with hindsight. Wilbert's first reaction was one of disappointment: 'When I first saw Reginald Payne's illustrations,' he says, 'I was annoyed at his version of Thomas, which was quite different from the drawings I had made, which had admittedly been based on Christopher's push-along toy.'

Wilbert's agents were also less than happy about the finished pictures:

> We went to great trouble and no small expense to procure really accurate drawings for this second book; only to find that Messrs Ward have once more prettified and vulgarised them, and rendered them inaccurate. Despite repeated efforts, we cannot inculcate in them any respect for engineering accuracy.

Later, Wilbert discovered that Reginald Payne's pictures of Thomas were based on a real locomotive design, namely an E2 0-6-0 tank engine, with extended tanks, which was built for the London Brighton & South Coast Railway by their Locomotive Superintendent, Lawson Billington. Knowing this, Wilbert was then content for that design to be followed in subsequent books.

Just as William Middleton received no credit for the pictures in the first edition of *The Three Railway Engines* (it was not until C. Reginald Dalby had redrawn them, in 1949, that an illustrator was named), Payne's illustrations to *Thomas the Tank Engine* likewise went uncredited. It is curious that the most famous volume in the Railway Series – containing key images of one of the central characters – gives credit to no one other than the author. Even when, in 1950, Dalby was paid £60 for 'improving' Payne's original pictures for a new edition of the book, no artist was named on the title page.

Yet, uncredited though they are, Reginald Payne's illustrations are as inseparably linked with Wilbert Awdry's *Thomas the Tank Engine* as are the drawings of John Tenniel with *Alice's Adventures in Wonderland* or those of E. H. Shepard with *Winnie-the-Pooh*. Despite the agents' view that the illustrations had been 'prettified and vulgarised', Payne (with some later assistance from Dalby) is responsible for having created one of the icons of our age.

Consider, for example, the illustration of Thomas rushing out of a tunnel, highlights gleaming on his paint work, 'speed lines' indicating his enthusiastic haste, his beaming face (large, round, excited eyes and a smile as wide as his smoke-box) all combining to create a portrait of good-natured optimism, of a character in love with life. Small wonder that such powerful imagery has found a place in the mythology of the late twentieth century.

Although no one could have known that Thomas would become the engine character with whom children would most readily identify, Payne instinctively illustrated Thomas with the features of a young child. In his first appearance in print, Thomas looks anxious, alarmed, sorry, sad and, in one picture, like a tired five-year-old, screwing up his eyes and giving a big, open-mouthed yawn. And, in the majority of illustrations, Thomas has an eager, innocent, wide-awake expression that recalls the ever-smiling, circular face of that other naive character, Mickey Mouse. And, like that carefree cartoon creation, Thomas the Tank Engine has gone on to become a powerful emblematic device reproduced on a million items of merchandise.

Although Wilbert did not think Reginald Payne's track and point work were up to the standard of his drawings of the engines and rolling stock, he conceded that the general effect of the illustrations was 'immeasurably superior' to those drawn for *The Three Railway Engines* by William Middleton (who, ironically, was employed to design a silhouette of Thomas and his coaches which was gold blocked onto the cloth bindings of early editions of the books).

There was talk of correcting inaccuracies in the pictures if it went to a reprint, but what was really important was that the book had at least been published. Wilbert now had two books in print and, with the war over and paper supplies less restricted, those books might well prove to be the beginning of a successful writing career.

In December 1946, however, this was not the uppermost thought in Wilbert's mind. He had plenty of other things to occupy him, especially since he was, by that time, seven or eight months into a new appointment as rector of Elsworth in Cambridgeshire; a job which looked as if it was going to allow little time for the writing of children's books.

CHAPTER SEVEN

"A Splendid Red Engine"

IN a way, the Awdrys were sorry to leave Birmingham: Wilbert's time there as a curate had been happy and he had begun to learn the skills necessary for running a parish. Wilbert's vicar at King's Norton, Canon Thomas Dunn, was a good man to work for – he had allowed Wilbert to take responsibility and had supported him with sound advice and plenty of encouragement. Wilbert had been there six years, which was a long time for a curacy, and didn't really want to go. Now, however, it was time to move on. Like a number of Canon Dunn's other curates, however, Wilbert took a little persuading. 'Sometimes,' Wilbert remembers him saying, 'I think I'll have to chuck my boot at you to get you to go!'

The question, however, was *where* to go? Nowadays, a curate can answer advertisements; but in Wilbert's day, you had to be recommended. When H. J. Scott, the vicar of a neighbouring parish, moved to Bourn in Cambridgeshire, Canon Dunn recommended Wilbert for the living, but he wasn't selected. Then, after one or two other unsuccessful recommendations, H. J. Scott himself proposed Wilbert's name for another Cambridgeshire parish, that of Elsworth with Knapwell.

A farming community, Elsworth lies south of the Cambridge Fens and about nine miles from the city itself. Built on limestone rock dating back 160 million years to the Jurassic period, Elsworth is an ancient village listed in the Domesday Book, in 1086, as 'Elesworde'. The Church of the Holy Trinity, for which Wilbert Awdry became responsible, was built during the early 1500s, but there had been a church in Elsworth since the tenth century.

Christopher Awdry has rather romantic memories of the village and recalls thatched cottages drowsing beside the brook; while, to his father, it seemed 'rather isolated'. He certainly inherited a number of problems: the retiring Rector, Lawrence Iggulden, had been at Elsworth for nineteen years and the parish had, latterly, become rather run down with both its church and school in need of repair.

Some repairs had been carried out in 1934, but during the war years little could be done and by 1946 it was, says Wilbert, 'in a pretty bad state'. So, too, was the Rectory. In fact, Wilbert soon discovered that the building, into which he was supposed to move with his young family, was infested. 'The place,' he recalls, 'was crawling with bugs of some sort – I didn't stop to enquire what their names were!' Margaret took the newborn Hilary and went to stay with her mother in Worcestershire, while Christopher and Veronica stayed with Wilbert's mother in London. Wilbert himself took lodgings in the village until the house had been de-loused and could be made habitable. 'The first thing I had to do was clean the kitchen floor, scraping off thick grease with a broken knife.' It was to be three months before Wilbert had the Rectory in a fit – if still primitive – condition for his family to move into. Margaret and the children joined him in July 1946, but so much still needed to be done to the property, that they felt as if they were 'camping out' in the building.

Although at first there was no mains water supply, there was a remarkably efficient – if somewhat eccentric – water system. All the rain water from the roofs of the Rectory and the adjacent church was piped down into a cistern. There was a hand-pump at the back end of the house by which this water could be pumped up to a tank in the roof.

'Pinned above the taps,' says Christopher Awdry, 'was a relic of the war: a handwritten card warning users not to waste water.' The pumping operation had to be carried out each morning to ensure the tank was full. 'While we were there,' says Wilbert, 'I only remember one year when that water system ran dry.' However, one of the first improvements was the installation of an electric pump to replace the antiquated hand-pumping method.

The Rectory, of yellowish-grey brick, stood beside the church at the summit of Elsworth Causeway in grounds extensive enough for the holding of such events as church fetes. Veronica remembers the house as having 'a lovely big porch with a door and stone seats' which the children occasionally commandeered in order to play 'house'.

Christopher recalls the Rectory as 'a large building, no doubt seeming larger to my young eyes than it actually was'. Nevertheless, it was certainly large enough to house the Awdry family of five with room enough to spare.

Wilbert, realising that the costs of repairing and maintaining the Rectory would be high, wanted to divide off part of the house and take in tenants, whose rent would help with the household expenses. Although, at the time, it was impossible to make repairs or alterations to a house without official permits, Wilbert hoped that his plan to provide a homeless family with somewhere to live might well receive the necessary approval.

It did not, however, prove easy to realise these plans and Wilbert soon found himself entrenched in a seemingly endless correspondence with two grant-giving bodies: Queen Anne's Bounty, concerned with the structure and maintenance of parsonages, and the Ecclesiastical Commissioners who gave grants for improvements.

Although neither organization would send representatives to assess the state of the Rectory, they both required estimates for the proposed work. The building trade, however, faced so many problems – such as shortage of materials – that Wilbert could not find anyone willing to give an estimate for the job. Eventually, a local builder agreed to provide the necessary piece of paper – on condition that he would not be expected to carry out the work!

The Rectory was T-shaped, the horizontal part representing the front of the building. An architect who lived in the parish, drew up plans showing how the house could be divided into two self-contained dwellings simply and cheaply. But it was when these plans were submitted to Queen Anne's Bounty and the Ecclesiastical Commissioners that battle really commenced.

The proposal was for the Awdrys to live in the rear of the building where the heating and water systems were based. The church charities, however, preferred a more expensive plan to convert the front of the building into what they considered 'a dignified residence' for a rector. But Wilbert wasn't concerned with dignity: 'I simply wanted somewhere for my family to live that would be easy and economic to run.'

Wilbert found himself caught up in wrangling arguments that lasted at least six months and were only ended when Margaret took a hand in the affair. Yet another letter had been received from one of the charitable bodies that had so infuriated Wilbert that, while he was out at a parish meeting, Margaret wrote a letter to the secretary. 'She said,' recalls Wilbert, 'that it was high time they did their job and enabled me to have a home in which I could live and do my job, without endless, futile correspondence about the so-called dignity of the Rectory.' The matter was then referred to the Bishop who, after a visit to Elsworth with the Archdeacon of Ely, supported Wilbert's plans and work went forward.

The church fabric also required attention: there was a leak (which took years to locate) in the roof above the organ and the chancel floor was dangerously uneven. The flooring was tackled by a do-it-yourself team from the parish who helped Wilbert with lifting the large paving-stones and adding a levelling layer of sand.

The heating system – invariably a problem in old churches – comprised underground coke stoves with a flue that went up through the tower. This flue was difficult to keep clear, until a local engineer (despite professing himself to be an atheist) was persuaded by Wilbert to install a device called an 'impeller' which drew the hot gases into the flue and up the tower.

Not all of Wilbert's difficulties were to do with buildings. He was thirty-five years old and whilst the Parish adopted what he calls a 'Wait and See' policy, some parishioners decided fairly swiftly what they thought of the 'new man', and Wilbert repeatedly found his views and opinions at odds with those of one of his church wardens.

Being a small rural community, many of the Elsworth families had intermarried and Wilbert soon learned to be careful what he said, since almost everyone in the village was related to everybody else. In addition to which, the inevitable comparisons with 'the old vicar' were heightened by the fact that his predecessor was still living nearby.

'It was my first parish,' he explains, 'and if things didn't go right – it was always the Rector's fault!' One such thing which was 'the Rector's fault' was a disastrous outing to Ely, when everything that could go wrong, went wrong. It was Whit Monday, 1947, and the Bourn Deanery had arranged to share a bus to take a party to a service in Ely Cathedral for young people who had recently been confirmed.

Post-war rationing of food and petrol made organised outings difficult. To add to their problems, a harsh winter in the Fens had resulted in a lot of melting snow and ice, followed by severe flooding. It also turned out that they were having to share the bus with several other parties which resulted in a circuitous route along water-logged country lanes. There were long delays on the outward journey and worse ones on the return so that the party arrived back at Elsworth in the early hours of the next morning, cold and hungry.

Wilbert admits to having been 'a bit of a worrier' and – despite strong support from Margaret, who got on well with people and had a gift for making friends – he tended to take such run-of-the-mill parish disasters very much to heart even if he sometimes appeared to be laughing them off. The fateful trip to Ely, for example, was commemorated by a light-hearted piece of doggerel that was published in the *Bourn Deanery Magazine* for July 1947, under the title, 'The Tale of a Bus':

On Whit Monday we started for Ely
Full of hope on a lovely fine day;
But, alas for our care, the bus was not there,
It had stuck in the floods on the way.

Wilbert and Margaret Awdry with their young family on holiday at Bredhurst in August 1948.

Wilbert and the children on the front steps of Emneth Vicarage.

The Awdry children with their father on the beach at Towyn, summer 1952.

Wilbert Awdry with Hilary and Veronica in 1952 on their way to Towyn in 'Jeeves' the car.

Family group: Veronica, Wilbert, Christopher, Margaret and Hilary Awdry in 1961.

Wilbert outside St Edmund's Church at Emneth, Cambridgeshire, of which he became Vicar in 1953.

'F. E. W.', Franklin Edmund Ward, who began a publishing phenomenon with the publication, in 1945, of *The Three Railway Engines.*

Eric Marriott, who edited the Railway Series from *James the Red Engine* to the last of Wilbert Awdry's books, *Tramway Engines.*

Edmund Ward's Sales Manager, John Welch, who carried a battered case filled with early copies of the Railway Series from shop to shop.

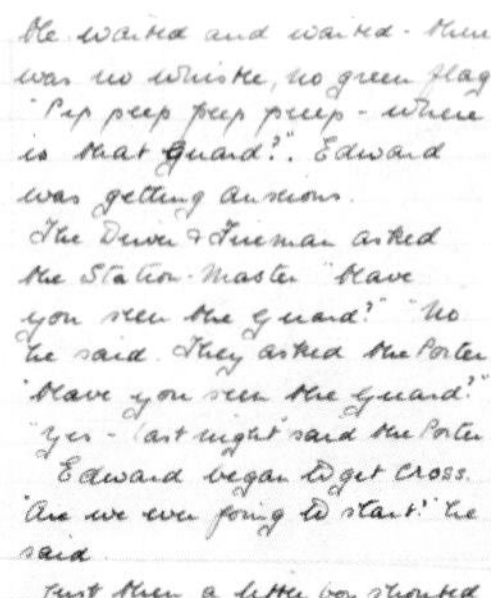

He waited and waited - there was no whistle, no green flag. "Peep peep peep peep - where is that Guard?". Edward was getting anxious.
The Driver & Fireman asked the Station-Master "Have you seen the guard?" "No" he said. They asked the Porter "Have you seen the guard?" "Yes - last night" said the Porter.
Edward began to get cross. "Are we ever going to start!" he said.
Just then a little boy shouted "Here he comes!", and there the guard was, running down the hill with his flags in one hand and a sandwich in the other.

The original manuscript with one of Wilbert Awdry's illustrations for what was to become pages 14 and 15 of *The Three Railway Engines.*

87 II.

There were ~~sometimes~~ sixteen heavy coaches full of important people like the Fat Director who ~~had~~ punished Henry.
Gordon was seeing how fast he could go. "Hurry Hurry Hurry" he panted.
Trickety Trock, Trickety Trock sang the coaches.
Gordon could see Henry's tunnel in front.
"In a minute" he thought "I'll 'Poop Poop Poop' at Henry, and rush through & out into the open again.
Closer and closer he came - he was almost there when Crack Wheee --- eeshshsh he was in a cloud of steam and going slower and slower.

eady to hand over
le authority and
f she is not
stian women about
nan to think and
that now members
e of the Eng-
;e to prevent
e evil heathen
life. A
ny localities
a respectable
led with hor-
m, the proud
while the
he gift!
s to those
to them.

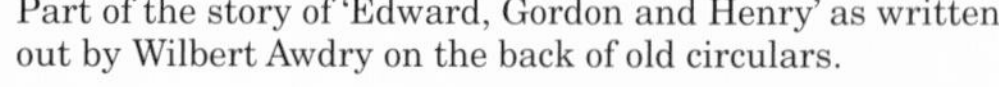

Part of the story of 'Edward, Gordon and Henry' as written out by Wilbert Awdry on the back of old circulars.

First editions, in illustrated dust-wrappers, of *The Three Railway Engines, Thomas the Tank Engine* and *James the Red Engine.*

One of the sketches made by Wilbert Awdry for the guidance of the illustrator, together with the finished artwork by William Middleton.

The original illustrations to *The Three Railway Engines* by William Middleton (left) were re-drawn (centre and right) in 1949 by the Railway Series' then illustrator, C. Reginald Dalby.

Wilbert Awdry at work on one of his stories in his study at Emneth. On the table are models of Henry, James and Edward.

The Three Railway Engines

A page from Edmund Ward's financial record-book showing the costs of producing *The Three Railway Engines.*

Wilbert, who was obliged to provide guide sketches for the illustrator of *Thomas the Tank Engine*, cut corners by using the same basic angle in several pictures. These are the finished illustrations for pages 17 and 29.

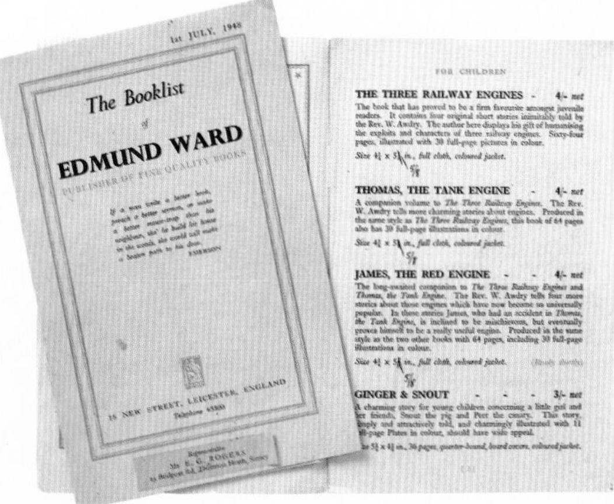

1st JULY, 1948

The Booklist of EDMUND WARD

PUBLISHER OF FINE QUALITY BOOKS

If a man write a better book, preach a better sermon, or make a better mouse-trap than his neighbour, tho' he build his house in the woods, the world will make a beaten path to his door.
EMERSON

15 NEW STREET, LEICESTER, ENGLAND

Representative
Mr. E. G. ROGERS

FOR CHILDREN

THE THREE RAILWAY ENGINES - 4/- net
The book that has proved to be a firm favourite amongst juvenile readers. It contains four original short stories inimitably told by the Rev. W. Awdry. The author here displays his gift of humanising the exploits and characters of three railway engines. Sixty-four pages, illustrated with 30 full-page pictures in colour.
Size 4¼ × 5[illegible] in., full cloth, coloured jacket.

THOMAS, THE TANK ENGINE - 4/- net
A companion volume to *The Three Railway Engines*. The Rev. W. Awdry tells more charming stories about engines. Produced in the same style as *The Three Railway Engines*, this book of 64 pages also has 30 full-page illustrations in colour.
Size 4¼ × 5[illegible] in., full cloth, coloured jacket.

JAMES, THE RED ENGINE - - 4/- net
The long-awaited companion to *The Three Railway Engines* and *Thomas, the Tank Engine*. The Rev. W. Awdry tells four more stories about these engines which have now become so universally popular. In these stories James, who had an accident in *Thomas, the Tank Engine*, is inclined to be mischievous, but eventually proves himself to be a really useful engine. Produced in the same style as the two other books with 64 pages, including 30 full-page illustrations in colour.
Size 4¼ × 5⅝ in., full cloth, coloured jacket. (Ready shortly)

GINGER & SNOUT - - - 3/- net
A charming story for young children concerning a little girl and her friends, Snout the pig and Peet the canary. This story, simply and attractively told, and charmingly illustrated with 11 full-page Plates in colour, should have wide appeal.
Size 5½ × 4¼ in., 36 pages, quarter-bound, board covers, coloured jacket.

Publisher Edmund Ward's Booklist for July 1948 announcing the publication of what was to become the most famous of the Railway Series books.

C. REGINALD DALBY (1904-1983), who studied at Leicester College of Art and worked as a freelance commercial designer, illustrated nine volumes of the Railway Series from *James the Red Engine* (1948) to *Percy the Small Engine* (1956), as well as re-drawing the original illustrations for *The Three Railway Engines* and 'improving' those for *Thomas the Tank Engine*.

ABOVE 'Come on! Come on! dontbesilly! —- dontbesilly!' puffed Henry.
Henry the Green Engine (1951)

LEFT The passenger sitting down with a cup of tea in this illustration to *Troublesome Engines* (1950) is a self-portrait of the artist (the nearby suitcase carries the initials 'C.R.D.') and the little girl with pigtails is Reginald Dalby's daughter, Kate, with her pet corgi, Chloe.

The illustration in *Tank Engine Thomas Again* (1949) which gave Wilbert Awdry so many headaches: Why is Henry wearing Gordon's buffers?

The Awdry family – Margaret, Wilbert, Christopher Veronica and Hilary – wave to Percy in *Troublesome Engines* (1950).

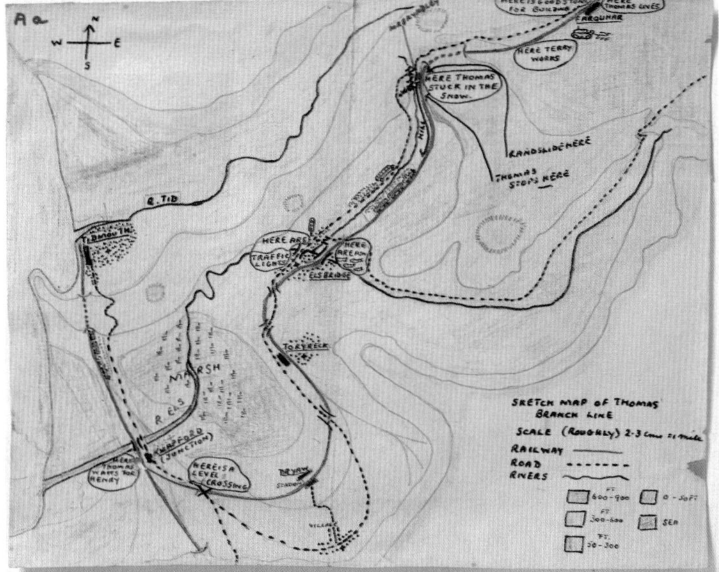

In *Thomas the Tank Engine Again* (1949) Wilbert Awdry described a race between Thomas and Bertie the Bus. To prove to his children that the race was fairly won, the author drew this map. It was the beginning of a series of inventions about the settings for the stories which led to the 'discovery' of the Island of Sodor.

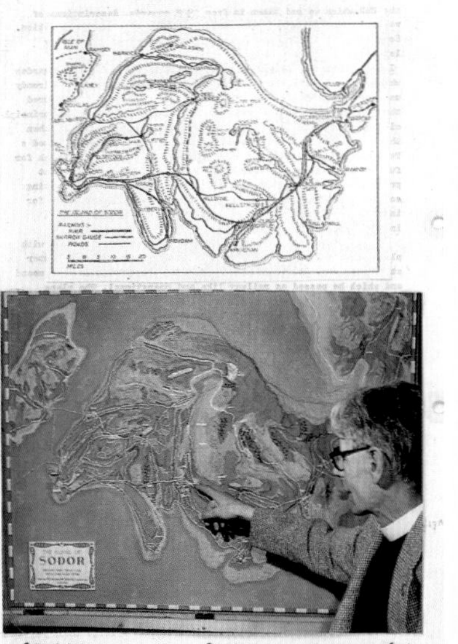

An early sketch of the Island of Sodor by the author who is shown standing beside a later relief map of the Island made by P. R. Wickham.

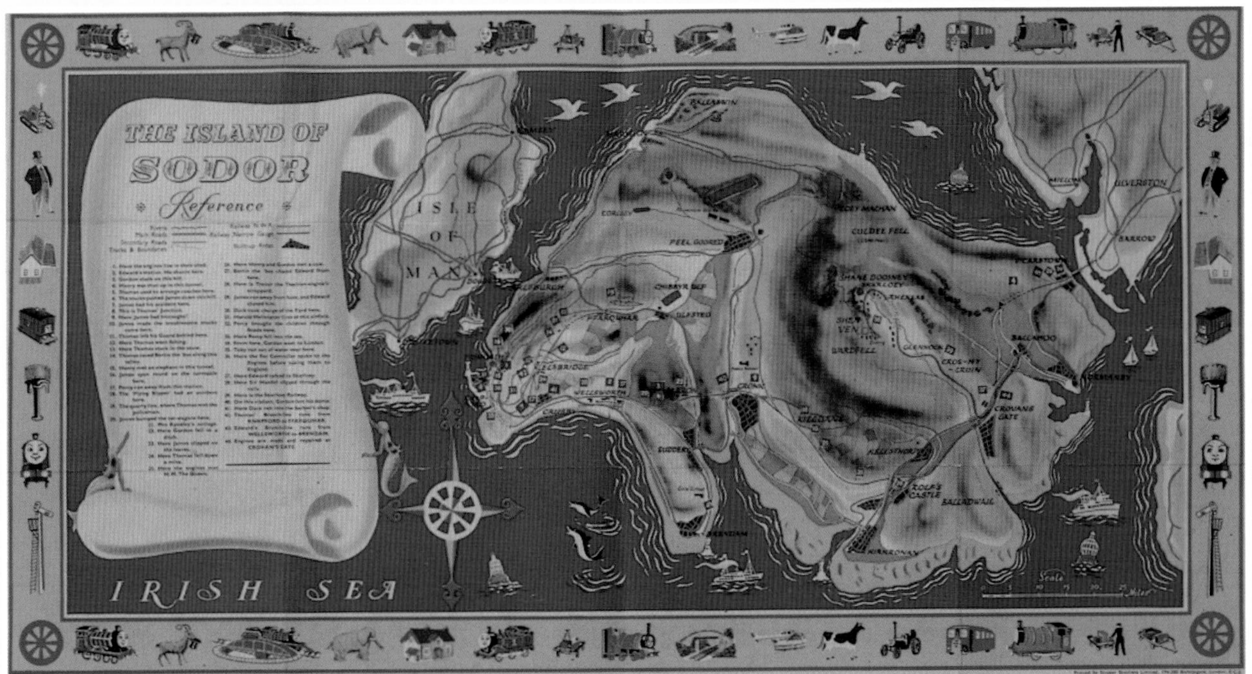

'It all happens here.' The first – and rather fanciful – map of the Island of Sodor (Complete with such un-Awdry like embellishments as mermaids) published in 1958.

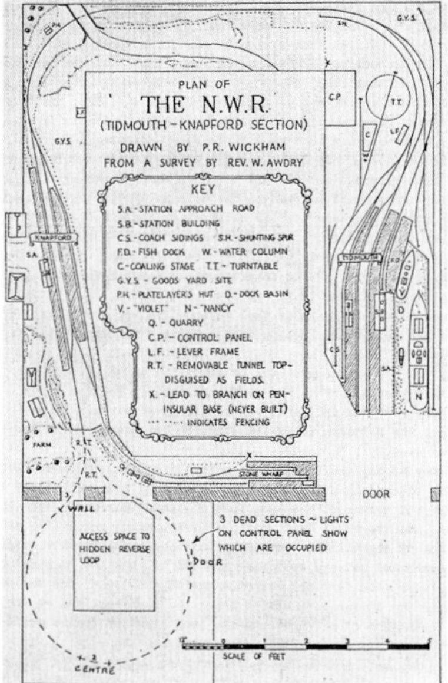

A scale drawing by P. R. Wickham of Wilbert's model railway layout for 'The N. W. R.', the railway featured in his famous stories.

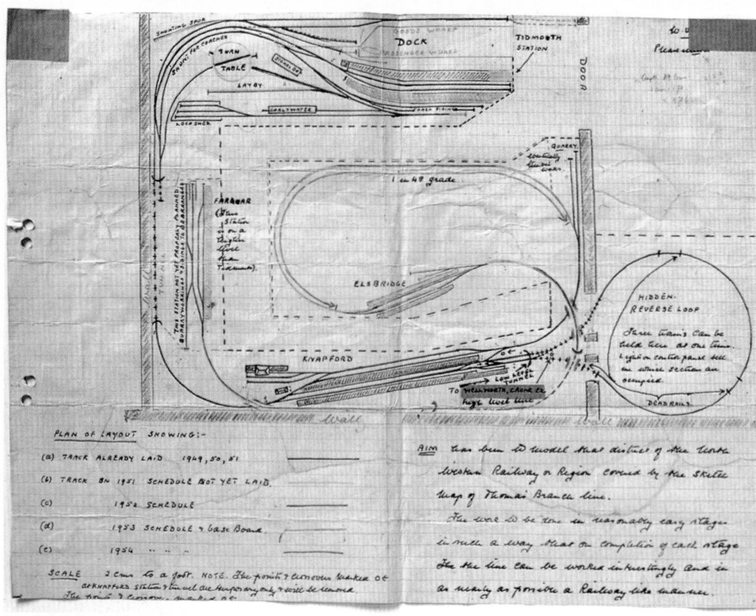

Wilbert Awdry's layout for his model railway which he began to build at Elsworth in 1949.

Wilbert Awdry's model railways were three-dimensional, working illustrations of the railways of Sodor. This section of the layout shows the harbour at Tidmouth.

A working model of Thomas the Tank Engine (with his coaches Annie and Clarabel) used on the Ffarquhar Branch.

Wilbert Awdry laying track on his model railway layout in the attics at Emneth Vicarage in 1954.

The Thin Clergyman, who also served as Controller of the N. W. R., is seen experimenting with point motors to control the two return loops automatically.

'The end of the Line': a busy day at Ffarquhar Station on the N. W. R. as depicted by Wilbert Awdry's 6 x 4 ft folding layout.

Hackenbeck Corner in 1959: The Three Beetles Inn, the bowling green, Thomas Cousins' workshop and (bottom right) the home of the Kneetly family who appear in Wilbert Awdry's story 'The Little People' – Mr. Kneetly (as usual) is under the car.

Keeping a sense of proportion: unhappy with some of Reginald Dalby's drawings, Wilbert Awdry sent the illustrator this photograph as a scale reference.

Part of the landscape of the Ffarquhar Branch Mark II, built when Wilbert Awdry retired to Stroud in 1965, and exhibited on many occasions over the following years. Here Thomas brings the 10.30 up to Ffarquhar station.

A glimpse of railway traffic on the Ffarquhar Branch Mark II.

Ulfstead Road station on Wilbert Awdry's model of the Mid-Sodor Narrow Gauge Railway, as it would have looked in the 1890s. Note the confrontation between Bill Shuvvel's traction engine and Josh Herder's cows on the road-bridge over the line.

George Awdry standing by a radio control marker on the Ravenglass and Eskdale Railway in Cumbria – a photograph later used as an illustration in *The Island of Sodor*, written by his brother and himself in 1987, when the location was said to be the Arlesdale Railway on Sodor.

By the 'Great Tree' we sat down and waited,
Thinking vainly of something to do,
But at last rose a cheer: 'The bus has got here!'
Not 12.20, but twenty to two!

We wandered through Toft and the Eversdens,
Picking up the good folk on the way:
And with Eversden past, on the main road at last
We rejoiced to be out and away.

But alas! All our earnest intentions
Were shattered, and hard was our fate;
With pedal well down, we reached Ely town
Not early, but ten minutes late.

The Cathedral Service you'll find
Described on a different page.
It's meaning was clear, it was simple, sincere,
And impressive to youth and to age.

When the Service was finally over,
We trooped out in a mass in the sun;
To the Cornmarket we, made off for some tea,
And queued up for a cup and a bun.

We had hoped when we'd done all we wanted
To set off for our homes in good time.
But the Driver said: 'No,' he'd a long way to go;
But would fetch us for certain at nine!

We climbed the Cathedral tower
And wandered the City around:
But in spite of our need there was nowhere to feed,
Not a bite nor a sup could be found.

At last a Hotel we invaded
And everything seemed very nice;
They gave us it's true, a sandwich to chew
And some tea, but 'Oh, dear! what a price!'

At nine we returned to the bus stop,
And awaited our Driver again;
But a mudguard that fell, a wrong turning as well
Delayed him till half after ten!

We climbed in and started off homeward
We got out to Goose Hall and then
Were again up the spout for the petrol ran out
And marooned us in Waterbeach Fen.

With singing and talking and laughter
We passed the time slowly away
Till a fresh bus had come, to take us all home
Not on Monday, but early next day!

There's a moral in this little story,
Which, if you are wise, you will learn:
If you go on a 'Day Trip' to Ely
You should take out a 'Monthly Return'!

There were all too few opportunities to get a break from the pressures of parish life and with little cash to spare, the family could not afford proper holidays. For several years, Wilbert did holiday duty for clergymen in other parts of the country: one year it might be Preston in Lancashire, the next Bredhurst in Kent. 'You simply went and lived in another vicarage,' recalls Wilbert, 'always making sure you took along some of your old sermons!' Although no weekday duties were expected of a visiting clergyman, for Wilbert and Margaret (who still had to 'keep house') these were really working holidays. As for Christopher, Veronica and Hilary, they – as children do – invariably made the best of things.

With all his parish work, Wilbert had no time for writing; apart from which, he was feeling more than a little disenchanted with the whole business of publishing. He had been particularly peeved by what he considered the 'pettifogging criticisms' of his text for *Thomas the Tank Engine*, and his agent's inability to get Edmund Ward – or the artists employed to illustrate the books – to take seriously his insistence on engineering accuracy.

Miss Gregorson had written, on the eventual publication of *Thomas the Tank Engine*: 'We should like the position to be that you had a third book accepted by the Oxford University Press or some other publisher. Were that the case, we could be rather rude to Messrs Ward about the inaccuracies. As it is, we dare not be, lest we have to have recourse to them again in the event of other possibilities failing, as other possibilities so commonly do.'

It was early in 1948 that Wilbert had a telephone call which suggested that it wasn't so much a matter of his having recourse to the publishers, as of them having recourse to him. Ward had, apparently, received many letters from young readers asking for another railway book. Was there, he wondered, any chance of Mr Awdry writing some more stories 'along the same lines'?

In view of the response from readers, sales figures for the first two books and the general popularity of railway stories – Diana Ross' *The Little Red Engine Goes to Market* and Graham Greene's first children's book, *The Little Train*, had both recently been published – it might seem unsurprising that there should have been an eagerness for a successor to *Thomas the Tank Engine*. However, the decision to take the series on was, as much as anything, due to the vision and persistence of one man.

Eric Marriott had trained in the editorial and print departments of Cambridge University Press before six years service with the army, during the Second World War. With the return of peace, Marriott rejoined C.U.P. in order to expand his knowledge of the administrative aspects of publishing. His ambition, however, was to work for a more commercial publisher, 'away from the cloistered atmosphere of the University Press'.

Answering an advertisement in the *Times Literary Supplement*, Eric Marriott went to Leicester to meet Edmund Ward. The interview began with Ward asking Marriott for full details of his birth – date, time and place – information which he required in order to consult with an astrologer. Whether due to Marriott's previous experience, or because it was written in the stars, Ward offered him the job of editor.

Edmund Ward was a relatively small-scale operation, publishing only a handful of titles a year and lacking the sophisticated equipment used by larger companies. For example, when Eric Marriott joined the company, in January 1947, books were still being sewn by hand; and, whilst his formal title may have been 'Editor', he was also expected to handle rights and publicity as well as to oversee the printing and marketing of the titles on Edmund Ward's list.

Two of those titles were *The Three Railway Engines* and *Thomas the Tank Engine*. At his interview with Ward, Marriott had been shown the first book and the text and artwork for the second. 'I could see a future for these humanised engines,' Marriott recalls, 'having a young daughter who had already expressed great interest in books, the idea of a series of "small books for small hands" was immensely attractive to me.'

Edmund Ward did not share Marriott's enthusiastic response; he was content to keep reprinting the two titles he already had, but did not want to pursue a series. His new editor, however, was similarly adamant: 'Ward's policy of reprinting existing books rather than publishing new ones may have been sound thinking at the time, but not something, perhaps, that was right for the future when conditions might become better and when publishing houses would have to compete more regularly with new titles. So, I said: "No. We must do a new book each year and go on reprinting the first two as well." ' And that is exactly what was to happen.

'To me,' recalls Wilbert, 'this was marvellous. I couldn't get over my amazement that a publisher should actually *ask me* to write a book for him!' What is more, that publisher was offering a fee of £75. Such a request, obviously, had to be given some very serious thought.

The first question was: what – or, rather, who – should the book be about? Perhaps something could be done with that new engine which had crashed into the story of *Thomas the Tank Engine*. His name was James, he was black with red stripes, and when readers had first met him, he was hurtling along with his brake blocks on fire. Ending up in a field of cows, James was rescued by Thomas, and promised 'some proper brakes and a new coat of paint'.

A new coat of paint suggested a fresh start; so, over the next few months, Wilbert began writing a story about James:

> *James was a new engine who lived at a station at the other end of the line. He had two small wheels in front and six driving wheels behind. They weren't as big as Gordon's, and they weren't as small as Thomas's.*
> *'You're a special Mixed-Traffic engine,' the Fat Controller told him. 'You'll be able to pull coaches and trucks quite easily.'*

The opening paragraph reinforced the hierarchical themes inherent in the stories from the beginning. There are big, powerful, impressive engines like Gordon and Henry; middle-sized engines, such as Edward and James and smaller engines like Thomas and, later, Percy. Each has (and *knows*) his place – or, perhaps one should say, his station. Nevertheless, the smaller engines often aspire to being able to do what big engines can do – usually with disastrous results, although they are sometimes permitted minor acts of heroism; while the big engines occasionally overreach themselves, do foolish things and have to endure the humiliation of receiving assistance from a lower class of engine.

At the time Wilbert Awdry was writing his stories, the concept of society being divided into upper, middle and working-classes was still generally accepted, and that structure is clearly present in the Railway Series. Being in charge of an express passenger-train is seen as being a superior occupation to hauling a goods-train: 'Instead of nice shining coaches, he was pulling a lot of very dirty coal trucks.'

And what of those lesser railway beings who are hustled and bustled about by bossy engines? Coaches are cross, cantankerous things that grumble: 'Where have you been? Where have you been?' and 'There's plenty of time, there's plenty of time'; while, further down the social scale, there are trucks – silly, noisy objects that clatter and bang and need to be 'kept in their place':

> *They talk a lot and don't attend to what they are doing. They don't listen to their engine, and when he stops they bump into each other screaming. 'Oh! Oh! Oh! Oh! Whatever is happening?' And I am sorry to say, they play tricks on an engine who is not used to them.*

The railway hierarchy brings responsibility and privilege; but, if an engine chooses to ignore his duties or is disobedient, he is stripped of all those benefits to which his position normally entitles him. When an engine misbehaves – such as Henry refusing to come out of his tunnel – he loses his standing in society (at least until he shows himself to be sorry) and may well see other, seemingly inferior, engines doing his work.

In our contemporary – less obviously class-conscious – society, this hierarchical sub-text is now probably understood by children in rather different terms. 'The adventures, moods and conversations of the engines,' observes Brian Doyle, 'often reflect those experienced by small children. After all, small engines are very like small boys and girls in many ways; and big, old engines are, perhaps, sometimes like grown-ups.' And those grown-ups are capable of being pompous and autocratic and yet, sometimes, of coming terribly unstuck.

As for James, his career does not get off to a particularly good start: resplendent in his new coat of red paint, he showers water on the Fat Controller's top hat (an incident based on one which Wilbert had witnessed at Ghent in Belgium). 'If you can't behave,' the Fat Controller warns James, 'I shall take away your red coat and have you painted blue.'

The hardest thing about writing a third volume (and the twenty-three titles which were to follow) was coming up with story ideas that were fresh, funny and had really happened. At the time Wilbert was telling the stories that became *The Three Railway Engines*, he had no idea that he would have to find more and more things for his engines to do, but with each book requiring four new adventures, the search for suitable plots was of paramount importance.

Wilbert had begun reading railway books which occasionally contained anecdotes that were to inspire stories. Another source of possible ideas was provided by George Awdry, who was then librarian of the National Liberal Club in London, and who passed on unwanted copies of *The Railway Gazette* to his brother.

'Before British Rail lost the ability to laugh at themselves,' says Wilbert, 'they had a page in that official magazine which they called "The Scrap Heap", in which were recorded off-beat incidents that had happened to some engine, somewhere, sometime. I started using some of these things as incidents in my books and that became the discipline: whatever happened to Thomas, Gordon, Henry and the others had to have actually happened and have a railway-like explanation which fitted.'

The Railway Gazette articles which, said George, 'invariably had a smile in them', provided the idea for 'James and the Boot-lace', the second story in the new book in which James develops a leak in the coach brake-pipe (which is mended using newspaper and a pair of leather bootlaces). 'You have given me a lot of trouble,' the Fat Controller reprimands James. 'People are laughing at my Railway, and I do not like that at all.'

In the next story, James learns the hard lesson about troublesome trucks and coaches, and then shares an adventure with the arrogant Gordon who loses his way when he is 'switched off the main line on to the loop'. Like an engine to which this had actually happened in Birmingham's New Street Station, Gordon 'had to go all round and back again'. By pulling Gordon's Express, James wins the gratitude of the passengers and, more importantly, the approbation of the Fat Controller. At last, James is on his way to becoming a Really Useful Engine.

With the manuscript complete, the thorny subject of illustrations arose. Despite the few reservations he had about the pictures in *Thomas the Tank Engine*, Wilbert would have been happy to continue using Reginald Payne, whose work was far superior to that of the artist responsible for *The Three Railway Engines*. This, however, was not to be. 'The artist,' Edith Gregorson advised Wilbert, 'has since had a nervous breakdown (due, I believe, to work at the Admiralty) and has disappeared from view.'

With no artist in prospect, Wilbert once more pondered the possibility of producing his own illustrations. Edmund Ward suggested that he try his hand

and Wilbert began making drawings that were technically far superior to the rough sketches he had made for the earlier books.

'I could make shift to draw engines,' says Wilbert, 'but people and scenery were beyond me.' Then a possible solution presented itself. A new Headmistress, Barbara Bean, had recently been appointed to the nearby Knapwell Church of England School, and one of her hobbies was sketching. Although Miss Bean knew nothing of railways, she agreed to collaborate with Wilbert on the illustrations.

'I did the engineering side of things,' Wilbert explains, 'including the bridges and tracks, while Barbara filled in the scenic details and the people and added watercolour to the illustrations.' The work took time, but the artists were pleased with the results and 'posted them off with great pride'. Their labour, however, had been in vain: Eric Marriott wrote to thank Wilbert for his 'rough pictures' and said that an artist had been engaged to re-draw them for publication! As a result, Wilbert was, as he puts it, 'forced to accept' Edmund Ward's choice of illustrator, C. Reginald Dalby.

Specimen illustrations in the possession of the publishers, suggest that several artists may well have been considered; they also suggest that the choice of Dalby was a good one. However, the collaboration between Wilbert Awdry and Reginald Dalby, which began with *James the Red Engine* and lasted until *Percy the Small Engine* in 1956, proved an uneasy alliance.

C. Reginald Dalby (the 'C' was for Clarence, a name he disliked and never used) was a commercial artist who had trained at Leicester College of Art. Writing in his unpublished autobiography, *Me: The Odyssey of a Nobody,* Dalby described his working relationship with Wilbert Awdry as 'not of the Gilbert and Sullivan kind', although it should perhaps be remembered that even that partnership was also not without its ups and downs.

'During the whole of our ten or eleven year association,' recalled the illustrator (it was actually only eight years) 'I only met him twice.' Reginald Dalby's reaction to the author of the Railway Series was forthright: in his eyes Wilbert Awdry was 'a pedantic, remote man with whom co-operation was difficult'.

In contrast, Wilbert remembers Dalby as 'a pleasant enough fellow', but adds that he showed little interest in railway engines. Certainly Dalby did not share the author's passion for them: 'To him,' says Wilbert, 'one engine was very like another.' The author prepared detailed sketches for the artist to follow, making extensive use of pictures from previous volumes; so having traced a picture, on page 63 of *Thomas the Tank Engine*, James and Edward were substituted for Gordon and Edward and this became the basis of Dalby's illustration for page 13 of *James the Red Engine*.

Wilbert would have liked the engines in the books to have been drawn 'from life', but this was something the artist declined to do. 'Living in Leicester,' says Wilbert, 'Dalby could have gone to Leicester Midland or Central any day and seen real engines, but he preferred to sit in his studio and draw what he *thought* was a good picture.'

In many respects, Dalby's illustrations certainly were good pictures: their lively energy and gem-like colours undoubtedly helped capture and hold the imagination of young readers. Children's writer, Michael Rosen recalls the impact of these books in the forties and fifties: 'Most books were fairly grey, and those books that weren't, were printed on a kind of browny paper with just two or three colours. But there was something about these *Tank Engine* books: they were incredibly vivid, bright – almost glowing!'

The illustrations are very much a part of the affectionate memories people have of the books: the critic John Churcher speaks of the limitlessness of 'the "blue-remembered hills" of C. Reginald Dalby's exquisite illustrations'. But however charming and evocative they are, Dalby's pictures nevertheless show a certain complacency about engineering accuracy!

'In his favour,' Dalby wrote of Wilbert Awdry in his memoirs, 'it should be said that he had accurate knowledge of rail techniques and engines. This knowledge I was grateful to accept.' It was as well that he did, for a glimpse at James' wheels reveal them to have a connecting rod that passes through the centre of the axles, making it impossible for them to turn!

'They were,' Wilbert admits, 'brightly coloured pictures, but they were to cause me an immense amount of trouble, and puzzled many young readers.' Those problems, however, had yet to emerge when Edmund Ward's 1948 catalogue announced the publication of *James the Red Engine:*

> The long-awaited companion to *The Three Railway Engines* and *Thomas the Tank Engine*. The Reverend W. Awdry tells four more stories about those engines which have now become so universally popular.

James the Red Engine was published in September 1948, with an introductory letter addressed to 'Dear Friends of Edward, Gordon, Henry and Thomas', in which the Author wrote: 'Thank you for your kind letters; here is the new book for which you asked.' Wilbert then commented on the recent nationalisation of the railways of Britain:

> We are nationalised now, but the same engines still work the Region. I am glad to tell you that the Fat Director, who understands our friends' ways, is still in charge, but is now the Fat Controller.

When, a few years later, Wilbert decided to create – or, perhaps, a better word would be 'excavate' – a history for his railway, he revealed that this character was named Sir Topham Hatt. Having served an apprenticeship at Swindon Works, this gentleman had risen through the ranks to Engineer, General Manager and, in 1936, Managing Director.

With nationalisation in 1948, Hatt was appointed Chairman of the Regional Executive and made a Baronet. 'It is no exaggeration to say,' wrote Wilbert, 'that the present prosperity of the Region is almost entirely due to his initiative and resource.' Notwithstanding which, it might also be said, in the words of the critic Margery Fisher, that Sir Topham Hatt is 'the epitome of all self-important frogs in small ponds'!

Whenever Wilbert is asked which of his books in the Railway Series is his favourite book, he refuses to be drawn; but he will admit that *James the Red Engine* is his *least* favourite. 'It was written,' he explains, 'at high speed, not from inspiration, but in order to meet a pressing deadline.'

Wilbert considers the book poorly crafted: 'The stories do not have the quality of those in the other books, and I always feel squirmy inside when I have to read them. They offend my sense of craftsmanship.' Even if *James the Red Engine* does show some weakness of style, its eponymous hero quickly proved a popular character with young readers and the book confirmed the fact that Wilbert had certainly not exhausted his powers as a storyteller.

It also revived his passion for railways. His interest was, as he puts it, still 'running in the background', but his model railway had been packed away in a crate in 1936 and, having neither time nor money to indulge his hobby, that is where it remained.

He had pursued a vicarious interest through Christopher who, on a visit to Cambridge had 'splashed out £2 2s. of saved-up pocket money on an O-gauge Hornby clockwork railway'. The original purchase, Christopher recalls was of 'a red, four-wheeled tank engine; three wagons and an oval of tin-plate track. With various additions through the years, it became quite an extensive layout, stretching the full length of the Rectory's upstairs landing, with enough track for a return loop in the box room.'

The publication of *James the Red Engine* and the prospect of writing even more railway stories, motivated Wilbert to unpack his own model railway. With so many parish problems and anxieties on his mind, Wilbert wanted, he says, 'something to think about which wasn't quite so important!' But once unpacked, where was the railway to go? In the grounds of the Rectory, were a number of outhouses – one of which Wilbert had already made into a workshop – and he decided that an adjoining one would make an ideal venue for his model railway.

At the end of *Thomas the Tank Engine*, 'the cheeky little engine' had been given his own branch line and when, in the autumn of 1948, Wilbert and Christopher began planning the layout for the model railway, they took this line as their inspiration. A few months later, Eric Marriott approached Wilbert (who had now split with his agent – despite their 'dire prophecies of woe') and requested a fourth book of railway stories. After some thought, Wilbert decided that Thomas' branch line would be a good place to start:

> *Thomas the Tank Engine is very proud of his branch line. He thinks it is the most important part of the whole railway.*
> *He has two coaches. They are old, and need new paint, but he loves them very much. He calls them Annie and Clarabel. Annie can only take passengers, but Clarabel can take passengers, luggage and the Guard.*

The problem with *James the Red Engine* was, as Wilbert saw it, that he didn't have 'a system'. That 'system' is what he attempted to establish in writing his new book, and he would follow it in writing all subsequent volumes. It began with what was to be the first of numerous drafts, since Wilbert usually rewrote his stories many times in order to reach the required word-length of 80 - 90 words on each page.

'It was no good,' he says, 'thinking you could get the right number of words straight away. You had to write the story down as it came. But eventually you had to reach a stage where each page became the equivalent of a chapter.'

Each of these mini-chapters had to feature action and incident that could be summarized by the picture that would appear on the page opposite, and those pictures had to be different from the pictures on the preceding and following pages. This was particularly important in order to avoid the kind of pictorial repetition found in the very first of the railway stories, 'Edward's Day Out', where a picture of Edward standing in the station waiting for the guard was followed by a picture with the guard running down the road that is so very similar that the illustrations look like a 'spot-the-difference' puzzle.

Until 1953, Wilbert could not afford a typewriter, so he wrote a longhand draft which he then corrected and often reworked many times, either in its entirety or in part, as he struggled to keep within the maximum word length, whilst still remaining true to his ideas. 'Sometimes,' he recalls, 'I'd have about 160 - 200 words and that would have to be cut down to 80 - 90 words. What is surprising is that if you go over a piece of writing again and again and again, you really can succeed in creating the same impression with fewer words.'

Wilbert kept a note of the number of rewrites he made, his all-time record being 26 revisions for just one page. Often he would leave the manuscript for several days, coming back to it with a fresh eye. Sometimes – as with *James the Red Engine* – when the deadline was close, he simply had to keep at it.

Veronica recalls how hard her father worked in writing the Railway Series: 'It makes me so angry when people say such things as, "There's only a few words on a page, anybody could write those stories!" They don't know what they're talking about! I well remember the care and preparation that went into the making of the books and the choosing of every word.'

One element in the writing which, at all costs, had to be preserved was the use of the rhymes and rhythms that, from the beginning, had marked out his style. So, in his new book, he began the very first story by telling his readers that Thomas sang 'little songs' to Annie and Clarabel as they ran backwards and forwards along his branch line:

> *When Thomas starts from a station he sings, 'Oh, come along! We're rather late. Oh, come along! We're rather late.' And the coaches sing, 'We're coming along, we're coming along.'*

The new book was to be called *Tank Engine Thomas Again* and, for many years, Thomas was the only engine in the shed to be given the honour of having more than one book named after him. It opened with the now familiar author's letter:

> Dear Friends,
> Here is news from Thomas's branch line. It is clearly no ordinary line, and life on it is far from dull.
> Thomas asks me to say that, if you are ever in the Region, you must be sure to visit him and travel on his line. 'They will have never seen anything like it,' he says proudly.
> I know I haven't!
> THE AUTHOR

It is interesting that Wilbert seems to be suggesting that the stories are fantastical while, at the same time, being based on a *real* branch line in a *real* railway Region. Although, at that time, even the author didn't know where Thomas and the other engines were supposed to be running, he did, once again, base his stories on accounts of real railway happenings.

Thomas' first adventure, drawn from an incident recorded in *The Railway Gazette*, sees him 'steaming out of the station' without his guard, who has tripped over an old lady's umbrella and fallen flat on his face!

> *'Come along! Come along!' puffed Thomas, but Clarabel didn't want to come. 'I've lost my nice Guard, I've lost my nice Guard,' she sobbed. Annie tried to tell Thomas 'We haven't a Guard, we haven't a Guard,' but he was hurrying, and wouldn't listen.*

The next story, 'Thomas Goes Fishing', was inspired by an account, recorded by David Smith, of a fireman on the Glasgow & South Western Railway who used to keep fish in the tender tank of his engine to eat the fungus and keep it clean. It was an eccentric idea and, at first, Wilbert wasn't sure how to work it into a story. However, with help from Eric Marriott (a rare instance of Wilbert accepting assistance with the creation of a storyline) Thomas embarked on one of his most bizarre exploits!

Every time Thomas travels along his branch line, he crosses a bridge over a river, and here he daydreams about going fishing. Then, one day, he runs low on water and, when his Driver and Fireman find the water tower empty, they stop on the bridge and fill Thomas' tanks with river water collected in a bucket on a rope. Thomas continues his journey, but he hasn't gone far before he develops a pain and groans: 'I'm going to burst! I'm going to burst!'

An inspection of Thomas' tanks reveals that he has, inadvertently 'gone fishing' – the bucket having contained more than just water. Supervised by the Fat Controller, the Driver and Fireman also go fishing and with their catch (and some potatoes supplied by the Station Master) make themselves a fish and chip supper beside the line:

> *'That was good,' said the Fat Controller as he finished his share, 'but fish don't suit you, Thomas, so you mustn't do it again.'*
> *'No, sir, I won't,' said Thomas sadly, 'engines don't go fishing, it's too uncomfortable.'*

In addition to finding new story ideas, Wilbert also began to expand the number of characters who might be worked into his little scenarios. The third story in *Tank Engine Thomas Again* introduced the Railway Series' first anthropomorphic, non-engine character. It begins in autumn, when Thomas happens to see a tractor working in a nearby field:

> *'Hullo!' said the tractor, 'I'm Terence; I'm ploughing.'*
> *'I'm Thomas; I'm pulling a train. What ugly wheels you've got.'*
> *'They're not ugly, they're caterpillars,' said Terence. 'I can go anywhere; I don't need rails.'*
> *'I don't want to go anywhere,' said Thomas huffily, 'I like my rails, thank you!'*

Then comes winter with 'dark heavy clouds full of snow', just as it had come during the Awdry family's first winter in Elsworth when the snow was so thick that Christopher remembers 'tunnelling through a deep drift that lay against our front door'. At first, Thomas is contemptuous of the snow, calling it: 'Silly soft stuff! Silly soft stuff!' When, however, he rushes out of a tunnel and finds himself stuck in a snowdrift, it is Terence, with his ugly caterpillars, who comes to his rescue.

While Terence 'tugged and slipped, and slipped and tugged' in pulling Thomas out of the snowdrift, a bus came tooting along in order to take his passengers to their destination. Although Wilbert had some uncomfortable memories of buses, this particular vehicle was to make another appearance in the final story in *Tank Engine Thomas Again*; and, as a result, the world inhabited by Thomas and his friends was to take on a completely new dimension.

CHAPTER EIGHT

The Discovery of Sodor

'ONE day Thomas was waiting at the junction, when a 'bus came into the yard.'

That was how the fourth story in *Tank Engine Thomas Again* had begun:

'Hullo!' said Thomas, 'who are you?'

'I'm Bertie, who are you?'

'I'm Thomas; I run this line.'

The characteristically immodest Thomas is soon boasting that he can go faster than Bertie, and the bus responds by challenging the engine to a race. The events which follow, unlike most incidents in the Railway Series, were not based on a specific event. 'I don't imagine,' says Wilbert, 'that there ever was such a race – for fear of reprisals from authority!'

Wilbert had written the first few pages and was reading it to Christopher, Hilary and Veronica. He was in the habit of trying out new stories on his children: 'If they laughed in the right places, well and good; if they showed signs of disapproval, I would have to try again!' On this occasion, Wilbert described the beginning of the race: 'The Station Master said, "Are you ready? – Go!" and they were off!' But when he reached the point where Bertie was left fuming at the level crossing gates while Thomas 'sailed gaily through', all three – as one child – said, 'Daddy, that's not fair!'

Hilary remembers the occasion clearly: 'We thought that Thomas had got all the advantages, and that there were far more hazards facing Bertie on the road.'

'In fact,' says Wilbert, 'in order to be fair, I'd given the bus and the train an equal number of hazards – such as stations, traffic lights and the level crossing – and, in the end, the race really takes place up the final valley where road and rail run side by side.' In order to prove his point, Wilbert drew a map to show the children that neither vehicle had been favoured in the race. 'He proved to us,' says Hilary, 'that, stupid though it was – an engine and a bus having a race – it was, actually, *fair*!'

Wilbert's map shows the road and the railway line marked with specific sites – 'Here are traffic lights' and 'Here is a level crossing' – as well as much else besides, such as the location of other stories in *Tank Engine Thomas Again*: 'Here Thomas waits for Henry' (in the story 'Thomas and the Guard'), 'Here Thomas stuck in the snow' and, not far away, 'Here Terry works', referring to the tractor character who eventually became known by the more formal name of Terence.

The map also shows bridges, tunnels and rivers – one of which is marked with the note: 'Here are fish' (as, indeed, Thomas had already discovered in the story 'Thomas Goes Fishing'). In addition, there were contour lines from sea level to 900 feet, and a variety of interesting place names: Dryaw (an anagram of Awdry); Toryreck (from Rectory), Knapford (from the real Knapwell) and Elsbridge, so named because it stood at the point where the road north crossed the River Els (from Wilbert's parish of Elsworth). The name Ffarquhar was much older in origin, being the name chosen in 1928 by the young Wilbert and George for the terminus of their never-completed model railway. The double 'f' which suggests Welsh connections was a reference to the fact that, during the early days of the Great Western Railway, there had been plans to site a railway in a remote corner of Wales – hence the literal meaning of Ffarquhar as 'far away quarry'.

There is something fascinating about every map: perhaps it is the romance of place names, or the mystery of symbols; or the fact that a map is a record of a specific moment in time that is itself the end product of centuries of history, geography and language; maybe it is the sense of holding a solution to the puzzle of Where Things Are, of taking a God's-eye view of the world, or simply a need to know how to get There from Here.

Also, on looking at any map, there is an urge to know what lies beyond its borders, and the earliest maps showed unexplored areas as empty blanks, marked with such cautions as 'Here there be dragons'. So, having made a map to show the race between Thomas and Bertie, Wilbert Awdry decided to explore further and the results of those explorations were to have a far-reaching effect on the Railway Series.

In publishing *Tank Engine Thomas Again*, Edmund Ward referred to it as 'One of the outstanding modern series of children's books which are in constant demand'; and the advertising copy which Eric Marriott wrote for the publisher's catalogue reflected the popularity which, in just four years, the series had achieved:

> Most young children know of Thomas, Henry, Gordon, Edward and James, of their almost human antics and the troubles into which they get themselves.

> The Reverend W. Awdry understands most easily and successfully the child's mind and, aided by the full colour illustrations, these books make a compelling and lively series which no bookseller can afford to overlook.

The task of ensuring that no bookseller overlooked the Railway Series fell to representative, later Sales Manager, John Welch: 'Edmund Ward asked me if I had two suitcases, and when I said "Yes," he said, "Well, put these samples into one, and some clothes into the other and go off and sell some books – especially W. Awdry's Railway Series." This was just after the war when the ability to sell children's books was expanding enormously and the big publishers, who had marvellous lists before the war, were coming back into their own. However, Edmund Ward was a very small publishing house and it was extremely difficult to get them placed.'

One or two booksellers (including W. H. Smith) suggested that Ward should drop the words 'The Rev.' from the cover, as it might deter some purchasers; but the chief difficulty was over their size: 'Four-and-a-quarter inches by five-and-five-eighths inches,' admits John Welch, 'was an extremely unconventional shape!' Some booksellers found the books awkward to display; others argued that they were so small they could be easily shoplifted.

The books' great selling point, however, was the illustrations – well-printed, in sharp colours on every page. Reginald Dalby's pictures for *Tank Engine Thomas Again* were a great improvement on those made for *James the Red Engine*; particularly evocative are Dalby's winter scenes for 'Thomas, Terence and the Snow'. There are grey skies; snowdrifts with blue shadows; bright, reflected light and the brickwork of sheds and tunnel entrances dusted with a powdering of white. Dalby created this last effect by using an almost dry brush – a technique which he also used when painting the clouds of steam that chuffed from the engines' funnels.

From correspondence forwarded to the author, it soon became clear that the Railway Series was proving a great success with readers of all ages, and Wilbert was particularly delighted by letters of appreciation from professional railwaymen who wrote to say that, because Wilbert's engine stories were all based on real railway incidents, they were the only ones they could read to their children without squirming with embarrassment. Since such correspondents often supplied Wilbert with new story ideas, he was careful about the way in which railwaymen were represented in the books: 'I made it a rule that no shadow of blame should fall on them for any mishap. It was always the engine's fault!'

With the publication of the fourth title, Eric Marriott decided that something had to be done about the illustrations in *The Three Railway Engines*, which he had never liked and which fell far short of the standard established with later volumes. Reginald Dalby was commissioned to re-draw the pictures and, whilst he simply followed the original designs by William Middleton (which were themselves merely interpretations of Wilbert's first sketches), they were a vast improvement.

The re-illustrated edition of *The Three Railway Engines* was published in October 1949. The following month, Wilbert decided to send a copy, together with the other three books as a first birthday present to Prince Charles. 'I have reason to believe,' Wilbert wrote to the then Princess Elizabeth, 'that they have given pleasure to many children, and I hope that in due course he will enjoy them too.'

In acknowledgement, came a reply from Jean Elphinstone, Lady-in-Waiting, who wrote: 'Her Royal Highness was deeply touched that you should have sent her son such an interesting present, and the Princess bids me express to you her warmest thanks on his behalf.'

Forty-five years later, in a letter to the present writer, the recipient of that gift, now His Royal Highness The Prince of Wales, recollected the pleasure it had given: 'I adored the books and remember so well the joy of those stories. In fact, I seem to recall reading them to my younger brothers when they were small too! I dare say the books are still in the nursery cupboard somewhere.'

Although remembered with similar affection by millions, it has now become fashionable to denounce the Railway Series. In 1994, journalist, Craig Brown dismissed them as: 'Very, very, very boring books. The prose quality is completely non-existent: it's a kind of plodding, plodding prose . . . there's no zest, there's no love of words, there's nothing that you'd find in any competent – or, certainly not any great – children's author.'

Children, however, have always found – and made completely their own – the books they love; and there are numerous episodes which demonstrate the excellence of Wilbert Awdry's writing:

> *Thomas had not crossed the bridge when Bertie started with a roar, and soon shot ahead. Excited passengers in train and 'bus cheered and shouted across the valley. Now Thomas reached his full speed and foot by foot, yard by yard he gained, till they were running level. Bertie tried hard, but Thomas was too fast; slowly but surely he drew ahead, till whistling triumphantly he plunged into the tunnel, leaving Bertie toiling far behind.*

Although Wilbert's books were a proven success, that was not, at first, reflected in the author's earnings, since he had parted with the copyright for a flat fee. Then, following the publication of the fourth title, Wilbert received a letter from his publisher. 'Edmund Ward wrote to me,' he recalls, 'saying that he was feeling rather guilty and had decided that he was going to make me an *ex gratia* payment out of the profits from the book sales.'

This sum, around £200, was a godsend to the struggling Rectory family and it provided some help with what was essentially a 'shoe-string existence' at Elsworth. It also enabled Wilbert to spend a little money on the 'luxury' of a model railway and the necessary workshop equipment.

Wilbert began planning the layout early in 1948, but was handicapped by the fact that whilst he had read about models in the *Model Railway News*, he had never actually seen one in operation. Nevertheless, there was a suitable site – one of two adjoining outbuildings – and Wilbert had a clear vision of what kind of line he intended to build:

> I wanted a Terminal station, capable of handling main line trains and which, for further interest, could be a port. Neighbouring industries would provide an economic reason for the line's existence, and by siting these on a branch line I could justify the introduction of a junction station which would provide further operational interest.

After filling 'several large size wastepaper baskets' with rejected schemes, a plan was devised that, when submitted to the Stationmaster at neighbouring St Ives, was passed as being 'railway-like and operational'. Late in 1948, work was begun on the baseboard. Track laying started the following January and, 'somewhat optimistically', the layout was promised to be ready for showing at the Church Fete, the following July. 'A week before the event,' says Wilbert, 'the only things down on the baseboard were the track and the wiring – there were no station buildings, platforms or scenic effects, and a gap in the baseboard indicated where the dock was to be.'

Time was fast running out, but when George Awdry came to stay at Elsworth for a week's holiday, the brothers tackled the task together, working until eleven or twelve o'clock most nights. Eventually, the job was done, and to their amazement and relief the line worked throughout the appointed afternoon, almost without a hitch.

Admission money for that first public exhibition went to the Fete; subsequently, the railway could be viewed by appointment and contributions were invited to help towards various items for the church, such as an altar frontal and an oak box for Communion wafers, which carried an engraved plate commemorating the fact that the money to buy it had been raised by Thomas the Tank Engine!

To begin with, the only engine working the line was Thomas – a commercial model bought 'off the shelf' from the model-maker Stuart Reidpath and painted in the same colours as those used in the illustrations to the book.

The railway system, built to 16.5 mm. gauge, began on a wide shelf with Tidmouth, the line's terminus and headquarters, its marshalling yards and its harbour. 'The track,' Christopher Awdry recalls, 'then followed the wall anti-clockwise, passing through a tunnel and rounding a curve into Knapford, a country station and the proposed junction for Thomas' branch line to Ffarquhar. The branch to a stone quarry, followed the wall, while the main line went through it and into the workshop, where it swept round in a large return loop.'

The tunnel between Tidmouth and Knapford, which was constructed from a wooden frame covered in old pipe-lagging, was the cause of an entertaining incident. Wilbert had gone into the railway room to do some running one evening and, as he had not used the line for some time, sent Thomas on a test run. When the engine entered the tunnel Wilbert heard 'a sort of scrabbling noise' and, when it emerged from the other side, it was followed by a mouse, which looked round and then shot back into the tunnel.

'Next time through,' Wilbert recalls, 'Thomas and the mouse had a dead heat at the opposite tunnel mouth – Thomas rocked and nearly came off the rails, but had the best of it.' Once again, the mouse retreated into the tunnel but, when Thomas next passed through, the mouse did not appear. However, when Thomas reached Knapford, he was reversed and – given full regulator – thundered into the tunnel: 'This time the mouse did not wait; it shot from the opposite entrance, streaked along the track, dived into the dock, leapt 3 feet 6 inches from the baseboard to the floor and was never seen again!'

Christopher Awdry remembers spending many hours with his father in that outhouse and other enthusiasts soon found their way to the Rectory. Even Bishop Wynn of Ely, during a visit to Elsworth, was taken to see the model railway and asked Wilbert whether there was any particular significance in the naming of 'Edward' and 'Gordon': *his* name happened to be Edward, while that of his Suffragan – Bishop Walsh – was Gordon; it must have come as something of a disappointment to his Lordship to find that this was simply a coincidence!

Another visitor was E. R. ('Teddy') Boston, an undergraduate at Cambridge who had heard about Wilbert Awdry's railway from a local model shop. He arrived at the Rectory without warning, but his enthusiasm was such that he and Wilbert struck up an immediate friendship that was to last until Teddy's death in 1986.

Teddy Boston, who eventually entered the ordained ministry, was a frequent visitor to Elsworth, helping to build the model railway and lending bits of rolling-stock. He later joined Wilbert on several railway holidays and was immortalised in the Railway Series as the 'Fat Clergyman' to Wilbert's 'Thin Clergyman'. Wilbert also wrote the foreword to Teddy Boston's posthumously published autobiography, *Font to Footplate*.

On his first visit, Teddy Boston had watched Wilbert running Thomas together with a new model engine, Percy, which had been scratch built by Wilbert from brass and template and sent to Stuart Reidpath to have a chassis built. The completed engine was photographed for the benefit of Reginald Dalby who was about to start work on illustrating the book in which Percy made his debut, a volume ominously entitled *Troublesome Engines*.

'News from the Line,' wrote Wilbert in his introductory letter, 'has not been good. The Fat Controller has been having trouble. A short while ago he gave Henry a coat of green paint; but as soon as he got his old colour back again, Henry became conceited. Gordon and James, too, have been Getting Above Themselves. I am glad to say, however, that the Fat Controller has, quite kindly but very firmly, put them In Their Place; and the trains are running as usual.'

Nevertheless, at the beginning of the book, things are really quite unusual. Henry, who is jealous of the fact that James has been given the job of pulling a circus train, has to take some workmen and their tools to a blocked tunnel: ' "Pushing trucks! Pushing trucks!" he muttered in a sulky sort of way.' Soon, however, it is Henry who is getting the push, when the blockage in the tunnel turns out to be one of the circus elephants!

Although, as with all the stories in the Railway Series, this adventure was inspired by a real event – on this occasion recounted to the author by an ex-Indian Railways engineer – Wilbert added imaginative touches that were all his own:

> *The elephant stopped pushing and came towards them. They gave him some sandwiches and cake, so he forgot he was cross and remembered he was hungry. He drank three buckets of water without stopping, and was just going to drink another when Henry let off steam.*

The elephant jumped, and 'hoo– – -oosh', he squirted the water over Henry by mistake . . .
'An elephant pushed me! An elephant hooshed me!' he hissed.

In the next story, once again inspired by actual incidents, Gordon and James both experience problems with a turntable. Gordon, who has been putting Thomas down because he is not a Tender Engine and, therefore, not as Important, gets stuck on a turntable and has to pull his next train backwards – as if he were no better than a tank engine. Then James has trouble with the same turntable when the wind catches him and spins him round and round until he's giddy! That night the three engines decide to hold an 'indignation meeting':

'It's shameful to treat Tender Engines like this! Henry gets "hooshed" by elephants; Gordon has to go backwards and people think he's a Tank Engine. James spins round like a top, and everyone laughs at us. And added to that, the Fat Controller makes us shunt in dirty sidings. Ugh– – – - !!' said all three engines together.

Gordon, Henry and James decide to go on strike. 'Most steam engine drivers,' says Wilbert, 'have the feeling that a steam locomotive has a personality and can express it; hence it is possible to imagine a strike of engines and the Fat Controller dealing with it calmly but firmly as a nanny might deal with sulky children in the nursery!'

The three engines having withdrawn their labour, Edward is enlisted to help with the shunting – despite being accused of having 'black wheels' (the engine equivalent of being a 'blackleg') by the striking engines. Eventually, the Fat Controller decides that the line really does need a tank engine and so goes to the Engine Workshop:

They showed him all sorts of Tank Engines. There were big ones, and little ones; some looked happy, and some sad, and some looked at him anxiously, hoping he would choose them.
At last he saw a smart little green engine with four wheels.
'That's the one,' he thought.
'If I choose you, will you work hard?'
'Oh Sir! Yes Sir!'
'That's a good engine; I'll call you Percy.'
'Yes Sir! Thank you Sir!' said Percy happily.

Percy is one of the most engaging engines in the shed with his slightly roly-poly appearance and the look of wide-eyed innocence given him by Reginald Dalby. The artist had visited Elsworth while *Troublesome Engines* was being written and he included the entire Awdry family – Wilbert, Margaret, Christopher, Veronica and Hilary – in one of his pictures for the story 'Percy runs away', in which they are shown, standing on a station platform, waving to the engine. When it came to the matter of pictorial consistency, however, Reginald Dalby remained unrepentant. 'He was,' says Wilbert, 'quite unconcerned about matters of detail.' According to the author, Dalby saw no future in the railway stories: 'What does it matter?' he asked, when Wilbert tackled him on some technical point. 'These books will fade out in a few years time. It isn't as if there's going to be a long series of them.' He couldn't have been more wrong.

The tensions between artist and writer showed no sign of easing, as can be seen from the opening paragraph of *The Island of Sodor*:

> *By 1950 letters began to come from sharp-eyed youngsters pointing out that engines and buildings often looked different in different books, and sometimes in the same one. It is quite useless to tell a five- or six-year-old that a mistake had been allowed to go into print. That sort of answer wouldn't satisfy them at all. To them the stories and pictures are real, and they are entitled to an explanation; so, in my replies, I had to make up a story to account for the discrepancy. I soon developed standard answers for the commonest questions, but even so there were so many letters that life began to get too short.*

One such 'standard answer' concerned the changing appearance of the troublesome Henry. At the end of *The Three Railway Engines,* the green Henry had been repainted blue; but, because he had been wrongly drawn with the same wheel arrangement as Gordon, the two engines were almost impossible to tell apart.

'I was furious about this,' Wilbert recalls, 'and my first reaction was to abolish Henry! To this end I gave him only one mention in *Thomas the Tank Engine* and that as an invalid. I hoped this would give the Fat Director (as he then was) a good excuse for scrapping him. I ignored Henry entirely in *James the Red Engine*. But I had reckoned without my readers. I had so many enquiries after Henry's health that I had to give him a reprieve and he appeared, still in blue and still in a delicate state of health, in *Tank Engine Thomas Again*.' This decision was to give Wilbert his worst headache yet.

Reginald Dalby was not responsible for Henry's appearance in either *The Three Railway Engines* or *Thomas the Tank Engine*, although he did later re-draw the illustrations for the first book. However, when, in 1949, Henry fleetingly looked in on page 9 of *Tank Engine Thomas Again*, Dalby inexplicably showed him as having a cab with two small windows instead of one, and with oblong – rather than round – buffers.

That one illustration, says Wilbert, 'raised a furore of indignation' among young readers who complained that although the text said the engine was Henry, the picture showed Gordon. 'Dear Rev. Awdry,' began one typical letter, written on behalf of a puzzled three-year-old, 'It's Henry again. He goes from green to blue and then to green again. He won't come out in the rain . . . and now he's made me have a row with Daddy! In *Tank Engine Thomas Again* Daddy came to page 8, and I said it wasn't Henry, it was GORDON. Daddy said it *was* Henry. I said it wasn't. "It is, it isn't, it is, it isn't" went on till Mummy intervened. "It is Henry," she said; but I said it couldn't be because "ONLY GORDON HAS SQUARE BUFFERS AND TWO WINDOWS IN HIS CAB". I can't read yet so I don't believe either of them, and I'm writing to you to tell them they're both wrong.'

'I had to tell a story,' says Wilbert, 'explaining that when Henry finally came out of the tunnel, his cab and buffers had got rusty because tunnels are damp and dirty places.' As a result, Henry was sent to the works and it was there, as Wilbert's answer explains, that the confusion really began:

> 'Who does Henry think he is?' said the Works Foreman. 'We can't afford to keep special buffers and cabs for him. He'll have to make do with spare parts we've got for Gordon.' So Henry came out of the works looking like Gordon. He was pleased, but Gordon was cross, especially when people like you mixed them up! Gordon was so rude to poor Henry that Henry got quite ill.

Another observant youngster received an alternative explanation in a letter, dated February 1951:

> Here is the sad story of Henry's buffers. One day after he had come out of the tunnel he was so pleased and excited that he didn't look where he was going and ran into a buffer-stop and broke his round buffers. The Fat Controller was very cross with him and when he was sent to the workshop they hadn't any round buffers left so they had to put on square buffers like Gordon. This made Henry very pleased but Gordon was

> dreadfully jealous because he was proud of being the only engine on the line with square buffers.
> Henry was proud of his square buffers: 'Buff-buff-buffers,' he would puff proudly and to try make everyone admire them. One day when he came to the Big Station at the end of the line, a crowd of people were on the platform. They were really waiting for a train but Henry thought they were waiting to see him. 'Buff-buff-buff-ers! Buff-buff-buff-ers!' he chanted proudly and forgot to look where he was going 'Buff-buff-' CRASH! He bumped into the buffer-stop and his beautiful buffers were broken. So the Fat Controller was cross with him again and sent him to be mended. This time in the workshop they had no square buffers left. 'N-no s-s-s-square b-b-b-buffers!' sobbed Henry 'Oh dear, oh dear!' 'Cheer up Henry,' said the Fat Controller and he patted his boiler kindly. 'Your paint is getting dirty, would you like a nice coat of green then the little boys won't mistake you for Gordon any more?' Henry was pleased, 'Oh, thank you, sir,' he said at once. So that is why in *The Three Railway Engines* Henry has round buffers, he has square buffers in *Tank Engine Thomas Again* and in *Troublesome Engines* he has green paint and round buffers. I hope you like this little story.

Answering so many letters was a repetitive, time-consuming business. 'Nevertheless,' says Wilbert, 'all the letters received were a delight. I learnt much from them about the art of story-telling, and enjoyed exercising my ingenuity in devising suitable answers.' One such answer (again a little story in its own right) explains why Gordon had different-shaped buffers in the first place. Written in January 1949, the letter picks up on an event described in the story 'Edward, Gordon and Henry' in *The Three Railway Engines*:

> You want to know why Gordon has long buffers. I will tell you a great Secret. We have to keep it a Secret because if he knew I had told you, Gordon would be very cross, and when Gordon is cross something always happens to the Express! You remember he burst his safety valve? He had to go to the 'Works' and have a new one. He was so proud of this new safety valve that one day he was 'showing off' and forgot to look where he was going and he ran into the buffers at the Big Station at the end of the line. So he had to go and have new buffers but we hadn't got any round ones left, so he had to have long ones which he didn't like at all. Presumably he got used to them and was proud of being the only engine with long buffers. Then a dreadful thing happened, Henry broke his buffers and had to have long ones too.

> Gordon got so cross: 'Why should Henry have long buffers like me?' he asked. So we don't mention buffers to Gordon now. So please, if ever you see Gordon, don't talk to him about buffers, it will offend him dreadfully and he really is a nice engine to talk to, if you remember not to talk about buffers!

At the beginning of *Troublesome Engines*, the next volume in the series, the Fat Controller tries to cheer up Henry and Gordon – who are feeling lonely when Thomas goes off to run his branch line – with new coats of paint, and (in the hope of sorting out some of the confusion about his identity) Henry wisely chooses to return to his original green! 'I also hoped,' says Wilbert, 'that by giving the engines numbers, Gordon and Henry could be more easily distinguished, but it didn't work that way; even then I had letters still mixing them up and asking why *Gordon* was now green instead of his former blue!'

Many years later, a young reader wrote to point out that in one illustration (on page 63 of *The Three Railway Engines*), Gordon *also* appeared to have had buffer trouble, temporarily exchanging his highly-treasured square buffers for round ones! It is scarcely surprising that the author should have been keen to regulate the appearance of his engines.

Wilbert was also thinking of trying to fix certain details of the landscape through which the engines travelled and remembered his map of the Thomas-Bertie race. He had given a copy to Reginald Dalby and the artist had used it as a reference in making his illustrations. 'This encouraged me to hope,' wrote Wilbert, 'that if I could find a suitable location for the Fat Controller's Railway and map it, I could, so to speak, standardise the scenery at any given spot, and so avoid any more troublesome questions on that score.'

The artist, it should be said, didn't altogether agree that his illustrations raised 'troublesome questions'. 'I did object,' wrote Reginald Dalby in his unpublished autobiography, 'when [Awdry] made adverse comments concerning certain natural landscape features which I introduced, such as a distant village, a spinney, hills on the horizon, even a glimpse of the sea or a church spire. All things of interest to children. It was a long time before I found out that such things didn't agree with some imaginary island in his mind where his railway was supposedly situated.'

But then it was some time before the author knew that himself. 'When Wilbert began the stories,' commented George Awdry, 'we didn't think there was anything to work out, but as they became more complicated, we had to put the railway within a framework.' The question was, *where*? 'We had to have somewhere,' recalled George, 'which was reasonably separate from British Rail which could have its own railway system, history, economics and industries.'

And yet it also had to be somewhere *within* the British Isles since it had been announced, in *James the Red Engine*, that the fictional railway – like the real one – had been nationalised. Although Wilbert and George pored over maps, nowhere seemed quite right. Then, in 1950, Wilbert visited Douglas on the Isle of Man to preach at a Sunday School Festival. 'In a long weekend,' he recalls, 'I was able to see something of the island which I had never visited before. I was also intrigued to find that although the Bishop had the title "Sodor and Man", he only had Man for his diocese. There is, of course, a historical reason for this, but as you have to go back some 700 years to find it, George and I decided that we could safely ignore it!'

That 'historical reason' was that the Isle of Man (together with the Western side of Scotland, the Hebrides, the Orkneys and large chunks of Ireland) had once been part of the Norwegian Empire, until, as Wilbert puts it, Alexander III of Scotland 'kicked the Norse out'. The name Sodor was derived from The Sudreys, the ancient word for the islands to the west of Scotland (just as those to the north were called The Nordreys) and when the area had been Christianised, the Isle of Man was chosen as a centre with a Cathedral and a Bishop whose title was 'Sodor and Man'.

'Everybody,' says Wilbert, 'knew that there was an Isle of Man, but we decided to "discover" *another* island – the Island of Sodor and so give the poor deprived Bishop the other half of his diocese!'

Ever since men have been making maps of the world around them, they have also been mapping the worlds of the imagination: from Eden to Hell, from Thomas More's Utopia to John Bunyan's Celestial City. No place has been too fantastical for the imaginative map-maker, be it Oz, Middle-earth, Narnia, Earthsea or Discworld.

Although the majority of such maps are purely fantastic, others have attempted to give geographic authenticity to fictional places. For example, an early edition of *Gulliver's Travels* contained a crude map showing the island of Lilliput as being a little south-west of Sumatra; and, years later, Robert Louis Stevenson included a map in Treasure Island on which the latitude and longitude had originally been marked and then, subsequently, 'struck out by J. Hawkins'!

Wilbert drew a map of Sodor (incorporating the area already plotted on the Thomas-Bertie race map) and located his island between Barrow-in-Furness on the British mainland and the Isle of Man. With the first map drawn, Wilbert and his brother began a unique collaboration; setting out, over the next few years, to discover and chronicle the geography, history, industry and agriculture of this fictional island.

What began, for Wilbert, as a necessary way of plotting and planning his stories soon developed into a highly enjoyable game of intellect that tested his and George's powers of imaginative invention and logical deduction. Rather as J. R. R. Tolkien explored and excavated the realm of Middle-earth – creating much more historical detail than ever featured in his books *The Hobbit* and *The Lord of the Rings* – so the Awdry brothers pieced together every aspect of life on Sodor, past and present, as well as the character of the Sudrian people and their language, Sudric.

When, in 1987, Wilbert and George Awdry published *The Island of Sodor: Its people, history and railways* they included an entry on the Rev. Canon Nicholas Dreswick (Historian):

> *Canon Dreswick's* History of Sodor*, 4 vols. (Chatter & Windows, Suddery 1899-1912), is the standard history of the Island, and still recognised as a masterpiece of scholarship and research. Its bulk makes it appear somewhat daunting; but it is written with such lightness of touch and subtle humour as to grip the general reader.*

According to the editors, this scholar began his work in 1889 'during a period of convalescence at Cronk Abbey following a severe illness. Nicholas Dreswick with his cousin and host, Albert Regaby, explored the Abbey library together and were disappointed to find little information about Sodor's history.' As a result, they determined that a book should be written about the Island: 'Nicholas agreed to undertake the writing if Albert, who had useful friends all over the island, would be responsible for research.' Clearly the Dreswick-Regaby partnership was modelled on that of Wilbert and George Awdry.

'It started off,' recalled George, 'with letters . . .' Actually, they were rather more than letters; they were screeds of highly-detailed – but totally fictitious – history which passed back and forth between the brothers for comment and amendment. From one of Wilbert's hand-written manuscripts here are a few early 'facts' about Sodor:

> About half the land is cultivated, oats, barley and turnips are the chief crops. Fishing is important, and the Tidmouth Kipper is a much prized breakfast delicacy. Lead, zinc and silver is mined, and the island stone has excellent weather-resisting properties.

> The language, Sudric, is fast dying out and is akin to Manx and Gaelic.
> The rugged and beautiful scenery, the fishing particularly in the mountain lakes attract holiday-makers from all parts.
> Tidmouth – once the haunt of Smugglers – now contributes much to the country's revenues by being its excellent port. The Docks are owned by the N. W. R. and as it is nearer to Douglas and Belfast many travellers prefer to embark there rather than at Liverpool or Fleetwood.

Having no typewriter, Wilbert wrote his historical essays on Sodor in a neat hand on lined foolscap paper (using only every other line) and making a carbon copy for his brother. Then, after George had read and commented on the piece, Wilbert would make corrections and amendments in red ink, using the alternating empty lines. Another of his early manuscripts is headed 'The Island of Sodor – Notes on its History and Development' and begins:

> The Romans apparently did not bother with it, they looked at it from their camp at Lancaster, made a landing at what is now Ballahoo, but were driven off, and retired. The inhabitants gave no trouble so were left alone.

'Before long,' Wilbert later wrote, 'we found ourselves evolving a political, social and economic history of the island. To do this we had delve into Irish, Scots, Norwegian, Icelandic, Manx and English history besides discovering Sudric sources of our own.' So, for example, a reference by Wilbert to an attempted invasion of Sodor by the Normans in 1085, led George to identify the site of this event as a coastal town named Normanby at the mouth of the Ballahoo river. Subsequently, like much of Sodor's history, this 'discovery' was revised: the river being named the Hoo, the town Norramby and the date of the attack recalculated first to 1116 and then to 1089.

Not surprisingly, perhaps, a great deal of ecclesiastical background was invented, such as an account of a sixty year period in Sodor's history during the twelfth century when the Island had no less than three bishops: one consecrated by the Norwegian Bishop of Trondheim, another by the Bishop of Argyll and a third by the Archbishop of York. Eventually, according to Wilbert, Henry III of England 'intervened and ordered that the three parties who claimed the right to appoint should agree on a common choice'. As a result, Sodor lost its separate bishop and had to share with Man. Beside this passage, George Awdry added a pencil note to the effect that on the strength of having once been the seat of a bishop, Suddery 'has always described itself as a city'.

George's comments (or, as he called them, 'Observations') on his brother's growing manuscript, were typed onto the blank backs of old pages of teleprinter paper from the National Liberal Club, where George was Librarian. If you turn over detailed accounts of such Sudrian matters as 'The Use of Mechanical Power on or near Roads', you find the ghosts of old news bulletins which, minute by minute, had come through on the Liberal Club's teleprinter.

Interwoven with the leaves of Sodor's history are momentous world events: '6.25 PM. WASHINGTON, FRIDAY. THE HOUSE OF REPRESENTATIVES TODAY OVERWHELMINGLY APPROVED A RESOLUTION TO END THE STATE OF WAR WITH GERMANY'. There are also a good many smaller domestic issues: '1.36 PM. COMMONS. THE LORDS AMENDMENTS TO THE FIREWORK BILL WERE AGREED TO.'; as well as what, in any London club, was considered the really crucial news: '1.41 PM. CRICKET. LUNCH SCORES. HAMPSHIRE 179 FOR FIVE WICKETS. LEICESTERSHIRE 183 FOR TWO WICKETS . . .'

The use of this unusual paper supply resulted in a curious juxtaposition of fiction and reality: for example, notes on the lineage of Sodor's monarchs finds close proximity to an ominous new bulletin, probably dating from the closing months of 1951: '7.35 PM. THE DOCTORS PAID A SECOND VISIT THIS EVENING TO THE KING AT BUCKINGHAM PALACE. NO FURTHER STATEMENT WAS ISSUED.'

As time went by, extensive background information about Sodor amassed. Wilbert noted the various types of inhabitants: those who were regarded as 'slightly "superior" people', and those considered 'tough & hard-headed' and who had originally pursued occupations in 'wrecking & smuggling, with fishing and mining in their leisure moments'! George, meanwhile, listed some of the features of the Island's castles:

> Rolf's Castle began as merely a church fortified, and the curtain wall is a relatively late addition.
> Ulfstead was established as a fortress, but once the Scots were out it fell into decay. Archaeologists find it especially interesting as it is all of one period.
> Suddery, as the capital, was a fortified town, but the castle was relatively late. This is the only 'Norman' castle, and it was always held by the city, not by a baron. The site was re-fortified in Napoleonic times, but the batteries built then have not spoiled its appearance.

Some inclusions owed their existence to highly personal jokes – such as the Tidmouth firm, A. W. Dry & Co. – other matters required extensive research and George made good use of his expertise as a librarian. When, for example, Wilbert chose the Manx word 'cronk' as a place name (site of Cronk Abbey) and needed to know its origin, George informed him: 'We have no Manx dictionary but a book on the Isle, containing several "cronk" place names, obligingly translates them. I deduce it means "hill", as this is the only word common to all the translations. No doubt the abbey was built on a knoll by the stream.'

Wilbert then further developed this theme, writing back to George to say that 'on consulting a larger scale map, it is now clearly established that there is a hill of some extent in the valley'. This place, he told his brother, was originally called, in Sudric, 'The Hill in the valley', which name 'being too long for everyday use . . . has been dropped for several Centuries'.

Although much of this material was eventually distilled into the book, *The Island of Sodor*, the fascinating process by which the story was roughed-out, set down, polished and refined can only be seen from the original unpublished manuscripts, with all their corrections and emendations.

For example, in an early note on Sudrian industry, George commented that 'the map shows several promising valleys for hydroelectric ventures' and added the query: 'Aluminium industry?' Back came Wilbert's response: 'Aluminium – sounds useful – what ores are required? And what sort of plant? Is electricity necessary for extraction?' George, who, before the war, had worked for the Institute of Mining and Metallurgy, duly supplied the required information:

> Aluminium. Ore is bauxite, not native in U.K. Some in Antrim, I see, but I have never heard of its being mined there.
> 2 tons of bauxite after purification give 1 ton of alumina (the oxide), and this is reduced by electrolysis, dissolved in fused cryolite (this is sodium aluminium fluoride).
> It is done in large tanks, molten aluminium at the bottom forming the cathode, with carbon anodes. Enormous currents at low voltage are used, 8,000 - 20,000 amp at about 6 volts.

Railways serve towns, villages and industries,' wrote Wilbert in *The Island of Sodor*, 'and while place names are wrapped up in geography and/or history, the siting of industry depends largely on geology.' Drawing on George's research, Wilbert recorded the forming, in 1923, of the Peel Godred Power Company, 'a subsidiary of the British Aluminium Company' to build a hydroelectric station. It is an indication of the successful way in which the Awdry brothers interwove fact and fiction that when, a few years later, a newspaper article about Wilbert and his stories contained a reference to the

British Aluminium Company's operations on Sodor, the B.A.C. invited the author to write an article on the island's aluminium industry for their house magazine!

In the opening pages of *The Island of Sodor*, Wilbert described the book as combining 'the activities of historical characters and events with fictitious ones in what we hope is a convincing way'. Among the real characters referred to are numerous kings and one or two would-be kings such as Henry Stuart who, in 1788, on the death of his elder brother, Charles Edward ('The Young Pretender'), proclaimed himself King Henry IX. During the Jacobite rebellion forty years earlier, he had supported his brother's claim to the throne but had subsequently been made Cardinal of York by the Pope, a position which, for many Jacobites, made him unacceptable as a potential monarch.

So what was the view of the Jacobites on eighteenth century Sodor? George Awdry suggested that a Sudrian noble ('Sir ? , head of a very ancient family') had undertaken a journey to Rome on behalf of the Jacobites on Sodor to tell Cardinal York that while 'they owed him all respect as a king's brother', they could not accept him as king. Wilbert then noted: 'A suitable name for [the] Ambassador to Cardinal York would be Sir Crosby Marown (Place names in I.O.M.). Sounds sufficiently aristocratic. In fact, I shouldn't be surprised if someone hasn't bagged it already – perhaps it would be as well to look [it] up in Telephone Directory & Dictionary of National Biography.'

George replied that Marown was cleared for use, since he couldn't trace it as a surname. He also suggested that Regaby, another place on the Isle of Man, 'somewhat farther North', might also provide a useful name, which indeed it did as Sir Geoffrey Regaby who, in 1540, became Lieutenant Governor and King's Agent on Sodor and whose son, Harold Regaby, became Bishop of Suddery. And it was a later descendant of this family who assisted Canon Dreswick in chronicling the Island's history.

The first essays on Sodor contain early accounts of the Island's railway history and this area of Wilbert and George's 'research' was to remain the most fruitful, since every time Wilbert's books introduced a new railway line, it had to be made to fit, with jigsaw precision, into what they already knew about Sodor.

'The island's railway system,' begins one early document, 'has contributed much to its present prosperity . . .' This is something of an understatement, since it could be said that *without* the railway system there would not be an Island of Sodor! The first event to be recorded in the history of Sodor's railways is particularly significant, since it concerns an attempt to link Sodor with England – just as the Awdry brothers were linking the fictional with the factual:

In 1850 a line was projected to link Barrow-in-Furness with Suddery, the ancient port and Capital. There was plenty of local enthusiasm, but no interest in the service on the mainland while the Admiralty were obstructive about the proposed low level Bridge across the Straits.

Early attempts at erecting this bridge were, apparently, dogged with difficulties: first, foundations were destroyed by the tide; then part of one of the spans was lost when cranes broke while hoisting it into position; and, eventually, the almost completed bridge was wrecked by a gale. Following the celebrated Tay Bridge disaster of 1879, further bridge-building plans were indefinitely shelved. According to the official published history of the N.W.R. Main Line, included in *The Island of Sodor*, it was not until many years later, in 1915, that 'a Schertzer Rolling Lift Bridge of some 120 ft span' was designed and successfully erected by no less a railway authority than Mr Topham Hatt.

Wilbert went on to list significant railway events such as the laying of a single track between Ballahoo and Rolf's Castle and the first of many closely written pages of notes about the various lines:

The Wellsworth and Suddery Rly. – Standard gauge – originally for lead & zinc mines – passenger light railway service too – steam worked.
Knapford lead mines had a line 4 ft 8½ from workings to harbour – horse traction – Knapford harbour shallow – continual dredging needed. Free trade – receipts diminishing – costs of dredging prohibitive.
A. W. Dry & Co. Boat Builders Tidmouth – finance extension as light railway along roadside to Tidmouth. Topham Hatt with Railway experience in charge of this work. Line too long to be worked by Horse Traction – 'Coffee pot' tram engine bought . . .

Anything and everything might be of relevance – even weather conditions on the island:

1909. March, a great storm destroyed not only the coastal railway (Tidmouth Knapford) but the road as well. Transport completely disrupted. Petition from Knapford Elsbridge Tidmouth results in A. W. Dry & Co. being granted loan from Treasury to help in urgent construction of Tunnel between Knapford and Tidmouth. Out of work quarrymen and miners cut tunnel under direction of quarry engineers. Opened in 1910.

Events in the world at large also affected life on Sodor. Under a heading 'Further prosperity of Tidmouth', Wilbert records: '1914 - 8 War Office at last awaken to possibilities of invasion [and] insist on the Construction of a strategic railway along the South Coast flanking the approach to the Mersey.'

Looking back on this extraordinary creative process, Wilbert was to write: 'Once we had started to develop Sodor, we found we had begun something of absorbing interest, without which subsequent books in the series could never have been written.'

And more of those books were soon on the way . . .

CHAPTER NINE

Branching Out

'THE Henry problem,' says Wilbert, 'was growing with every book.' In an attempt to resolve the difficulties surrounding the Railway Series' most troublesome engine, Wilbert devoted the next volume to settling Henry's future. Published in 1951, *Henry the Green Engine* opened with what seemed like gloomy news for Henry, who is told by the Fat Controller that he is too expensive: 'You have had lots of new parts and new paint too, but they've done you no good. If we can't make you better, we must get another engine instead of you.'

Exchanging his top hat and frock coat for overalls, the Fat Controller rides Henry's footplate, but the engine is such a 'bad steamer' that he soon runs out of puff. Things look decidedly bad for Henry until he is given one last chance – using a supply of expensive coal fetched specially for him from Wales. Fired up with the right fuel, Henry might just redeem himself. It was in a book by J. C. Bowen-Cooke, for many years Locomotive Superintendent of the London & North Western Railway, that Wilbert had first come across the idea that coal contained the equivalent of calories in food and it is another example of the way in which he incorporated authentic railway lore into his little books.

In one of his most engaging illustrations, Reginald Dalby showed Henry getting up steam beside his own exclusive coal-bunker marked with a NOTICE:

STRICTLY PRIVATE
BEST WELSH COAL
FOR HENRY ONLY
BY ORDER

The Welsh coal does the trick and Henry is soon steaming ahead once more, but it proves to be just the lull before the storm, because Wilbert had something terrible in store for poor Henry: 'It was time to be ruthless,' he says, 'If I couldn't scrap Henry, he must have a severe accident which would necessitate his complete rebuilding.'

Teddy Boston, who was at Lincoln Theological College at the time, told Wilbert of an accident that had happened on a nearby loop line during wintry weather and this became the basis of the events recounted in the second story in *Henry the Green Engine*. On a snowy, frosty night, Henry is given the task of pulling a train-load of fish from the harbour – 'The Flying Kipper' – when he is overtaken by disaster.

The journey begins with an idyllic image of winter, and Dalby's superb illustration perfectly depicts Wilbert's text: Henry rushes through the frosty night, the light of his fire illuminating the clouds of smoke and steam pouring from his funnel and shining out of the cab window, with a yellow glow, onto the snowy ground.

The points from the main line to a siding are frozen and the signal set up at 'danger'; however, the signal arm – forced down by a heavy fall of snow – appears to show the line ahead as 'all clear'. But all is far from clear because, standing in the siding, is a goods train waiting for 'The Flying Kipper' to pass. Instead, Henry goes flying into the back of the other train and finds himself sprawling in the snow. The Fat Controller comes to see Henry and tells him what is going to happen:

> *'Cheer up, Henry! It wasn't your fault. Ice and snow caused the accident. I'm sending you to Crewe, a fine place for sick engines. They'll give you a new shape and a larger firebox. Then you'll feel a different engine, and won't need special coal any more. Won't that be nice?'*
> *'Yes, sir,' said Henry doubtfully.*

Henry's problematic appearance was about to be resolved once and for all. Back he comes from Crewe in his new shape looking 'splendid and strong' and, as the author wrote in his introductory letter to the book, 'ready for anything'. As Wilbert now puts it: 'The operation was entirely successful. Henry became a reformed character and has since been no trouble!'

The saga, however, was not quite over, because Wilbert was soon receiving letters from young readers asking why the signal in the story went *down* to let a train pass when the signals they were familiar with went *up*! 'Once upon a time,' replied Wilbert to one such enquiry, 'a long, long while ago, when the Fat Controller and I were little boys, all the signals went down for trains to pass, and then some people thought it was better if the signals pointed up and so they made them point upwards on their railways, but the Fat Controller and I have always liked to have them point down, so in our Region we stick to the old way because we like it better.'

Henry the Green Engine was the sixth title in what the publishers referred to as 'the Reverend Awdry's lively and ever popular series'. So well-known were the engine characters, that Eric Marriott's advertising copy for the new book referred back to an event in the first volume, confident that readers would understand: 'Henry has now recovered from his silly habit of staying inside tunnels whenever it rains, but he is still causing considerable trouble to that strict but kind-hearted Fat Controller.'

The Railway Series showed every indication of having the makings of a British institution! It also showed early signs of having marketing potential. In 1950, Edmund Ward had published (price 2s. each) 'Two well-produced painting books containing scenes from the Reverend Awdry's Railway Series . . . with simplified outline drawings for children to paint and advice on how to mix the colours.'

The same year saw the publication of the first – and, for many years, the only – translations of the books. Welsh minister, Sir Ben Bowen Thomas had suggested that Edmund Ward publish the engines' adventures in the Welsh language. As a result, J. T. Jones, a former winner of two National Eisteddfod literary awards, was paid seven guineas to translate the first four titles – *Y Tri Injian Tren, Thomas yr Injian Danc, James yr Injian Coch* and *Thomas Injian-Danc Eto* – each of which were produced in a modest print-run of 5,000 copies.

1951 saw the publication of two more Painting Books and a novel innovation. One day, as Eric Marriott was looking through the illustrations in the Railway Series, he realised that their shape reminded him of something else. Hence the following announcement in Edmund Ward's catalogue:

> Three sets of postcards, each of six cards showing scenes from the popular Awdry railway books, printed in full-colour and varnished. Supplied in half-gross and gross sets of 18 different cards. 18/6 per gross, less normal discounts plus purchase tax.

As a result of the books' growing popularity, 'The Rev. W. Awdry' (as he appeared on all the dust-wrappers) was becoming a household name, enabling him to publish a rather different little book. It appeared in 1951, the same year as *Henry the Green Engine,* and the title on its sky-blue cover was *Our Child Begins to Pray.* Illustrated with colour plates and line drawings by Rene Cloke, the book was described on its jacket as: 'a serious attempt to satisfy a demand by many parents for a manual which will help them to teach their children how to pray.'

Wilbert wrote in the same economic and seemingly effortless prose as he used for the Railway Series: 'Little children learn most easily, not by instruction, but by copying what "grown-ups" do,' his introduction begins,

'Little children learn to pray by seeing "grown-ups" pray: at morning and evening prayers, and at Grace at meals. We cannot start too soon.'

What is immediately clear in reading *Our Child Begins to Pray*, is that Wilbert was writing from personal experience: 'When our children were tiny, almost as soon as they were born, either my wife or myself would tuck them up at night; then kneeling by the cot we would say a prayer, and sing a few verses of a hymn.' By so doing, Wilbert believed, parents were beginning a process of 'storing up in Baby's mind happy, comforting and loving thoughts of God'.

All three Awdry children – Christopher, Veronica and Hilary – have clear recollections of their father's attitude towards their spiritual life: he led by example, but exerted absolutely no pressure on them to conform to his rule. The only religious obligations were (as they would have been in many households of that time) grace at meals and simple prayers at bedtime.

Veronica recalls her father coming upstairs to say goodnight to Hilary and herself. The girls would be reading in bed and they would hear him coming because one of his legs made a cracking sound ('A bone in the leg,' he used to say); then he would call out, in rhyme: 'Now that Daddy's come upstairs, its time for you to say your prayers.' 'But,' says Veronica, 'I never felt that we had to do anything we didn't want to do.'

'Prayer time,' wrote Wilbert in *Our Child Begins to Pray*, 'should be happy and not a compulsory routine. Sometimes he will not want at this stage to say his little prayer. If so, do not worry, say it for him; be content to go on building up in his mind by your own manner that talking to God is a happy and natural thing to do and before long he will want to join you regularly.'

When answering youngsters' questions, Wilbert advocated the simple, uncomplicated approach which he and Margaret had adopted: 'Our two elder children asked at prayer time, "Mummy, what are you doing?" "Talking to God" was the simple answer. Some days later at prayer time came the question. "Mummy, can I talk to God?" Here was the opportunity, and Mummy taught them their first simple prayer.'

Since Wilbert saw spirituality as a vital – yet everyday – part of life, it is small wonder that so many of the stories in the Railway Series are little parables on such themes as reward and punishment, or contrition and forgiveness. In *Henry the Green Engine*, the hapless Henry has scarcely settled back down in the shed when Gordon is picking on him:

'Why should Henry have a new shape?' he grumbled. 'A shape good enough for ME is good enough for him. He goes gallivanting off to Crewe, leaving us to

do all his work. It's disgraceful!'

'And there's another thing. Henry whistles too much. No respectable *engine ever whistles loudly at stations.'*

'It isn't wrong,' said Gordon, 'but we just don't do it.'

Poor Henry didn't feel happy any more.

But just two pages later, it is Gordon who has problems with his whistle valve and comes rushing down the hill at great speed, 'purple in the boiler and whistling fit to burst'. There is an even-handedness about life in the Railway Series; in the same volume, Percy foolishly envies the workmen who wear scarves – 'My funnel's cold, my funnel's cold!' – then collides with a porter's trolley, loaded with luggage belonging to the Fat Controller, and ends up, not with a scarf, but with Topham Hatt's best trousers wound round his funnel and looking very silly; while a group of boys who think it is fun to drop stones on Henry from a bridge, are paid out when a well-timed 'sneeze' from Henry covers them with soot and ash. On Sodor, justice is fair, punishment is swift and forgiveness (to those who are sorry) unreserved.

The first draft of the history of Sodor contains a brief, but telling, observation by the Fat Controller: ' "There are, of course, other regions and other Railways," he often remarks, "but no one has ever seen anything like ours." ' Maybe not, but we might easily wish that we had. Two seemingly conflicting concepts coexist on the Island of Sodor: endless opportunity for adventurousness (even recklessness) and a powerful sense of order and moral fairness. This combination, together with an ethos that stresses the importance of the individual and tolerance for others, creates a world into which we might well wish to escape in the certain knowledge that life there, however full of incident, is ultimately safe and secure.

The Awdry brothers continued chronicling Sodor's past; in August 1951, for example, Wilbert wrote to George telling him that he had 'been reading up the Reformation' and, whilst 'not entirely satisfied with the result', had composed several new pages of historical notes:

1534 – Sir Geoffrey Regaby – moderate – in favour of reform – trusted by Henry VIII – Formerly a Privy Councillor – friend of Cranmer & Latimer. [He] knew what was coming and because of moderate views [was] hated by Cromwell & Co., who had manoeuvred Henry VIII into getting rid of him by appointing him Governor of Sodor (a good long way from London).

He knew it was Henry's wish (he had seen the memorandum in Henry's own

writing) to convert some 13 of the Abbeys into Cathedrals for new dioceses.
Regaby knew that the Dissolution of the Monasteries was inevitable, and had a shrewd idea as to who would get the plunder. Back in Sodor he discussed the matter with the Abbot of Cronk, Michael Colden, for whom he had a great respect. Together they evolved a plan which would give the appearance of Reforming zeal, be in accordance with Henry's real wishes, secure the greater part of the revenues of Cronk and Well[s]worth for the Church, and at the same time be not unprofitable for themselves.
1540 – The Second Act of Suppression. Armed with his warrant and with a suitably impressive following, Sir Geoffrey presented himself at the Abbey Gate. The Abbot received him gravely and with a suitable show of reluctance in order to impress observers . . . was apparently forced to hand over the deeds of the Abbey.
That done, while Sir [Geoffrey] Regaby's men 'searched' the buildings, the Abbot retired to the parlour where, over a glass of wine, Sir [Geoffrey] Regaby showed him three documents.

The first of these documents gave the church of St Luoc in the city of Suddery the status of a Cathedral; the second, 'issued by the newly constituted Chapter', elected 'Henry's "well beloved" Michael Colden' as first Bishop of Sodor; while the third, a conveyance, gave Cronk Abbey, its buildings and half its revenues, to Sir Geoffrey Regaby – the other half going to endow the new Bishopric! A neat example of pragmatism and a will to survive.

George Awdry, meanwhile, was exploring matters of heraldry and coats of arms: 'A real beauty occurred to me for Tidmouth,' he wrote to his brother, 'It ought to be rather elaborate, as it is relatively new, and the simple ones are doubtless allotted already.' The proposed arms for Tidmouth were to feature a smith's hammer and tongs, a lymphad (an heraldic ship), three herrings and a wheel. 'This,' George explained, 'covers all Tidmouth's titles to importance: shipping, transport, fishing, engineering . . .'

As the brothers' 'researches' continued, the Island of Sodor aroused the interest of Edmund Ward. Wilbert had approached his publisher with the idea of producing a relief map of the Island for use at exhibitions and displays. Writing to George in August 1951, Wilbert reported that, 'Edmund Ward has taken up the idea of Sodor with enthusiasm, and is having a relief map made for us about 4 ft square.'

The artist commissioned to make the map, P. R. Wickham, worked from various maps made by Wilbert and sketched a draft drawing of the island.

This, Wilbert told George, raised questions of detail which they had not previously covered: 'windings of roads and rivers, the position of Cronk Abbey and Peel Godred Aluminium Works & so on. He also wants a list of the principal towns & villages with their main features and approximate sizes.'

In fact, George had already given thought to the question of Sodor's population: 'By rough triangulation,' he advised Wilbert, 'the area is 1,298 sq. m. [square miles], or 830,720 acres.' To arrive at a population figure, George made comparisons with Pembroke, an area with similar conditions: 'Some industry, a main rail artery, a considerable tourist traffic.' Working from the fact that Pembroke's 393,003 acres supported a population of 88,539, George calculated that if that figure were doubled – 'and writing off Sodor's excess area as mountain or sparsely inhabited for other good reason' – the Island would have an estimated population of about 177,000.

Using George's computations, Wilbert drew up a list of twenty places with appropriate information:

> TIDMOUTH. Borough; Pop. 35,000. Port for I.O.M. & N. Ireland. H.Q. N.W.R. Borough, Royal Charter 1918. Shipbuilding, factories, kippers, heavy industry.
> KNAPFORD. Small Town; Pop. 2,200. Farming, fishing, fowling. Former lead mines. Now junction for Farquar, extensive stone traffic. Dormitory for Tidmouth.
> ELSBRIDGE. Village; Pop. 500. Ancient church and bridge. Market farming, fishing, boating.
> WELL[S]WORTH. Village; Pop. 550. St Tibba's Nunnery, 1150. Large modern hospital – serves whole Island.

By October 1951, Wilbert was able to report to George that the relief map was complete and – despite showing up one or two errors in his original design – 'seems very good'. When, some years later, a brightly coloured pictorial version of the map was published, Wilbert sent a copy to the Bishop of Sodor and Man explaining that he was restoring to him the other half of his diocese. The Bishop replied, thanking Wilbert for the entertainment his stories had given, and adding: 'I am both interested and amused by your alleged discoveries.'

For Wilbert, writing the stories and researching the history of Sodor was more than a mere entertainment, it was a form of therapy. The endless problems of parish life at Elsworth were wearing him down. 'If I hadn't had the books to write,' he reflects, 'I should have gone crackers!'

Not that it was easy to find the time to write, or even to think up new ideas – particularly since they had to be based on authentic incidents. Inspiration for the stories in *Henry the Green Engine* had come from various sources including Teddy Boston, *The Railway Gazette* and C. Hamilton Ellis' book, *The Trains We Loved*; however, Wilbert was already reaching the stage of needing not just new stories but also new characters to keep the series going.

The idea for a new character came in 1951, during the Awdry family's summer holiday in Gorleston, Norfolk. Wilbert and Christopher were wandering around nearby Great Yarmouth, when they came upon a tram engine, became friends with his crew and took some photographs. Both father and son were intrigued by what Wilbert was later to describe in one of his books as the 'funny little engine with a queer shape'. When the holiday was over, Wilbert began looking for a way to incorporate this curious 'character' into his railway books.

Further inspiration came, shortly afterwards, from another tram engine. Teddy Boston, then curate of Wisbech, near Cambridge, arranged for Wilbert to ride the footplate of one of the last surviving Wisbech and Upwell Steam Tramway engines. Wilbert was fascinated by the stories he heard about these unusual engines, some of which he later incorporated into a series of articles about 'Remarkable Railways':

> On the day the line was opened, a horse pulling a Midland Railway cart met a tram in Elm High Road. It bolted through a quickset hedge into a garden. Midland supporters said that a monstrosity like the Wisbech Tram was enough to upset any horse; but others claimed that since the Midland horse was 'raiding' Great Eastern territory, the sight of the tram must have shown him that the game was up and accordingly he fled!

With these obviously highly individual engines running through his mind, Wilbert began writing a new story: 'Toby is a tram engine. He is short and sturdy. He has cow-catchers and side-plates, and doesn't look like a steam engine at all . . .' Just as Wilbert and Christopher encountered their tram engine while on holiday, so Toby is discovered by the Fat Controller and his grandchildren on their holiday.

The question – since, as always, authenticity was vitally important – was how to justify Toby being employed to work with the railways of Sodor. George researched details of tramway regulations and the solution was for Thomas to fall foul of the law by travelling on the line running along the road to the quarry without having the regulation cow-catcher and side-plates. Remembering Toby, the Fat Controller sends for him and gives him a job.

Like any new engine, of course, Toby (together with Henrietta, his coach) runs the usual gauntlet of mean comments: 'Toby and Henrietta were shabby when they first came, and needed new paint. James was very rude. "Ugh! What dirty objects!" he would say . . . You never see my paint dirty." '

But shortly afterwards – due to Wilbert's unwavering sense of fairness – James duplicates another real-life railway occurrence and has an unfortunate accident with two tar wagons:

> *Toby and Percy were sent to help, and came as quickly as they could.*
> *'Look here, Percy!' exclaimed Toby, 'whatever is that dirty object?'*
> *'That's James; didn't you know?'*
> *'It's James's shape,' said Toby thoughtfully, 'but James is a splendid red engine, and you never see* his *paint dirty.'*
> *James shut his eyes, and pretended he hadn't heard.*

Toby the Tram Engine made his appearance in 1952, at a time when publisher, Edmund Ward, was experiencing difficulties because of rising costs and essential materials being in short supply. In an introduction to the annual trade-catalogue, Eric Marriott told booksellers that, despite these problems, Ward was 'determined to maintain the high standard' for which they were 'well known throughout the world':

> With this determination in mind, and with your continued recognition of it, we look forward to a future in which our books may continue to bring not only benefits to those who trade in them but also profit and pleasure to those who read them.

Wilbert Awdry's books were certainly among those which resulted in profit and pleasure; but, with seven titles in print, the need for fresh inspiration was crucial. It came, in the end, from a scrap of newspaper that was to radically effect the Island of Sodor and the Railway Series.

In 1951, somebody had sent Wilbert an article clipped from the *Birmingham Mail.* The headline, published on 11th February, read: 'EIGHT MILES OF RAILWAY TO PLAY WITH – AND REAL TRAINS – FOR £1 A YEAR.' The article explained that one pound was the cost of becoming 'part-owner of a complete railway in Wales'.

That railway was the narrow (2 ft 3 in.) gauge line running from Towyn, Merioneth in West Wales (now Tywyn, Gwynedd) towards Talyllyn Lake at the foot of Cader Idris. It was more than eighty years since an act of Parliament, in 1865, gave the Talyllyn Railway Company powers to construct and run a

railway from a wharf alongside the then Aberystwyth & Welsh Coast Railway for a distance of 6 $^{3}/_{4}$ miles to Abergynolwyn and, from there, a further line to the quarries at Bryn Eglwys.

Quarrying at this remote site, 700 feet up in the mountains, had begun eighteen years earlier, in 1847, when a Welshman named John Pughe had found substantial quantities of fine slate. Pughe's enterprise, however, was severely restricted by his having to use packhorses to transport the slate over the mountains to the nearest small port at Aberdovey, twelve miles away. It was a slow, costly process and, *en route*, many slates got broken. John Pughe's difficulties were heightened when competitors, working slate at Corris on the other side of the mountain, were able to cut their costs by building a horse tramway to Derwenlas on the River Dovey.

In 1864, Pughe gave up the struggle and sold out. The quarry was bought by William and Thomas McConnel, heading a group of Manchester cotton merchants. The American Civil War having severely affected the cotton trade, they had decided to diversify their interests into mining. They were especially attracted to John Pughe's quarry because he maintained that there was more than just slate to be found at Bryn Eglwys. Only a few years earlier, the Clogau Mine, near Dolgelly had struck a sizeable vein of gold, and Pughe believed that his quarry contained similar riches. The McConnel brothers formed the Aberdovey Slate Company and gave immediate thought to the problem of transportation.

The company engaged James Swinton Spooner, whose father had built the Festiniog Railway, to survey a railway line that would serve the quarry. As a secondary consideration it was decided to use the line to provide transport for the residents of Abergynolwyn (many of whom worked in the quarry) and the hamlets of Rhydyronen and Pandy. Spooner chose a gauge of 2 feet 3 inches, probably because the quarry was already using trams with this gauge. Construction of the line, running along the valley slopes to Towyn, was relatively straightforward – except where it had to pass over a deep ravine, near Dolgoch, and a three-arch viaduct had to be built.

The Talyllyn Railway Company purchased from Fletcher, Jennings & Company of Whitehaven, two steam locomotives, which after many years of faithful service, came to be known as 'The Old Ladies of Towyn'. The first to arrive, in 1865, was christened Talyllyn. 'She was needed to help build the line,' Wilbert wrote in an article about the Old Ladies, 'But would she? Not a bit of it. Once off-loaded from a standard gauge railway truck she sat on Wharf [Station], and refused to budge.'

No one at Towyn, it seems, could do anything with her so a request for assistance was sent to Fletcher, Jennings & Company, who despatched a fitter, Mr Robert Bousted, to sort out the problems. 'He came to Towyn,' says Wilbert, 'for a few weeks, but liked the place so much he stayed for eighteen years!'

Despite Bousted's best efforts, Talyllyn remained temperamental and when Captain Tyler from the Board of Trade carried out an inspection, prior to passing the line for passenger-carrying, the engine rocked and rolled so much that he insisted that a pair of trailing wheels be fitted in order to steady her. As soon as the second engine, Dolgoch, arrived, Talyllyn went back to Whitehaven and returned, as Wilbert puts it, 'a reformed character'.

Three trains a day ran each way between Towyn and Abergynolwyn. On the outward – and upward – journey, empty trucks were pulled behind the four four-wheeled carriages; then, at the foot of the quarry, these were exchanged for trucks loaded with slate to be carried back to Towyn on the return journey. In winter months, with the exception of market days, there were never many passengers; but, during the summer, the line was a popular attraction for Victorian and Edwardian holiday makers who took outings on the 'Toy Railway' to see Dolgoch falls or to walk from Abergynolwyn to Talyllyn Lake and Cader Idris.

With the passing years it became clear that the Aberdovey Slate Company was not going to prove the financial success for which its founders had hoped. 'Alas,' wrote the railway historian, L. T. C. (Tom) Rolt, 'the rosy dream of mineral wealth soon faded. There was no gold, and slate of good quality proved increasingly difficult to get.' In 1879, the concern was put up for auction but found no takers. The Aberdovey Slate Company was wound up and the McConnel family operated the quarry as a more modest operation until, in 1911, they decided to sell.

The quarry and the railway were bought by Mr (later Sir) Henry Haydn Jones, the principal landowner in the valley who became Member of Parliament for Merioneth. Abergynolwyn, in the valley below the quarry, was now a mining village of some size and a decision to close the quarry would have been disastrous for the local community. The new owner was determined that quarrying was to continue and so it did, even during the depression years when it made Sir Haydn nothing but a loss. By the 1940s, with no money for maintenance, many of the underground workings had become dangerous and, had the Inspector of Mines not turned a blind eye to this fact, quarrying might easily have been halted.

The railway also suffered. The 'reformed' Talyllyn was, says Wilbert, a 'more willing worker' than Dolgoch. As a result, she was worked the hardest and with no money for repairs, time took its toll on the engines. In 1944, 'leaking steam from every joint', Talyllyn was retired, leaving Dolgoch to run the line alone. The quarry finally closed in 1947, but not the railway. 'We'll continue to run it,' said Sir Haydn, 'if it costs us £5 a week.' Three years later, however, the Talyllyn Railway's benefactor died.

Although Sir Haydn's manager, Mr Edward Thomas, kept things running throughout 1950, it seemed increasingly inevitable that the little railway had reached the end of the line. 'Because of the failure of the quarry to fulfil expectations,' writes Tom Rolt, 'there had been no incentive to modernise or improve the railway; the original locomotives and passenger coaches – even the original rails – were still in use. All were in a deplorable condition.'

The post-war mood in Britain was one centred on optimistic visions of a future of limitless prospects. There may have been a certain nostalgia for Britain's local railways, but it was largely as something quaint, even eccentric. It is interesting that one of the most popular attractions at Battersea Park during the 1951 Festival of Britain was the outlandish Far Tottering & Oyster Creek Railway based on the fragile, spidery designs of *Punch* artist Rowland Emett, whose engines were comic creations made from such unlikely component parts as kettles, weather-vanes, garden fencing and divers' helmets!

In sharp contrast to this attitude towards railways – an affectionate memory of an outmoded concept – was that of a group of rail enthusiasts who met together in order to explore the possibility of saving a railway that was a remarkable survivor from Victorian times, but which required almost as much patching together as Emett's railway. The prime movers in this brave attempt to save the Talyllyn were Tom Rolt – railway engineer turned author – and three friends: David Curwen, W. G. Trinder and James Russell.

Many discussions took place with Lady Haydn Jones, Edward Thomas and others and, in February 1951, it was announced that Sir Haydn's executors were handing over the railway to a non-profit making organisation called 'The Talyllyn Railway Preservation Society'. The idea was unique; no one had previously tried to preserve a passenger-carrying railway and there was, as Tom Rolt later recalled, 'a great deal of head-shaking', while journalists were quick to describe the enthusiasts as 'playing trains'.

The opening paragraph of the newspaper report, received by Wilbert, described the venture as being 'every boy's dream – and most men's'. It certainly caught Wilbert's imagination: 'I was out of sympathy with British Railways' nationalisation and felt that anything which could be done to preserve an independent railway was worthy of support.' The name of Towyn was already known to Wilbert since it was the home of a distant cousin, Frank Awdry. Although Wilbert had never met Frank, he knew Frank's three sisters who lived in Clevedon, Somerset.

As boys, Wilbert and his brother, George, had often visited Clevedon, experiencing the delights and vagaries of the late Weston, Clevedon & Portishead Railway, and being regaled by the sisters with stories that had been told to them by Frank about another 'somewhat wayward little railway' at Towyn. If, thought Wilbert, it were proved 'as eccentric and individualistic' as the Weston, Clevedon & Portishead, then it might be worthwhile making its acquaintance – and might even provide a few offbeat stories for use in the Railway Series.

Wilbert wrote at once to The Talyllyn Railway Preservation Society asking for details of membership. These were duly received, and off went a cheque for two pounds: 'one for membership,' Wilbert explained, 'and the other for initial donation, I am sorry I can't afford more.' The receipt for this payment carries the number 79, which places Wilbert within the first one hundred people to respond to the appeal. By May 1951, there were 664 members and almost £2,000 had been raised.

In acknowledging Wilbert's donation the Society's Treasurer, Patrick Garland, wrote that they had acquired from British Railways two further locomotives – both saddle-tank engines – that had worked the now defunct Corris Railway. These engines were to be re-named Sir Haydn and Edward Thomas in honour of the owner and manager of the Talyllyn. 'So you will see,' wrote Patrick Garland, 'that there is a possibility that a "Thomas the Tank Engine" will finish up on the Talyllyn Railway!!', to which Wilbert replied: 'I hope that "Edward Thomas" will behave, and not follow the example of my "Thomas"!' Neither correspondent could have imagined quite how close an association would eventually be formed between Thomas and his friends and the engines on the Talyllyn.

In 1951, Wilbert's chief desire was to visit and work on the railway, but this was not immediately possible. As soon as he heard about the Talyllyn, Wilbert suggested to Margaret that they might go to Towyn for their annual family holiday, only to find that she had already booked for them to go to Gorleston. Without that holiday, of course, Toby might never have joined the railways of Sodor; for Wilbert, however, it was still a disappointment: 'I should have liked to have helped in a working party,' he wrote when sending his first subscription, 'but distance and previous plans make that impossible this year, but if all goes well I may be able to do something next year.'

Despite her unceasing support and encouragement for Wilbert's writing, Margaret Awdry did not share her husband's passion for railways and, in 1951, she may well have given a sigh of relief that those holiday arrangements had already been made. The following August, however, the Awdrys went to Towyn.

The family arrived at their 'digs': 'Monfa', Beach Road, Towyn, the home of Miss Katie Pugh and – for several summer holidays to follow – that of Wilbert Awdry and his family. Leaving Margaret to put the girls to bed, Wilbert and Christopher went straight to Wharf station where Tom Rolt, then General Manager of the Talyllyn, and his wife Sonia were awaiting the arrival of the Saturday evening train. Wilbert introduced himself as a volunteer and was booked to do duty as Guard during the second week of their holiday.

The following day, with Tom Rolt's permission, Wilbert and Christopher walked the newly laid track from Wharf to Pendre. Although Wilbert was drawn to the workshop – intrigued by sounds of interesting activity going on within – his customary reserve prevented him. 'As very "new boys",' he later recalled, 'I felt a bit shy of pushing our way in to see. I was afraid, wrongly as I discovered later, that our curiosity would be resented.'

Wilbert and Christopher looked, instead, at the wagons standing out in the open and peered into the shed at the ancient coaches. Then 'a sheeted something' caught Wilbert's eye: it was Talyllyn – the line's first engine – which they uncovered, photographed, and carefully recovered before going on with their walk, through the crossing gates, and along another stretch of re-laid track 'disappearing enticingly under Ty Mawr bridge'.

Despite being stopped by an officious policeman – who had been detailed to patrol the line in order to prevent vandalism and who had not been informed about anyone having permission to walk the line – Wilbert and Christopher continued their first expedition along this remarkable little railway.

For Wilbert many memories must have been evoked and, with them, many emotions stirred. Memories of helping – and hindering – his father and Carol as they ran the model railway in the garden at Ampfield Vicarage; memories of those walks with his father along the railway line: waiting for a new engine to pass on its running-trials, watching the plate-layers at work or sitting in the line-side hut, made from old sleepers, littered with tools and filled with tobacco-smoke, while vicar and railwaymen enjoyed long conversations.

If the Railway Series had, perhaps unintentionally, provided Wilbert with a means of expressing his deep love of railways, as well as keeping alive the memory of vitally important experiences from his past, then the Talyllyn was to provide a similar, real-life, opportunity.

Come Monday morning, the Awdry family assembled at Wharf station in time to catch the 10.25 a.m. train: 'For the first time we experienced the peculiar bumping, rolling gait exhibited by the four-wheel coaches in those early days. The children enjoyed it and so did I, but my wife did not. She said it made her feel sea-sick, so we returned by the same train, and that afternoon, while my wife took the girls to the seashore, Christopher and I went to the British Railways station and invested in Cambrian Coast Runabout tickets.'

For Margaret Awdry the holiday perhaps fell a little short of expectations – or, more accurately, lived up to her worst fears. Asked how his mother coped with this and subsequent railway holidays, Christopher Awdry replies: 'With fortitude!' Hilary was six years old; Veronica was nine and Christopher, twelve. Small wonder, with a young family making demands on her, that Margaret Awdry, rail-widow, should have become, in Christopher's words, 'a bit jaded'. Veronica didn't think a great deal about the holiday at the time: 'It only struck me afterwards,' she says, 'that we went to Towyn because that was what Dad wanted to do.' Even Christopher – for whom it was the first holiday of which he was to have clear memories – began to feel, after a week, that he had 'had about enough'. Whereas for Wilbert, the fun and fascination were only just beginning . . .

Not that the experience was pure unalloyed pleasure – it also brought its problems! When, on the following Monday, Wilbert reported for work at Wharf station, he learned from Tom Rolt that, in addition to being Guard, he would have to carry out the duties of Booking-Clerk *en route*. 'His instructions were no doubt thorough, covering most eventualities,' Wilbert later wrote, 'but they went right over my head. I had never done anything of the sort before, and could not visualise the situations and problems he was enumerating. When it came to the crunch, I had to learn the job by doing it, making mistakes and taking the consequences . . .' Rather like his own fictional engines.

In a draft for an article written in 1989, and published, in shortened form, in a commemorative newspaper, *Talyllyn 125*, Wilbert recalled some of those mistakes:

> As Guard, my chief boobs at first concerned the van brake. At that time, apart from the brake on the engine, the van had the only other brake on the

> train. I would forget to put it on at stations, thus sometimes making starting a heavily loaded 'up train' difficult with tight couplings. Sometimes, conversely, having screwed it on when stopping, I would forget to ease it off after giving the Right Away. This lapse . . . would be followed by the unmistakable sound of locomotive slip. Indignant whistles from up front would remind me of my error which I quickly corrected.

As Booking-Clerk, Wilbert had one or two problems with tickets, partly because – through unfamiliarity – he muddled up the various halts along the line (Hendy, Fach Goch, Cynfal, Tynyllwyn) but mostly because, he says, 'I was not, and still am not, an agile mental arithmetician.' Sometimes he didn't charge passengers enough, sometimes he gave them back too much change; the result, however, was always the same: on his return to Wharf, he found himself making up the shortfall! 'My biggest boob of all,' recalls Wilbert, 'and one which I was not for some time allowed to forget, was when I left the Refreshment Lady behind at Abergynolwyn . . .'

The Talyllyn had recently introduced an innovation: a lady volunteer would take the first 'up train' with an ice-box, soft drinks and various other refreshments. At Abergynolwyn she would install herself in the former Booking Office from where she sold her refreshments to travellers throughout the day, before returning on the last 'down train' in the afternoon. The lady in charge during Wilbert's week as Guard was Mrs Davies, the mother-in-law of one of the Talyllyn drivers, Bill Oliver. Wilbert remembers her as a stout lady with a forthright manner – just how forthright, he discovered that day!

> While I was checking tickets and firmly fastening doors she would usually stand in the station door in full view. On that fateful evening she was not in full view, having been delayed in her packing up by a last minute customer. This must have happened on the Wednesday, as on that day during the peak season an extra evening train was run, and it was important that our departure should not be late. I was so concerned about this that after ticket and door duty, I forgot Mrs Davies and gave Bill the Right Away.
>
> Bill ought to have remembered, but he was probably bothered about the time too, so he opened up and off we went. We had barely cleared the platform when I heard a frantic yell and there was Mrs Davies, red in the face, arms waving, bustling down the platform. I whistled to attract Bill's attention, but my whistling was evidently drowned by No. 4's [Edward Thomas'] clatter, so I tried screwing down the brake. This had the desired effect. It didn't stop

> the train, but the drag attracted Bill's attention by the time we'd gone about 300 yards down the line, and he propelled the train back to collect his fermenting mother-in-law.
> We picked up her gear, depositing both it and her in the van, apologising profusely the while. She was too much out of breath to say much at first, but by the time we reached Wharf, I'd heard plenty!
> By Friday morning . . . Mrs Davies was threatening Bill and myself with dire penalties if ever we left her behind again, so I knew she'd seen the funny side and that all was now forgiven.

This story was too good to waste and Wilbert filed it away for future use.

As the creator of the Railway Series, Wilbert found that he had a certain amount of kudos. Indeed, when the Preservation Society's Treasurer, Patrick Garland, had first written to Wilbert, in February 1951, he concluded his letter: 'I need not tell you how much enjoyment your books have brought to my children and incidentally to their parents and many other grown ups. More strength to your elbow in this great work!!' It is, therefore, not too surprising that, while Wilbert was working as Guard and Booking-Clerk, Tom Rolt should have suggested to him that the Talyllyn Railway engines might be incorporated into the Railway Series. Although Wilbert admits that, when he arranged to visit Towyn, he was wondering whether it might prove possible to base a story on the Talyllyn Railway, it was to take him another two years to work out how to do it.

In the meantime, Wilbert had discovered an entirely new world and one – like his model railway layouts or the imaginary railway system on Sodor – which was still far from complete; for, although The Talyllyn Railway Preservation Society had achieved much in just over a year, a great deal still remained to be done. Throughout the whole of 1950, the railway had carried only 5,200 passengers; by 1951 that figure had increased to 15,600 and, by 1952, to 22,800. Revenue had also risen, in two years, from £400 to £1,000. Nevertheless, as Wilbert recalls, much money and effort were still required:

> I recall that relaying had been done from Wharf as far as Ty Mawr. Beyond that, except at stations, the track mostly appeared to be in its primitive – almost primaeval – state, overgrown with grass and brambles from untrimmed hedges.
> This was particularly evident on the open hillside stretch between Dolgoch Woods, Quarry Siding and beyond.

> Here railtops were sometimes invisible, and were it not for the slate fencing, the trackbed was barely distinguishable from neighbouring fields, with our locomotive finding her way, as it were, by faith alone.

The analogy was one not lost on a priest.

However the rest of the family may have viewed the holiday in Towyn, for Wilbert it was a singular experience. Overcoming his natural diffidence, he had made friends with many of the other volunteers and enjoyed the camaraderie that existed among them: 'I found that most were as amateur as myself and, like me, learning by doing and enjoying the process, in spite of mistakes.'

Reminiscing, thirty-seven years later, about his first journeys as a Guard on the Talyllyn, Wilbert wrote:

> I found it an unforgettable experience, between stations, to sit on the van floor, with my feet on the step, watching the train make its leisurely snake-like progress along the line, seeing the locomotive followed by each vehicle in turn negotiate inequalities in the track.
>
> First the engine would roll from one side to another, followed, like the joints of a caterpillar, by each coach all down the train so that it was often possible to see, at any one time, the various vehicles each leaning in an opposite direction to the one in front of it.
>
> Added to this, loose rail joints would make themselves felt in the resounding bumps they gave to all four wheels of the van.

It was with feelings of regret that Wilbert left Towyn and he may well have been hoping to make a return visit the following year. In 1953, however, there would be no holiday for the Awdry family due to a change in their circumstances.

Wilbert had been at Elsworth for six years and had never been very happy. It is indicative of Wilbert's character that this unhappiness was shared only with Margaret. The Awdry children have only good memories of their time at Elsworth, and Veronica, looking back, says that they were totally unaware of their father's discontent, or of the various struggles which he and Margaret had endured.

However, those struggles – especially over making changes to the Rectory – had not gone unrecognised in Diocesan circles and, in 1950, Wilbert had been appointed Rural Dean of Bourn. The previous Rural Dean, Harold J. Scott – through whom Wilbert had come to Elsworth – was moving to another parish and the then Bishop of Ely, Edward Wynne, offered the job to Wilbert.

The duties of Rural Dean were to visit the churches in the Deanery and make friends with their incumbents, as well as looking at their buildings to see what condition they were in and what repairs might be recommended. Wilbert demurred, pointing out his lack of seniority, only to be told that the Bishop considered him 'a fine, determined sort of fellow', and that he had much admired Wilbert's recent battles with the bureaucrats. 'I hope,' said the Bishop, 'that you will be able to help some others in the Deanery who are beleaguered in the same way that you were.'

Nevertheless, by 1952, Wilbert was looking to move on. Christopher (who had been educated at a local primary school) had a good singing voice and, three years earlier, had got a place at St Chad's Choir School (now Lichfield Cathedral School); Veronica was approaching secondary school age but the Awdrys weren't happy with the local secondary schools. From enquiries they learned that the Wisbech High School would provide a good secondary school education and began visiting various parishes in the vicinity that either were, or might become, vacant.

One of these was in the ancient Cambridgeshire village of Emneth, whose vicar was thinking of retiring. The name Emneth originally meant 'the village in the meadows'; it was listed in the Domesday Book as one of the seven towns of Marshland, and parts of St Edmund's Church date back to Norman times. More importantly, Emneth was an easy three-mile bus journey from Wisbech; so, in January 1953, the Awdrys moved to 'the village in the meadows' which was to become their family home – and that of Thomas & Co. – for almost the next thirteen years.

CHAPTER TEN

New Lines on Old Lines

IT was the year 869, and Edmund, King of the East Angles, led his army against a horde of invading Danes. The English lost the battle, Edmund was taken prisoner and – when he refused to share his Christian kingdom with those whom he considered heathen – was tied to a tree, shot with arrows until his body looked 'like a thistle covered with prickles' and then had his head cut off.

King Edmund was made a saint and many churches were named after him, one of which stands in Emneth. The oldest part of St Edmund's Church is the chancel, dating back to the twelfth century, and beneath the one remaining Norman clerestory window, is a carved wolf's head. This, according to the *Notes for Visitors* (written by 'W. Awdry, Vicar'), is 'a reminder of the legend that St Edmund's friends, searching, after his martyrdom, for his severed head were guided to the place by the howling of a wolf, which had taken charge of it, and protected it against all comers'.

Wilbert Awdry never could resist a good story and there are several in the little three-page leaflet – like the tale of the two tombs inscribed with identically worded epitaphs:

Here Thomas Dove lies, whose name alone
The pulpit will preserve without this stone

Here Henry Johnson lies, whose name alone
The pulpit will preserve without this stone

Both these gentlemen were puritan ministers foisted onto the church during Oliver Cromwell's Commonwealth. Thomas Dove held office from 1646 to 1651, followed by Henry Johnson who, with the Restoration in 1660, decided to conform and accept the Prayer Book. 'Puritan divines,' wrote Wilbert, 'prided themselves on their preaching; but, in spite of their boastful epitaphs, their stones are now the only record of this pair's eloquence!'

As for Wilbert's eloquence in the pulpit, his sermons tended to be short and to the point. His daughter, Veronica, recalls him saying: 'If you've got something to say, you don't have to take half-an-hour to say it!' In consequence, his sermons tended to be more memorable than those of many other preachers. However, it is not for his words from the pulpit, but for those contained in twenty-six small volumes of stories about railway engines, that the Reverend W. V. Awdry will ultimately be remembered.

There were only seven in print when he and his family moved to Emneth in 1953. Although still within Cambridgeshire – and, indeed, within the same diocese of Ely – Emneth was a very different area to Elsworth. A village with a population between one and two thousand, Emneth was flat drainage country which had, long ago, been reclaimed from the fens and transformed into a great region for fruit-growing.

It seems likely that it was the monks of Thorney Abbey, arriving by boat along the River Nene, who first brought Christianity to Emneth, and the earliest church was probably a rough Saxon building made from timber or even wattle and daub. The church, as Wilbert Awdry found it, was the usual amalgam of periods but with a number of fine fifteenth-century features: an elaborate carved font; a rood screen (scarred by several deep gashes that were probably made by Puritan swords); and some fragments of stained glass that were further survivors of the Civil War. An attempt was made in 1865 to restore these windows, but the result was not entirely successful – especially when it came to the likeness of St Edmund. 'Although the restorers did their best with the pieces,' wrote Wilbert in his leaflet about the church, 'they could not make St Edmund's head fit on properly.' Appropriate, it might be thought, in view of the fact that St Edmund really did lose his head, but what those responsible for the Victorian restoration actually did was to put his head back on in such a way as to give him what Wilbert describes as 'a somewhat rakish look'.

Also dating from the fifteenth century is the nave roof, which is one of the finest in the Marshland churches. Fourteen upright figures show the Apostles, Christ and St Edmund, while above them, on the hammer beams, fly fourteen angels depicted as serving at the Mass. It was eight years after Wilbert's arrival at St Edmund's that the true magnificence of these carvings was discovered when scaffolding was erected to treat the roof for deathwatch beetle. 'I persuaded the local photographer to climb up and take some pictures,' recalls Wilbert. 'Since it was a rather rickety framework, he was worried about falling. I told him not to worry because I'd give him a free funeral, but the offer wasn't altogether well received!'

The parish had been well looked after by the previous incumbent and two long-serving churchwardens, Arthur Image and Henry Ayres. Every Sunday evening, these gentlemen would count the day's offerings and then take it in turns to dip into their own pocket for whatever small change might be needed to bring up the total to a convenient round figure.

A local fruit-farmer, Mr Ayres was also the church treasurer and Wilbert commemorated his work, in limerick form, at a Parish annual general meeting:

St Edmund's financial affairs
Need cause him no trouble or cares,
He can leave the whole lot,
Every penny he's got,
In the capable hands of his Ayres.

After the problems they had experienced with Elsworth Rectory, Wilbert and Margaret were relieved to find the Vicarage 'wind and weather-proof' and in good repair. Veronica remembers it as: 'a big house with a large drawing room that was seldom used; a large dining room, which we used as a living room; a study for father; five bedrooms; a kitchen and scullery, with back stairs; and – oh, joy! – three attics at the very top of the house.'

Attics! What better location for a model railway? 'It had taken four years to lay out the railway at Elsworth,' recalls Wilbert, 'but it was dismantled in three or four days!' Now, the engines could run once more and not in a cold, damp outhouse. One attic became a playroom for Veronica and Hilary; the other two were commandeered by Wilbert, who knocked holes in the wall to let the trains pass through!

A system of electric bells was installed so that when Wilbert was in the attic, the family were able to communicate with him without having to run up several flights of stairs. In this way, he knew when meals were ready or when he was required by visitors or telephone callers. Whilst never neglectful of parish duties or family responsibilities, Wilbert devoted as much spare time as he could to his new layout:

> I had visions of a model railway empire. It was planned as a main-line section with two return loops, out of sight in the adjoining attic that was also my workshop. One loop represented the Tidmouth end of the line; the other, that at Barrow-in-Furness. The loops met at the junction station of Knapford, where the controls for the line were to be. Each loop had four dead sections, so that it should have been possible to have eight trains on line at any one time. The trains on the loops were controlled by relays, so that a train coming in would switch on the one ahead of it on the loop which, by going on a certain distance, would then trigger the train ahead of that.

It was model railway engineering on a grand scale. The system, however, was not without problems. 'It was,' says Wilbert, 'all right in theory and it worked well enough when I was operating the line from the other room where the loops were, but when I tried to operate it from the room where the station was, something invariably went wrong; and the trouble almost always happened when somebody came to see the line! Suddenly, out of sight, you would hear a "CLONK!" and a "CRASH!" '

The layout featured engines from the Railway Series, adapted from existing commercial models. However, whilst Wilbert had a Hornby tank engine painted blue and red with the number 1 on its side, there was no attempt to add that expressive face which is an essential feature of Thomas as illustrated in the books. This raises, perhaps, an interesting philosophical question: Do the engines of Sodor *really* have faces – and who, other than the reader, can see them – or are they nothing more than an imaginary device for displaying the personality and mood of the various engine characters?

'My rule,' says Wilbert, 'is that faces are allowable in the books since the engines are in Sodor, where anything can happen and usually does. But that is not so in England.' So, whilst in *Duck and the Diesel Engine*, City of Truro was drawn in such a position that it was impossible to see whether or not he had a face, the illustrator of a much later volume, *Enterprising Engines*, was permitted to give Flying Scotsman a face during his visit to the Island; similarly, Stepney the 'Bluebell' Engine (in the book of that name) has a face while on Sodor, while the other Bluebell Line engines, whom he describes living on their railway in England, are shown as being faceless. Whether young readers understood this premise is a matter of conjecture and there is, anyway, a notable exception to Wilbert's rule – when, in 1957, the Eight Famous Engines all show their faces on the British mainland.

Although, in recent years, various authentic steam locomotives on preserved railway lines have been permitted to put on 'masks' in order to look like the engines of Sodor for young visitors, Wilbert never indulged any such fancies with his model railway layouts, which were intended solely for the entertainment of himself and fellow modellers.

As for the family, Christopher was now away at school and Veronica and Hilary, who had passed their Eleven Plus exams and were attending Wisbech High School, only took an occasional interest in the activities in the adjacent attic. 'There was,' says Veronica, 'no expectation that we had to be interested; it was like the writings – it was simply there.'

Veronica recalls those 'writings' as being 'just part of life, an accepted thing'. To the children – who were now getting a little too old for them – a new volume in the Railway Series wasn't anything particularly important: 'it was what father did once a year!' Nevertheless, Wilbert still used the family as guinea-pigs, testing out each new story in draft form.

Wilbert says his readings were invariably greeted with universal groans of 'Not another one!' which may have occasionally been the case, although any such response, says Veronica, would have been 'tinged with a bit of humour!'

'Father would bring out what he had written,' she recalls, 'and try it out on us. We would be asked for our comments: Was it too long? Should any of the words be changed?' These story appraisal sessions usually took place just before the Awdry family's evening meal and often – to Margaret's exasperation – the food sat on the table until it got cold!

Nevertheless, she also gave her views on what her husband had written and, at a subsequent meal, Wilbert would return to the table with a revised draft. 'Even though they weren't written for our age group,' says Veronica, 'we always listened and we always told him what we thought.' Revisions were duly made and another reading session would follow: Hilary remembers hearing some of the stories as many as six times!

Although they were only small books, writing them seemed to Wilbert a never-ending process: 'I had no sooner finished the manuscript for one volume – usually around May, for publication in September – than I had to start thinking about possible stories and looking for new characters for the next book. There was a gap in parish life, between the end of July and Harvest Festival, and it was then that I would start getting things down on paper. Eventually, I began to wonder how much longer it was going to go on!' The answer to which was, longer than he could ever have imagined.

The first title to be published following the Awdrys' move to Emneth, was also the first book to be named after the bossiest engine on the line:

> *Gordon was resting in a siding.*
> *'Peep peep! Peep peep! Hullo, Fatface!' whistled Henry.*
> *'What a cheek!' spluttered Gordon. 'That Henry is too big for his wheels; fancy speaking to me like that! Me e e e e!' he went on, letting off steam. 'Me e e e, who has never had an accident!'*

This was the beginning of the eighth title in the Railway Series, *Gordon the Big Engine*. Gordon soon pays a price for his cockiness when he has a mishap, inspired by an incident described in a news-cutting sent to Wilbert by a young reader named Richard, from Thorpe, near Norwich. It was entitled 'Engine No. 43142 takes the wrong turn at Lynn':

> The 43142, a 90-ton 4 MT engine, used for goods and passenger work, should have taken the 12.30 train from South Lynn to Yarmouth on Saturday.

Driver B. Fisher and Fireman D. Hudson were operating the turntable and had the engine half-way round the turn when it began to move forward off the turntable and down a 7 ft embankment, its nose becoming embedded in a ditch.

Wilbert's story follows the real-life event in detail, adding a characteristic reaction for Gordon: ' "Oooosh!" he hissed as his wheels churned the mud. "Get me out! Get me out!" '

The author sent his young researcher a copy of the published book and the boy's reply is an indication of the extent to which many children felt an involvement – even a sense of collaboration – with the stories:

Dear Mr Awdry,
I was very excited and pleased to receive your letter and the Book. Thank you very much indeed.
I shall always keep it very carefully.
I took it to school and showed it to my teacher and headmaster.
When I see any more Interesting things about trains I will send the cuttings to you.
Love
Richard

Apart from the events described in the first story, *Gordon the Big Engine* turned out to be one of the most accident-filled books in the series: James is soon in trouble with leaves on the line, which cause him to slip and slide; and Thomas (after being rude to Gordon about falling into the ditch) takes a nose dive himself down a disused lead mine: ' "Fire and Smoke!" said Thomas, "I'm sunk!" – and he was!'

The year of publication, 1953, saw the Coronation of Queen Elizabeth II and, in the book's final story, Wilbert Awdry imagined the new monarch making a royal visit to the Island of Sodor. This event led to more problems – this time for Henry, who is convinced that he will be chosen to pull the Royal Train. However, disaster strikes when a cloud of smoke from Henry's funnel causes a painter, working up a ladder at the big station, to drop a paint pot on the engine:

The Fat Controller pushed through the crowd.
'You look like an iced cake, Henry,' he said. 'That *won't do for the Royal Train.*
I must make other arrangements.'

Those arrangements result in Gordon (who, with Thomas, has been in disgrace) pulling Her Majesty's train: his brass gleaming, his buffer beam decorated with flags and the Royal Arms. Reginald Dalby's illustration of the Fat Controller welcoming the Queen shows an open carriage door with an emerging arm and gloved hand, but the text is less coy: ' "We have read," said the Queen to the Fat Controller, "a great deal about your engines. May we see them, please?" '

This story, with the Queen meeting and talking to Gordon, Thomas, Edward and the others is an indication of the extent to which, within just eight years, the engines of Sodor had entered popular mythology: even the Queen of England, it suggests, knew all about Thomas the Tank Engine and friends; and – since her son liked the books so much – she may well have done!

The new book, however, was not without problems – and, once again, they were to do with the illustrations. It was Edmund Ward's editor, Eric Marriott, who had insisted that for every book from *Troublesome Engines* onwards, Wilbert should prepare a 'word picture' for each page of text which Reginald Dalby could follow in making his rough drawings. These were then submitted to the author for comment and correction, as was the final artwork prior to publication. In addition, Wilbert photographed some of his engine models in appropriate set-ups (such as Thomas head-down in the mine) in order to aid the illustrator.

Despite everyone's best endeavours, errors still occurred, such as the illustration on page 51 of *Gordon the Big Engine*, which shows Gordon, Henry, James and Edward standing in their shed: the central pillar supporting the roof is directly in front of Henry's right buffer, making it impossible for the engine to leave the shed without bringing about its demolition!

Long after publication, it was discovered that this illustration contained another mistake. Jonathan Atkinson, aged 7¼, wrote to point out that 'James' wheels were wrong'; and, indeed, Dalby had depicted the red engine as having a four-wheel leading bogie, making it a 4-6-0 instead of the 2-6-0 which it had previously been, and *still was* in other illustrations in the same book!

'You were very clever indeed to see that mistake,' Wilbert replied in July 1965. 'I never noticed it and the book first came out in 1953, twelve years ago. You are the first person ever to write to me about it. It is lucky that James' wheels are dark and not many people notice the mistake, because it would be very expensive indeed to alter the picture.'

1953 turned out to be something of a year for railway catastrophes. In May, the B.B.C. wrote to Eric Marriott at Edmund Ward: 'Our television department has in mind televising, on 14th and 28th June, two stories from the book *The Three Railway Engines* by the Reverend Awdry.' In offering the

standard fee of £1.00 per minute, R. G. Walford, of the B.B.C.'s copyright department, pointed out that it had not yet been decided which stories were to be used and that, as they had to fit a ten-minute slot, they might require some editing in order to allow for the 'animation'.

The 'animation' would involve the use of Gauge 00 miniature reproduction railway-stock with 'scenic backings' based on the illustrations. Although in principle, terms were agreed, Wilbert was understandably concerned about authenticity. The B.B.C. explained that they intended to use electrically operated Hornby models, based on British Rail designs which were 'similar if not almost identical with the illustrations in the book.' The letter then went on to qualify that statement: 'It is true that there are certain differences, for example, the illustrations do not show any smoke deflector plates which are present on the Hornby models but there is very little difference between the Hornby tank engine and the tank engine used for the illustrations.'

Since the B.B.C. explained that 'it is of immense value having somebody controlling the engines electrically, so that they can be moved forwards and backwards at will, by means of switches,' it can be assumed that they were unaware that Wilbert Awdry was himself a model railway enthusiast. Certainly, an expression such as 'similar if not almost identical' was unlikely to have slipped past him unnoticed. Eric Marriott therefore arranged that the models to be used in the series should be sent to the publisher's offices in Leicester, so he could arrange for them to be suitably 'adapted'.

Meccano Ltd of Liverpool (who manufactured the Hornby engines) duly dispatched 'three Duchess of Athol locomotives with tenders', while Douglas Mair, who was to direct the films, sent the tank engine – all of which had to be suitably adapted and delivered to the B.B.C.'s Lime Grove studio in time for a rehearsal on Wednesday 10th June.

The cosmetic surgery – which also involved repainting the engines in their appropriate liveries – was undertaken by P. R. Wickham, who had been responsible for making the relief map of the Island of Sodor. On the appointed day, Eric Marriott escorted the engines to London and, on arriving at the studio, was immediately 'shunted into a cubicle' and given a pile of railway sound effects records and asked to select the necessary sounds for use in the programme. When he emerged, some hours later, Marriott expected to see the engines going through their paces only to find that Douglas Mair was still some hours away from a rehearsal.

Marriott's disappointment was nothing compared with what he, Wilbert Awdry and millions of viewers were to experience on the following Sunday afternoon. Perhaps it was an ill-omen that the story chosen for the first broadcast was 'The Sad Story of Henry' . . .

Although the programme was only ten minutes long, it was highly technical – and was televised live. In addition to controlling the model engines (and the studio cameras) the director had to cope with technical effects such as superimposed rain (of which Henry was to be afraid), music and effects cues and live narration by Julia Lang of the then popular Home Service radio programme, *Listen With Mother*.

'The trains,' Wilbert recalls, 'were soon jerking about all over the place,' and the script (as a press report, two days later, put it) 'had to be freely adapted to meet the contingencies'. 'Once,' says Wilbert, 'the operator made the elementary mistake of not switching the points, and there was a nasty derailment.' Eric Marriott also remembers the moment when disaster struck: 'I settled down – with my wife, Dorothy, and my two children, Jennifer and David – in front of our 12-inch Pye television, expecting great things. Julia Lang began telling the story, a train came down the line – and fell off the track! And, *then*, a huge hand came into shot, picked it up and put it back on the rails!'

On the morning of Tuesday 23rd June, the disaster was fully reported in the newspapers. The *Daily Telegraph* revealed: 'The Rev. Wilbert Awdry, Vicar of Emneth, Norfolk, has sent an ultimatum to the B.B.C. He says that permission for the programme will not be granted unless an assurance is given against a recurrence of mistakes. Mr Awdry complains that one of the engines, James, was allowed to "gate-crash" a story about the other two locomotives, Edward and Henry. As a result, the adventures became merely "playing at trains".'

In the *Daily Mail*, the story made the front page – even taking precedence over 'Old Bailey drama – "HANGED MAN ACCUSED CHRISTIE" ', a report on the 10 Rillington Place murders trial:

CHAOS CLOSES THE CHILDREN'S LINE

What a way to run a (television) railway

As railwaymen, the B.B.C. are not even good television broadcasters. They admit it freely. And in a suitably secluded room somewhere in the Lime Grove television studios, a senior programme assistant will probably be spending much time running model trains in the next few weeks.

The highly qualified technicians who run the TV service, taking complicated outside broadcasts and ingenious camera effects in their stride, have found

> that operating a model railway can be hazardous.
> So much so that they have cancelled the second of the children's programmes, *Three Little Engines* [sic] due to be televised next Sunday, until they have 'overcome certain technical difficulties'.
> Said a frank B.B.C. spokesman: 'There was a bit of a mess up . . .'

The 'mess up' was not to be repeated. Practice did not make perfect, and the B.B.C. eventually decided to abandon the project. Meanwhile, the fate of the televised Railway Series had become as Wilbert put it 'a matter of almost National concern!'

The author received many letters of sympathy from outraged viewers: 'All the trains in all your books,' wrote Margaret Adams of Caterham, 'are live personalities in our house. Imagine the horror when we saw the disgraceful way the B.B.C. dealt with [them]. A child seeing this for the first time could not have any idea of the depth of Henry's tragedy and the thrill when they lit his fire up and steamed out again. It just seemed an ordinary weak little train story for very small children.'

Another correspondent, Harold Wagg of Claverdon, near Warwick, wrote to say that whilst he and his family never tired of Mr Awdry's stories, they had been 'sorely disappointed' in the televising of 'The Sad Story of Henry': 'We write thus, to assure you that we can always switch the television off, get one of your stories from the shelf, and by the "television" of our minds, conjure up a far better viewing of Thomas and his friends than the B.B.C.'s effort.'

In an attempt to make amends, the B.B.C. suggested that if the publishers could arrange a hall, and Wilbert Awdry could set up a working layout, they would be willing to prepare scripts, take their cameras, and film any number of episodes. However, Edmund Ward was not really interested in the wider exploitation of the books, repeatedly reminding Eric Marriott: 'We are *book publishers*.' Whilst (with some persuasion) he agreed to the production of a few modest spin-offs, the idea of assisting with the creation of a television series was not favourably received, and it was to be another thirty years before Henry and his compatriots were again seen on television.

'Dear Mr Awdry,' wrote a young man from Cheltenham, named Clive Holland, 'I have got all your books as I have just had *Edward the Blue Engine* for my 6th birthday. They are my favourite stories and I can read most of them myself.' For the ninth book in the Railway Series, published in 1955, Wilbert returned to the engine that had started the whole thing off in *The Three Railway Engines*. 'I think most of you are fond of Edward,' wrote Wilbert in his introductory letter to *Edward the Blue Engine*, 'His Driver and Fireman, Charlie Sand and Sidney Hever, are fond of him too. They were very pleased when they knew I was giving Edward a book all to himself.'

Human characters in the Railway Series are rarely spoken of by name, and those who are, have names which came, says Wilbert, 'off the top of my head'. However, Edward's driver and fireman were inspired by a real 'Charlie' and 'Sidney' who worked on the Wisbech and Upwell Line, which ran through the parish at Emneth.

Edward the Blue Engine reintroduces Bertie the bus (who has another race – this time, not in competition with an engine, but in order to ensure that delayed passengers catch their train); and features another non-railway engine character . . .

> *There is a scrap-yard near Edward's station. It is full of rusty old cars and machinery . . .*
> *One day Edward saw a Traction-engine in the Yard.*
> *'Hullo!' he said, 'you're not broken and rusty. What are you doing there?'*
> *'I'm Trevor,' said the Traction-engine sadly, 'they are going to break me up next week.'*
> *'What a shame!' said Edward.*
> *'My driver says I only need some paint, Brasso, and oil, to be as good as new,' Trevor went on sadly, 'but it's no good, my Master doesn't want me. I suppose it's because I'm old-fashioned.'*
> *Edward snorted indignantly, 'People say I'm old-fashioned, but I don't care. The Fat Controller says I'm a Useful Engine.'*

Trevor (who is 'Saved from Scrap' by a kindly clergyman) was inspired by a real traction-engine living with the Vicar of the East Anglian village of Magdelen. The conversation between Trevor and Edward about being old-fashioned was symptomatic of a growing attitude in Britain towards steam locomotion that, within a few years, would lead to the decimation of those services that had originally inspired the Railway Series. In a talk, given to the Downham and District Rotary Club in 1963, Wilbert passionately expressed his views:

> 'Outdated rubbish!' say the streamline efficiency boys. 'Sweep it all away!' Inefficient by modern terms, undoubtedly, but efficiency should also be measured in terms of long life and reliability.

Wilbert was speaking, specifically, of the Talyllyn Railway, the only railway in the world which has the whole of its original locomotive and passenger stock not only in working order, but in regular service.

In 1954 the Awdry family had returned to Towyn for their summer holiday. It was Christopher's first experience of working on the Talyllyn: 'Father and I went up the line with an oilcan, brushes and spanners, tightening up the bolts on the fishplates. By the time we'd finished we must have covered most of the whole length of the line as it then was, and we did some ditching in Pendre Cutting.'

In his talk about the Talyllyn, Wilbert described his involvement with the railway as having given him 'a new, intensely creative and rewarding experience in life'. It was inevitable that, at some point, he would find a way of meeting Tom Rolt's request to immortalise the Talyllyn engines in the Railway Series. Although it took Wilbert a few years of irregular thought (followed by lengthy correspondence with his brother, George), he eventually devised an imaginary railway that would be complimentary with the Talyllyn.

It was 1953, and Wilbert wrote to George: 'I have just worked out some notes on the History etc. of the Skarloey Railway. On the whole it has developed well, and I have drawn freely on the Festiniog, Corris, Welsh Highland, Croesor, and Tal-y-llyn Railways for inspiration.'

Attached were nine pages of typed foolscap (Wilbert was now using a typewriter), bearing the title: 'Notes on the Development and Working of the Skarloey Narrow Gauge Railway in the Island of Sodor':

> SCARLOEY (Wooded lake) is situated in the East Central district, and as its name implies, is surrounded by woods. It is a well-known beauty spot, visited by Anglers and Tourists. The lake drains at Rheneas ('divided waterfall') into the Hawin Dooey ('black river'), so called because for the first part of its course its bed is of slate in which this region abounds.

'Facts,' Wilbert told George in his letter, 'haven't bothered me as much as names.' Not surprisingly, George Awdry was soon writing back, responding to those names: 'With all hesitation,' he replied, 'I suggest that Scarloey is a scribe's error.' Wilbert agreed, although, in doing so, amended the spelling:

> As you say, Skarloey is a scribe's error, it should be SCACALOEY, a corruption of Skogarloey = the wooded lake. The name with its Scandinavian prefix and Celtic suffix is a philological curiosity which, though unusual, is found elsewhere in Sodor . . . The current theory is that while Norse settlers often accepted and adopted some Celtic place names,

NEW BOOKS

THE RAILWAY SERIES (also on pp. 8 and 9)

Toby the Tram Engine by THE REV. W. AWDRY

In this seventh title in the popular Railway Series, we meet a new engine called Toby the Tram Engine who makes himself as lovable as the well-known Thomas the Tank Engine.

Size 4½ × 5⅝ in., fully bound, 64 pages, 30 full-page plates in full colour by C. REGINALD DALBY 4/6 *net* (U.S.A. $1.00)

Scenes from **The Three Railway Engines**
Scenes from **Troublesome Engines**

Painting Books 3 and 4 are in the same style as the first two.

Crown 4to, 16 pages in full colour 2/- *net* (U.S.A. $0.65)

The Railway Series Postcards

After many requests, we have produced three sets of Postcards, each of six cards, showing scenes in colour from the popular Awdry Railway Books.

18/6 *per gross + P.T. in Gt. Britain*

Series 101 *Thomas the Tank Engine*
Series 301 *Henry the Green Engine*
Series 201, *James the Red Engine*

page two

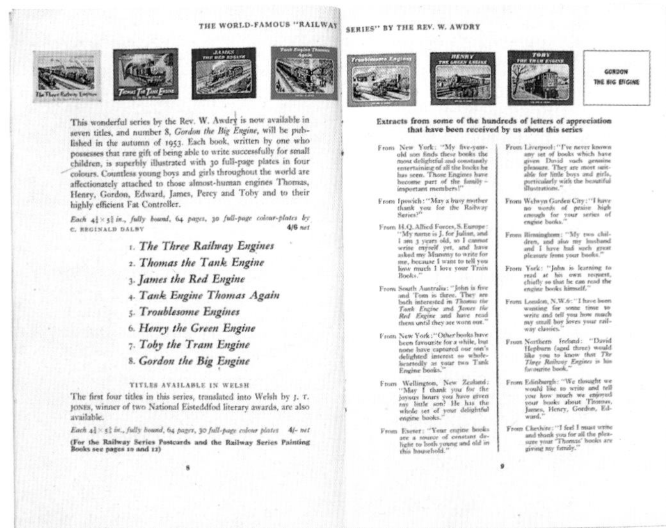

THE WORLD-FAMOUS "RAILWAY SERIES" BY THE REV. W. AWDRY

This wonderful series by the Rev. W. Awdry is now available in seven titles, and number 8, *Gordon the Big Engine*, will be published in the autumn of 1953. Each book, written by one who possesses that rare gift of being able to write successfully for small children, is superbly illustrated with 30 full-page plates in four colours. Countless young boys and girls throughout the world are affectionately attached to those almost-human engines Thomas, Henry, Gordon, Edward, James, Percy and Toby and to their highly efficient Fat Controller.

Each 4½ × 5½ in., fully bound, 64 pages, 30 full-page colour-plates by C. REGINALD DALBY 4/6 *net*

1. *The Three Railway Engines*
2. *Thomas the Tank Engine*
3. *James the Red Engine*
4. *Tank Engine Thomas Again*
5. *Troublesome Engines*
6. *Henry the Green Engine*
7. *Toby the Tram Engine*
8. *Gordon the Big Engine*

TITLES AVAILABLE IN WELSH

The first four titles in this series, translated into Welsh by J. T. JONES, winner of two National Eisteddfod literary awards, are also available.

Each 4½ × 5½ in., fully bound, 64 pages, 30 full-page colour plates 4/- *net*

(For the Railway Series Postcards and the Railway Series Painting Books see pages 10 and 12)

8

Extracts from some of the hundreds of letters of appreciation that have been received by us about this series

From New York: "My five-year-old son finds these books the most delightful and constantly entertaining of all the books he has seen. Those Engines have become part of the family – important members!"

From Ipswich: "May a busy mother thank you for the Railway Series?"

From H.Q. Allied Forces, S. Europe: "My name is J. for Julian, and I am 3 years old, so I cannot write myself yet, and have asked my Mummy to write for me, because I want to tell you how much I love your Train Books."

From South Australia: "John is five and Tom is three. They are both interested in *Thomas the Tank Engine* and *James the Red Engine* and have read them until they are worn out."

From New York: "Other books have been favourite for a while, but none have captured our son's delighted interest so wholeheartedly as your two Tank Engine books."

From Wellington, New Zealand: "May I thank you for the joyous hours you have given my little son? He has the whole set of your delightful engine books."

From Exeter: "Your engine books are a source of constant delight to both young and old in this household."

From Liverpool: "I've never known any set of books which have given David such genuine pleasure. They are most suitable for little boys and girls, particularly with the beautiful illustrations."

From Welwyn Garden City: "I have no words of praise high enough for your series of engine books."

From Birmingham: "My two children, and also my husband and I have had such great pleasure from your books."

From York: "John is learning to read at his own request, chiefly so that he can read the engine books himself."

From London, N.W.6: "I have been wanting for some time to write and tell you how much my small boy loves your railway classics."

From Northern Ireland: "David Hepburn (aged three) would like you to know that *The Three Railway Engines* is his favourite book."

From Edinburgh: "We thought we would like to write and tell you how much we enjoyed your books about Thomas, James, Henry, Gordon, Edward."

From Cheshire: "I feel I must write and thank you for all the pleasure your 'Thomas' books are giving my family."

9

Pages from Edmund Ward's catalogues for 1952/53 showing an early example of Thomas merchandising, the Railway Series Postcards, and 1953/54, the year in which *Gordon the Big Engine* was published.

Henry and Edward as depicted by C. Reginald Dalby in *Henry the Green Engine* (1951); Gordon losing his dome in *Duck and the Diesel Engine* (1958), illustrated by John T. Kenney; the Fat Controller with some of his *Enterprising Engines* in the 1968 volume illustrated by Peter Edwards.

In the last volume to be illustrated by Reginald Dalby, Percy is shown steaming past a ships chandlers named after the editor of the Railway Series E. T. L Marriott.

Wilbert Awdry's stories reached a new audience through a series of gramophone recordings of readings by the B.B.C. radio and television personality, Johnny Morris.

The cover of the first *Railway Map of the Island of Sodor,* published in 1958, and an advertisement for for the new Percy Train Set produced by Meccano/Hornby in 1966.

There is a quite striking similarity between many of the engines running on the Island of Sodor and real engines which once ran on the railways of Britain. Here are just a few of them.

R. M. Casserley Collection.

'EDWARD the blue engine was getting old.' Edward, whose adventures began the Railway Series, bears a resemblance to the 'Larger Seagull' type 4-4-0s, built by Sharp Stewart in 1896, which once worked the Furness Railway. The example shown in this picture is No. 45 (original F.R. No. 22), photographed at Moor Row on 24th March, 1924.

R. M. Casserley Collection.

GORDON was originally described by Wilbert Awdry as being 'very big and very proud', as was the engine shown in this photograph. No. 1472 is an unnamed example of Nigel Gresley's Class A1 4-6-2 locomotive, originally designed for the Great Northern Railway, but introduced just before the London & North Eastern Railway was formed in 1923. The photograph was probably taken shortly after the engine had received its L.N.E.R. livery, and may be standing near King's Cross shed.

Colour-Rail.

THOMAS is based on the Class E2 type 0-6-0 tank engine designed by Lawson B. Billington, Locomotive Superintendent of the London, Brighton & South Coast Railway between 1911 and 1922. The E2s were introduced in 1915 to replace earlier members of the Class E1 engines which had been scrapped. The last five in the ten-strong series had extended side-tanks to give a greater water capacity but all engines had two inside cylinders and driving wheels 4' 6" in diameter. Illustrated are the wooden model of Thomas made by Wilbert Awdry for his son Christopher and the model engine representing Thomas which ran on the Ffarquhar Branch Railway.

'TOBY is a tram engine. He is short and sturdy. He has cow-catchers and side-plates and doesn't look like a steam engine at all . . .' The J70 Class, which inspired the creation of Toby, were 0-6-0 locomotives, slightly more powerful than the early 0-4-0 Class Y6 engines and were introduced in 1903. Designed by James Holden for working on the docks at Great Yarmouth, Ipswich and Lowestoft, they carried a mere 15 cwt of coal. Their water-tanks – built between the boiler and the axles and known as well-tanks – were also small, holding only 625 gallons. Because of his small water-tank, Toby needs to stop for a refill at Elsbridge during each journey, which then brings the fourteen mile trip well within his capacity.

W. V. Awdry Collection.

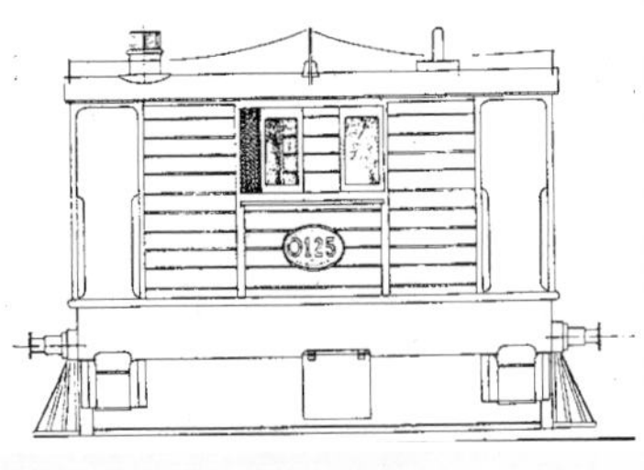

C. V. Awdry.

Sir Topham Hatt once ordered an engine similar to this. It is a Great Central Railway 'Atlantic' engine, that is an engine with a 4-4-2 wheel arrangement. The photograph here shows G.C.R. 4-4-2 No. 706 at Scarborough shed in August 1938, moving out to take an excursion train home. What the Fat Controller received was HENRY, who was something like a cross between Gordon and a nightmare!

C. V. Awdry

After his accident while pulling the Flying Kipper, HENRY was sent to the Works at Crewe where he underwent a transformation and returned looking 'splendid and strong' rather like this preserved example of the Class No. 44871, seen on the Bo'ness & Kinneil Railway at Bo'ness on 5th November, 1992. It should be noted that 44871 is coupled to a Stanier high-capacity tender; however, on the Island of Sodor there are no really long runs and the Fat Controller prefers to use the smaller Fowler tender.

JOHN T. KENNEY (1911-1972) who, like Reginald Dalby, studied at Leicester College of Art, worked as a commercial artist, illustrator and, in later life, became a distinguished painter of animal studies and sporting scenes. Kenney illustrated six books in the Railway Series from *The Eight Famous Engines* (1957) to *Gallant Old Engine* (1962).

'We mustn't go past it,' he said. 'That's Orders.' *The Eight Famous Engines* (1957)

Toby was out on the Main Line. *The Eight Famous Engines* (1957)

The two engines greeted him cheerfully. *The Twin Engines* (1960)

John Kenney drew Wilbert Awdry (in flat cap and clerical collar) in this illustration to *Duck and the Diesel Engine* (1958). Is the man in the bow-tie beside him, Kenney's predecessor, C. Reginald Dalby?

'My funnel feels wobbly . . .' *Gallant Old Engine* (1962)

In 1951, the success of the Railway Series by 'The Rev. W. Awdry' resulted in Edmund Ward publishing *Our Child Begins to Pray* an 'attempt to satisfy a demand by many parents for a manual which will help them to teach their children how to pray'. The colour plates and line illustrations were by Rene Cloke.

Two illustrations by 'R. G. F.' for a children's story about 'The Little People' who live on a model railway layout, serialised in the *Church of England Newspaper* during 1959 and 1960.

As a departure from his famous engines, Wilbert Awdry wrote two books about a little red, three-wheeled car called Belinda. The author disliked the illustrations by Ionicus (left) to the first book, *Belinda the Beetle* (1958), so the sequel, *Belinda Beats the Band* (1961) was illustrated by Railway Series artist, John T. Kenney (above). When the books were republished in paperback in 1992, Belinda became a Volkswagen (right) and the illustrations were by Val Biro.

Fellow railway enthusiasts: George Awdry with his nephew, Christopher, and brother, Wilbert.

Quite a mouthful! George Awdry on a Welsh village platform during a railway holiday with his brother in the 1960s.

On the Talyllyn Railway, 1952, Wilbert Awdry as guard gives the right away watched by his daughter, Hilary.

Edmund Ward celebrated the sale of the two millionth copy of the Railway Series in 1961 with a party on the Bluebell Line in Sussex. Among those present are Wilbert Awdry, Eric Marriott (far right) and the Fat Controller.

Dolgoch, one of the 'Two Old Ladies of Towyn', photographed at Towyn by Wilbert Awdry in 1954.

The Reverend E. R. ('Teddy') Boston who was immortalised as the Fat Clergyman in such books as *Oliver the Western Engine,* demonstrating his model railway layout at a Wisbech Trade Fair in 1953.

Real railways provided inspiration for railway developments on the Island of Sodor. The Snowdon Mountain Railway, in Wales (left) inspired Wilbert's nineteenth book, *Mountain Engines*, while the Ravenglass and Eskdale Railway, in Cumbria, was the model for a Sodor counterpart in several books beginning with *Small Railway Engines* in 1967.

The last of the Canadian Pacific's Selkirk engines (5934) photographed by Wilbert Awdry at Calgary, Canada, in June 1980 during a railway holiday with his brother, George.

A CN4-8-2 which Wilbert and George found 'stuffed and caged' in Assinboine Park, Winnipeg.

GOOD FOR ONE CONTINUOUS PASSAGE
FROM St. James, Manitoba
TO Grosse Isle, Manitoba
AND RETURN
—Passage Subject To Rules Of The Society—
Not Good After Date of Issue
No Stop over Allowed Not Transferable
Property taken into cars will be entirely at owner's risk
General Passenger Traffic Manager
COACH
VOID IF NO STUBS ATTACHED

PRAIRIE DOG CENTRAL

№ 00127 A ADULT

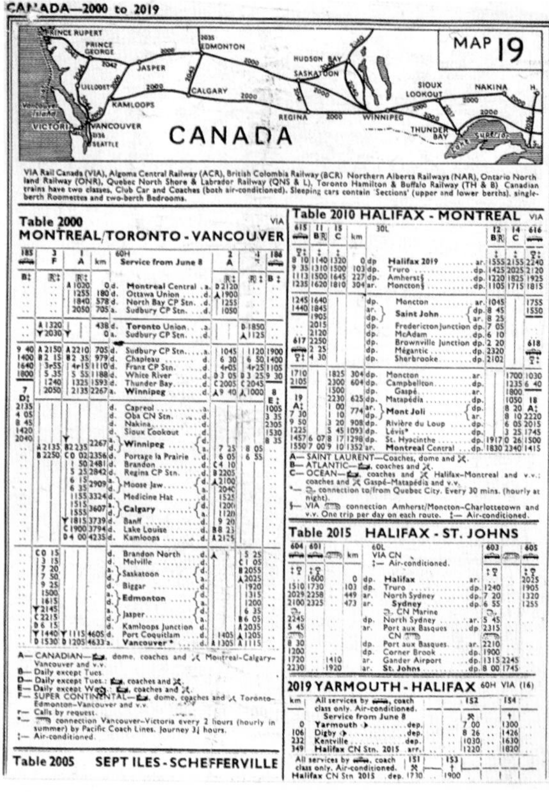

CANADA—2000 to 2019

VIA Rail Canada (VIA), Algoma Central Railway (ACR), British Colombia Railway (BCR) Northern Alberta Railways (NAR), Ontario Northland Railway (ONR), Quebec North Shore & Labrador Railway (QNS & L), Toronto Hamilton & Buffalo Railway (TH & B). Canadian trains have two classes, Club Car and Coaches (both air-conditioned). Sleeping cars contain 'Sections' (upper and lower berths), single-berth Roomettes and two-berth Bedrooms.

Table 2000 VIA
MONTREAL/TORONTO - VANCOUVER

185	3 F	1 A	km	60H Service from June 8	2 A	4	186
B	R	R			R	R	B
..	..	A 1020	0 d.	Montreal Central . . a.	D 2120	..	..
..	..	1255	180 d.	Ottawa Union . . . . d.	1900	..	..
..	..	1840	578 d.	North Bay CP Stn. . d.	1255	..	..
..	..	2050	705 a.	Sudbury CP Stn. . . . d.	1050	..	..
..	A 1320		438 d.	Toronto Union . . . a.		D 1850	..
..	2030		0 a.	Sudbury CP Stn. . . . d.		1125	..
9 40	A 2150	A 2210	705 d.	Sudbury CP Stn. . . . a.	1045	1120	1900
1400	B 2 15	B 2 35	979 d.	Chapleau . . . . . d.	6 30	6 50	1400
1640	3r55	4r15	1110 d.	Franz CP Stn. . . . d.	4r05	4r25	1105
1800	5 35	5 55	1188 d.	White River . . . . d.	D 3 05	D 3 25	9 30
7 D	1240	1325	1593 d.	Thunder Bay . . . . d.	C 2005	C 2045	
	2050	2135	2267 a.	Winnipeg . . . . . d.	9 40	1000	8 E
2135			d.	Capreol . . . . . . a.			1005
4 05			d.	Oba CN Stn. . . . . d.			3 35
8 45			d.	Nakina . . . . d.			2305
1420			d.	Sioux Lookout . . . d.			1530
2040			2267 a.	Winnipeg . . . . . d.			8 35
..	A 2135	B 2 35	d.	Winnipeg . . . . . a.	7 25	8 05	..
..	B 2250	C 0 02	2356 d.	Portage la Prairie . . d.	6 05	6 55	..
..		1 50	2481 d.	Brandon . . . . . . d.	C 4 10		..
..		5 25	2842 d.	Regina CP Stn. . . . d.	B 2205		..
..		6 15	2909 a.	Moose Jaw . . . . . d.	2100		..
..		6 35	d.	Moose Jaw . . . . . a.	2040		..
..		1155	3324 d.	Medicine Hat . . . . d.	1525		..
..		1515	3607 a.	Calgary . . . . . . d.	1200		..
..		1555	d.	Calgary . . . . . . a.	1120		..
..		1815	3739 d.	Banff . . . . d.	9 20		..
..		C 1900	3794 d.	Lake Louise . . . . d.	B 8 23		..
..		D 4 00	4235 d.	Kamloops . . . . . d.	A 2125		..
..	C 0 15		d.	Brandon North . . . d.		5 25	..
..	3 15		d.	Melville . . . . . . d.		C 1 05	..
..	7 20		a.	Saskatoon . . . . . d.		B 2055	..
..	7 50		d.	Saskatoon . . . . . a.		2025	..
..	9 25		d.	Biggar . . . . d.		1920	..
..	1500		a.	Edmonton . . . . . d.		1315	..
..	1615		d.	Edmonton . . . . . a.		1200	..
..	2145		a.	Jasper . . . . d.		6 35	..
..	C 2215		d.	Jasper . . . . a.		B 6 05	..
..	D 6 15		d.	Kamloops Junction . d.		A 2035	..
..	1440	1115	4605 d.	Port Coquitlam . . . d.	1405	1205	..
..	D 1530	D 1205	4633 a.	Vancouver * . . . . d.	A 1305	A 1115	..

A— CANADIAN— , dome, coaches and ✕ Montreal–Calgary–Vancouver and v.v.
B— Daily except Tues.
D— Daily except Tues.: , coaches and ✕.
E— Daily except Wed.: , coaches and ✕.
F— SUPER CONTINENTAL— , dome, coaches and ✕ Toronto–Edmonton–Vancouver and v.v.
r— Calls by request.
*— connection Vancouver–Victoria every 2 hours (hourly in summer) by Pacific Coach Lines. Journey 3¼ hours.
‡— Air-conditioned.

Table 2005 SEPT ILES - SCHEFFERVILLE

Table 2010 HALIFAX - MONTREAL VIA

615	11 B R	15 C	km	30L	12 B R	14 C	616
‡	‡	‡			‡	‡	‡
8 10	1140	1320	0 dp	Halifax 2019 . . . . . . ar.	1555	2155	2240
9 35	1310	1500	103 dp.	Truro . . . . dp.	1425	2025	2120
1113	1500	1645	227 dp.	Amherst§ . . . . dp.	1220	1825	1925
1235	1620	1810	304 ar.	Moncton§ . . . . dp.	1105	1715	1815
1245	1640			dp. Moncton . . . . ar.	1045		1755
1440	1845			ar. Saint John . . . . dp.	8 45		1550
	1905			dp. Saint John . . . . ar.	8 25		
..	2015			dp. Fredericton Junction dp.	7 05		..
..	2120			dp. McAdam . . . . dp.	6 10		..
617	2250			dp. Brownville Junction dp.	2 20		618
	2 25			dp. Mégantic . . . . dp.	2320		
‡	4 30			dp. Sherbrooke . . . . dp.	2102		‡
1710		1825	304 dp.	Moncton . . . . ar.		1700	1030
2105		2300	604 dp.	Campbellton . . . . dp.		1235	6 40
		1500	dp.	Gaspé . . . . ar.		1800	
19		2230	625 dp.	Matapédia . . . . dp.		1050	18
A‡		1 00	774 ar.	Mont Joli . . . . dp.		8 20	A‡
7 30		1 10	dp.	Mont Joli . . . . ar.		8 10	2220
9 50		3 20	908 dp.	Rivière du Loup . . . . . dp.		6 05	2015
1225		5 45	1093 dp.	Lévis* . . . . dp.		3 25	1745
1457	6 07	8 17	1298 dp.	St. Hyacinthe . . . . . . dp.	1917	0 26	1500
1550	7 00	9 10	1352 ar.	Montreal Central . . . dp.	1830	2340	1415

A— SAINT LAURENT—Coaches, dome and ✕.
B— ATLANTIC— , coaches and ✕.
C— OCEAN— , coaches and ✕ Halifax–Montreal and v.v.; coaches and ✕ Gaspé–Matapédia and v.v.
*— connection to/from Quebec City. Every 30 mins. (hourly at night).
§— VIA connection Amherst/Moncton–Charlottetown and v.v. One trip per day on each route. ‡— Air-conditioned.

Table 2015 HALIFAX - ST. JOHNS

604	601		km	60L VIA CN ‡— Air-conditioned.	603		605
‡	‡				‡		‡
..	1600	..	0	dp. Halifax . . . . ar.	..	..	2025
1510	1730	..	103	dp. Truro . . . . dp.	1240	..	1905
2029	2258	..	449	ar. North Sydney . . . . . . dp.	7 20	..	1320
2100	2325	..	473	ar. Sydney . . . . dp.	6 55	..	1255
				CN Marine			
2245	..	..		dp. North Sydney . . . . . . ar.	5 45	..	..
5 45	..	..		ar. Port aux Basques . . . . dp.	2315	..	..
				CN			
8 30	..	..		dp. Port aux Basques . . . . ar.	2210	..	..
1200	..	..		dp. Corner Brook . . . . . . dp.	1900	..	..
1720	..	1410		ar. Gander Airport . . . . . dp.	1315	2245	..
2230	..	1920		ar. St. Johns . . . . dp.	8 00	1745	..

2019 YARMOUTH - HALIFAX 60H VIA (16)

km	All services by , coach class only. Air-conditioned. Service from June 8			152		154	
				✕		†	
0	Yarmouth . . . . dep.	..	..	7 00	..	1300	..
106	Digby . . . . dep.	..	..	8 26	..	1426	..
232	Kentville . . . . dep.	..	..	1030	..	1630	..
349	Halifax CN Stn. 2015 arr.	..	..	1220	..	1820	..

All services by , coach class only. Air-conditioned.	151		153				
	✕		†				
Halifax CN Stn 2015 . dep.	1730	..	1900				

ABOVE A time-table for VIA Rail Canada, showing some of the places visited by Wilbert and George Awdry during their holiday.

LEFT Ticket for the Prairie Dog Central railroad in Winnipeg where the Awdry brothers rode vintage steam locomotives of the Canadian Northern Railway.

BELOW George Awdry at the summit of Whistlers Mountain (alt. 7,500 ft) reached by the Jasper Tramway in Canada's Mountain National Parks.

The Prairie Dog's No. 3 locomotive, photographed by Wilbert in Winnipeg in June 1980, two years before the engine celebrated its one hundredth birthday.

they also adapted others to suit themselves when the Celtic name was hard for a Nordic tongue to pronounce. What the original Celtic prefix was we have no means of knowing.

Other names had to be found: Sudrian counterparts for Welsh place names such as Rhyd-y-rhonen (the ford of Ash tree) and Brynglas (Blue hill). In Wilbert's original draft, these places appear as blanks, against which he typed the words: 'Any suggestions?' In tiny handwriting, George penned his proposals: 'Crossag-ny-cuirn (Little crossing of the mountain ash)' and 'Glennock. Gleih-knock (Gleih = ? blue. See Blue hill)'. The Awdry brothers were once more engaged in their fascinating private game of origins and derivations that, like the bulk of an iceberg, is hidden beneath the surface of the Railway Series.

There were strong links between the Skarloey Railway and the Talyllyn: the locomotives – Skarloey and Rheneas – were identical with Talyllyn and Dolgoch. The Skarloey guard's van even had 'a compartment specially fitted up for the Guard as a travelling ticket office, with a little window through which the passengers could buy their tickets'. Wilbert had sold tickets from just such a van on the Talyllyn – although he pointed out that the Welsh railway 'did not make this alteration until 1902'.

In comparison with these extensive notes, the description of the Skarloey Railway in *The Island of Sodor*, published in 1987, is remarkably succinct (and includes later history which, in 1953, had not yet occurred):

> *This is the oldest railway in the Island. Begun in 1806 as a horse-worked line between Cros-ny-Cuirn and Balladwail by the Crovan's Gate Mining Company, it was extended to their mines on Ward Fell by a series of inclined planes and finally in 1864/65 realigned for steam traction. In 1909 the company was sold out to Mr [later Sir] Handel Brown. It stayed in private ownership till 1966 when a Share Issue was floated and it became a Company. It went through hard times before that, however, and on the first Sir Handel's death it was under threat of closure, but now it more than pays its way. Sir Handel Brown II is Chairman, Mr Peter Sam (The Thin Controller) is General Manager with Mr Ivo Hugh as Chief Engineer.*

Ivo Hugh was based on Hugh Jones, a Talyllyn employee for many years, while Peter Sam was based on Tom Rolt: 'Just as the Thin Controller had faith in the future of the Skarloey and refused to let it die,' says Wilbert, 'so also it was Tom, above all, who had faith in the future of the Talyllyn.'

As for Sir Handel Brown: his character was obviously inspired by the owner of the Talyllyn Railway – Sir Haydn Jones – although the fictional counterpart was originally going to be named Sir Handel *Smith*, 'a young man who [in 1906] had just succeeded his father as a principal shareholder and owner of much of the land through which the railway passed.' Like Haydn Jones, Handel Smith proved to be the saviour of a railway line. Although the copper mines, which the railway had originally been built to serve, were exhausted, Sir Handel decided to develop the excavation of slate and to keep the line running. But by 1953, things were looking gloomy for the Skarloey Railway. In October of that year, Wilbert was writing to George as if reporting real current events:

> I am not certain what the position of the Skarloey Railway is at the moment. Sir Handel died last January, aged 75. He had no sons, but there are five daughters: Agnes, Lucy, Ruth, Hilda, and Beatrice. Neither they nor their husbands are at all interested in the railway or the quarries as such. Too much capital locked up with too little return, sums up their view I feel; and they really want, either to sell the undertakings, or get an Abandonment order, and get as much as they can for scrap.

It should be noted that Sir Handel's daughters eventually gave their names to Skarloey's coaches (with the exception of 'Hilda', who was replaced by 'Jemima').

As an afterthought to his letter, Wilbert added: 'Oh, by the way, Sir Handel Smith was Liberal MP for (I think) Sodor East from 1908 to 1923. Perhaps the Club Archives can throw some light.' The 'Club' was the National Liberal Club, where George was Librarian and his 'researches' were soon on their way back to Wilbert. Under the heading 'Landmarks in the Political Career of the Late Sir Handel Smith', George Awdry charted Sir Handel's unsuccessful attempts to be elected in 1895 and 1900, his first triumph in 1906 and the ups and downs of his later career in politics, leading to his receiving a baronetcy in 1937.

A year of such delving into Sodor history led to the writing of the tenth title in the Railway Series, *Four Little Engines*. To introduce readers to the first of those engines – described in Edmund Ward's catalogue as 'the delightfully named Skarloey' – Wilbert used the first (and oldest) of his railway characters:

> *The Fat Controller had sent Edward to the Works to be mended. Near the Works Station, Edward noticed a narrow-gauge engine standing in an open-sided shed.*

'That's Skarloey,' he thought, 'what's he doing there?' He remembered Skarloey and his brother Rheneas, because in the old days he had often brought passengers who wanted to travel up to the Lake in their little train.

Although called *Four Little Engines* the book is really about only three engines, since on the second page of the first story, Skarloey tells Edward that Rheneas has been taken away to be mended.

As a result, and because Skarloey is a Very Old Engine and deserves a good rest, the Owner has bought two more engines, Sir Handel and Peter Sam. Just as Skarloey and Rheneas correspond to Talyllyn and Dolgoch, the newcomers are clearly related to the two engines which The Talyllyn Railway Preservation Society had purchased and renamed Sir Haydn and Edward Thomas. Apart from 'guest appearances' by Edward, Gordon and Henry, the success of the new volume of stories rested on its three new, superbly delineated, characters.

There is Skarloey: an elderly engine, gracious and modest. He dozes and dreams – 'as old engines will' – of days gone by; but, when called upon in an hour of crisis, finds the strength and courage to save the day. The two 'new' old engines are sharply contrasting: Peter Sam is a helpful, easy-going engine, always ready to pour oil on troubled waters, while Sir Handel is irritable, pompous, bombastic and sarcastic:

'Now Sir Handel,' said the Fireman next morning, 'we'll get you ready.'
'I'm tired,' he yawned, 'let Peter Sam go, he'd love it.'

Sir Handel always finds something to complain about: ' "What a small shed!" grumbled Sir Handel. "This won't do at all!" ' or ' "Trucks!" snorted Sir Handel, "TRUCKS!" ' Indeed, despite Sir Handel's aristocratic bearing, the Thin Controller soon has him marked down as a Troublesome Engine who is too big for his wheels. Rude and conceited he may be, but readers of *Four Little Engines* were in no doubt that the author had created another memorable engine character and demonstrated that, a decade on from his first book, his powers of invention were as fresh as ever.

All Wilbert's stories in the new book had some connection with real events occurring on the Talyllyn; but the third story, 'Peter Sam and the Refreshment Lady', had a particularly personal inspiration:

The last passengers arrived. The Guard was ready with his flag and whistle.
The Refreshment Lady walked across the platform.

> *Then it happened! . . .*
> *The Guard says that Peter Sam was too impatient; Peter Sam says he was sure he heard a whistle . . . . Anyway, he started.*
> *'Come quickly, come quickly!' he puffed.*
> *'Stop! . . . Stop! . . . STOP!' wailed the coaches. 'You've . . . left . . . her . . . behind . . . ! YOU'VE . . . LEFT . . . HER . . . BEHIND . . . !'*
> *The Guard whistled and waved his red flag. The Driver, looking back, saw the Refreshment Lady shouting and running after the train.*

It is interesting that Wilbert's policy of protecting the reputation of railwaymen by ensuring that anything that goes wrong with the Railways of Sodor is always due to the engines rather than the staff, should have been extended to cover his own error in leaving the Talyllyn's refreshment lady, Mrs Davies, at Abergynolwyn!

The illustrations accompanying these charming stories are far from being Reginald Dalby's best work, although the engines were accurately drawn (using photographs of the Talyllyn originals) and the artist introduced some pleasant new scenic views with pines, hills and purple-headed mountains.

The Edmund Ward catalogue which, in 1955, announced the publication of *Four Little Engines* also listed another book, *Tales of Flitterwick Harbour* 'by the artist of the Railway Series', which Dalby may have hoped would rival the popularity of Wilbert Awdry's engines:

> The first title in a new series of stories for young children contains four gay little stories about a bustling sea port told by the town clock who, as he has four faces, sees everything. The charm of the stories is echoed by the full colour and black and white illustrations by the author.

Those who hold that the Railway Series' success is solely due to Dalby's illustrations should reflect on the fact that, despite being created by the same artist, Flitterwick Harbour and its central character, Tubby the Tugboat, did not survive to become a series, and are now long forgotten.

Curiously, the next volume in the Railway Series was to be the last with illustrations by Dalby. It was, perhaps, an inevitable result of what had been a year of change. In 1955, Edmund Ward – who had retired from day-to-day involvement in the business several years earlier – sold the company to the London printers, Straker Brothers Ltd, who had also taken over another small publisher, Nicholas Kaye. Although they retained the imprint 'Edmund Ward' (with its logo of Aquarius, the water-carrier, and the slogan 'The sign of a good book'), the company – with its editor, Eric Marriott, and sales manager, John Welch – moved to Bishopsgate in London; while Edmund Ward remained in Leicester, to quote a local press report, 'as a director of the firm in an advisory and consultative capacity'.

When the publisher and the illustrator had both been based in Leicester, Eric Marriott had always successfully managed to mediate between Wilbert and Dalby. He not only smoothed over their occasional disputes, but prevented others from arising, by spotting errors in some of Dalby's pictures before Wilbert ever saw them. Now, however, problems had to be dealt with at long-distance, which proved far from easy; and, with the eleventh book in the series, things finally came to a head. That book was about Percy.

One of Wilbert's young correspondents, six-year-old Clive Holland, had written to his favourite author with a request: 'Will you please write a new book called Percy the Polite Engine with another story in it about Trevor. We think Percy is very polite because he always says "Yes, sir, please, sir".' Clive was not alone, there were similar requests from a Christopher, a Giles and a Peter – to whom (with Clive) the book's introductory letter would eventually be addressed:

> Thank you for writing to ask for a book about Percy. He is still cheeky, and we were afraid (the Fat Controller and I) that if he had a book to himself, it might make him cheekier than ever, and that would never do!
> But Percy has been such a Really Useful Engine that we both think he deserves a book. Here it is.

The book was not called *Percy the Polite Engine*, but *Percy the SMALL Engine*; and, far from being polite, Percy plays tricks on Gordon and James. However, like so many of the stories in the Railway Series, this is a rites-of-passage story and Percy matures from being a mischievous prankster to receiving the Fat Controller's ultimate accolade for being 'a Really Useful Engine'.

As for Trevor, he did not make the requested return appearance; but the book does introduce two interesting new characters, one of whom is a curiously shaped engine with the letters G.W.R. (for Great Western Railway) on its large oblong side-tanks:

> *'What is your name?' asked the Fat Controller kindly.*
> *'Montague, Sir; but I'm usually called "Duck". They say I waddle; I don't really, Sir, but I like "Duck" better than Montague.'*
> *'Good!' said the Fat Controller. ' "Duck" it shall be.'*

Percy quickly becomes good friends with Duck, who soon shows himself to be a determined engine, well able to uphold the good name and no-nonsense tradition of the G.W.R.: 'I'm a Great Western Engine. We Great Western Engines do our work without Fuss . . .'

The other newcomer has 'whirly great arms' and answers to the name of Harold. Proud of being able to 'hover like a bird', Harold Helicopter looks down on railways as being slow and out of date. In a variation on Thomas' famous contest with Bertie the bus, Percy races Harold – and wins. The following story, however, sees engine and helicopter working together to ensure that the Vicar's Sunday School Outing arrives safely home despite torrential rain and terrible floods.

That story – containing such exciting sounds as those made by Harold's whirling arms: 'Buzzzzzzzzzzzzzzzzz! Buzzzzzzzzzzzzzzzzz! Buzzzzzzzzzzzzzzzzz!' or Percy steaming along, with the floodwaters lapping around his wheels: 'Oooooooooooooshshshshshshshshshshsh!' – ends with Percy and Harold (like so many Railway Series rivals) learning to coexist harmoniously. Their earlier race, however, concluded with Percy's fireman making up a song of triumph in the engine's honour. The song needed music, and although Wilbert knew how he wanted the tune to sound, he couldn't write it down: 'So, I whistled it to Ernie Trundle, the organist at Emneth and he took down the notation.'

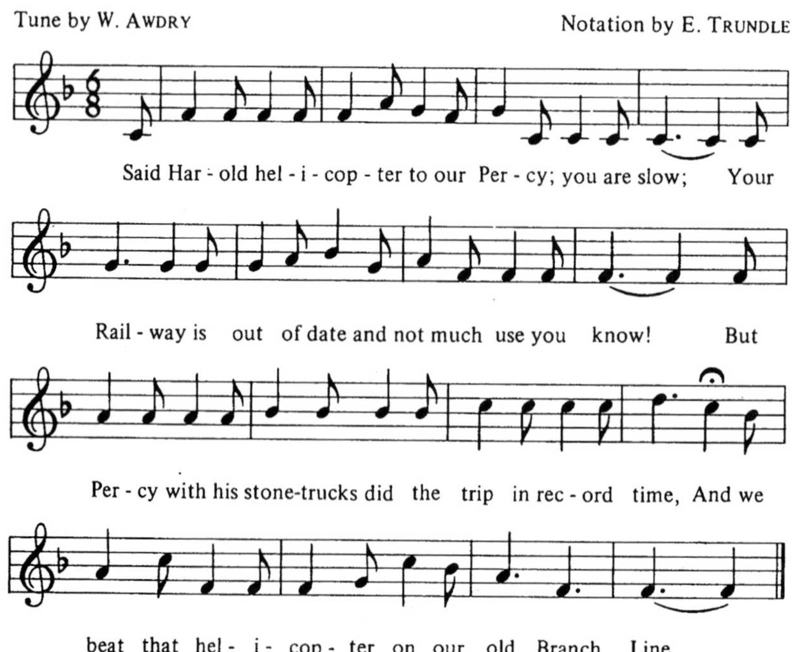

'Edmund Ward,' says Wilbert, 'had grave doubts about the "music" and consulted a music publisher who took a pretty poor view of it!' Although the words and music eventually appeared on the final page of *Percy the Small Engine*, the innovation generated some Troublesome Correspondence for Wilbert: 'My little boy has read *Percy the Small Engine*, No.11 in your delightful Railway Series,' began one letter. 'But when Mark came to play the tune at the end of the book, he found that, as printed, the song did not make very good sense. I therefore send you what I believe to be the correct notation for your song.'

More concerning, in 1955, was the final breach between Wilbert Awdry and Reginald Dalby. The illustrator produced some of his best pictures for *Percy the Small Engine*: the station interior, with steam from Percy's funnel lit by shafts of early evening sunlight coming through the glass roof; the view of the harbour, with ships, tugs and cranes (as well as a compliment to the Series' editor in the form of a sign on a warehouse: 'E.T.L. MARRIOTT, SHIPS CHANDLERS'); or the picture of Percy 'Ooooshing' his way through flooded fields while Harold whirls through a sky dark with storm clouds.

Nevertheless, elements of Dalby's pictures continued to give Wilbert and Eric Marriott concern. On a tracing paper overlay, the author and editor made detailed annotations. For example on one of Dalby's original illustrations for *Percy the Small Engine*, Marriott pointed out that the Fat Controller, wearing spats, had 'FROGMAN'S FEET!', while Wilbert commented that the support for Percy's funnel was 'NOT VISIBLE'. On a subsequent illustration, Wilbert complained: 'Henry's front too large and his funnel is small in consequence. He has a taper boiler not parallel sided (see your previous drawings throughout *Henry the Green Engine*). It appears that there are trees growing where the signal box should be.'

The trees were duly uprooted and Henry's front re-worked, but Wilbert's chief objection was to the way in which Dalby drew Percy: 'I wrote to him and said: "I beg, pray and exhort you not to make Percy look like a green caterpillar with red stripes!" '

Wilbert's memory of these events is that the artist took umbrage and resigned. Reginald Dalby, writing in his unpublished autobiography, tells the story differently: 'Press dates were of major importance yet it became later and later before I received the script, despite many requests. Finally, it was so late that I returned the copy and our association ended.'

Eric Marriott, who had often had to act as peacemaker between the two men (justifying Wilbert's seemingly pernickety attitude to an artist who simply did not understand the need for technical accuracy), sees a degree of self-justification in Dalby's account. It is true that, as the series progressed,

Wilbert found it harder to devise, write and deliver the next manuscript, but Dalby did not dramatically reject a manuscript; it was simply that *Percy the Small Engine* was, for him, the end of the line.

'I was sorry to give up,' wrote Dalby, 'as I had become intimately involved with my engines, their characters and personalities; but, like that other famous "artist", Adolf Hitler, "my patience became exhausted".' Wilbert's patience had also worn thin, but the pressing problem was where to find an artist to take over the series. A new book had been written and was announced, in Ward's catalogue for 1957, under the title *The Fat Controller's Engines*. When it eventually appeared it was as *The Eight Famous Engines* 'with illustrations by John T. Kenney'.

The choice of John Theodore Eardley Kenney – who like Dalby had studied at Leicester College of Art – was a happy one: he brought a freshness and a new liveliness to the twelfth title in the series with pictures that combine a lightness of touch with a more realistic look. Remembering John Kenney, Wilbert says: 'We got on splendidly. He was as different from Dalby as chalk from cheese. He was interested in the work and used to go down to his station and draw railway engines from life.' The engines which Kenney drew appear longer, larger, and more svelte – in fact, far less like the 'toy trains' of Dalby's pictures. As for his human characters, they are *real* people: pushing barrows, leaning on shovels and running along station platforms; and the scenery recalls those airy, luminous country scenes that featured on 1950's railway posters.

Kenney, who had illustrated numerous titles for Ladybird books, produced several memorable images for *The Eight Famous Engines*, such as his picture of wheeling seagulls looking down on Thomas and Percy as they gaze at the 'DANGER' notice on the Quay, their steam being blown away horizontally by the wind that is whipping the sea into angry breakers; or the idyllic autumn scene in which Toby chuffs along beside a farm with its haystack and chicken coops, while a horse and cart (accompanied by an eager dog) wends its way down a nearby lane.

The Eight Famous Engines is very much a continuation of the preceding book, since Percy (puffed up by his heroic navigation of the floods) boasts that he is unafraid of water and even cheeks Henry by singing:

Once an engine attached to a train
Was afraid of a few drops of rain . . .

A few pages later, Percy overshoots the buffers on the Quay and slithers helplessly into the sea. John Kenney's illustration shows the unfortunate engine up to his nose in sea water being severely reprimanded by the Fat Controller:

> *'Please, Sir, get me out Sir, I'm truly sorry Sir.'*
> *'No, Percy, we cannot do that till high tide. I hope it will teach you to obey Orders.'*
> *'Yes, Sir,' Percy shivered miserably. He was cold. Fish were playing hide and seek through his wheels. The tide rose higher and higher.*

In the book's final story, the eight famous engines of the title – Edward, Gordon, Henry, Thomas, James, Toby, Percy and Duck – discover that the Fat Controller has 'a plan':

> *'The people of England,' he said, 'read about Us in the Books; but they do not think that we are real . . . .'*
> *'Shame!' squeaked Percy. The Fat Controller glared. Percy subsided.*
> *' . . . so,' he continued, 'I am taking My Engines to England to show them.'*
> *'Hooray! Hooray!' the engines whistled.*

Led by Gordon, the cavalcade puffs off to London: a metaphor for the way in which the twelve small books that had made those engines famous had steamed out of Wilbert Awdry's imagination and into our collective consciousness.

CHAPTER ELEVEN

Steaming On!

It was April 1957 and Wilbert was required to give the Vicar's report at the Annual Parochial Church Meeting at St Edmund's, Emneth. He decided to do so – in verse – as if written, not by himself, but by his congregation. He entitled it 'Our Vicar':

It's four years since our vicar came,
And we have gone on much the same.
He isn't either prim or grim,
And we are getting used to him.
He's neither High, nor very Low,
Some people think him rather slow,
Sometimes he forgets his lines –
Announces things for curious times!

That particular confession was probably inspired by an occasion when, as he was giving out notices of service times for the coming week, he inadvertently announced Evensong at four-thirty instead of the usual six-thirty. Later in the service, a note was passed to him from a member of the congregation containing a rhymed observation on this change:

Sunday next, oh, dear, oh Lor'
Evensong's at half past four!

As he smiled and tucked the verse into his cassock, Wilbert probably reflected on the fact that this little jest was indicative of the rapport that he had established with the people of Emneth. 'Fen-men,' he says, 'have something of a dire reputation, and I decided if I hadn't made an impression of some sort within six years I would move. Instead, I found that, after four years, I could walk into any house in the parish without having to be invited.' Wilbert had earned that freedom.

'Anything that he took on,' says Veronica, 'was treated as having equal importance with everything else.' He introduced Children's Church on Sunday afternoons, which gave young parishioners a shortened form of service and – through electing their own churchwardens and other officials – taught them something of how a parish church was run. Wilbert also ran a youth club and a cricket team and helped choirman, Cyril Taylor, organise a concert party – which he also participated in – to raise money for building a church hall. And, in all these activities, he never forgot one important thing: always to give credit where credit was due – even if it were paid in the form of limericks:

> If you have to arrange for a 'Feed',
> And expert assistance you need;
> You can always say gaily
> 'We'll ask Mrs Bailey,'
> And she'll get it all done at top speed!

> In a house that is swarming with cats
> Live the Buttricks who beat the church mats.
> They sweep out the floor
> And wage ceaseless war
> On spiders, and woodworm and bats.

Margaret – herself a member of the church's team of polishers and broom-wielders – also made a strong impression on the people of Emneth. Veronica, who describes her mother as the 'doer' in the family, believes that the secret of Margaret's success was that whilst she appeared to be a dutiful vicar's wife, involved with running the Mother's Union and the Sunday School, she never actually did anything simply out of duty.

In addition to running a home and helping with parish work, Margaret was employed, for ten years, as a supply teacher. Having declined an invitation to teach at Wisbech High School, because her own daughters were pupils there, she accepted a post at the Queen's Girls Secondary Modern school. 'It was,' says Veronica, 'a rather tough school, and she was only a little lady, but she had such an aura of sincerity and quiet strength about her that she never experienced any problems; and when, years later, a former pupil confessed to having been in awe of her, she was utterly astonished.'

As in any vicarage marriage, Margaret encountered a great many people; her unique gifts, as the present writer can testify, were an ability to make people feel instantly at ease and to show genuine interest in everyone she met. These qualities were to earn her, over the years, a great deal of respect and love.

Recalling his childhood, Christopher Awdry once described the atmosphere of the family home as 'fairly quiet and pretty contented' and said that he remembers looking up to his father, not just as a parent, but also as a clergyman, since, 'in those days, a clergyman of a parish was still pretty important'. Whilst admiting that 'if he said "Behave", then we behaved', Christopher added: 'He wasn't a "Victorian" father by any means, but he was the head of the house and what he said went.'

Even Margaret – who very occasionally objected to being thought of as the wife of Thomas the Tank Engine and pointed out that she was a person in her own right – staunchly supported Wilbert in all aspects of his ministry, even in his persistent, sometimes stubborn, determination to achieve something (however remote) on which he had set his sights. Two such issues are jokingly referred to in that poem which he delivered in 1957; one was Wilbert's wish that Christenings should be held not, as they then tended to be, privately on a Sunday afternoon, 'but right in public, during Church' at morning or evening prayer, where the entire congregation would be witness to the promises made by the godparents. The other matter concerned the low attendance at early morning services of Holy Communion:

Now in his bonnet there's a bee!
He often tells us straight that we
Should all be present at H. C.
But really! There he goes too far
We're much more comfy as we are
Staying in bed on Sunday late
We cannot struggle forth for eight.

The poem ends with an admission of his tendency towards resoluteness:

It might be worth our while to try it
At least 'twill keep our Vicar quiet!
He'll talk and talk and talk till we
Observe both sacraments, you see.

Wilbert's humanity, his simple (but never simplistic) faith and his straightforward philosophy of life, aided by Margaret's warmth, humour and gregariousness, meant that the Awdrys – two very committed people, complementing one another – not only got on well with people, but were fondly regarded:

Our Vicar certainly would be
Not everybody's cup of tea
Some people cannot stand the bloke;
But one thing, he *can* take a joke.

Wilbert shared the sense of humour of many of his parishioners, among whom there was a decided fondness for practical jokes. Most of the japes and leg-pulling went on in the local hostelries, The Duke of Wellington and The Queen's Head, in both of which Wilbert was always a welcome visitor, enjoying a half-pint of mild-and-bitter and puffing on his beloved pipe:

He's seldom seen without his pipe,
It bubbles and is rather ripe!
It's old and crusted, had hard knocks,
Some say he smokes old army socks!

Mrs Wellbourn, the landlady of The Duke of Wellington was especially noted for her cooking. 'There was always a plate on the bar counter,' says Wilbert, 'piled up with home-made meat pies – and very good they were too!' Customers would pay for their pies with their beer, but one particular regular would come in, pick up a pie, take a bite, call out: 'I'll have one of these, Missus,' and then always try to leave without paying.

The landlady eventually tired of this and, one day, tipped off her regulars not to eat any of the pies which were set out, as usual, on the counter. 'In bustled the reluctant payer,' says Wilbert, 'seized a pie, took a bite and then, with a look of horror on his face, yelled: "Cor! What have you got in this pie, Missus?" ' The answer was a very special pie-filling using meat caught with mouse-traps in the cellar!

The landlord of The Queen's Head, Charlie Thompson, also relished a good joke, and, on one occasion, decided to take the rise out of George Claxton, a market gardener who habitually claimed to grow the best beans, peas and other produce in the area. One Market Day, Charlie went to Wisbech and returned with some cod's roes which his wife baked until they were tiny round pellets. When George Claxton next came into the pub, the landlord showed these to him and asked if he knew what they were. Falling for the gag, George confidently declared them to be seeds and, in view of his legendary green fingers, offered to take some home and plant them.

Those in on the ruse were so pleased at having fooled George, they told the story a little too freely so that George also got to hear the truth and decided to turn the joke on the jokers. A few days later, when asked how the seeds were doing, George replied: 'They're coming along fine! Couldn't be better!' Charlie Thompson and the others were astonished and when, eventually, they were invited to go and see for themselves, they simply couldn't resist. On arriving at George's garden, however, they found row upon row of sprats, planted tail downwards in the soil!

Wilbert enjoyed sharing a laugh with the locals and although he may have been viewed as something of an eccentric, the fact that people laughed *with* him, rather than *at* him was undoubtedly due to his ability to laugh at himself – as the self-mocking doggerel of 'Our Vicar' testifies:

> Sometimes he preaches rather well,
> At others, he's as dull as . . . . !
> Some wonder if he's any brains –
> He's int'rested in railway trains!
> That's not as soft though as it looks;
> He writes a lot of little books
> Which children like, so he must be
> Just as intelligent as you and me.
> He must do this, for, sad but true,
> It's hard to live on parson's Screw.

Indeed, raising a family and paying for the upkeep of a large vicarage left the Awdrys – even allowing for Margaret's earnings – with little spare cash; in fact, the children quite often had to make do with second-hand clothes, although, looking back, all three of them say that any anxieties which their parents may have been experiencing were kept well hidden from them. The money earned by Wilbert's 'little books' was, therefore, a welcome addition to the family income.

Although, to begin with, the titles had been purchased outright for a flat fee – the usual practice at the time, especially for picture books – Edmund Ward nevertheless acknowledged the Railway Series' success with occasional gifts of money. However, as more books continued to appear, Ward's editor, Eric Marriott, felt that there was an injustice in Wilbert being paid a flat fee for what was rapidly becoming a best-selling series. As a result, Ward agreed to give Wilbert, *ex gratia*, a royalty of one penny a copy on every book sold. 'Which,' says Wilbert, 'with the books then selling for four shillings each, was really not so bad.' It was, in fact, a very generous gesture since the arrangement was also to apply to back titles.

Ward prominently promoted each new addition to the Railway Series in its catalogues – the cover of one has a list of notable authors headed by 'A. A. Milne and the Rev. W Awdry' – but the backlist was also vitally important since, at the time, it represented some 70% of the company's income. The Railway Series, now comprising a dozen titles, was a national institution as well as being widely known in English-speaking countries around the world.

John Welch, who had been appointed Sales Manager in 1949, vigorously pursued sales, not just within the United Kingdom, but also overseas; and, by 1950, the year of *Troublesome Engines*, Ward had sales representation in Australia, Canada, New Zealand, South Africa and the U.S.A. Two years later they had added India and the Rhodesias; and, by 1955, there were representatives in Argentina, Uruguay, Europe and the Far East. The following year, that in which *Percy the Small Engine* was published, Ward had expanded their overseas markets into Ceylon, Pakistan, West and East Africa, Mauritius, Iraq, Persia, Malta, Gibraltar, the British West Indies and the Pacific Islands.

This development is reflected in a selection of unsolicited testimonials which Eric Marriott included in one of Ward's catalogues. In addition to letters from London, Edinburgh, Liverpool, York and Ipswich ('May a busy mother thank you for the Railway Series?'), there were as many others from far flung locations:

> HQ Allied Forces S. EUROPE: 'My name is J for Julian and I am three years old so I cannot write myself yet and have asked my Mummy to write for me because I want to tell you how much I enjoy your train books.'
>
> S. AUSTRALIA: 'John is five and Tom is three, they are both interested in *Thomas the Tank Engine* and *James the Red Engine* and have read them until they are worn out!'
>
> WELLINGTON, NEW ZEALAND: 'May I thank you for the joyous hours you have given our little son? He has the whole set of your delightful engine books.'
>
> NEW YORK: 'My five-year-old son finds these books the most delightful and constantly entertaining of all the books he has ever seen. Those engines have become part of the family – important members!'

Two more appreciative (but exhausted) American parents – Mr and Mrs A. J. Moffatt, of Hewlett, New York – wrote to the author, describing the effect the books had had on their four-year-old son, Robert: 'We are bombarded with questions *ad infinitum*. For instance, "What would Henry say if he were coupled on behind Gordon and Gordon was going too fast?" Gordon would sing: "Oh come along we're rather late!" and the coaches would sing: "You can't get away etc." These questions and conjectures go on and on, early and late, day after day! Other books have been favourites for a while but none have captured his delighted interest so wholeheartedly as your tank engine books, so thanks from him and from us.'

The stories even achieved popularity in countries where children have little, if any, personal experience of railway trains. George Awdry recalled his brother receiving 'a bitter complaint from someone in Switzerland who had had to drag her infant all across county to find a working engine!'

It became clear that the success of the Railway Series was twofold: the stories were not simply loved by young readers, they were also approved of by parents (the chief purchasers of children's books) as being entertaining, morally correct – they were, after all, written by a clergyman – and even educational: 'John,' wrote one grateful parent, 'is learning to read at his own request, chiefly so he can read the books for himself.'

Although Edmund Ward had never favoured producing 'spin-offs' to those books, Eric Marriott saw the sales potential offered by such an enthusiastic world market and, with the death of Edmund Ward in 1957, began a programme of diversification that can now be seen as having laid the foundations for the present day merchandising of Thomas the Tank Engine and Friends.

Inspired by the publisher Sir Stanley Unwin's observation that 'Trade follows the book', Marriott launched several ingenious by-products based on the Railway Series. One such idea was 'The Railway Press-Out Model Books', advertised as 'a wish come true for thousands of young children!' That wish was then identified by an enthusiastic copywriter: 'How many young followers of the Rev. Awdry's famous Railway Series have not at some time or other wished for actual models of the jolly engine characters to play with?'

The question was, of course, rhetorical; what mattered was that, for two shillings and sixpence, those 'young followers' could purchase models of Thomas, Percy, Gordon and James, complete with coaches or tenders, 'all ready to press-out, fold and glue'. As well as 'full instructions for assembling the engine', each book was advertised as containing 'a short story' – although what customers did not know was that this was for the totally pragmatic reason that, without a story, it would have been classified as an item of stationery, rather a book, and would, therefore, have been liable to Purchase Tax!

Edmund Ward's 1958 catalogue also announced the publication of *The Rev. Awdry's Railway Map of the Island of Sodor*. Also priced at 2s. 6d., it was (like the best Ordnance Survey Maps) linen-backed, but printed (unlike Ordnance Survey Maps) in bright colours with distinctive 1950s lettering. There was a nursery wallpaper border of engines, elephants, cows, turntables and Fat Controllers, and the map itself was fancifully embellished with boats, buoys, seagulls, dolphins and mermaids. 'When completely open,' read the advertising blurb, 'it will make an excellent decoration for a child's bedroom wall.' It also had a key to locations in the stories – 'Mrs Kyndley's Cottage',

'Harold the Helicopter lives at this airfield', 'Here is Trevor the Traction-engine's scrap yard' – as well as showing the sites of the various exploits: 'Here James had hiccoughs!' – 'Here Gordon fell in a ditch.' – 'Here Percy fell into the sea.' – 'Here Thomas fell down a mine.' – 'Here the engines met H. M. The Queen.'

The same catalogue contained a photograph of two boys and a girl (with a teddy bear and a Labrador dog) sitting round a gramophone. 'Now records too!' ran the copy, 'What a bedtime thrill for children, the Rev. W. Awdry, *in his own voice*, telling two of the railway stories with the background effects of *real* engines.' For thirteen shillings, you could buy a 7-inch, long-playing record on which – in a precise, slightly singsong voice – Wilbert narrated the stories of 'Edward's Day Out' and 'Edward and Gordon' from *The Three Railway Engines*. These readings were spasmodically (and rather crudely) interrupted by various authentic-sounding chuffings, puffings, steamings and whistlings as well as such unlikely sounds as a few coughs and mumbles in illustration of a line about the driver and fireman coming along to start work.

It is an extraordinary thing that the Church of England vicar who had first told this little story, fifteen years earlier, to his young son who was ill in bed, should have found himself telling that same story – on a commercial gramophone recording – for an entire generation of other people's children.

In the same year in which Wilbert cut his first (and only) disc, he came up with a new idea for a book that was *not* about railway engines. It was a story about a motor car and, appropriately enough, the inspiration for it had come during a car journey. 'We were driving through Atherstone, near Tamworth, in the Midlands,' says Wilbert, 'and we met a lot of three-wheeled cars driving away from the works where they were made. Our children decided they looked like beetles, so that is what we called them.' Whenever, thereafter, the family went out in their car, they played a game of car-spotting and Hilary remembers getting extra points each time she saw 'a beetle'.

Belinda the Beetle was published in 1958 – not by Ward, but by Brockhampton Press, who had approached Wilbert with a request to write a children's book. As the title reveals, the central character was a heroine rather than a hero, which was an interesting development, after all those male engines:

> *Mr William Whisker finished his breakfast, and came down to open the showroom. He pushed up the shutters, and unlocked the door. Then, in the morning light, he looked at his cars.*
> *There were Maisie the Minx, Jacky the Jaguar, and Susie the Snipe . . . He*

thought how much he loved them, and how he hated having to sell them . . . 'One good thing,' he thought, 'I shan't lose Belinda. No one will want to buy her,' And he went over to the corner where she stood, and stroked her lovingly. Belinda was a little car with three wheels, she was painted red, and her number plate was BLN 111.
Mr Whisker was fond of Belinda. He was sorry for her too. She had had an accident with a lorry and had never been the same car since.

With the help of George Egg (a decidedly 'good egg') Belinda is soon back in the prime of vehicular life and the suitably bewhiskered Mr Whisker eventually sells her to a friendly local family: Mr Exel, the Vicar of Arlstead, his wife and two children, Susan and John. It isn't long, however, before Belinda and her new owners are caught up in an exciting adventure involving stolen jewels and two shady villains called Brown and Snoop.

As a full-length children's novel, *Belinda the Beetle* proved that Wilbert could handle a sustained narrative in an engaging style, full of lively exploits and featuring a range of human characters as diverse as the denizens of the railway shed. The children's characters were particularly well drawn:

First came Susan, hop-skip-and-jumping. She looked excited about something. Susan was ten. She had pig-tails, a round face, a broad grin, and a long tongue. Her Brother John came behind. He was eight, and smaller, slower and dreamier than Susan, but he was a very solid little boy. He adored Susan, though he didn't let her boss him.

The little red car's adventures were flamboyantly illustrated by Ionicus (Joshua Charles Armitage), a prolific artist and illustrator closely associated with books by P. G. Wodehouse, R. G. G. Price and Ogden Nash. Wilbert Awdry asked to see the 'roughs' for Ionicus' illustrations, in much the same way as he was then seeing all the illustrations for the Railway Series. The artist, however, refused to submit his pictures for comment and they were published without the author's approval.

Ionicus' illustrations, like all his work, were drawn with a strong bold line, but Wilbert disliked what he felt to be a caricature style unsuited to the story. When, therefore, a sequel – *Belinda Beats the Band* – was commissioned in 1961, Wilbert agreed to write it on the strict understanding that John Kenney, the artist of the Railway Series, be asked to provide the illustrations, which he duly did in a more realistic, homely style.

Belinda Beats the Band opens with a dramatic flourish that demonstrates Wilbert's increasing confidence as a storyteller: 'The lorry swerved, bumping on the grass verge, then swung back to the road. The driver mopped his face. "That was a near thing," he exclaimed. "Lucky that car was red or I wouldn't have seen it in time . . ." ' The red car, of course, is Belinda, and she and the Excel family are soon being bumped into a new adventure featuring a gang of crooks, a kidnapping, stolen goods and secret underground passageways.

Wilbert drew on personal experiences to provide some of the detail for the story. For example, the Exel family are about to set off on holiday, exchanging parishes with another Vicar, as the Awdrys themselves did on several occasions; their destination is Tinwell, a fictionalised version of Knapwell (Wilbert's other parish when he was Vicar of Elsworth) complete with a ruined rectory and a history of having once been a Black Death village.

Belinda Beats the Band is full of action and suspense but, as with the first book, the real strength of the story lies in its anthropomorphic heroine and her two young friends, whose behaviour is clearly drawn from first-hand observation of children:

> *'Wait for me, Susan!'*
> *'We can't wait, John. You must hurry.'*
> *'How can I hurry?' panted the little boy. 'I've got a stitch.'*
> *'Bother your stitches,' said his unsympathetic sister. 'You're always getting them.'*
> *'I'm not.'*
> *'You are.'*
> *'I'm not.'*
> *'Well anyway,' said Susan, 'you always seem to get them when we have to hurry. I bet you only pretend, so's I have to wait for you like I'm doing now.'*
> *'I don't pretend,' said John indignantly. 'Mummy says I'm braver than you when I hurt myself.'*
> *Susan knew this was true, and she was rather ashamed of it; but she wasn't going to admit it.*
> *'Anyway,' she argued, 'I'm bigger than you, so my pains must be bigger than yours. So I feel them more.'*
> *'How do you know?' countered John. 'You can't feel my feels.'*

Belinda herself is slightly temperamental and – like many a real car – sometimes has to be coaxed into doing what she is supposed to do. Her fusspot personality is as deftly (and effortlessly) drawn as those of the Awdry railway engines. Languishing in a ditch, her pride more dented than her bodywork,

Belinda complains to George Egg about the indignity of her position: 'Please get me out, George. I don't like being sideways. It's not what I'm used to . . . It's so upsetting. I don't like being upset, I don't. These lorries! They shouldn't be allowed . . . Do you know what I'm going to do with the next one? I'm going to toot my horn at him, telling him to get out of my way, and I'm going to go straight for him and make him go in a ditch and see how he likes it.'

'It is not always easy,' wrote the head of a one-teacher school in Yorkshire, 'to find stories to suit a group of children aged 5-11, but yours absolutely fill the bill and hold them all enthralled, particularly your "Belinda" books. Will you please let me know when you are having another one published?' There wasn't to be a third book about Belinda; but, even if the little car never achieved the same popularity as Thomas and his cohorts, Wilbert never lost his affection for her.

Several years later, Richard Chambers recalls driving home to Birmingham from Exeter University in his own car – 'If,' he says, 'you could call it a car!' – a make of three-wheeler called a Frisky. *En route*, he dropped off his girlfriend, Veronica Awdry, at her parents' home, then in Stroud: 'It was my first encounter with Wilbert, and I will never forget the sight of this tall clergyman with shortish grey hair, ignoring his daughter who he hadn't seen for some time, and walking round the car saying, "It's a Belinda!" '

When both books were republished in paperback for young readers of the 1990s, Belinda was modified into a less imaginative vehicle – 'a little Volkswagen Beetle' – and her adventures were re-drawn by the artist Val Biro who, some years earlier, had begun writing and illustrating a series of picture books about another anthropomorphic motor – Gumdrop the Vintage Car.

In one of Belinda's impassioned protests about lorries, she describes them as, 'Nasty, smelly, dieselly things, taking up all the road,' and another nasty, dieselly object made its appearance in the thirteenth title in the Railway Series, *Duck and the Diesel Engine*:

> *'Good morning,' purred Diesel in an oily voice, 'pleased to meet you, Duck. Is that James?* – and *Henry?* –and *Gordon too? I am delighted to meet such famous engines.' And he purred towards them.*

The introduction of Diesel marks the end of an age of innocence on the Island of Sodor. Despite passing references to Nationalisation and links between the railways of Sodor and those on the mainland, the average reader would scarcely have given thought to the time period in which the stories were set; the various adventures just happened – whether in the past or the present couldn't have mattered less. Now, however, an engine arrived in the yard that was very much of its day.

The Railway Series' editor, Eric Marriott was conscious of the fact that more and more diesels were being seen on the railway tracks of Britain and thought that, 'in order to keep the Series up to date', it would be a good idea if a diesel were to join the Fat Controller's engines. Marriott put this suggestion to Wilbert Awdry on several occasions and, for a long time, the author resisted. 'I kept being pestered,' recalls Wilbert, 'and I eventually agreed to introduce a diesel.'

The engine which appeared in *Duck and the Diesel Engine* was not, however, quite what Eric Marriott had been expecting. The Fat Controller introduces Diesel, who has arrived on Sodor for a trial period and details Duck to teach him about the yard. However, the new engine quickly displays an arrogant attitude:

> *'Your worthy Sir Topham Hatt thinks I need to learn. He is mistaken. We Diesels don't need to learn. We know everything. We come into a yard and improve it. We are revolutionary.'*
> *'Oh!' said Duck, 'If you're revo-thingummy, perhaps you would collect my trucks, while I fetch Gordon's coaches.'*
> *Diesel, delighted to show off, purred away.*

Wilbert's personal dislike of diesel locomotion undoubtedly coloured the characterisation of Diesel, and the smooth-talking engine is revealed to be a thoroughly bad lot. Significantly, Diesel is the only engine character without a personal name; he is simply called by the name of what he is.

Diesel is soon making trouble: telling lies, siding with the trucks against the engines and spreading rumours of bad things which poor Duck is supposed to have said about the other engines. John Kenney, now well into his stride as illustrator with his second book, depicts Diesel as looking as smooth and oily as Wilbert describes and having a face capable of a range of angry, malicious, contemptuous and sneeringly vindictive expressions.

After the difficulties experienced in dealing with Reginald Dalby, Wilbert enjoyed a much happier relationship with John Kenney. Wilbert paid several visits to the artist and his wife at their home in Leicestershire and Mrs Peggy Kenney remembers her first impression of the author as 'tall, thin and scholarly with a long woolly scarf'. John and Peggy Kenney also visited the Awdrys at Emneth Vicarage where they played croquet – a game constantly interrupted by the family's hens which had taken up residence on the lawn and declined to be moved!

The *Times Educational Supplement* praised *Duck and the Diesel Engine*, saying: 'the Reverend Awdry is more ingenious than ever'; and the book was significant not just for its inclusion of a non-steam locomotive, but because it was also the first book in the series to feature a real-life engine.

The book opens with an illustration by John Kenney showing members of a Railway Society eagerly taking photographs of Duck and the other engines. Looking at this picture, the present writer spotted amongst the rail enthusiasts, a clergyman – wearing glasses, flat-cap and vicar's collar – introducing someone, wearing a bow tie, to the green distinctive shape of Duck with his G.W.R. letters. The clergyman is clearly Wilbert Awdry, but who is the man in the bow tie? A possible answer was provided by Eric Marriott who, by chance, had also just recently noticed the two men pictured in the crowd, and who immediately recalled someone who *always* wore a bow tie – Reginald Dalby. Did Kenney, as a little joke, include his predecessor in this picture? If so – and if Wilbert had told him about his ups and downs with Dalby – then maybe the Vicar in the picture is saying to the artist: 'Now, *that* is what Duck is supposed to look like!'

Duck soon discovers that the Railway Society have travelled to Sodor hauled by another (and very famous) Great Western Railway engine, City of Truro, the first engine to go 100 miles an hour.

City of Truro was a two-cylinder 4-4-0, built at Swindon by G. J. Churchward with the capability of steaming steadily for hours at a stretch; the 'famous run' had taken place on 9th May, 1904, when Driver Clements took the Ocean Mail special from Plymouth to Bristol at speeds which touched at least 100 miles an hour. It was a record that was to hold for almost thirty years; although, at the time, the achievement was not publicised by Paddington in case the thought of travelling at such speeds should alarm the public!

Writing of this event in one of a series of articles entitled 'Locomotives Which Made History', for the *Church of England Newspaper*, Wilbert Awdry described the final stages of the run after City of Truro had reached what has been claimed as a speed of 102.3 miles an hour:

> After a slight check to 68 m.p.h. at Taunton, driver Clements rapidly accelerated: 74 m.p.h. at Bridgewater became 77 over the flats and 'City of Truro' brought her train to Pyle Hill, Bristol, in just over 120 minutes for the 128 miles from Plymouth.
>
> She was sound in steam and cool in bearing as when she had left the shed that morning. In fact, she could have taken the train on to Paddington with

no trouble at all, but as she was short of coal, they brought on 'Duke of Connaught' instead.

Wilbert, who wrote that piece nearly sixty years after City of Truro had made her record-breaking run, had first seen the engine, as he puts it, 'stuffed' in the old York Railway Museum. At that time there was no expectation of its ever running again; however, during the 1950s, special trains pulled by historic locomotives became popular with rail enthusiasts and, in 1957, City of Truro enjoyed a renewed (albeit short) lease of life. The following year, the engine met Duck with whom he became firm friends 'and talked "Great Western" till late at night'.

Before long, Gordon is rocketing down the track panting: 'He did it! I'll do it! He did it! I'll do it!' One of John Kenney's finest pictures shows the result of Gordon's attempt 'to do a "City of Truro" ': autumn trees on the hillside bend in the wind as Gordon, trailing clouds of steam and smoke, races over the viaduct. But disaster strikes for the would-be record-breaker when the wind creeps under his loose dome, lifts it off and blows it away – leaving him, like City of Truro, a domeless engine!

Gordon, however, is not the only casualty in *Duck and the Diesel Engine*. Drawing on a real-life railway incident at Hull that had been reported in *The Railway Gazette*, Wilbert shows Duck – having prevented a more serious accident but still in desperate straits – overshooting the buffers and crashing into a barber's shop: 'There was a sliding groaning crash, and part of the wall caved in. The customer jumped nervously; but the barber held him down. "It's only an engine," he said calmly, and went on lathering.'

As for Diesel, if Eric Marriott had once entertained hopes of that 'revo-thingummy' engine becoming a regular character in the Railway Series, he was to be disappointed. At the end of the book, after getting Duck into trouble and telling more lies about Henry, Diesel is sent away. Some may have regretted the passing of one of the few real villains to appear in the series, but as far as Wilbert was concerned, there was no choice in the matter: not only did Diesel have to go, there was absolutely no chance of his ever coming back. 'Diesel,' says Wilbert emphatically, 'had put himself beyond the pale.'

Nevertheless, the author's introductory letter quotes the Fat Controller as saying: 'I do not believe that all Diesels are troublesome', and, as if to prove his point, a really useful diesel engine, called Rusty, made his appearance in the very next book. The eponymous hero of *The Little Old Engine*, published in 1959, was Skarloey and the book was the second title to be inspired by the Talyllyn Railway.

From 1952, the Awdrys had continued to visit the Talyllyn for their annual holidays and, on and off, spent five summers at Towyn in Wales. The children, however, were now growing up and a compromise arrangement had to be arrived at for the sake of Margaret and the girls, who were becoming increasingly bored by railway visits. As a result, visits to the Talyllyn (on which they were sometimes joined by Wilbert's brother, George) were alternated with family holidays elsewhere.

Christopher who, in 1954, had got a choral exhibition to Worksop College, a public school in north Nottinghamshire, retained his inherited interest in railways, but recalls that very few of the non-railway holidays were completely free of them! He remembers, for example, a holiday when he was eighteen and the family was going to be together for the last time before the children went off to do different things: 'It was on the Isle of Man and was certainly never intended to be a specifically railway holiday; but, inevitably, there turned out to be a fair number of trains in it!' There was also a year when Christopher and his uncle George went to Towyn without Wilbert: 'Probably because Mum insisted he had a holiday with her for a change!'

Photographs taken on railway holidays often show Margaret looking at various 'dirty objects' beside some abandoned line with what can only be described as a bemused expression; but, however difficult Margaret found it to muster much excitement for some of their expeditions, she was extremely tolerant of all aspects of her husband's passion for railways, and doubtless realised that the Talyllyn was providing much needed inspiration to keep the Railway Series running.

The Little Old Engine contained all the usual *un*usual adventures such as the accident which occurs when a line of trucks, loaded with slate, hurtle down a rope-worked incline (in the hope of playing a trick on Sir Handel) and smash into poor Peter Sam by mistake. With hindsight, some of these later titles might be thought to lack the excitement found in the first ten books, but since Wilbert was no longer writing to entertain his own children, or even trying out the stories on them, there is a feeling that the books – although *never* without their railway authenticity – are being more driven by industry than by inspiration.

Nevertheless, because Wilbert knew that his stories would be read aloud, it remained vital that they sound right and flow smoothly. When, therefore, his live audience had grown up and left home, he began reading the stories onto a tape recorder in order to be able to hear them on the ear. Margaret's judgement remained invaluable: 'She could always tell me if it was a good story or not,' says Wilbert, 'she was not a great railway enthusiast, but – maybe because of that – she was a good audience.'

As for *The Little Old Engine*, the verdict of a contemporary reviewer was that the author had written 'a captivating book that will not disappoint his followers'. For one thing, the book introduces several interesting new characters: in addition to the inelegant, but well-meaning, Rusty, there is Duncan, a rude, bouncy engine with a fondness – in the lingo of the fifties – for doing 'Rock 'n' Roll'. Having previously worked in a factory, Duncan also uses strong language – especially when, as a result of his rocking 'n' rolling, he gets stuck in a tunnel: 'I'm a plain blunt engine . . . I speak as I find. Tunnels should be tunnels, and not rabbit holes. This Railway is no good at all.'

There are also a variety of new coaches and guard's vans going under such names as Cora, Ada, Jane, Mabel, Gertrude and Millicent, who has a seat for passengers and a tiny cupboard-like space for the Guard – an arrangement of which Peter Sam does not approve: 'Guards are very important. They need Vans. They shouldn't be put into cupboards.'

Skarloey, the little old engine itself, returns to the line, fully mended and is visited by a television crew who film him and the other engines at work on the line. Just such a programme about the Talyllyn Railway had been televised in 1956 with Wilbert taking part in the film as a guard. The photographs which Wilbert took on that occasion formed the basis for John Kenney's illustrations.

Sir Handel, it should be noted, refuses to take part – 'Vulgar, I call it. Fancy traipsing about making an exhibition of yourselves. I won't do it, I tell you. Tellysomething indeed!' – and, as a punishment, is kept in the shed and taken to pieces for the benefit of the cameras! It is rare to find oneself in sympathy with the cantankerous old engine, but the introduction of such contemporary concepts as television and rock and roll are oddly anachronistic in what, hitherto, had seemed to be a timeless world.

The Little Old Engine contains a further acknowledgment of a world outside that which is inhabited by the famous railway engines when Skarloey's Owner tells everyone how proud the railway is of its Little Old Engine, who is ninety-five years old and as good as new; there is, he says, 'nothing like him anywhere'. Skarloey, of course, knows better; and, on a page facing a fine illustration of Talyllyn by John Kenney, he explains: 'Another engine came to be mended too, called Talyllyn. When the workmen saw us together, they laughed and called us their "little old twins". Talyllyn told me about his Railway. It is a lovely one, at Towyn in Wales.'

It could be argued that anything taking the limelight from the engines of Sodor represents a negative aspect to the careful creation of authentic links between the Island and our world. However, the inclusion of occasional eulogies in praise of railway preservation societies such as the Talyllyn have undoubtedly given a tremendous boost to their work.

'. . . I often think of Talyllyn. He's 95 years old too, just like me.
'Please go and see him, all of you, and wish him "Dry rails and good running" from Skarloey, his "Little Old Twin".'

The next volume in the Railway Series featured a very different pair of twins. Published in 1960, *The Twin Engines* opens with Henry, Gordon and James making 'boiler-aching' complaints about having to pull goods trains: 'Dirty trucks, dirty sidings. Ugh!' The Fat Controller, however, has a solution – he has ordered, from Scotland, a new engine for goods work. But problems begin when not one but *two* engines arrive. Since neither has a number, it proves difficult for Sir Topham Hatt to know which engine ought to be kept and which returned:

Donald and Douglas, who do not want to be separated, spend the rest of the book trying *not* to reveal which of them is which. Eventually, after various mishaps (including a signal box which is accidentally demolished and a spiteful Brakevan that is smashed to smithereens) the Twins prove themselves Useful Engines and, thanks to a Deputation (or as Percy calls it a 'Desperation') from the other engines, are allowed to stay.

'I wanted a couple of goods engines,' recalls Wilbert, 'and decided that Caledonian twins might be particularly suitable. As for their accents, Scottish friends who read the story said that Donald and Douglas were a couple of typical Glaswegians!'

Not that everyone, however, was able to understand what they were saying. Their very first words, when asked by the Fat Controller how they had lost their numbers, were: 'They maun hae slyly slippit aff Sirr. Ye ken hoo it is.' Wilbert admits to having received at least one protest: 'I had a letter from a very harassed German lady who wrote and said, "English I know, but what is THIS?" '

Another complaint – not about the text, but about the illustrations – was received from Mrs Theresa Stewart of Doncaster: 'Our small son aged five bought *The Twin Engines* and found to his great disappointment that you have a new illustrator and, sadly, he doesn't seem to understand about lamps on the front of engines. One of the pleasures for me, as well as being the mouthpiece of reading your books, is their correctness of detail. We do hope this is only an oversight and not a precedent.'

Such a letter obviously demanded a serious response: 'Thank you for your letter pointing out the deficiencies in the illustrations of *The Twin Engines*. I checked through the pictures immediately after reading your letter and was astonished to find it correct. It is indeed a shocking oversight. In only one picture, that is on page 21, is there a headlamp drawn. Will you please give your son my most humble apologies and tell him that I will do my very best to see that the shocking mistake doesn't occur again.'

In closing, Wilbert defended his 'new illustrator' (who was responsible for far fewer errors than his predecessor): 'The present illustrator has been on the job since 1957, he's really very good and takes an endless amount of trouble.' As, indeed he did. John Kenney's pictures for *The Twin Engines*, even if they are *sans* headlamps, are among his best work: there are superbly drawn pictures of the Twins (combining strong engine shapes and engaging personalities) and a splendid portrait of the Fat Controller in his office, the very image of power and authority. Elsewhere, in Kenney's evocative snow scenes, Sir Topham Hatt perhaps betrays an underlying humorousness by sporting a long black and yellow scarf that looks all the more startling for being worn with morning suit and topper.

The continuing success of the Railway Series led Wilbert, in 1960, to branch out into journalism and begin a long-running association with the *Church of England Newspaper*. It was in November 1959 that the newspaper changed hands and Wilbert Awdry received a letter from the Reverend John King who, the following year, was to take over as editor:

> One of the things I am keen about is that the C.E.N. shall appeal to laymen as well as clergy, and particularly to young people – young married couples with children, etc. I am wondering whether there is any possibility of your contributing some children's stories – not necessarily religious? The only ground on which I can approach a complete stranger like yourself is that we – like everyone else – immensely enjoy your engine books (and I believe we also both are St Peter's Hall men).

Wilbert responded, showing interest, but asking a number of questions: 'What would be the position with regard to the copyright of the things which I might write for you? Would you want short stories weekly? or a serial? and what sort of length? Would you want continuous regular contributions, or so to speak, in spasms, letting others have a go from time to time?'

John King replied that his ideas about the Children's Page he was planning for the *Church of England Newspaper* were 'as yet extremely fluid', but proposing 'a series of, say, 500 word stories that would be suitable for parents to read to their children'. The suggestion was for either a three month series of weekly stories or a serial in twelve weekly instalments to which Wilbert would retain copyright and for which he would be paid (the one question he *hadn't* asked) 3½ guineas per story or instalment. 'Perhaps,' wrote King, 'a theme quite different from railway engines would commend itself to you.' In the event, inspiration came not from railway engines but from *model* railway engines.

CHAPTER TWELVE

All Change!

WILBERT had dreamt of becoming the Brunel of model railway engineering. But the problems he experienced with his ambitious railway layout in the attics at Emneth Vicarage eventually became too much for him: 'I was mostly occupied with maintenance and, since the layout was constantly under repair, it consequently never approached completion!'

The opportunity to embark on a potentially less troublesome project had come in 1955, when Wilbert was asked to build a simple 4 mm. scale layout for the following year's Wisbech Trades Fair. The result was the Ffarquhar Branch layout Mark I (Mark II would be built many years later, when Wilbert moved to Stroud). The 6 ft by 4 ft layout, which could be folded for transport into a box 6 ft by 2 ft by 1 ft 6 in., featured Ffarquhar Station and the smaller Hackenbeck Halt as well as various local landmarks of that charming little hamlet, such as the stream, the hill (complete with a ventilation shaft for the railway tunnel passing underneath), The Three Beetles inn and the workshop of agricultural engineer, Thomas Cousins (named after two Emneth personalities: garage mechanic, Robert *Thomas*, and blacksmith Norman *Cousins*). The Ffarquhar Branch was first exhibited in a marquee for the seven days of the Wisbech Fair. 'When it rained,' recalls Wilbert, 'we were cold and damp; when the sun shone we were roasted!'

There were some 34,000 visitors to the fair, a great many of whom found their way to Ffarquhar where Wilbert and two or three local helpers ran the line every day from two o'clock in the afternoon until ten o'clock at night:

> All types came. There were the young children, not under proper control, who would creep under the barrier and prod and poke, and try to pick things up. When the harassed operator let out a bellow their mothers would take them away in a huff, making remarks about it being only a toy railway anyway!
>
> Other youngsters, well-behaved and interested, followed the doings of one particular engine with breathless interest, and could not bear to lose sight of it for a moment. 'Toby', being local, was the greatest favourite. 'Where's Toby? Why has he gone? Why doesn't he come out again? I want to see Toby!'

That particularly popular engine had been specially built to run on the Ffarquhar Branch with the models of Thomas and Percy which Wilbert had made while he was at Elsworth. Writing in *Railway Modeller* in 1961, Wilbert recalled how he and Christopher had first encountered the J70 tram engine at Yarmouth which had been the inspiration for Toby: 'She was exceedingly dilapidated but, nevertheless, there was a certain dignity about her as she trundled along the street ringing her bell.'

For the Ffarquhar Branch, Wilbert based his Toby not on the 0-6-0 tram which they had originally seen, but on an 0-4-0 variety (known as a Y6) which was better suited to the four-wheel motor-bogie he used to power the model. However, since the last Y6 tram had been scrapped in 1952, Wilbert created his Toby with the help of old photographs and blueprints supplied by Eastern Region's Stratford works. This model – made in card and plywood – would last until 1979, when it 'went into preservation'.

Railway Modeller published detailed instructions by Wilbert for building a model of Toby ('Railway Modeller Shows You How!') from which it is possible to gain a sense of just how much skill and patience the creator of the Railway Series brought to the intricate business of modelling: 'The bell chain is soldered, in middle, to top of staple holding bell (tricky this), and at each end to lil pins projecting from roof.' Persistent though Wilbert was when confronted by fiddly jobs, he was always disarmingly honest in advising others:

> COWCATCHERS. Take a sheet of pins in paper. Mark out say four or five rows of 36 mm. length. These pins are the bars of your cowcatchers. Why so many rows? Well, if you are as ham-handed as I am, you are sure to spoil your first attempts, and it saves time and annoyance to have others ready in reserve. Insert an extra pin between each two pins in each row. By the way, the official drawing shows twenty-four bars on each cowcatcher. I only managed to squeeze in eighteen. You may do better!

During its first exhibition at Wisbech, the Ffarquhar Branch – in contrast with Wilbert's other layout – operated faultlessly. Having proved itself as a Really Useful Railway it soon became a popular attraction at fetes and Trades Fairs in the countryside around Emneth, raising much-needed funds for St Edmund's Church.

The settings and scenery on the layout were extremely realistic and in an article for *Railway Modeller* in 1959, Wilbert revealed some of the building secrets, such as a hill made from medical lint soaked in size, wrung out and pinned, 'furry side up' over a skeleton shape constructed from scraps of pulp-board. Pipe-lagging was turned into hedges; carpet underlay became the rough grass along the roadsides; and 'a stiff paste of black Bostick moulded round the heads of pins' produced woods for a bowling green ('the jack is a pin head with a dab of white paint').

When it came to the inn sign for The Three Beetles, Wilbert received some assistance from Christopher:

> In warm weather, my son's bedroom is invaded by ladybirds. They crawl in swarms over the windows and have to be 'Flitted'. He decided to use some for the inn sign. He prepared the card, stuck on the three dead beetles and left them to set. Half an hour later he came back and found they had not set at all. There was the card, but no beetles! This happened several times till we found three really dead ones! Perhaps Durofix is to ladybirds as smelling salts are to ladies!

The layout also boasted what, for a model railway, was an unusual landscaping feature:

> Has anybody ever tried to model *a bog*? We have; but not apparently with much success! We point it out to visitors, and they say 'Ah, yes,' and then look at something else! All the same, we are proud of our bog. It took several evenings to make, and the clumps of rushes were very troublesome to plant. It is a great pity they are not better appreciated!

Folding up as it did into an oblong box, Wilbert was able to transport the Ffarquhar Branch in the back of his Bedford van. One day, returning from an exhibition, Wilbert saw a hitchhiker thumbing for a lift on the Great North Road. Wilbert stopped, but the hitchhiker, seeing what looked suspiciously like a coffin in the back of the van, declined the ride!

For three years running from 1963, the Ffarquhar Branch was given the accolade of an invitation to the Model Railway Club exhibition at Central Hall, Westminster. Wilbert's experience, since 1956, had taught him that visitors to the annual exhibition weren't simply content to see trains running around, they wanted to know where those trains were going and why. So Wilbert visited his friend Teddy Boston, and together they worked out a time-table to cover, in simulation, an entire day's work from 6 a.m. till midnight which could be shown, with a spoken commentary, in three twenty-minute sequences.

A typical programme might begin with Toby taking workmen to the quarry and Percy busying himself with shunting and collecting loads of stone from the wharf, while Thomas pulled the commuter train to Tidmouth. At the end of the 'day', Wilbert had so arranged everything that all the rolling stock was back where it had started, and was ready to begin again.

The exhibition ran for a week, by the end of which Wilbert had lost his voice; so, the following year, he introduced the idea of operating the layout to a tape-recorded commentary, a practice he continued for as long as he exhibited.

'The commentary,' says Wilbert, 'served three purposes. First, it helped the viewer know what was happening and why. It also helped the operator by reminding him – particularly if he were new to the job – what comes next, without having to pause and look it up on the time sheet. Finally, it helped those who might know the commentary by heart but who – if operating alone for long periods – were apt to lose the thread! If that happened (and it often did) the tape kept you going without disaster.'

'Someone said,' Wilbert told the *Evening Standard* in 1964, ' "happy is the man who has got a world of his own". With model railways you have your own private world where you make things go the way you want, without the frustrations of real life.' It was a candid admission.

It was this private world that inspired the story which Wilbert submitted to the *Church of England Newspaper*. Provisionally entitled 'The Little People', it was, explained Wilbert, 'concerned with what might happen, did the people etc on a model railway come to life'. A young boy named Roger is allowed to help his father operate the model railway in the garden shed. One day, his father has to leave the room and Roger finds himself alone with the railway:

> He sat on the chair, waiting for Daddy, and looked at the Railway.
> He loved the hills and trees and houses, the river, and gardens, and stations.
> He liked the animals and the people who lived there. They looked real. In fact, to Roger, they were real people with real names doing real things . . .
> Roger half closed his eyes. 'They look realer like this,' he thought. The room was warm, and he felt sleepy.
> 'It's scandalous!' said a small squeaky voice, 'I buy a ticket, and get in the train. Do they take me to the Junction? No! They bang me, they bump me, they whirl me round and round, and leave me in the tunnel. Faugh!'
> 'I'm going straight to the station,' said another voice. 'I shall demand my money back and . . .'
> 'So shall I.'
> 'And I.'
> 'And I.'
> Roger rubbed his eyes and stared. A crowd of little people surged out of the tunnel, all talking at once in shrill, angry voices.

The story has obvious connections with the Railway Series (there are attempts to get the train out of the tunnel which recall the problems with Henry in *The Three Railway Engines)* and there is clearly some kinship with *Gulliver's Travels*. But there are also many moments of original, comic invention, as when one of the characters borrows the Postman's bicycle but finds, when he is half way down a steep hill, that it doesn't have any brakes, because Roger's father hadn't bothered to put any on the bike when he made it!

The characters whom Roger observes in the story were already well known to Wilbert for, as he explained in a footnote to the first episode: 'The story is based on the scenery and population of the Author's own model railway.' In his article about the Ffarquhar Branch for *Railway Modeller* in 1959, Wilbert had identified various members of that 'population', such as the occupants of an old thatched cottage at the foot of the hill:

> The Horker family have only just moved in. The garden, though dug over, has not yet been planted. There is a fine old apple tree in blossom. Amos Horker, a sheep farmer, is walking up the hill with his dog to see to his sheep grazing on the summit. His wife Hepsibah, an old-fashioned body, is walking over the plank bridge. She has her shopping basket.
>
> Ellen, their daughter, is feeding the pigs. She and her father made a sty for them from some old shingles and bits of corrugated iron. There are three pigs, a black and two whites, and they seem to be in prime condition. Ellen's brother, Simon, is a lazy young man. He is happiest when watching others work and giving them advice. He is supposed to be planting the garden; but that, he feels, can wait, so he strolls over, hands in pockets, to watch Ellen instead.

The Horker family were featured – doing exactly those things – in the first episode of 'The Little People'; and, in the third instalment, another local family – living in a neat little house with a neat little garden – made their appearance. In *Railway Modeller*, Wilbert had already created a scenario for them:

> Mother, father and the two children have just started their holiday. That, at least, is their idea, but the car has decided to be awkward! All we can see of father is a pair of legs. He has been underneath the car for some time! The children are fidgeting about asking irritating questions, and mother stands impatiently by the pile of luggage. She is getting crosser and crosser every minute.

In 'The Little People', the family are given a name – the Kneetlys (later changed to the Neatleys) – and when Peter Fryer ('Station-Master, Porter,

Ticket-Collector and everything else' at Hackenbeck Halt) finds there is a train stuck in the tunnel, he asks whether Mr Kneetly will drive him to the Station:

> 'Mmm!' said Mrs Kneetly doubtfully. 'We ought to have started an hour ago, but my husband has to keep mending things. He says he won't be long, but every time the car starts, something else goes wrong and that has to be mended. I'm getting just a little bit impatient.'
>
> Mr Kneetly wriggled out. His name didn't suit him. He was dirty and untidy, but he greeted Peter cheerfully.
>
> 'You're in luck! I've just finished.' He tested the engine, listening with his head cocked on one side. 'Beautiful,' he said. 'We'll start now. The Station's on our way.'
>
> He left the engine running while he went to wash. The family and Peter got in. Mr Kneetly came back still untidy, but full of enthusiasm.
>
> 'I've just put in a Gadget, Fryer,' he said proudly. 'My own invention too. It'll save us pounds. I'm going to patent it.' He raced the engine. 'Just smashing!' he crowed. 'We'll be at the Station in two ticks.'
>
> Mrs Kneetly wondered, but didn't say so.
>
> They backed towards the lane. BANG – CLANG. The engine roared. Peter jumped. Mr Kneetly got out. 'Bad luck!' he announced cheerfully. 'The exhaust-pipe's off. I shan't be long.' He collected some tools and slid under the car again.
>
> 'I'm sorry,' whispered Mrs Kneetly, 'but you'd better walk. I think it's quicker!'

Mr Kneetly's comment about his gadget being his 'own invention' calls to mind the White Knight from Lewis Carroll's *Through the Looking-Glass and what Alice found there*, a book that clearly inspired another episode in the story of 'The Little People'. On first encountering the White King and Queen in Looking-Glass House, Alice is so huge in relation to the chesspieces, that when she picks them up, they get a terrible shock and the White Queen concludes that she must have been blown up by a volcano! The young hero of Wilbert's story causes similar alarm when he prevents two of the little people from falling off a roof; and, indeed, he has only to speak or laugh to have a devastating effect:

> 'Are you ready?' asked the little fat man. 'One, Two, Three, HEAVE!'
>
> They all pulled, but nothing happened. They tried again and again. At last the coach moved a little. Roger got so excited that he called out, 'One, Two, Three, HEAVE!'

> This was a mistake.
> Roger's voice sounded so loud to the little people that they dropped the ropes and ran to the tunnel. The little fat man was the first to get there.
> Bill came to the tunnel mouth to speak to him. 'Why did you stop pulling, Sir?' he asked. 'With me and my mates pushing, and you pulling, we had her just started nicely.'
> 'There was an explosion,' said the little fat man with dignity. 'It – er – exploded quite close to us. We came to take shelter.'

On receiving the first episode, the *Church of England Newspaper*'s editor, John King, responded enthusiastically: 'I am absolutely delighted. It is exactly what I hoped for. I took the liberty of trying it out on my older boy (aged four) and he is now itching to know what happens next.'

What happens next, is that Roger discovers that his train has been stopped in the tunnel by a gang of crooks because there is a jeweller on board with some valuable gems. The ventilating shaft from the tunnel is used as a getaway and the stolen jewels are hidden in that unusual (and underestimated) feature of the Ffarquhar Branch landscaping, the bog:

> Bud felt pleased. 'Now I'll collect those sparklers.'
> He left the shaft and knelt on a stone at the edge of the bog. He found the thing he was looking for, and pulled. Soon a parcel appeared. He pulled off the waterproof bag, made sure that the jewels were safe, and put them in his pocket.

Aided by Roger, the little people successfully frustrate the dastardly plans of the villains and order is restored – only seconds before Roger's father comes back into the shed.

When 'The Little People' completed its serialisation in 1960, there was talk of Wilbert revising the story so that it might be published in book form by Edmund Ward. Managing Director, Stanley Pickard, even considered introducing an unusual form of illustration for the book, comprising 'a photographic picture . . . taken especially, with a dramatic lighting effect, of an aspect of your layout appropriate to an incident in that chapter'. Pickard also had a further imaginative elaboration in mind:

> We then see these photographs having drawn on them by an artist, in a flat second colour, some of the characters of the little people, and perhaps occasionally a suggestion of the proportionately gigantic hand of Roger. We

think that some children would enjoy looking at these characters and this also would enable others to study the layout of the actual model system with great interest.

Nothing, however, came of the idea and the little story which might well have immortalised Wilbert Awdry's 'other railway' remains a curiosity locked away in the yellowing pages of the *Church of England Newspaper*.

As for the model railway itself, the Ffarquhar Branch continued to be shown in its original form on the exhibition circuit till 1965 (later, rebuilt at Stroud as Mark II, it did the same rounds until 1988), giving its creator far more pleasure than he had ever got from trying to build his 'great model railway empire', which had consistently broken down and gone wrong.

Meanwhile, traffic still occasionally ran on the Emneth layout, as can be seen from a newspaper article in 1961, penned by a journalist with a distinct taste for hyperbole: 'At his rambling vicarage, yards and yards of railway track trail through the loft, trains chuff happily backwards and forwards past stations and signals – the dream world of Mr Awdry.'

The clipping, from one of Wilbert's numerous files, has gone brown with age, the journalist's name (along with that of the paper in which the article appeared) lost in the process of cutting-out. The surrounding news-stories drift in and out of focus like insubstantial ghosts: a power-cut in the City of London which plunged the Stock Exchange into darkness for half-an-hour; a Croydon ear, nose and throat specialist who committed adultery with a nurse, gave up his profession and became a credit account agent for the Co-operative Society . . .

The article, which can be dated as July 1961, was entitled by its writer PARSON PUFFER HITS 2,000,000: 'Wilbert Awdry is a Cambridgeshire parson with a passion for model railways and a gift for thinking, and writing, of trains as if they were people . . . It is indicative of the passion which trains arouse in small boys (and in big boys too) that this week the two millionth copy of a Rev. W. Awdry railway book will be sold. It is one of the phenomena of the publishing world.'

Such phenomena needed to be celebrated, so the grateful publishers, (who allegedly told the 'Parson Puffer' journalist that Mr Awdry's books 'have earned a lot of money'), organised a party. It was held aboard the Bluebell Railway in Sheffield Park, Sussex, on 29th September, 1961. Two million books represent a lot of raw material and a great many production processes – 2,000 separate colour half-tones, 4,000 reams (or 125 tons) of art paper, tons of board and thousands of yards of cloth – so Eric Marriott (Kaye & Ward's editor and, now assistant Managing Director) ensured that among the guests (who were conveyed to various 'special diversions' in coaches dating from 1898) were representatives of all those who had contributed to the success story which the Railway Series had become: paper-makers, block-makers, printers, bookbinders and the publishers themselves.

Also clambering aboard the train that day were booksellers, editors of literary journals and officials from the National Union of Railwaymen and the National Coal Board (who provided the fuel for the trip and had an advertisement on the back of the invitation: 'Use solid fuel, more heat at less cost – and it's British!'); as well a number of celebrities and personalities, including David Davies (B.B.C. *Children's Hour*'s 'Uncle David'); Leslie Daiken, founder of the Toy Museum and Institute of Play; Captain W. G. Smith, owner of an ex-Great Northern Tank Engine, restored to its original working condition; Geoffrey Warde, Retired Bishop of Lewes and President of the Bluebell Railway; Captain Anthony Kimmins R.N., author of the popular farce, *The Amorous Prawn*; and Mrs Isabella Wallich, whose company, Delyse Records, was about to launch a series of readings from the railway books by another guest – 'B.B.C. and TV artiste', Johnny Morris.

The author and artist were also present, along with a sizable contingent of children from the London Railwaymen's Orphans Fund and Chailey Heritage Craft School and Hospital, Sussex. 'By means of this Celebration Party,' read the invitation, 'the producers hope to provide an opportunity for children of this jet-age – the orphans of Railwaymen among them – to meet rail pioneers who used steam, to talk to the author, and to inspect the engines "Bluebell" and "Stepney".'

Writing an account of the occasion for *The Bookseller* a few months later, in October 1961, Eric Marriott wrote of the Railway Series' undying popularity: 'There still come letters from Australia, requests from Africa, notes from Canada, memos from America, picture postcards from Blackpool, Birmingham and Berwick; and British Railways are emptying the water from the boilers. Thomas the Tank Engine chuckles in his shed at nights and thinks of the millions of children's children to come. After all, he will always be vintage.'

Thomas was again a prominent player in the next book of stories, the sixteenth in the series, *Branch Line Engines.* Getting too big for his wheels once more and believing he can manage without his driver, Thomas goes for a run, finds he can't stop (that popular prelude to one of Wilbert's rail disasters) and ends up – covered with plaster and festooned with a window frame –

peering through a large hole in the Station-master's house, just as the family are sitting down to breakfast. As a result, Thomas has to be sent to the works and a replacement engine employed to do his work.

In the 'Parson Puffer' article, Wilbert's publisher (presumably Eric Marriott) was quoted as saying: 'We tried to get him to introduce a diesel, but he killed it off in the same story. Anyway, in his latest book he has introduced another diesel and not killed it off, so perhaps he's mellowing towards them.' Thomas, however, was not. On finding that his duties are to be carried out by a diesel, he is scandalised:

> *'A D-D-Diesel, Sir?' Thomas spluttered.*
> *'Yes, Thomas. Diesels* always *stay in their sheds until they're wanted. Diesels* never *gallivant off to breakfast in Station-masters' houses.'*

This paragon of an engine turns out to be a temperamental diesel railcar named Daisy. In our world, steam-engines, like ships, are usually referred as feminine, whereas on the Island of Sodor – at least until the arrival of Daisy – they are male. Gender difference, however, makes little impression on the other engines, who are hostile towards Daisy on the grounds of the source of her locomotive force and – as with most newcomers to the railway – simply because she is an outsider.

Not that, to begin with, Daisy has many endearing qualities; in fact, she is soon complaining about the conditions in the yard – 'This shed is dreadfully smelly' – and refusing to pull the milk van because it is against 'Fitter's orders':

> *'My Fitter is a very nice man. He is interested in my case. He comes every week, and examines me carefully. "Daisy," he says, "never, never pull. You're highly sprung, and pulling is bad for your swerves." '*

Daisy continues to cause problems, has an embarrassing encounter with a bull and seems set to go the same way as Diesel, but is eventually saved by the predicament of another. When Percy ignores a notice saying: 'ALL TRAINS STOP TO PIN DOWN BRAKES' and ends up perched on top of a truckload of stone from the quarry (an incident which happened, in 1876, on the London, Chatham and Dover Railway) Daisy helps Toby clear up the mess and, in so doing, sufficiently redeems herself to be given one of the Fat Controller's merciful second chances.

When Daisy appeared on the Ffarquhar Branch at the 38th Model Railway Club Exhibition in 1963, a commentator in the *Daily Telegraph* described the Diesel railcar as looking 'very much the wallflower of the show'. However, this may have been a somewhat prejudiced view, since the same journalist reported that, despite the line closures being introduced by the Chairman of British Railways, Dr Richard Beeching, there was a 'defiantly reactionary' atmosphere at the Exhibition, one model even including a wall 'realistically scrawled in white paint with the slogan "Down with Diesels" '.

A similar article the following year, in the *Guardian*, described the engines running on the Ffarquhar Branch, and added that for most of the 40,000 visitors to the Model Railway Club Exhibition, 'Thomas the Tank Engine is perfection in a sadly imperfect railway world.'

However perfect a world Wilbert's Ffarquhar Branch may have been, the 'Parson Puffer' journalist revealed that it was 'never allowed to interfere with his parish affairs', reassuring readers that 'an urgent summons from his publishers goes unheeded if it clashes with a meeting of the Housewives' Guild'.

In one small sphere, however, church and rail interests were to combine. In 1960, Wilbert had contributed his story of 'The Little People' to the children's pages of the *Church of England Newspaper*. He and Christopher also regularly entered the paper's crossword competition – sometimes with success: 'We had notification that Christopher had won a prize, but they were always very slow about paying these things and, as Christopher wanted the prize money before he went back to school, I wrote to bustle them up. They replied with an invitation to write some articles.'

'Try to imagine a time in England when no one could travel any faster than the fastest horse . . . ' That was how, on 23rd December, 1960, Wilbert began the first of several long-running series for the *Church of England Newspaper*. 'The First Railway Engine in the World' told the story of the building of Richard Trevithick's tramway locomotive which, in 1804, had 'chugged cheerfully along at about five miles an hour' and begun the railway revolution.

Other 'Locomotives With a Story' followed, and were succeeded by series about 'Narrow-Gauge Railways', 'Remarkable Railways' (among whom were those Wisbech trams that had inspired Toby), 'Some Solitary Locomotives' (including The Great Bear, one of the engines that Wilbert and his father used to go and watch for beside the line at Box), 'Locomotives That Have Made History' (such as The Rocket, Actium, City of Truro, Flying Scotsman, Silver Link and Mallard), and – a typical Wilbert title – 'Railway Odds and Ends'.

'I exploited my talent,' says Wilbert, 'for being able to tell a story in as few words as possible.' Apart from an economic prose style, the *Church of England Newspaper* articles, which ran until 1967, showed Wilbert's eye for a good story; a story such as the one told him by the railway historian, C. Hamilton

Ellis, about a tank engine on the Southern Railway named Victoria – it is called 'Victoria's Vengeance':

> When war started, Victoria was an old lady, as engines go. She took her share of the extra hard work. She suffered too, as all other engines did, from lack of maintenance . . . November 28 1942 was the day which lifted Victoria out of the ranks of ordinary engines to a place in history. It was dull and cloudy. Victoria was on her usual Ashford-Hastings run when, somewhere on Romney Marsh, a 'tip-and-run' raider zoomed from the clouds and gunned her train. He began at the rear and worked forward, then giving Victoria a burst, he turned, presumably planning to gun the train from the other side before making off.
>
> This was too much for Victoria. Like her name-sake, the Old Queen, she had a short way with those who took liberties. Part of the aircraft may have touched her, or a bullet may have found a weak spot in her boiler; at all events, Victoria exploded upwards and sideways, hurling her funnel, her dome, and her left-hand side tank into the belly of the aircraft, which crashed in the Marsh, a total wreck.
>
> The engine men were unhurt, and one of them danced with excitement on the track when he saw what had happened. Victoria, covered with honourable wounds, was towed away and put to rights.

In the second of a series entitled 'Famous Locomotives', in January 1962, Wilbert wrote about Dolgoch, one of 'The Two Old Ladies of Towyn' who, after 84 years, was still working on the Talyllyn Railway. The article recalled a time when the fate of the railway depended entirely on Dolgoch: 'If the "Old Lady" failed, so also would the railway. Its end would be the scrap-heap or, at best, a museum. Dolgoch was a temperamental old lady, but a very gallant one.'

And that phrase was to provide the title for the next volume of stories, published later the same year, *Gallant Old Engine*. At the beginning of the first of the Railway Series books to be inspired by the Talyllyn, *Four Little Engines*, Rheneas – Dolgoch's alter ego on Sodor – had been sent away to be mended; now he returns – although not until the last page of the book! However, the story of how Rheneas saved the Skarloey railway (which mirrors the story of Dolgoch, and was inspired by an episode in Tom Rolt's book *Railway Adventure*) is told, in 'flashback', as an object lesson in dedicated service for the benefit of Duncan, who is forever grumbling about life on the line: 'Passengers are just nuisances.' As Skarloey explains – and the comment should be read within the context of the line closures that were taking place on what the Sodor engines refer to as the 'Other Railway': 'Passengers are our coal and water. No passengers means no trains. No trains means no Railway. Then we'd be on the scrap-heap, my engine, and don't you forget it.'

Gallant Old Engine is crammed full of exploits, such as the various indignities which Peter Sam has to undergo when he collides with a low hanging icicle at a tunnel mouth and then has to make do with a piece of wired-on drainpipe for a funnel. The story was drawn from one of those amusing anecdotes recounted in *Railway Gazette*'s 'Scrap Heap' column; although a subconscious childhood memory from the winter of 1919 may have coloured the incident. Writing in her diary, his mother recorded: 'Feb. 10 Wilbert went with Daddy to Corsham to see icicles hanging over the tunnel. They came back by train. The coldest day since 1895.'

The solution to Peter Sam's problems is a Giesl funnel: up-to-date, but flat and funny-looking – 'Sir Handel and Duncan asked him why he had sat on it, and then hooted with laughter.' This is a typical Awdry touch: introducing, and explaining, a new item of locomotive technology that few of his readers would have heard of – whilst still making it fun.

Arguments about sexist attitudes in the Railway Series were still some twenty years away, but – in recognition of the fact that the books were enjoyed as much by girls as by boys – Wilbert introduced a female human character, Nancy, the guard's daughter, who helps polish up the old engines in readiness for Rheneas' triumphant return to Sodor.

John Kenney draws Nancy, dressed in jeans and a red and white bobble-hat, shining the brass-work on Skarloey, who has just woken up and looks sleepily at the yellow duster, tickling his nose. It is one of several splendid illustrations – others include Peter Sam puffing anxiously along through cold, grey, wintry weather and the frosty scene when he loses his funnel. Although *Gallant Old Engine* was only the sixth title to be illustrated by John Kenney (compared with the eleven books illustrated by Reginald Dalby), it was to be his last. Problems with his eyesight, combined with the exacting technical precision demanded by the Railway Series, resulted in Kenney's resignation.

Wilbert was finding it increasingly difficult to come up with ideas for new books, but spurred on by demands from Eric Marriott, and prodded into action by Margaret, he still, somehow, managed to find subjects to write about. In 1961, Wilbert had gone to speak at an event organised by the Bluebell Railway Preservation Society, in Sussex – where, the same year, celebrations to mark the sale of the two-millionth copy had been held. During these visits, Wilbert saw Stepney, a London, Brighton & South Coast Railway Terrier Class, who had been one of the first engines to be preserved on the line. He decided to take Stepney on an imaginary visit to the Island of Sodor, so that he could tell the engines (and the book's readers) something of the Bluebell Railway's story.

There was, therefore, a new book, *Stepney the 'Bluebell' Engine*, but no one to illustrate it. So, Eric Marriott asked Swedish-born illustrator, Gunvor Edwards if she would try her hand at some illustrations for the Railway Series. Although Kenney's illustrations were markedly different in technique to those by Dalby, there was sufficient similarity for the pictures to be thought of as having a particular 'style'. The first requirement of a new artist would be to capture that style.

'In those days,' recalls Gunvor's British artist husband, Peter Edwards, 'we knew nothing was impossible for us, so Gunvor agreed at once.' She decided to start well into the book with a difficult picture showing the big Diesel standing alongside four of the engines in their shed.

The painting had to be quite small, about ten by six inches, and Gunvor soon realised that duplicating the sort of pictures used for the series was not going to be easy. 'We all have our own handwriting,' says Peter Edwards, 'and it is very hard to consistently imitate another. Also there were some mathematical problems; it seemed important, for example, that the same number of wheels would appear on one side of the train as on the other!'

Gunvor was unhappy and although Peter, as he puts it, was 'trying to be a "serious" artist', he tried one of the pictures himself. 'I could no more imitate the earlier books than Gunvor, but Eric Marriott seemed happy enough to let me continue with a few more drawings.' Since, however, Wilbert had been told that Gunvor was to be the new illustrator, it was felt that Peter Edwards should pay a visit to the author, 'to sort things out'.

Late one murky, winter night, Eric Marriott and Peter Edwards travelled to Emneth. Sitting in the Wisbech train, Marriott told Edwards he was going to meet 'a very important author'. At that time, illustrators dealt with publishers and art editors, but seldom, if ever, met an author: 'Perhaps,' says Edwards, 'some people still remembered the clashes between Lewis Carroll and his illustrator, John Tenniel.' It was, therefore with 'a slight sense of trepidation' that Edwards found himself face to face with the Reverend W. Awdry.

The artist's first impression was of 'a tall, sombre, rather cadaverous man with a deep voice', who possibly viewed Peter Edwards with some suspicion: 'It was all a bit stiff and stilted to begin with and it was probably due to the friendly presence of Mrs Awdry that the atmosphere gradually warmed up. Then, I mentioned that we had been travelling on the Cambridge train where one could look out through the driver's cab and how I had liked some of the arches we had passed.' This proved a turning point in the conversation and Wilbert was soon talking enthusiastically about Brunel and the G. W. R. – or, as it was affectionately referred to, 'God's Wonderful Railway' – and telling Edwards some of his horror stories about the illustrative errors perpetrated by Reginald Dalby.

'One of the big issues,' says Edwards, 'seemed to be the chequered career of Henry; and, since I wasn't quite clear who Henry was, I was taken to see the model railway and introduced to the Green Engine.' It is interesting to note that the Henry model engine proved as troublesome as his literary counterpart and was eventually scrapped – the only one of Wilbert character models to go without 'preservation or replacement'.

The visit to the Awdrys was a success and by the time Edwards left, Wilbert had accepted him as the new illustrator of the Railway Series. Perhaps surprisingly, in view of the fact that Edwards' style was more impressionistic than his predecessors, Wilbert liked the artist's work – 'He drew from life and obviously had an affection for the characters' – and became fond of him and his family.

Published in 1963, *Stepney the 'Bluebell' Engine* carried the joint credit: 'with illustrations by Gunvor & Peter Edwards', but it was almost entirely Peter's work. It was not the easiest book on which an illustrator might make his debut, containing, as it does, more conversation and description than action. In fact, the book's most adventurous episode is the race between Caroline Car and Stepney, who has accidentally carried off a well-hit cricket ball while passing what the artist identifies as the 'Elsbridge Cricket Club'.

Peter Edwards visited the Bluebell Railway to draw some of the engines referred to in the story, including the twins, Bluebell and Primrose, and the tough-talking Captain Baxter: 'He's worked in a Quarry, and you know what *that* does to an engine's language and manners.'

The resulting illustrations are lively and colourful, but a mix of styles is, perhaps, an indication of the fact that Peter Edwards was still attempting to approximate the look of the earlier books. His pictures, for example, of Stepney and the cricket match have a Dalbyesque realism, while others have a freer approach to landscape that is closer to Kenney. One or two show the emergence of a style that is uniquely Edwards' own; a good example of which is his atmospheric drawing of old engines abandoned on a desolate siding on the 'Other Railway' – a picture which, incidentally, breaks Wilbert's self-imposed rule about engines not having faces in England. At the time that Edwards began illustrating the Railway Series, he was working on a set of covers for the complete novels of Graham Greene and took his inspiration for this picture from a cover he had designed for Greene's *A Gun for Sale* which has a chase in a railway siding.

The Railway Series sometimes resembles a long-running television soap opera: new characters are introduced, some of whom prove so popular they become 'regulars', while others make only occasional appearances and quite a few are never seen or heard of again. There was George the steamroller in *Gallant Old Engine* – depicted by John Kenney as being a livid green individual with a sour expression and bug-eyes; and, in *Stepney the 'Bluebell' Engine*, the passing character is 'the big Diesel', who – like his infamous predecessor – has no other name.

The Diesel, who has a large, square, yellow face with a supercilious expression, tells the other engines: 'Your Controller should scrap you, and get engines like me. A fill of oil, a touch on the starter, and I'm off, with no bother, no waiting.' Shortly afterwards, he inadvertently swallows the Inspector's hat and, having been rendered useless *and* a laughing stock, slips away into the night: 'He said Goodbye to no one, but left two things behind: the nasty smell of bad manners, and a battered bowler hat.'

Although Stepney eventually returns to the Bluebell line, another unusual railway was to inspire the setting for Wilbert's nineteenth book, *Mountain Engines*. In May 1963, Wilbert wrote a two-part article for the *Church of England Newspaper* in his series on 'Remarkable Railways'. The subject was the Snowdon Mountain Railway which was particularly remarkable for the altitude to which it climbed, and because its engines *push*, rather than *pull* their coaches. Two months before, Wilbert had visited Snowdon with his friend and fellow cleric, E. R. 'Teddy' Boston:

> The little engine panted and snorted, clawing its way up the slope. It was a novel sensation to hear the engine's vociferous remarks coming at us from behind. From the window, as we looked back, we caught occasional glimpses of the fireman hard at work feeding the fire, and we wondered how many hundredweights of coal he needed for the hour's journey up four-and-three-quarter miles of mountain side.
>
> We watched the ribbon of track unrolling before us, sometimes seeming to go down, at others apparently rearing up before us like the side of a house, but we knew our eyes were playing tricks for there is no downward or even level stretch in the whole ascent and our engine was working hard the whole time. Upward, inexorably, she pushed our coach over viaduct, past waterfall and

isolated farms until we reached the timber line at Halfway, above which nothing seems to grow but grass and coarse scrub. Higher still to Clogwyn where even the grass failed, and only on favourable days are trains allowed to cross the windswept ridge from which we looked down 2,000 shadowy feet to the Pass of Llanberis below.

We left the ridge and struck the steepest climb of all, up which the engine barked and bellowed in her effort to lift us 1,000 feet in something less than a mile. The line rose above us steeply disappearing into the skyline. Shouting her challenge to this obstacle, the little engine brought the skyline ever nearer till its grim edge faded into a magnificent landscape and we trundled over the last and easier stretch into Summit Station, the highest in the British Isles.

A. O. E. Davis, then Director of the Snowdon Mountain Railway, suggested that Wilbert might care to give the Island of Sodor a similar rack railway. A suitable location existed on Culdee Fell (marked on the first published map of Sodor at 2,046 feet). With a little 'research', Wilbert pieced together the history of the Culdee Fell Railway, which had begun construction in 1897 and opened three years later. In his entry on the railway in *The Island of Sodor: Its People, History and Railways*, Wilbert noted that the Snowdon Mountain Railway had been opened shortly before work began on the Culdee Fell who, as a result, were able to benefit from Snowdon's advice and expertise:

It is not surprising therefore that the two railways are similar in many respects. The main difference is that while the Snowdon Railway's climb is short and sharp (4 3/4 miles only), the Culdee Fell line is twice that length with easy gradients at the foot steepening finally to a fierce 1 in 5 on the last half mile to Summit Station.

There were certainly a number of parallels between the two railways. The central character in *Mountain Engines*, Culdee, tells the terrible story of their No. 1 engine, Godred who 'never learnt sense' and, even after being taken to pieces to see if anything was wrong with him, still 'went on in the same old way' until a fateful day crossing a ridge called the Devil's Back:

'One day I was going up, and waited at a station for Godred, coming down, to pass me. As I waited, so it happened. One moment he was on the track; the next, his Driver and Fireman jumped clear as he rolled over. No one was hurt. His coach stayed on the rails, and the Guard braked her to a stop.'

In *The Island of Sodor* Wilbert gives another account of this incident, which occurred just over a month after the Railway's opening, adding that when the engine plunged into the ravine 'the passengers kept calm and no one was injured'. The source of this story – like virtually everything happening in the Railway Series – is revealed in the second of Wilbert's articles on the Snowdon Mountain Railway in the *Church of England Newspaper*:

> Opening day was April 6, 1896. No. 1, 'Ladas' went to the top with a train (two coaches). On the way down, near Clogwyn, she left the rails, fell down the ravine and ended up a total wreck. The driver and fireman jumped clear. The coach brakes held firm, and all the passengers who 'stayed put' were unhurt. Unfortunately, two passengers panicked, jumped out and were injured. One of them died.

The real fascination in reading *Mountain Engines* (as with other books in the series 'inspired' by real railways) is Wilbert's skill at presenting not just real-life engine incidents, but whole pages of railway history recast to fit within the context of Sodor, past and present. Nevertheless, it is hard not to miss the simplicity of the earlier stories with their rhythms and rhymes and their inexhaustible round of adventures and arguments, trick-playing and revenge-taking, disasters and rescues.

One of the pleasures of these later books, however, is the variety of landscape which comes as a welcome change to those endless lines running through fields of cows or beside the sea. In this, Wilbert was well served by Peter Edwards.

As well as the settings – rocky crags, black-shadowed drops, green cloud-darkened middle distances and far-off misty horizons – Edwards produced charming likenesses of the curious little engines with their forward-tilted smokestacks who, because their faces are usually hidden behind the engine they are pushing, have another face on the back of their cab. In one of his finest illustrations, Edwards shows No. 6 (formerly Lord Harry, but now stripped of his name for foolish behaviour) attempting to take a train across the Devil's Back to rescue some wounded climbers. Low cloud sweeps across the distant peaks, driving wind and hail lash the engine and its stalwart truck as they battle on with their eyes screwed-up and their teeth clenched.

'Peter was so keen on getting authentic drawings of the locomotives,' says Wilbert, 'that he went down to Llanberis in January to visit workshops of the Snowdon Mountain Railway.' Although illustrating the book alone, the artist continued to share title-page credit with his wife, Gunvor, who, along with their children, accompanied Edwards on this and subsequent research trips. 'At a time in our life,' says Edwards, 'of short funds and few breaks, the family had an excuse to explore the Welsh Coast, Lakeland, Cornwall and Devon, Sussex and Kent with a steam trip to cap it all!'

The Railway Series had been running for almost twenty years and in recognition of Wilbert's growing celebrity, the B.B.C. Home Service invited him to appear on Roy Plomley's radio programme, *Desert Island Discs*. Broadcast on 19th October, 1964, the interview included a brief history of the Railway Series and attempted, not too successfully, to show something of the man behind them.

'Now, Mr Awdry,' began Plomley, 'on a desert island what would you be happiest to have got away from?' 'The continual spate of circulars and forms,' answered Wilbert, 'which come every day by post.' And which, he might have added, had provided the writing materials for his first book, *The Three Railway Engines*.

Would he be lonely? Wilbert replied that he would hate it, but hoped it might be said of him, as it had been said of a great man with a strong faith in God: 'He was never less alone than when he was alone.' Would he, then, try to build a craft with which to escape? Explaining that he had inherited some of his father's woodworking skills, Wilbert thought he might try to get off the island, 'provided,' he added, 'I had some clue as to where the island was situated.' A reply which solicited one of those mock-serious jests with which Plomley carefully maintained the programme's premise: 'This is information we could give you only very roughly.'

Plomley asked what book (apart from the Bible and Shakespeare) Wilbert would wish to have on the island. 'I think I will plump for *Robinson Crusoe*, in the hope that I shall be able to pick up a lot of useful hints from Robinson's experience.' The urbane flow of conversation is deceptive: programme transcripts show that re-takes had to be made of several sections, suggesting that Wilbert may have found the experience rather nerve-wracking. Also, whilst Roy Plomley sounds coolly professional, he exhibits little indication of having any empathy with his castaway. Possibly, he was perplexed by some of the eight gramophone records which Wilbert had chosen to take with him to the mythical desert island.

True, there were several conventional choices, such as 'Jesu, Joy of Man's Desiring'; 'Baal, we cry to thee' from Mendelssohn's *Elijah*; and Sir Joseph Porter's song ('When I Was a Lad') from Gilbert and Sullivan's comic opera *H. M. S. Pinafore*. But Wilbert also asked for an episode from *The Buggins Family*, an old radio comedy show featuring Mabel Constanduros and Michael Hogan, that was much-loved by him and his brother; and no less than *three* railway recordings that Plomley no doubt thought a little specialist for the average listener: *Trains in the Hills*; *Rhythms of Steam* ('a two-cylinder engine in good condition, expertly driven, pulling a passenger train up a gradient') and a memory of Talyllyn – 'The Old Lady Drives to Dolgoch'.

Wilbert's remaining choice was part of a reading of 'Edward and Gordon' – modestly, not his own recording, but a version read by broadcaster, Johnny Morris, who had established a reputation as a story-teller for children with his television persona, 'The Hot Chestnut Man', and whose long-running radio and television series, *Johnny's Jaunts*, enjoyed perennial popularity. It was in 1962 that Johnny Morris had begun a series of recordings of the first eight titles in the Railway Series.

At first, Morris was not sure that he wanted to make the records: 'Funny thing about Thomas the Tank Engine,' he says, 'I was not all that mad about them. They were all right, but . . . ' However, Isabella Wallich, who had founded and ran Delyse Records, argued that the success of the books (then approaching the two million mark) augured well for record-sales; she also convinced Morris that he had the ability to bring the engines to life. This he did splendidly, each engine speaking with his own distinct voice: Thomas is young, bright and full of cheeky enthusiasm; Percy is rather perky and public school; James has a lilting Welsh accent; Henry evidently comes from the faded upper class; Toby speaks in a soft, slow, west-country voice, while his coach, Henrietta, adopts a pathetic, despairing tone; and Gordon sounds like a pompous, northern alderman in a play by J. B. Priestley. As for all those noisy trucks: they bump into one another with a rapid succession of startled 'Oh!' sounds, each hitting an individual note on what might be described as a musical scale of surprise.

Wilbert remembers arriving at the studio for the first recording session, having a list of proposed cuts in order to edit the text to the required length of an extended play disc, each of which would contain two stories. Johnny Morris had prepared his own version, but was happy to defer to the author. However, Wilbert asked to hear Morris' scripts and, at once, agreed that they were the versions to be used. Although the stories occasionally suffer from editing, they are more often sharpened, and Morris builds on the rhythmic patterns of dialogue and sounds by using Wilbert's device of repetitions (often adding many more than are found in the books), enhanced by his own unique range of whistles, puffings, chuggings and great bursts of steam.

Looking back on his meetings with Wilbert Awdry, Johnny Morris writes: 'He was a steam buff and so was I. He was highly technical and reserved, I was slightly emotional and extrovert. He sat in the control room, I was locked away in the recording cubicle, so, we weren't in very close contact; but he nodded and smiled at the characterisation of the Welsh engine and the troublesome trucks and seemed contented with the way his stories were interpreted. There was never any trouble or worry, he was very professional and did not tinker or nit-pick. He knew what he wanted and I knew what to do.'

The formula proved a highly successful one and, when, some years later Johnny Morris was unavailable to continue the series, the role of storyteller passed to William Rushton, who – in fruitiest tones – recorded another six books: 'I found it,' he says, 'all very exhausting, because I tried to do lots of different voices and, unlike Johnny Morris, I can only do about five or six. Everybody was terribly worried because the Rev. was going to attend the recordings. I suppose it was a bit alarming, but it didn't bother me too much because I come, on my mother's side, from a long line of Welsh clergymen and when they say "Cannons to the left of them and cannons to the right", well I had several canons *and* an archdeacon! Anyway, he turned out to be a sweetie; we got on very well and I remember that he laughed a lot at the recordings.'

The last Railway Series title to be recorded by Willie Rushton was *The Little Old Engine* and, in 1964, Wilbert began planning yet another book about the Skarloey railway. This book, like one or two of the stories in *Gallant Old Engine*, would tell something of the history of the line and, in so doing, mark the one hundredth anniversary of the Talyllyn, which had inspired the Skarloey Railway. The various episodes in the book – recounted to the guard's daughter, Nancy (now shown wearing slacks and a T-shirt) – were once again, based on authentic incidents from early days on Talyllyn, as told in Tom Rolt's book, *Railway Adventure*. The story begins with the building of Skarloey and Talyllyn, depicted in Peter Edwards' illustration standing side by side – one showing a face and one not – in the Whitehaven workshops of Fletcher Jennings. The book follows the problems in getting Skarloey (like Talyllyn) to work and the decision to give the engine two additional wheels and a cab – a change in appearance which much impresses the coaches:

> *'Such a handsome engine!' they tittered. 'Six wheels and a cab – so distinguished, my dears! It's a pleasure to see him.'*

In December 1964, Wilbert wrote to the railway historian C. Hamilton Ellis: 'My "latest", which I hope will be out very soon after Whitsun, celebrates the Talyllyn Centenary. *Very Old Engines* has given our artist quite a task in drawing Skarloey No. 1 and Rheneas No. 2 as near as possible to what Talyllyn and Dolgoch were like 100 years ago and I think he is making a very good job and hope the pundits will think the same.' In the event, Peter Edwards showed himself to be perfectly at ease drawing the top-hatted, frock-coated gentlemen of the 1860s and, since the book concluded with a plea from Rheneas for readers to visit the Talyllyn Railway, he painted a lively final picture of three of the little old engines steaming along at Towyn.

Writing in *Books*, the Journal of the National Book League, in the year in which *Very Old Engines* was to be published, Dennis Butts concluded an article on 'The Reverend's Railways' with this comment: 'Long ago in a memorable essay on *Boys' Weeklies*, George Orwell showed how the values and attributes embodied in children's literature are often extremely questionable, prone to xenophobia and snobbery. Today he might be even more concerned about the triviality and emptiness of many of the books for the youngest children. But in that border country between fantasy and fact, the Reverend W. Awdry's tales are some of the few honourable exceptions today.'

By the time *Very Old Engines* was published in 1965, a dramatic change had taken place in the life of its author. Wilbert Awdry had decided to retire.

CHAPTER THIRTEEN

End of the Line?

THE decision to leave Emneth had not been an easy one; the Awdrys were deeply involved with the community and Wilbert was on Christian-name terms with most of the local people, whether or not they attended church: 'I had, long ago, learned this lesson: in a country parish, a vicar has to be flexible. In a town there are probably several churches, and if someone doesn't like the vicar they can always go to another church; but in the country, you are on your own: *you* represent God to the whole of the parish, and if people take a dislike to you, or the way you do things, and decide to stop coming to church, there may very well be nowhere else for them to go.'

Nevertheless, Wilbert felt that the time had come for a change: 'After 12 years at Emneth, I began to feel that I was a getting a little tired of the place and that the people there were probably getting a little tired of me!' Besides, Wilbert's writing career was making many demands on him. To a journalist who commented that he was a publishing phenomenon, he replied: 'It is also jolly hard work!'

It was not just the growing burden of the research necessary to produce another book each year, but the extensive correspondence that Wilbert began receiving as a result of his career as a children's author. There was a quantity of fan mail, but there were other letters as well, written both in a belief that 'The Rev. W. Awdry' understood the working of the child mind and in the sure knowledge that, as a parson, he could be trusted with confidences. Perplexed parents wrote with questions about the spiritual upbringing of their children and, sometimes, about anxieties over 'problem children'. 'All these letters,' says Wilbert, 'had to be answered fully and carefully as part of my ministry. As a result, I found I had less and less time for parish work and felt that I ought to leave it.'

Wilbert consulted the Bishop of Ely who replied, in effect: 'It's your fault. You started this. It's important too, and you must go on with it.' Talking the situation over with Margaret, Wilbert came to the conclusion that he might be able to fulfil a more useful role if he were to go, as he puts it, 'into private practice'.

In an interview with the *Daily Express*, headlined THE 'PUFF-PUFF' PARSON, Wilbert explained: 'At first sight it might seem a bit frivolous, to give up a parish to write children's books and answer letters, but I think I do a good job. I have become a sort of confessional. In a way I've swapped the small parish for a country-wide one.'

In reaching the decision to retire, Wilbert must have reflected on his almost twenty years of parish life, first as Rector of Elsworth and Knapwell, then as Vicar of Emneth.

At Elsworth, it had been something of an uphill struggle. 'At first,' says Wilbert, 'I don't believe anyone actually thought I was doing any work. They supposed that, because I was Rector and lived in a great big house, that I had plenty of money and nothing to do all day!'

In reality, the opposite had been the case: Wilbert had done virtually everything himself, sometimes having to light the stoves in order to heat the church and ring the bell for services. He even found himself up a ladder with a piece of holly bush, trying to clear the chimney for an old lady living in one of the three parish almshouses. Unfortunately, just at the moment when Wilbert had dislodged a quantity of soot, the elderly resident put her head in the fireplace – in order to call up the chimney to the Rector – and got an unpleasant surprise!

It is an indication of how much work Wilbert and Margaret did at Elsworth – and the changes which they brought about in the parish – that, following the Awdrys' move to Emneth, one of the congregation should have written: 'Everything seems to have faded out since you have gone . . .'

Although Evensong was well-attended, it required accurate timing since the six o'clock service had to finish by 7.00 p.m. so that Wilbert could jump in his car and dash to Knapwell Church – collecting an organist *en route* – for another service, fifteen minutes later. Less successful were Wilbert's attempts to get his parishioners to attend services of Holy Communion: 'It was virtually impossible! I arranged service at all sorts of times between seven and ten o'clock in the morning, but it didn't make an atom of difference!'

In an attempt to have some kind of morning service, Wilbert had instituted a Junior Church. Every Sunday, Wilbert would drive his battered Ford van to collect children from Knapwell and take them to Elsworth in time for a service which started at 10.00 a.m. Junior Church, which was later to be a feature of Sunday afternoon life at Emneth, was a simplified version of the Church of England service of Morning Prayer, aimed at familiarising young people with church procedures. Wilbert's intention extended beyond the order of service to include the concept of how a parish church was run. Twice a year, the children elected two churchwardens and the sidesmen and women who took the collection and, in the vestry after the service, added up the money and entered the sums in an account book.

One of Wilbert's aims was to instil in children a sense of responsibility. For example, there was no Sunday School Attendance Register as such; instead, on a table near the door were index-cards for each child marked with his or her name and the children were responsible for 'clocking-in', as Wilbert puts it, by posting their card into a wooden box with a slot in the top. After the service, an elected attendance officer would open the box and date-stamp whatever cards were inside.

Junior Church services were, of course, about much more than church administration: in the address, which substituted for the sermon, Wilbert attempted to explain such basic issues of the Christian faith as 'The Lord's Prayer', 'The Creed', 'The Ten Commandments' and 'The Sacraments'. Wilbert wrote his talks, using red ink, in microscopic handwriting, on small pieces of paper cut up from old circulars and the unused back of letters. These pages had holes punched into them so that they could be made into little books, held together with treasury-tags.

Wilbert's talks featured stories about children with funny alliterative names such as Thomas Tickletrout, Fred Fiddlestring, Jennifer Jane Jelliband and Winifred Wilhelmena Whatnot. His illustrations, like Christ's parables, drew their inspiration from everyday life:

> Supposing you went into a field and picked toadstools, then cooked them and ate them because you believed they were mushrooms. You would have at least a tummy ache – probably something worse – because of a wrong belief.
>
> Lots of people, grown-ups as well as children, have pains in their souls which are far worse than tummy ache because they have wrong beliefs about God and the Christian religion.

'It was important,' says Wilbert, 'that you talked about things they could understand, rather than highfalutin' ideas that were beyond them.' Wilbert quite often spoke of experiences from his own childhood, such as this one used to introduce his talks about the Commandments:

> Once I had a clockwork car. In the box with it was a paper in which the maker said these things: keep the mechanism oiled, don't overwind it and don't push it about. I didn't bother about the rules, and the car was soon broken and no longer a good car – because I didn't obey the maker's rules.

Each week in many church Sunday Schools, children received an adhesive stamp with prettified pictures of Bible scenes. In Wilbert's Junior Church, however, the children were given home-made stamps with designs that either featured everyday objects or were inspired by newspaper and poster advertisements. The Bisto Kids were depicted on their way to church, while the Guinness strongman was redrawn, supporting a heavy chest with one hand, in illustration of the rewritten slogan: 'Confirmation gives you strength.'

The talk would give the children the words needed to complete the caption to each picture which could then be stuck in a little album and coloured. At Elsworth, where there was no money to spare, Wilbert reproduced his pictures using an early duplicating device and the children had to stick them in with paste; at Emneth, where Wilbert could afford to spend a little more, a local printer made blocks from his drawings and printed the stamps on gummed paper.

'I wanted children to know,' says Wilbert, 'that religion was something for every day.' And that is what his picture-stamps attempted to show. An aeroplane became a 'prayeroplane'; confession to a priest was shown as being God's telephone box; a set of traffic-lights was used to teach Wilbert's conviction that there are three, as opposed to two, answers to prayer: 'No', 'Wait' and 'Yes'; while a lighthouse, standing on the Rock of Christ, had a beam of light ('The Creed') which shone out across the water showing the way to a little sailboat called the 'H.M.S. Me'.

Of all Wilbert's work, he regarded that done with, and for, children as being among his most important. Once a week at Emneth, he set out with his twelve-seater Bedford Van to collect children from the local junior schools and take them to the Vicarage, where he conducted religious education classes which he always made sure the children enjoyed. He served on the governing boards of a number of schools and, for over ten years, had been Secretary of the Ely Diocesan Children's Council. In the years ahead, Wilbert would serve on the Central Children's Council, meeting at Church House, Westminster, but he realised that it would be the week-by-week contact with children that he and Margaret (who used to run a Sunday School for younger children at the Vicarage) would miss most about retirement.

As for the question of income, the loss of his professional earnings would be compensated for by the money he was now earning from the Railway Series. There had been new negotiations with the publishers, resulting from Wilbert's growing dissatisfaction with the agreed royalty rate of one penny per copy. The problem was that this arrangement had been made at a time when the books were selling for four shillings each; but gradually, over the years, prices had risen to 4s. 6d. by 1957 and, six years later, to five shillings. During the mid-sixties some titles were increased to 5s. 6d. and, by 1970, they were all selling at six shillings.

These rises were relatively modest, since controlling the price of the Railway Series was one of the prime concerns of Eric Marriott, who was not only editor, but also production manager. The books were small and contained only 28 pages of text; as a result, the books' size in relation to their price was something booksellers were constantly pointing out to the publisher's representatives. 'It was vital,' says Marriott, 'that we held acceptable prices if we wanted to build a successful series.'

For Wilbert, however, the price rises meant that his royalty had been devalued. 'I kicked up rather a fuss,' he says, 'and when I got a lot of hard-luck stories about rising costs of printing and about artist's fees having gone up, I said: "Well, how about the chap who creates the stories?" I didn't want a large amount, I just wanted a royalty that would reflect the retail price of the book.'

Eric Marriott doubts whether Wilbert was fully aware of what it was costing to maintain, promote and extend the Railway Series. 'Those "hard-luck stories" were certainly not figments of the imagination nor a device to avoid dealing fairly with Wilbert. I was having a continuous battle to keep production costs at a minimum. At the time, the printing, binding and processing unions were virtually in control and large increases in paper-costs happened regularly. Every year, we either had to bear higher costs or find economies.'

Those economies were constantly being made. Initially the books had been printed by Edmund Ward's own printing company, the De Montfort Press, which used letterpress and produced only one book per sheet of paper. As costs increased, Marriott changed printers and binders in order to get two books produced per sheet and finally opted for Jarrolds of Norwich, who used large offset litho machines that could print four books to one sheet. 'I am convinced,' says Marriott, 'that the constant attention to prices, editorial concern and production quality laid the foundation for the overall success of the Railway Series.'

Despite the publisher's problems, they sought to pacify their unhappy author. Whilst retaining the copyright in the characters, Wilbert was to be paid a 3⅓ % royalty. It was an extraordinary arrangement, since although, by present-day standards, the percentage was small, it nevertheless allowed the author to earn royalties on books for which, under the terms of his original contracts, the publishers had already paid.

By 1965, royalties from the Railway Series were earning him about £1000 a year, which was then a reasonable income on which to live. The only question was where? Wilbert's mother was living in London, Margaret's mother and family were in Worcester, so they began looking for a house somewhere in the 'Stroud-Gloucester-Cheltenham triangle'.

As for the children, they were now 'out in the world', and Margaret and Wilbert (who was determined not to repeat his mother's possessiveness) adopted a balanced attitude towards letting their children go: 'We always felt that they had got their own lives to live and, although at times they could be extremely irritating, they were personalities in their own right.'

Veronica, who had been at Leeds University where she had obtained a Degree in French and Latin, was now at Exeter University, studying for a Diploma in Education. Hilary, after a domestic science course at a college of Further Education in Oxford, was an Assistant Matron at a boys' preparatory school. If any of the children, in 1965, were causing Wilbert and Margaret any anxiety, it was the twenty-five-year-old Christopher.

It was seven years since, at the age of eighteen, Christopher had decided to leave Worksop College. After being there for four years, he felt that he had 'had enough of school'. Looking back, he recalls: 'It helped me to try and cope for myself and not depend on other people, but I wasn't brilliant academically – I was the plodder who does enough to get by. In retrospect, I regret that and wish that I had worked a bit harder; although whether the end result would ever have been any different, I don't know.'

That end result – five O Levels – did not please Christopher's father: 'It suggested,' says Wilbert, 'that he had not been doing a great deal of work, which was certainly annoying to his parents!' Since Wilbert remembers his son once saying that he wanted to be either a parson or to go into publishing, he no doubt hoped that Christopher would first go to university and then, possibly, end up in the church.

As it was, things worked out rather differently. Wilbert arranged for Christopher to work for the Wisbech printer, Balding and Mansell and, two years later, a job with the publishers Kaye & Ward who, under the imprint Edmund Ward, published the Railway Series.

'I worked in sales, production, accounts, and editorial,' says Christopher, 'and I particularly enjoyed the editorial side of the business. I was supposed to be at Kaye & Ward for a fixed trial period of two years, but after eighteen months I decided to leave. I was living in Toc H hostels in Hackney and St George's Square, and I simply couldn't stand London any more.'

Christopher got a job – 'Quite without informing me,' says Wilbert – with the East Midland Allied Press in Peterborough, who produced a number of newspapers, including the *Angling Times*, and who were attempting to branch out into book publishing, beginning with a series of titles on fishing.

At Peterborough, Christopher joined the Cathedral Voluntary Choir where he met and became friendly with another singer, Elaine Checkley.

As for Veronica and Hilary, they, in Wilbert's words, had 'collected a couple of nice young men'. In 1963, the three Awdry children had gone to Cornwall for a camping holiday. They were to have been accompanied by Veronica's current boyfriend, Michael (who was to have driven the car) but when their relationship cooled, the rest of the party found themselves without transportation. Christopher suggested they ask Alfred Fortnam, who had been at Worksop College with him. Alfred's father had just bought a new car and, as he had yet to sell his old one, was willing for his son to use it to transport the holidaymakers. 'Alfred,' says Wilbert, 'tagged along, and he's continued to tag along for the rest of his life, because he got on so well with Hilary that he decided he wanted to marry her.'

A few years later, Veronica developed a friendship with Richard Chambers, a fellow postgraduate, studying at Exeter University. One evening, at an informal meeting, a group of students were discussing childhood influences with one of their tutors: 'The name Enid Blyton came up,' recalls Veronica, 'but when conversation turned to the Railway Series, no one in the group could put a name to the author. I just sat there, getting more and more uncomfortable! It sounds absurd, but I think this was the first time I understood what those books meant to people. They were written by my Dad and I was proud of him, but I didn't realise how well-known his books were – partly because I don't think he fully realised it himself.'

Among the young men in the room, who were all enthusing about the stories, was Richard, who had been studying chemistry at Birmingham: 'As a child I did not read very much; in those postwar years there were not an awful lot of books around. I went from reading nothing to the early Thomas books and the next thing I remember reading was a Pictorial Encyclopedia when I was about ten years old. That evening at Exeter, I was passionately declaring my enthusiasm for the stories, but I would have been far too embarrassed to have done so if I'd have known that the author's daughter was sitting in that very room!' Eventually, Veronica told them the name of the Thomas the Tank Engine man and that evening saw the beginning of her friendship with Richard.

Wilbert and Margaret eventually settled on Stroud as their future home, buying a large, double-fronted house in Rodborough Avenue. The house number was thirty, so on the wall near the front door Wilbert fixed an oval London, Midland & Scottish bridge plate (used to give an identification number to bridges along a railway line) inscribed 'L. M. S. 30'. They also decided to give the house a name: 'Sodor'.

A wrought-iron gate into the front garden was a parting gift to Wilbert and Margaret from the people of Emneth and was the work of the local agricultural blacksmith, Norman Cousins, who (despite 'never showing his face in church') had always got on well with Wilbert and whose surname Wilbert had borrowed for the firm of Thomas Cousins, situated on the Ffarquhar Branch Model.

The garden, when the Awdrys moved to Rodborough Avenue, was virtually a wilderness: 'It was so terribly overgrown that you couldn't see out of the back windows! Anyway, we had three hale and hearty young men in Christopher, Alfred and Richard, so we just set them to work!'

'I enjoyed,' says Wilbert, 'the freedom of irresponsibility, in that I was no longer deluged by diocesan correspondence.' However, although retired, Wilbert had no intention of giving up his ministry and, having been duly licensed by the Bishop of Gloucester, Basil Guy, to take services anywhere in the Diocese, it wasn't long before he began receiving invitations to preach and requests to deputise for priests who were sick or were on holiday from their parishes.

Writing in an article for the *Church News* in 1985, Wilbert recalled:

> Taking occasional Sunday duty had its rewards – more valuable than the small fee! The friendships made, the welcoming smiles and handshakes from congregations at churches revisited perhaps after long intervals of time; the appreciation expressed (often quite out of proportion to services rendered); old jokes remembered, as when, on the occasion of my first visit to a certain church, I asked in the vestry which service they used and was told '1066, Sir,' by the churchwarden!

There was also the service in a church where the small lectern fitted to the pulpit worked loose, slid away and deposited Wilbert's sermon notes over the occupants of the front pew! No wonder Wilbert speaks of the 'great fun' which he has derived from the 'variety of bizarre situations' in which, over the years, he has found himself:

> On another occasion I had been invited to preach at Evensong in a very Victorian church in Cheltenham. I could see no pulpit, so I assumed that preaching was done either from the lectern or chancel steps. Not a bit of it. During the hymn after the Grace, a choirboy slipped quietly out of his place

> and started turning a large handle. Imagine my astonished amusement when, slowly and jerkily, a pulpit on wheels emerged from an alcove, and running along a special railway line, came ponderously to rest in the middle of the Chancel aisle. Fortunately I had time to compose myself before the vicar conducted me with due solemnity to the mechanical marvel. No one seemed to think it in the least odd, they were all so used to it, I suppose; but I certainly regarded having preached from a travelling pulpit as one of my more memorable experiences. Legend has it that, on one occasion, a preacher went on far too long, and a choirboy applied the closure by winding him away off stage!

Wilbert was also permitted to take services in Free Churches (provided there was no objection from the local Church of England incumbent) and he soon found himself doing duty at Methodist, Baptist and Congregational chapels – an experience which was to widen his perceptions of the 'church': 'When you are in a parish, you don't often come into contact with anyone outside your own little world; after moving to Stroud, I soon got to know most of the churches and just about everybody who went to them!'

Wilbert became one of the voluntary Chaplains of Gloucester Cathedral and took on visiting chaplaincies for several preparatory schools. Retirement, he discovered, was a complete misnomer: 'I was soon working virtually every Sunday and, eventually, our children started to get quite annoyed, because they would ask us to visit them and we couldn't, because I was always on duty!' Margaret was also busy, working as a supply teacher and a volunteer at the nearby Rodborough Child Health Clinic.

When Wilbert had appeared on *Desert Island Discs*, he had been asked (as were all Roy Plomley's castaways) what luxury he would like to take with him. 'I wanted to take my model railway,' responded Wilbert, 'but absence of electricity would make that useless.'

That model railway now underwent something of a transformation. In an article written in 1966 and published, two years later, in the magazine, *Railway Modeller*, Wilbert had announced: 'The Ffarquhar Branch is to be rebuilt. For one thing, my faithful "Bedford" which took it to many exhibitions has been sold, and for another, the 6 ft by 4 ft arrangement does not make the best use of the space available in the Railway Room of our new house.' The ambitious plans (in the event, never fully realised) included the addition of the Elsbridge loop line (passing the Dairy) and the Skarloey railway complete with 'village and tree-girt lake'. Certain alterations had had to be made, both to the upstairs room where the line was to run ('I have rehung the door to open outwards') and to the line itself: 'There is only one concession to the Beeching era. Hackenbeck Halt is closed, for lack of space to fit it in.' Otherwise, it was intended that life in and around Ffarquhar should go on as usual:

> You will still be able to get your pint at the 'Three Beetles' and play a game of bowls if you feel so inclined. Mr Neatly will probably be still tinkering with his car . . . Amos Horker, too, still keeps pigs and sheep at Tunnel Farm . . .

'It looks,' wrote Wilbert, 'as if I have got plenty to keep me busy. So the sooner I get going, the better.' What he was already busy at was a model of the Mid-Sodor Narrow Gauge Railway. The model was begun in 1966 and, since Wilbert had no experience of narrow gauge modelling, building it was largely a matter of a trial and error. Built to a scale of 4 mm. to the foot, with a track gauge of 9 mm., the model was to show 'the most spectacular part of the Mid-Sodor Railway, namely the incline from Cas-ny-Hawin to Ulfstead Road' as it would have looked in the 1890s.

The region depicted had to be compressed into an area that would divide into two baseboards: one, measuring 3 ft 6 in. by 2 ft, carrying the scenic display; the other, 3 ft 6 in. by 9 in., for the operating controls. This layout required complex planning and Wilbert experienced a lot of setbacks. Having constructed the baseboards and layout – which involved a lot of curving track with sharp gradients (one third of which would be hidden by the finished landscaping) in order to model a section of railway with a line summit of 867 feet above sea level – it was found that the model was a fraction too large to fit into the slightly tapered boot space of Wilbert's car. After an inch had been cut off each baseboard – an operation which changed the radius of one of the curves and sharpened its gradient to nearly 1 in 25 – it proved possible to transport the main baseboard in the boot and the control on the back seat of the car, the two sections being bolted together for exhibition.

The basic plan for the line was that it was to 'twist and turn from side to side of a river gorge in order to gain height'. Modelling the landscape took a long time, and the shaping of hills and moorlands were inspired by a variety of pictures of mountains, rocks and cliffs from railway posters which were juggled around until they jigsawed into an acceptable configuration.

The focal point of the layout was the station at Ulfstead Road. The road itself, which ran across a bridge over the line, was important, not just because it explained the name of the station, but because the road bridge on the model masked the fact that this was where the line exited through the backdrop into what Wilbert called in his working notes 'the outside world'. Wilbert was faced with a dilemma: the road needed traffic but it would have to be static. Instead of simply showing carts standing still on a bridge beneath which moving trains were passing, Wilbert devised a traffic jam! A traction engine and a herd of cows meet head-on, causing an *impasse* on the bridge:

> Bill Shuvvel with his traction engine and Josh Herder with his troupe of cows are old antagonists. Bill, in general, usually gets the best of it because Josh's cows soon lose interest and look for entertainment elsewhere. Then an anguished shout from Ulfstead Road's Station Master, Galahad Qualtrough makes Josh break off his pungent remarks about Bill and his blankety-blank steam kettle, and round up his strays from Station premises. Meanwhile, Bill, taking his chance, chunters through!

The Mid-Sodor model entered the exhibition circuit in September 1968, and continued to be popular at exhibitions, as an alternative to the Ffarquhar Branch Mark II, for the next twenty years, being shown as far afield as Worcester, Southampton, Plymouth, Harrogate and Nottingham.

In 1968, a month after the Mid-Sodor went on show, Wilbert was invited to be a judge at the Gloucestershire Model Railway Competition where he met co-judge, Iliffe Stokes, who, with his wife Doris, were a legendary railway modelling team. Stokes held a theory that in order to create an illusion of space, the railway modeller should avoid clutter. Wilbert, however, had found that in a very small area, such as that with which he was working on the Mid-Sodor model, space and distance could only be conveyed by cluttering up the landscape with mountains and trees. They argued about it at intervals during the competition and Stokes invited Wilbert to bring and show his model to him and his wife at their home in Dowdeswell, Gloucestershire.

The model was compact enough to be erected and operated successfully on the Stokes' sitting room table and, whilst Iliffe admitted that he liked what Wilbert had done with it, he pointed out that Ulfstead Road was too important to the layout to make do with a station house that was modelled out of a cardboard kit. Doris Stokes offered to make an authentic-looking model house for the layout. This she did using a photograph, supplied by Wilbert, of a station building at Escairgaeliog, on the defunct Corris Railway. The model – actually a mirror image of the original – fitted so well that, as Wilbert puts it, 'the house seems literally to have grown out of the landscape.' This addition to the scenery at Ulfstead Road was the beginning of what Wilbert refers to as the 'Mark II' stage of the Mid-Sodor, a model which continued to undergo refinements to both its scenery and its rolling-stock, which was improved to include a number of engines that were to make their appearance in the Railway Series over the next few years.

When, during the fanciful speculations required of Wilbert for *Desert Island Discs*, he relinquished the idea of taking his model railway with him as a luxury, he decided, instead, on 'a good supply of lined foolscap, plenty of pencils, and a rubber'. 'Lots more books?' asked Roy Plomley. 'Lots more books!' replied Wilbert.

Easy to say; another thing to do! Twenty titles was no mean achievement, but the eighty stories contained in them had used up a quantity of research, so there was a constant need to find new characters and stories: 'Christopher, George and I would go away visiting different lines and preserved railways, and we would try to collect possible material for the next book; then, at the end of each July, I would have to start trying to get things down on paper.'

In 1966, what Wilbert was getting down on paper was a book entitled *Main Line Engines* which featured old friends such as Thomas, Gordon and Duck and introduced two new characters:

> *Bill and Ben are tank-engines who live at a port on Edward's line, each has four wheels, a tiny chimney and dome, and a small squat cab.*
> *They are kept busy pulling trucks for ships in the harbour and engines on the main line.*
> *The trucks are filled with China Clay dug from the nearby hills. China Clay is important. It is needed for pottery, paper, paint, plastics and many other things.*

Wilbert had read about a pair of curiously-shaped tank engines working at the Port of Par, near Fowey in Cornwall, whose short chimneys and squat cabs were designed to clear a particularly low bridge on the line. 'I went to Cornwall in the hope of seeing them at work and, possibly, taking a trip on the footplate. I talked to the Harbour Master at the Port of Par, who told me that the driver was a very crusty old chap who did *not* like parsons!' However, he promised to see what could be done, stressing that Wilbert would have to make himself as 'inconspicuous as possible'.

Later that afternoon, Wilbert was riding the footplate – permission having been given, 'with a fairly bad grace', for strictly no more than half an hour. However, Wilbert had done his homework and was able to talk to the driver knowledgeably about his engine: 'He was absolutely wrapped up with it, and did everything that needed doing to it, except boiler repairs. You almost expected steam to come out of his ears!'

An hour went by with Wilbert still there while they shunted the yard; then, when they had finished work in the yard, the driver suggested they take a trip up the line. 'We travelled as far as the clay-dries and back,' recalls Wilbert, 'by which time I'd been on the footplate for about two hours! Then he said, "Well, I've got to put the engine in the shed now." So I got down off the footplate and, as I turned to thank him, he said: "Didn't you ever want to be an engine driver when you were young?" "Yes," I replied. "And then," he said, with a pitying look, "you went and spoilt it all by turning yourself into a parson! *What* an opportunity you missed!" '

Bill and Ben are likely little individuals – almost as irresponsible and prankish as Thomas and Percy once were – and are described in terms of young children, scampering about, chuckling, squeaking and making jokes:

Their Drivers examined a patch of oil. 'That's a diesel,' they said, wiping the rails clean.

'It's a what'll?' asked Bill.

'A diseasel, I think,' replied Ben. 'There's a notice about them in our Shed.'

'I remember, "Coughs and sneezles spread diseasels." '

'Who had a cough in his smokebox yesterday?'

'Fireman cleaned it, didn't he?'

'Yes, but the dust made him sneezle: so there you are. It's your fault the diseasel came.'

'It isn't!'

'It is!'

It was a return to the kind of banter at which Wilbert excelled (here making a joke at the expense of a medical poster of the times, which carried the slogan: 'Coughs and sneezes spread diseases'). The diesel in question is, at first, not even given the distinction of a capital 'D', but is later identified as a 'Metropolitan Vickers, diesel-electric, Type 2' – and, since he turns out to be really rather a good engine, is known by the friendly name of BoCo. The inspiration for BoCo was a real, experimental diesel known as CoBo, the name of which indicated an unusual four-wheel and six-wheel bogie arrangement. CoBos did not prove very successful and the only one still in existence is in preservation. 'I chose the CoBo,' says Wilbert, 'because it was distinctive and had character; but I changed the name around because I thought BoCo was easier to say and had the ring of an affectionate nickname.'

The book contains a mix of amusing and exciting escapades: James has problems with some busy bees; Edward bravely soldiers on when one of his crank-pins breaks; and Gordon, after sneering at branch lines, gets accidentally switched onto one, where he is mercilessly ragged by Bill and Ben:

> *'What's that?' asked Bill loudly.*
> *'Ssh!' whispered Ben. 'It's Gordon.'*
> *'It* looks *like Gordon, but it can't be. Gordon* never *comes on Branch Lines. He thinks them vulgar.'*
> *Gordon pretended he hadn't heard.*
> *'If it isn't Gordon,' said Ben, 'it's just a pile of old iron . . . '*
> *' . . . which we'd better take to the scrap-yard.'*
> *'No, Bill, this lot's useless for scrap. We'll take it to the harbour and dump it in the sea.'*

Peter Edwards' illustrations shows an alarmed Gordon with raised eyebrows and big, wide eyes in which the pupils have been reduced to tiny dots. 'Because of the limitations imposed by the size of the pictures,' writes Edwards, 'the face is all you've got with which to express anything. I had difficulty with the Scottish Twins – all I could think of to make them look different from the other engines was to give them whiskery eyebrows! But with most of the engines I had to go along with what was already drawn: rather round-eyed, bulbous-nosed characters, with no ears and no ability to turn the head, which really restricted what could be done with the facial expressions.'

Despite such restrictions, the faces in *Main Line Engines* are superb: an angry James going boss-eyed as he tries to look at the bee on his nose; or Edward, his faced screwed up with the excruciating pain of his broken crank-pin or with his tongue between his lips in concentration as he struggles on regardless. 'As to Gordon, who is obviously the most aristocratic engine of the lot,' says Edwards, 'I modelled him on Eric Marriott, who has rather a splendid nose!' The dignified features of Kaye & Ward's editor and Assistant Managing Director (including that nose!) are clearly to be seen in several of the illustrations in which Gordon appears.

Of his working relationship with Wilbert, Edwards writes: 'He was very clear and much more accommodating than I had expected. The preoccupation with engine details had been forced upon him by his gimlet-eyed young readers, but once I had learned which way round the engines must face (aided at times by the surprising number of turntables on the Island) it was soon possible to present him directly with finished drawings, to be touched up, if necessary, with little effort.'

Peter Edwards, like John Kenney, had regular meetings with Wilbert in which work and socialising happily blended. Wilbert recalls the first time the

ABOVE Often spotted at railway events, the Thomas the Tank Engine Man in cloth cap and clerical collar.

LEFT Wilbert Awdry, President of the Dean Forest Railway, with Margaret Radway and companion (the first female rail crew) in the late 1980s.

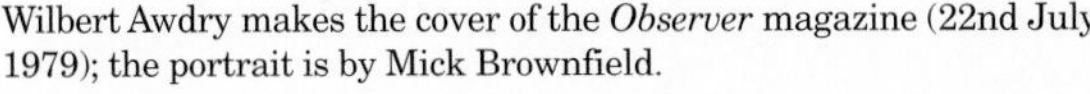

Wilbert Awdry makes the cover of the *Observer* magazine (22nd July, 1979); the portrait is by Mick Brownfield.

ABOVE Wilbert, in 1985 with a drawing of a Great Western 'Duke Dog' class engine by Rolf Harris.

LEFT The Reverends, E. R. ('Teddy') Boston and W. V. Awdry, the Fat and Thin Clergymen photographed on Teddy's locomotive, Pixie, at Cadeby in 1975.

The last book in the Railway Series to be written by Wilbert Awdry was published in 1972.

ABOVE Wilbert Awdry went into 'private practice' and moved to Stroud in Gloucestershire. He called his new home 'Sodor'.

RIGHT Margaret and Wilbert Awdry on their Ruby Wedding Anniversary in 1978 with Hilary, Christopher and Veronica.

BELOW RIGHT Wilbert Awdry with his brother George, son Christopher and two son-in-laws Richard Chambers and Alfred Fortnam.

Margaret and Wilbert Awdry celebrate their Golden Wedding Anniversary in August 1988.

PETER EDWARDS, born in London in 1934, studied illustration at Regent Street Polytechnic. In 1957, he married the Swedish illustrator and designer Gunvor Ovden who, five years later, was invited to take over illustrating the Railway Series. When the work proved not to be Gunvor's forte, it was carried on by her husband who illustrated nine books – *Stepney the 'Bluebell' Engine* (1963) to the last volume written by Wilbert Awdry, *Tramway Engines* (1972).

ABOVE End of the line . . . the sad demise of steam on the 'Other Railway' as pictured by Peter Edwards in *Stepney the "Bluebell" Engine* (1963).

LEFT The Reverend Teddy Boston and the author of the Railway Series, the Reverend Wilbert Awdry, depicted by Peter Edwards as The Fat and Thin Clergymen in *Duke the Lost Engine* (1970).

. . . the full force of the gale struck him like a blow. *Mountain Engines* (1964).

Peter Edward's portrait of Gordon in *Main Line Engines* (1966) was modelled on Railway Series editor, Eric Marriott.

The books about the engines of Sodor have made them famous all over the world, but the Railway Series has also featured occasional appearances by celebrated locomotives from mainland Britain.

John T. Kenney painted this meeting between Duck and another Great Western Railway engine, City of Truro, in *Duck and the Diesel Engine* (1958).

A portrait of Talyllyn by John T. Kenney in *Little Old Engine* (1959).

Captain Baxter one of the Bluebell Line engines depicted by Peter Edwards in *Stepney the 'Bluebell' Engine* (1963).

Bluebell and Primrose, two of the engines on the Bluebell Line, painted by Peter Edwards for *Stepney the 'Bluebell' Engine.*

Stepney the eponymous hero of *Stepney the 'Bluebell' Engine* who was only depicted as having a face when he was visiting the island of Sodor.

Peter Edwards' illustration of Flying Scotsman's visit to Sodor in *Enterprising Engines* (1968).

Peter Edwards shows Talyllyn and Dolgoch celebrating their 100th birthday with an exhibition run in *Very Old Engines* (1965).

Thomas meets Stephenson's Rocket at the National Railway Museum at York; an illustration by Clive Spong for *Thomas and the Great Railway Show* (1991).

While at the National Railway Museum, Thomas also meets Iron Duke.

Mallard and Duchess of Hamilton flank Thomas outside the railway shed in York.

Thomas and Green Arrow, another of Clive Spong's illustrations for *Thomas and the Great Railway Show*.

Wilbert, the engine on the Forest of Dean Railway named after the creator of the Railway Series, painted by Clive Spong in *Wilbert the Forest Engine* (1994).

CLIVE SPONG, born in Mickleover, Derby, in 1947, attended first Leicester College of Art (where Reginald Dalby and John Kenney had both studied) and then Coventry College of Art. Clive, who was given his first Thomas the Tank Engine book when he was about six years old, began illustrating the Railway Series with the twenty-seventh title in the Railway Series, and the first to be written by Christopher Awdry, *Really Useful Engines*.

ABOVE Poor Gordon was getting very breathless.
Gordon the High-Speed Engine (1987)

LEFT 'Undercoat!' muttered Henry in disgust.
Henry and the Express (1993)

The old and the new: James the Red Engine with Emma the Inter-City 125 in *Gordon the High Speed Engine* (1987).

The harbour was busy and Toby worked hard.
Thomas Comes Home (1992)

ABOVE The caption to this 1988 cartoon by Whittock simply read 'Holy Smoke'.

LEFT Wilbert Awdry attended many events during his retirement . Here he is reading a story to a young admirer, Emma Rouse, at the Swindon Model Railway Club Exhibition in November 1985.

The cover of *Really Useful Engines* the first Railway Series title to be written by Christopher Awdry and published in 1983.

Christopher Awdry with his wife Diana and son, Richard, photographed by his brother-in-law, Alfred Fortnam, in 1982 around the time Christopher was telling his own Thomas the Tank Engine stories to Richard.

Scenes from Britt Allcroft's television series *Thomas the Tank Engine and Friends.*

ABOVE Britt Allcroft and Wilbert Awdry in 1986.

LEFT Two generations of storytellers: Wilbert and Christopher Awdry pictured with some of the model engines from *Thomas the Tank Engine and Friends.*

BELOW The spectre of John Major confronts Thomas and the Fat Controller. An illustration by Nick Clark for Incledon/Clark's *Thomas the Privatised Tank Engine.* (1994).

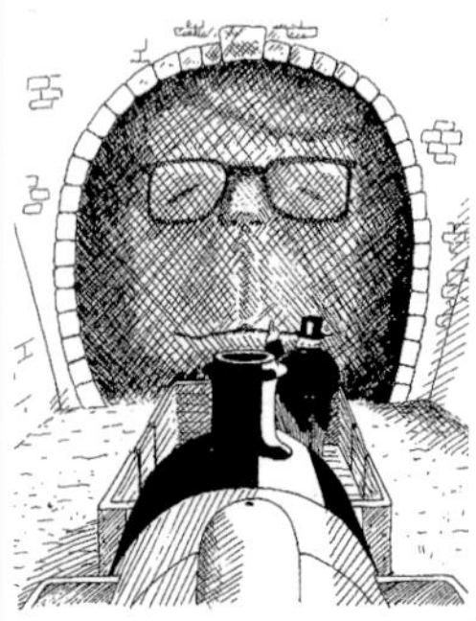

Edwards family arrived at Rodborough Avenue: 'We looked out of the window and saw first one child, and then another, and then another and then yet *another*, scrambling out of the car!'

'We had at least four of our six children with us,' remembers Gunvor Edwards, 'and when Mrs Awdry invited us to stay for tea (scones and home-made loganberry jam) there weren't enough chairs for us all. However, it didn't matter because Mr Awdry told them that it was quite all right to sit on the floor, cross-legged, like North American Indians, so that is what the older ones did. However, the little one, Gavin, perched on a chair and, in the middle of tea, suddenly toppled off and fell under the table! Mr Awdry was much amused by the fact that, after a while, Gavin came crawling out again, unhurt and quite unconcerned.'

'I will never forget,' says Peter Edwards, 'the consideration and sober respect paid by Wilbert to our children, Martina, Adrian, Josephine and Gavin. Wilbert introduced them to the Branch Line layout, which he had set up in his Model Railway room upstairs, with just the right tone of amused seriousness to keep the older ones absorbed by his railway world. Gavin, whose attention span was, at that time, more limited, spent most of the time under the tea table (again!) playing with a small railway set provided just for him.'

The train set which young Gavin Edwards played with was probably the new one from Meccano/Hornby (for which his father had designed the packaging). Wilbert had, for some years, been trying to persuade Hornby to make working models of the engines in the Railway Series, and, in 1966, they finally produced a model of Percy. 'Here's some really happy news,' announced an advertisement on the back-wrappers of the Railway Series:

> You can have Percy the Small Engine all to yourself! – Just like he looks in the stories. Same face, same colours – everything! The cheeky little engine can come puffing out of the pages and into your playroom, pulling his own gaily coloured train on his own rails . . . You could get him from the toyshop now – and you'll be sharing all Percy's exciting adventures tonight!

Wilbert had an exciting railway adventure of his own in 1967, when he and Teddy Boston were invited to the Isle of Man. The island's 3 foot, narrow-gauge railway, which had been started in 1874, had closed down in the autumn of 1965. 'For eighteen months,' says Wilbert, 'locomotives lay in their sheds, coaches stood dingy and decrepit in sidings, stations locked up and deserted. All became prey to vandals.' In March 1967, a company was formed by the Marquis of Ailsa to lease the line and a re-opening day was fixed for 3rd June.

Time was at a premium, former employees rallied round and Teddy Boston and Wilbert Awdry received the call!

A diary of events records all kinds of escapades as the two clergymen did their best to help. There was, for example, the Herculean labour of transporting station furniture and signs in an almost unmanageable three-ton motor truck: 'My remark that it is lucky they've got the sandbags out (for the T.T. races) was not well received!' They turned their hands to anything that needed doing whether it was cleaning out engine boiler-tubes or the men's lavatory. They polished up rusty brass-work with 'scrapers, emery paper and plenty of elbow grease', and cleared out fifty to sixty years accumulation of junk from the cab of one of the engines, Caledonia (which Teddy Boston was to drive at the opening ceremony):

> . . . Old spanners which fitted no nuts that we could find, decrepit oil lamps, paraffin cans, candle ends, bits of piping. One tin was a prize specimen. Of two to three pint size, it had originally held paint. The outside was rusted away, but [the] tin still kept its shape because of the film of paint inside. Unfortunately W.A. handled it unwarily, and broke it. We inspected cab fittings, and noted items for attention tomorrow, notably gauge glasses, which appear blocked, and regulator which, not unnaturally, is very stiff.

Eventually, the day of the opening ceremony dawned. Everywhere were crowds of 'grey top hats and morning coats', and Wilbert found himself inappropriately dressed: 'W.A.'s disreputable raincoat and cloth cap eyed askance ("Hasn't he heard of Moss Bros?"). However, his dog collar vouches for his respectability, and some of the "top hats" recognise him as Thomas the Tank Engine!'

While old lines were reopening on the Isle of Man, so too was a line on nearby Sodor:

> *Douglas and Donald disappeared regularly behind the Big Station, along a line on which none of the others had ever gone. They returned with loaded ballast trains, and were most mysterious about it.*
> *'Verra wee engines bring the ballast doun fra the hills,' was all they would say.*
> *Soon the engines could talk of nothing else. James and Henry thought the 'Verra wee engines' must be some kind of magic.*
> *'I don't believe it,' said Gordon. 'Donald and Douglas have pulled our wheels before.'*

The mystery was explained in the author's introductory letter to his twenty-second book:

Dear Friends,

Some leadmines up in the hills have long been closed, but their waste-heaps still spoil a lovely valley.

The Fat Controller has now found that the waste is good weed-killing railway ballast. He talked to the Owner and the Thin Controller of the Skarloey Railway, and other important people. They 'went shares' and built a Small Railway to fetch it away.

The Small Engines are managed by a Controller. They call him the Small Controller; but that is only in fun. He is bigger than either of the others!

However fanciful talk of small magical engines might have seemed, the inspiration for *Small Railway Engines*, published in 1967, had come from a real 15 in. gauge railway: the Ravenglass and Eskdale Railway, in Cumbria. Wilbert had visited Britain's oldest narrow gauge railway first, in 1966, with the Reverend Teddy Boston, and subsequently with Margaret.

Following what had become a tradition for places in Britain to have counterparts in Sodor, Wilbert named his new line (which, as Sodor's historical records later revealed, was built along the former track-bed of the defunct Mid-Sodor Railway) the Arlesdale Railway; while the engines on the Ravenglass and Eskdale – River Mite, River Irt and River Esk – were twinned with three endearing, if a little rough and ready, characters: Mike (newly painted red), Bert (who is blue) and Rex (green):

Rex introduced Duck to Bert and Mike. 'As you can see . . . the Small Controller's given us different coats.'

'Silly nonsense,' grumbled Mike.

'I like *being blue,' protested Bert.*

'It's all right for you,*' fumed Mike, 'but not for me. Passengers'll say I look like a pillar-box!'*

'Shocking!' said Rex, and winked at Duck. 'Consider my *feelings. When we were both green, passengers kept calling me Mike!'*

'You . . . you . . .' spluttered Mike.

'Stow it you two,' said Bert.

One of the stories in the book was based on a real incident experienced by Teddy Boston: Bert is splashed with mud by a passing car, and pays off the car's driver, when he takes a ride on the engine, by shooting so much steam up among the wet trees that they shower him with water. More than that, Teddy and Wilbert both appear as characters in the book.

The engines were being cleaned and polished for the day. Bert, who was going out first, had a tall chimney in his funnel to draw up his fire.
'We've got Visitors today,' said his Driver.
Rex yawned. 'We have 'em every day,' grunted Mike.
'But these are Special,' said the Driver. 'One takes "moving pictures", and the other writes books. So mind you all behave.'
'I don't want to be a moving picture in a book,' protested Bert. 'I want to stay as I am.'

The visitors turn out to be two clergymen: 'one fat, the other thin'. Although readers might have supposed the Fat and Thin Clergymen to be no more real than the Fat and Thin Controllers, Peter Edward's illustration of them meeting Bert shows Teddy Boston (drawn from photographs) and Wilbert Awdry (drawn from life).

Both Reginald Dalby and John Kenney had included likenesses of Wilbert (along with other 'real life' individuals) in occasional illustrations for the Railway Series; but Wilbert had never before been identified. Now the creator was making an appearance in his own created world; the writer was becoming a character in his own fiction. It is interesting to speculate why, at this point, Wilbert Awdry began writing himself into his texts.

Was it, perhaps, because, after so many years of 'archeology', the Island of Sodor had become, in a sense, a real place? Was it because the extending of Sodor's railway system to include new lines, with parallels in Britain, had simply made it possible for Wilbert to imagine himself there as easily as *here* – after all, having travelled on the Talyllyn, Snowdon, Ravenglass and Eskdale Railways, hadn't he also travelled the Skarloey, Culdee and Arlesdale Railways?

Or was the reason for Wilbert's appearance in the stories because he felt so alienated by what was happening on the railways of his own world?

'Cheer up, Gordon!' said the Fat Controller.
'I can't, Sir. The others say I've got boiler-ache, but I haven't, Sir. I keep thinking about the Dreadful State of the World, Sir. Is it true, Sir, what the diesels say?'
'What do they say?'
'They boast that they've abolished Steam, *Sir.'*
'Yes, Gordon. It is true.'

This shocking revelation came in the twenty-third title in the series (and the first to carry the imprint Kaye & Ward), *Enterprising Engines*. By the year of publication, 1968, the age of British steam was over. The fires were cold and the boilers drained; almost all the great giants – which had thundered along the iron road and ruled the world of transportation for over one hundred years – were scrapped and destroyed, their rusting remnants scattered like dinosaur bones. Lines had been axed and stations closed: Michael Flanders and Donald Swann, in their revue, *At the Drop of Another Hat*, sang a melancholic hymn to the 'Slow Train' and those places with haunting names – Miller's Dale, Tideswell, Ambergate, Chittening and Summercotes – to which no one would ever again take a train.

The Railway Series had foreseen the end. In *Gallant Old Engine* (1962), Skarloey had spoken of the threat of being scrapped; the following year, in *Stepney the 'Bluebell' Engine*, the author wrote that Percy 'feels sad because many fine steam engines are cut up on the Other Railway (B.R.)':

> *'Oh dear! I couldn't understand it all; but engines on the Other Railway aren't safe now. Their Controllers are cruel. They don't like engines any more. They put them on cold damp sidings, and then,' Percy nearly sobbed, 'they . . . they c-c-cut them up.'*

In *Enterprising Engines*, Flying Scotsman, one of the few engines to escape this terrible fate, visits Sodor. A few years earlier, Wilbert had written about this legendary engine in his *Church of England Newspaper* series, 'Locomotives Which Made History', recounting the story of how, in 1934, it had made the round trip journey of 371 miles from Kings Cross to Leeds in five hours, nine minutes, during which time it had reached, and held, a speed of 100 miles an hour.

Drawn from life at Doncaster by Peter Edwards, Flying Scotsman tells Gordon that he is lucky 'to have a Controller who knows how to run railways'. When the time eventually comes for Flying Scotsman to depart, there is an emotional leave-taking, illustrated by Peter Edwards in a celebratory picture which shows the great L. N. E. R. engine, wreathed in smiles, standing amongst a group of Sodor engines:

> *The Fat Controller said that they had all been honoured, and thanked Flying Scotsman and his Owner for their help. 'Please tell everyone,' he went on, 'that whatever happens elsewhere, steam will still be at work here. We shall be glad to welcome all who want to see, and travel behind,* real *engines.'*

In the same book, however, two 'unreal' diesel engines visit Sodor. These visitors have no names: they are not even called 'Diesel' or 'diesel', they are simply referred to by their numbers, 7101 and 199 – except that Henry refers to the latter as 'old Spamcan'.

Some years ago, Wilbert Awdry drew up a list of all the stories in his books and the source of their inspiration. Of the *Enterprising Engines* story 'Super Rescue' – in which a steam engine pulls two 'dead diesels' and their trains – he noted: 'Based on a reader's account with photos of a trip from Bournemouth to W'loo.' The reader, whose name was Richard and to whom the book is dedicated, had witnessed this extraordinary sight in April 1967; but it was a rare day on the Other Railway when a steam engine was able to play such a triumphant role.

Wilbert admits that the next story, 'Escape', is 'fiction', but adds that he believes it 'would *just be possible*':

> *Douglas had taken the 'Midnight Goods' to a station on the Other Railway. He was shunting ready for his return journey, when he heard a faint 'Hisssssssssssss'.*
> *'That sounds like an engine,' he thought.*
> *The 'Hisssss' came again. This time, it sounded almost despairing. 'Who's there?' he asked.*
> *A whisper came. 'Are you a Fat Controller's engine?'*
> *'Aye, and proud of it.'*
> *'Thank goodness! I'm Oliver. We're escaping to your railway, but we've run out of coal, and I've no more steam.'*

The book ends happily enough: Oliver, who is a Great Western Railway engine, manages his Colditz-like escape to Sodor and there joins Duck on the reopened Arlesburgh Line: 'It runs along the coast to the Small Railway. "We *re-open* Branches," they boast.'

As for the diesels: 199 is sent packing, while 7101 (who turns out to be better than most of his kind) is given the name Bear and encouraged to learn how railways are run on the Island of Sodor. A phrase used by Wilbert in this passage about Bear is a telling one: 'He had good manners for a start, so Henry didn't find it hard to teach him our ways.' Not the Fat Controller's ways, but '*our* ways'. For Wilbert, who had lived and breathed the world of railways since his earliest days, Sodor offered a retreat from a time with which he was out of joint.

What in its earliest manifestations was a reassuring image of all that is safe and secure in childhood, had now come to represent an adult haven: a place where a man might avoid, or at least ignore, the worst aspects of change, and to which any 'enterprising engine' worth its coal would want to escape.

The engine who, in such extraordinary fashion, had claimed the sanctuary of Sodor was to reappear in the next volume of stories which ran into a little trouble when it came to the question of a title. The usual author's letter was addressed to Margaret: 'Dear M., We both wanted to call this book Little Western Engines; but Publishers are stern men. They did not approve . . . '

It wasn't so much that Kaye & Ward's editor, Eric Marriott, didn't approve, as that he wanted something less anonymous than *Little Western Engines*, which was taken from the nickname given to the Arlesburgh Branch line by the other engines. Like *Mountain Engines*, *Main Line Engines* and *Small Railway Engines* the proposed title described the type of railway the stories were about, but lacked the impact of those initial titles which had begun with a name, such as *Thomas the Tank Engine*, *James the Red Engine*, *Henry the Green Engine* and *Gordon the Big Engine*. The last title that had featured an engine by name was *Stepney the 'Bluebell' Engine* which had appeared six years earlier.

Since Oliver had made his debut, in *Enterprising Engines*, in highly dramatic circumstances – hiding in disused quarry lines 'with diesels baying and growling like hounds outside' – Marriott thought the new book should have the engine's name in the title: it was called, therefore, *Oliver the Western Engine*. In his introductory letter to Margaret, Wilbert sniped mildly at the publishers:

> They, of course, don't know the trouble we've had with Oliver. We hope he has learnt sense, but goodness knows what will happen when he finds he has a book all to himself . . . .
>
> I know! If Oliver gets uppish, we'll set Messrs. Kaye & Ward on to him. That'll teach him!
>
> W.

The story in which Oliver gets himself into 'trouble' is a classic of its kind. So remarkable have been Oliver's adventures in escaping to Sodor, that he can scarcely avoid getting 'puffed up in the smokebox':

> *They all wanted to know about his adventures.*
> *'Amazing!' Henry would remark.*
> *'Oliver,' said James, 'has resource . . . '*
> *' . . . and sagacity,' put in Gordon. 'He is an example to us all.'*
> *'You're too kind,' giggled Oliver modestly.*

Like many another before him, Oliver is on track for disaster – even his coach, Isabel, can see it coming: 'He's proud, he's conceited; he's heading for trouble, I feel it in my frames.' Pushed and shoved by troublesome trucks, Oliver ends up, bunker downwards, in the well of the turntable:

> *Later that day, Donald and Douglas spoke pungently in Scots, and the Fat Controller spoke pointedly in English. All three left Oliver in no doubt at all, that so far from being sagacious, he was a very silly engine.*

Oliver manages to restore his reputation in a struggle of wills with Scruffey – a black, battered wagon with a vulgar, one-toothed leer – who eventually comes apart and, in one of the few frightening illustrations in the Railway Series, is shown lying in a heap with a fixed, terrible-eyed stare on its disembodied face.

The mood of *Oliver the Western Engine* is less doom-laden than some of the recent volumes and it opens with an escapade inspired by another story from *The Railway Gazette*'s 'Scrap Heap'. Donald having taunted Duck for 'quacking' on about being a Great Western engine, finds himself the butt of a practical joke:

> *A duckling popped out of Donald's tank at the first water-stop. Both Driver and Fireman goggled with surprise, but Donald laughed.*
> *'Na doot at a' who's behind this,' he said . . .*

Donald and his crew take their revenge and the following morning something is discovered beneath Duck's bunker – a nest box with an egg in it! It was the kind of prank that would have been much enjoyed by the locals at The Duke of Wellington or The Queen's Head in Emneth.

Such innocent goings-on are sharply contrasted by the political points made in the final story which takes its title from the name of an obnoxious character, 'Bulgy' – a huge and decidedly *red* bus:

> *The bus watched the passengers happily 'milling' round the Small Railway.*
> *'Stupid nonsense!' he grumbled. 'Wouldn't have brought 'em if I'd known. I'd have had a breakdown or something.'*
> *'I'm glad you didn't,' smiled Duck. 'You'd have spoilt their fun. Look how they're enjoying themselves!'*
> *'Pah!' snorted the bus. 'Enjoyment's all you engines live for, taking the petrol from the tanks of us workers. Come the Revolution,' he went on fiercely, 'railways'll be ripped up. Cars 'nd coaches'll trample their remains.'*
> *'Free the roads,' he growled. 'Free the roads from Railway Tyranny!'*

Bulgy, of course, comes to a much-deserved bad end – wedged under a low bridge and dumped in a field to live out his remaining days as a henhouse.

There is a terrible justice in the bus – emblazoned, in Peter Edward's illustrations, with such slogans as 'Free the Roads' and 'Join the Anti-Rail League' – meeting a similar fate to many steam engines.

The bringing low of Bulgy was Wilbert's last political statement in the Railway Series, and the next book provided altogether more gentle and genteel diversions. *Duke the Lost Engine* was the twenty-fifth title in the series (which had now sold three million copies and was being published in paperback) and the only book other than *The Three Railway Engines* to open with the magical words, 'Once upon a time . . . '

> *. . . three little engines lived in their own little shed on their own little railway. Duke was brown, Falcon blue, and Stuart green.*

Falcon and Stuart turn out to be Sir Handel and Peter Sam as 'youngsters'; while Duke (impudently nicknamed 'Granpuff' by the others) was named after His Grace, the Duke of Sodor, and was based on another veteran engine. Wilbert had first encountered the inspiration for Duke during a visit to Portmadoc with George in 1958. Here is how Wilbert described it, in 1961, in one of his 'Famous Locomotives' articles for the *Church of England Newspaper*:

> Who would expect a railway level-crossing on a hilltop? Yet one bars the steep road out of the village of Penrhyn near Portmadoc in North Wales.
> In the Station on the left you may see a narrow-gauge train. The low-slung coaches are attractive in ivory and green, but the engine holds our interest as it snorts away round the hillside. It is not only really clean, but an unusual type. It is a 0-4-0 tank engine with a tender.

The engine, named Prince is the oldest steam engine in regular passenger service anywhere and the Festiniog Railway, on which it runs, is the longest serving public narrow gauge railway in the world. The Awdry brothers had an opportunity to ride the footplate; although, as Wilbert's notes on the visit record, it wasn't the easiest of trips:

> W. had first go on Prince. He stood on the Fireman's side. Fireman was outside in tender looking in! With left elbow wedged on cotton waste pad on cylinder behind and right knee wedged against inside of Cab side sheets and right hand holding Cab handrail knob, he was fairly comfortable and preserved against lateral movement, though an occasional jolt at rail joints brought his head in sharp contact with Cab roof! Standing in cab, feeling the

motion, and listening to the exhaust beats gave one a great impression of speed – but this was dispelled on looking out and seeing the scenery ambling by at about 15 m.p.h.

Duke the Lost Engine contains another guest appearance by the Fat and Thin Clergymen and the Small Engines:

'Are you writing another book, Sir?'
'Yes,' said the Thin Clergyman, 'but not about you!' he smiled at their downcast faces.
'Cheer up!' he went on. 'It's about a nice old engine who is lost; but if you're good, the artist might put you in the pictures.'

As, of course, he did in one of the book's dreamy, soft-focus illustrations. It is a sunny, optimistic tale which, in a way, celebrates the work – dear to Wilbert's heart – of the various railway preservation societies who have found, saved and restored so many engines. Like several of the most recent titles, the book is set in both the past and the present, as it gradually pieces together its story of death and resurrection. First comes the closure of the local lead mines and the railway line; the sale of Falcon and Stuart and the abandonment of Duke, oiled, greased, covered and left in a shed; the passing years during which Duke becomes buried beneath landslides and rock-falls; then his discovery, by the two Clergymen, who restore him, Lazarus-like, to new life on the rails:

Peter Sam and Sir Handel were on 'early turn'. They peeped out of the shed.
'He's there!' they whispered, 'Shsh! Shsh! Shsh!'
Duke opened his eyes. 'You woke me,' he grumbled. 'In my young days engines were . . . '
' . . . seen and not heard, Granpuff. Remember?'
'I remember,' said Duke, 'two idle good-for-nothings called Falcon and Stuart . . .'
'Good for you, Granpuff! We're glad you've come. We can keep you in order now.'
'Keep me *in order! Impertinence! Be off!'*
The pair chuffed away, well content.
'Impudent scallywags,' murmured Duke; but his old eyes twinkled, and for the first time in years he smiled as he dozed in the sun.

Even the one dark episode in the book is more comic than alarming. There is talk of an unnamed American engine who 'rode roughly and often came off the rails', drawling: 'Listen, Bud, in the States we don't care a dime for a few spills.' Eventually the Manager took his wheels away and turned him into a pumping engine and Peter Edward's picture shows the hapless American, bricked up – like some unfortunate character in a story by Edgar Allan Poe – but with his nose resting on the top row of bricks!

Duke the Lost Engine is a testament to the longevity, not just of its central character but of the Railway Series itself. When the younger engines tired of listening to Duke's stories, they would 'wink at each other and chant solemnly':

> *'Engines come and engines go,*
> *Granpuff "goes on" for ever!'*

It must have seemed to many that the Reverend W. Awdry's stories would also 'go on for ever'. Other engine-stories had come along – some of them looking suspiciously like examples of plagiarism. There was, for example, Ursula Hourihane's *The Little Blue Engine That Wanted a Drink*, with pictures by Rene Cloke (the artist who had illustrated *Our Child Begins to Pray*), that had a very familiar ring to it:

> *There was once a little blue engine. It was a smart little engine with shiny brass fittings and with its number painted on its side in gold letters – 1234. The little blue engine was too small to pull heavy goods trains and it was too small to pull heavy passenger trains. It could only go on rather short journeys with just a few people in about two coaches*

When, however, little blue engine gets stuck going up a hill (because the driver has forgotten to give him any water) it behaves in a way which no engine on Sodor would ever do – it heaves and puffs itself off the rails and rumbles – 'very carefully and slowly' – over the grass and down into a water-filled ditch:

> *'Toot-toot! Water!' it shouted when it saw the cool pool in the ditch. Schloop! Schloop! Huish! The little blue engine drank and drank of the cool clear water.*

That done, the little blue engine returns to the railway line: 'U-PP, it struggled, puffing and grunting, till it was safely on the shiny rails once more.' As it had come, so the little blue engine (and others of its ilk) went, but Wilbert chugged on, year after year: twenty-five titles, containing 101 stories (each book has four stories, except *Henry the Green Engine* which has five). Now, however, it was beginning to look as if he was running out of steam . . .

Editor, Eric Marriott, had experienced increasing difficulty in obtaining the typescript for each new story; and illustrator, Peter Edwards, recalls finding himself with less and less time to work on the pictures. 'I had warned the publishers,' says Wilbert, 'that I felt I was getting rather stale: that it was up-hill work and was becoming difficult to find genuine events which hadn't been used before; but they were on to a good thing and they didn't want me to stop.' Indeed, Marriott annually found himself trying to encourage and cajole one of his company's most successful writers into writing a new book. In 1971, he failed . . .

Booksellers leafing through the latest book catalogue from Kaye & Ward, would have been surprised to find no mention of a new title in the Railway Series. Such a thing was unprecedented. *The Three Railway Engines* had been published in 1945, *Thomas the Tank Engine* had appeared the following year and *James the Red Engine* in 1948; each year, from then on, for twenty-three years, a new title had always been added to the series.

To fill the gap, the publishers issued some more titles in paperback and Peter Edwards redrew 'The Rev. W. Awdry's Railway Map of the Island of Sodor'. It was twelve years since the map had first been published, since when several additional railway lines had been opened, re-opened or 'discovered'. Gone were the dolphins and mermaids and the nursery colour-scheme; the map was now reproduced to look like an authentic Ordnance Survey Map – complete with contour lines, towns, roads, rivers and railways (each line marked in a different colour) – and it folded up into the tall, oblong shape so familiar to hikers and ramblers. It was a charming conceit, and some years later, Peter Edwards was astonished to see a copy of the map on show in the British Museum in an exhibition of imaginary cartography.

The following year, 1972, the Railway Series received a reprise, when a new title, *Tramway Engines*, was published. Although the author, in his 'Foreword', maintained that Thomas had been 'pestering' him to write about his Branch Line, it was really a combination of Eric Marriott and Margaret Awdry who persuaded Wilbert – who candidly admits to having got 'a bit fed up with it all' – to produce yet another volume for the Railway Series. It was, however, to be his last.

It is appropriate that for his subject matter, Wilbert should have returned to the most popular of his characters. Just as Beatrix Potter's books for children came to be known as 'The Peter Rabbit Books' (even though Peter appeared in only a few of the series), so the Railway Series was more commonly referred to as 'The Thomas the Tank Engine Books'.

According to Thomas, his Branch Line is 'the importantest part of the whole railway' and, even though he doesn't feature in the title, he has an important part to play in *Tramway Engines*. The first story has Percy telling the tale of a ghost train on the line that is so spooky that it makes his 'wheels wobble'. Thomas is suitably dismissive of such nonsense: 'Pooh! You're just a silly little engine, Percy. I'm not scared.'

When Percy collides with a farm-cart carrying a load of lime and ends up as white as a ghost, he and Toby devise an elaborate hoax as a result of which Thomas thinks he's seen a ghost – and is *terrified*. In the next story, however, he has the satisfaction of seeing Percy being made to look suitably ridiculous. The episode begins, however, with one of those exchanges not uncommon between the Fat Controller's engines:

> *'Wheeeeeeeeeeeesh!' Percy gave his ghostly whistle. 'Don't be frightened, Thomas,' he laughed, 'it's only me!'*
> *'Your ugly fizz is enough to frighten anyone,' said Thomas crossly. 'You're like–'*
> *'Ugly indeed! I'm–'*
> *'–a green caterpillar with red stripes,' continued Thomas firmly. 'You crawl like one too.'*

Thomas' insult was more than fifteen years old – it had first been used by Wilbert, in 1956, as a description of the way in which he felt Reginald Dalby was depicting the Small Engine. In *Tramway Engines* Percy lives up to the description when first a crate of treacle-cans drop on him, making him very sticky, and he then has to travel along a line where a lot of cut hay is being blown about by the wind. The resulting effect, to Thomas' great delight, is suitably comic:

> *'Look what's crawled out of the hay!' he chortled.*
> *'What's wrong?' asked Percy.*
> *'Talk about hairy caterpillars!' puffed Thomas as he started away.*

If these japes are typical of a type of story to be found in many books in the Railway Series, then the rest of *Tramway Engines* is also classic Awdry material: 'Mavis is a diesel engine belonging to the Ffarquhar Quarry Company . . . Mavis is young, and full of her own ideas. She is sure they are better than anybody else's.'

Peter Edwards first picture of Mavis shows the chunky black diesel with cowcatcher and side-plates, and black-and-yellow chevrons marked on her front. Her face has a pert, turned-up nose, a pair of lips tightly pursed into a bow and long eyelashes.

She loves re-arranging things, and put Toby's trucks in different places every day. This made Toby cross.
'Trucks,' he grumbled, 'should be where you want them, when you want them.'
'Fudge!' said Mavis and flounced away.

Lest it seem to those in search of sexist attitudes, that Mavis' character is being portrayed in this way because she is female, it should be remembered that almost every engine in the series has at some time or other behaved in a silly fashion and some of them – Thomas, Henry, Percy, Duncan and Sir Handel among them – continue to do so. However, the story does contain a trace of the battle, not between men and women, but between steam and diesel, with Daisy the diesel railcar advising Mavis: 'Depend upon it, my dear, anything steam engines do, we diesels do better.'

Having caused various problems for Toby, one of which almost results in the unfortunate tram engine falling into a raging torrent, Mavis eventually sees the error of her ways, helps rescue Toby, and afterwards – when praised for what she has done – bravely owns up to mistakes which might not have been discovered. The story ends for Mavis – as it had done for Daisy, Bear, Donald and/or Douglas and Patrick (formerly Lord Harry) – with forgiveness and a second chance:

Mavis is now a welcome visitor at Ffarquhar Shed. She is still young and still makes mistakes; but she is never too proud to ask Toby, and Toby always helps her to put things right.

These were to be the final words written by Wilbert Awdry in the Railway Series. Later the same year, Kaye & Ward published *The Reverend W. Awdry's Railway Series Surprise Packet*. Designed by Peter Edwards to look like a railwayman's satchel, the *Surprise Packet* opened up to reveal all manner of interesting and informative items: a vividly-coloured Sodor railway poster; puzzle pages; four Dalby illustrations in which to spot errors; information about signals and headcodes; diagrams showing how steam engines work; the story of 'The First Railway Engine in the World' (reprinted from the *Church of England Newspaper*); two board games – Knapford Junction and The Tidmouth Grand Tour ('Which Engine will get to the Sheds first?'); working models of Skarloey and friends – powered by cotton-reels and elastic bands; and pictures of all the major characters from Edward to Mavis.

Surprise Packet was originally conceived to serve as a spin-off and as a stop-gap measure until the possible publication of the twenty-seventh volume in the Railway Series, but Wilbert was now resolute: 'I was finding more and more difficulty in producing my kind of stories. I had a title for the next book, *Really Useful Engines*, but I had done enough. The publishers wanted me to continue, but I wasn't prepared to go on and, maybe, produce sub-standard stuff.' He had, as Lewis Carroll said of the business of storytelling, 'drained the wells of fancy dry'.

Eric Marriott now realised that the little books – which he had once had to convince Edmund Ward to develop into a series and which, latterly, he had had to persuade the author to keep writing – had, at last, reached the buffers. In August 1973, Marriott left Kaye & Ward to join the board of publisher, Michael Joseph and become Managing Director of Pelham Books. Wilbert wrote to congratulate Marriott:

> Margaret and I wish you every success, though I shall miss you very much at Kaye & Ward. It won't seem the same place after our 26+ years association over Thomas the Tank Engine. Thank you, too, for your friendship and enthusiasm and hard work you have put in over the years on behalf of the Engine series, without which I am quite certain they would not be the success they are. Margaret remarked, when I showed her your letter: 'One of the chores he won't have to do now is writing tactful letters to you trying to dig another book out!' You see she is still sticking pins into me now, just as she did over *Three Railway Engines*!
>
> I really will try and scrape the barrel for another one this Autumn!'

But, scrape as he might, the barrel was empty.

CHAPTER FOURTEEN

Full Steam Ahead!

'YOU will find the little cardboard stands in bookshops and sweetshops and newsagents at ankle level; they contain the fictional *oeuvre* of the Reverend W. Awdry – the Railway Series. The small books fit neatly in the hand and compare well in value with the Yorkies and Texans . . . '

It was 1979, and Wilbert found himself appearing on the cover of the *Observer* magazine. Artist Mick Brownfield depicted him as if he were on a railway bridge with that famous little tank engine visible in the background. Both creator and creation were shown wreathed in smiles and puffing contentedly away – Wilbert on his pipe, Thomas through his funnel. Inside the magazine were pictures of many of the other famous engines, about whom journalist Maureen Cleave wrote with a degree of enthusiasm that indicated their status as classic characters able to be effortlessly called to mind:

> For 25p there are four short stories about the mighty engine, Gordon, puffed up and boastful; Henry, wilful and disobedient; saucy, plucky Thomas, the tank engine; and the coaches Annie and Clarabel who twitter girlishly about the lip that Thomas gives Gordon . . .

There were, the writer observed, twenty-six books, 'all in print since their various publication dates'. There had not, however, been a new title for seven years. Rosemary Debnam, until recently the editor of the Railway Series (who was then working in the publicity department at Kaye & Ward) recalls that, for several years, booksellers continued to place orders for the next title in a series which everyone at the publishers now realised was at an end. Occasionally, a not-too-optimistic approach was made to see whether Wilbert had had any ideas for a new book; but Eric Marriott was no longer there to chivvy Wilbert along and the answer was always the same.

Even though, to all intents and purposes, the engines of Sodor had ceased running, Wilbert could never hope to escape his reputation as their creator – or avoid getting drawn into the controversies which they sometimes generated. In April 1972, a contentious issue had been raised by an article appearing in the 'Private Ear' column of the *Sunday Times*:

> Once upon a time, kiddies, the Rev. W. Awdry wrote a little story about Henry the Green Engine. In book form the story has sold 100,000 copies since 1951. Last week, someone noticed a 'naughty word' in the book, the sort of word you wouldn't expect from a gentleman of the cloth. Henry the Engine got cross with some boys for throwing stones, so he puffed smoke over them until they were 'as black as niggers'.

Henry the Green Engine had been published over twenty years earlier, in 1951, when such a phrase would have seemed innocuous. Shoe-polish was available in a shade called 'Nigger Brown'; children played a counting game which ran: 'Eeny, meeny, miney, mo, catch a nigger by his toe'; and Agatha Christie (taking her inspiration from a well known nursery story) had published a murder mystery entitled *Ten Little Niggers.* Wilbert rightly maintained that, in any age, words often do not mean what they have meant previously, but times were changing: Agatha Christie's *Ten Little Niggers* was retitled *Ten Little Indians* and people were questioning whether it was appropriate for the jam manufacturer, Robertson's to use a golliwog as its trademark.

It was all rather unfortunate. Eric Marriott had spoken to the *Sunday Times* journalist, Peter Dunn, assuming their conversation to be off the record, only to be told that it wasn't. Despite a strongly worded letter to the paper's editor, Harold Evans, Marriott found himself being quoted as saying: 'I'd have thought "nigger" was a sort of affectionate version of "negro" which is an unacceptable word isn't it?' Things, however, were to get worse. The following day, the *Daily Telegraph* ran a longer article carrying the headline: 'Henry the Engine author defends use of word "niggers" .' Wilbert was quoted as saying that the complaint was 'rubbish' and had probably come from what he called 'the Race Relations Industry' and which he intemperately dismissed as being 'a load of codswallop'.

Despite the fact that the Race Relations Board said it was nothing to do with them, a deluge of correspondence followed, most of which, it must be said, was in support of Wilbert. Quite a few of the letters, however, revealed extreme right-wing attitudes towards issues of race that were prevalent at the time.

People wrote that they were 'disgusted to read', or had 'read with horror' the article in the *Daily Telegraph*. 'Perhaps the same complainant,' wrote a bookseller from Norfolk, 'would like to start the machinery to investigate "The Father Brown Stories" or Barbara Cartland's *Black Panther*.' One correspondent complained about 'the pettiness and loss of direction of so many people who would be offended themselves if described as childish, petty, moronic or even trouble finders', adding: 'Traffic wardens are a similar class of parasites in the community whose main job is to bring their fellow citizens into trouble.'

A 79-year-old lady from Middleton-on-Sea, Sussex, wrote that she considered 'the Race Relations Industry' to be 'one of the most ridiculous movements that this country has ever sponsored', adding: 'I feel sure many members of other races must be laughing up their sleeves at it.' The writer appears to have thought that Wilbert Awdry was attempting to start a political pressure-group: 'Can anything be done to counter the thing? If so, I shall be only too happy to contribute.' Another impassioned correspondent obviously thought the same:

> If you can think of a way in which such nonsense as this could be put a stop to, I should be interested to hear from you. I for one would like to see an end put to such hair-splitting nonsense . . . It is time people got on with the spirit of living, instead of dissecting perfectly harmless phraseology. More power to your pen.

The magazine, *Gloucestershire Life*, also came to Wilbert's defence, illustrating their remarks with a cartoon of an engine with a smoke-box made-up in the style of the then popular television entertainers, the Black and White Minstrels; while a New Zealander, living in London, wrote: 'I thank God for the fact that there is a true Englishman left in dear old England.'

Wilbert himself, believing that the original complaint and its reporting had been engineered in order to fuel 'a witch hunt', remained unrepentant and resisted altering the phrase: 'I don't know what the alternative will be,' he told a newspaper reporter, 'If you say "as black as chimney sweeps or miners" you have their unions up in arms.' It is worth noting here that when, in the mid-sixties, Johnny Morris had read the story of 'Henry's Sneeze' on record, he had described the boys as running away 'smothered in soot and cinders'.

However, as the furore died down, Wilbert began receiving letters of complaint from what Kaye & Ward amusingly described as 'ordinary people'. One such correspondent who had two adopted children – 'one white and one of mixed race' – wrote to complain of Wilbert's 'shocking example of tastelessness', and went on to say that, in telling the story, she had suitably amended it to 'as black as coal'. Wilbert wrote to his publishers agreeing to change the offending word, not to 'coal' ('that doesn't read at all well'), but to 'as black as soot', which was deemed to 'come off the tongue far better'.

Two years after the initial fuss, letters were still being received. One anonymous writer (the postcard was signed 'Sir Borrobol the Diesel') wrote to tell Mr Ward (whose real name they assumed to be hidden behind the partial anagram 'Awdry') that his exhibition of racial discrimination was 'an un-Jewish and un-Christian thing'; while a lady from Norfolk wrote that she had bought a copy of *Henry the Green Engine* and before giving it to 'a little friend' had 'felt it necessary to substitute the word "tinker" pasted over, hoping it will not be noticed'. The writer's substitution of the word 'tinker' is interesting since, although at the time unaware of it, she was replacing what had come to be considered a derogatory term with another word that would itself, one day, become equally unacceptable.

In replying to this correspondent, Wilbert informed her that the phrase was to be changed, but couldn't resist pointing out: 'I don't think your alteration will succeed, for if I know anything about small boys or girls for that matter, sooner or later the alteration will be pulled off *just because it is an alteration, and he wants to see what is underneath*!'

The most telling episode in this affair was a letter received as late as 1976 when editions of the book were, for some unknown reason, still carrying the word 'niggers'. A lady wrote: 'I have just defaced a library book for the first time in my life.' On finding the phrase 'as black as niggers', she wrote, 'I blocked out the last two words as I find them highly offensive.' The writer clearly had deeply held personal views: 'I adopted a West Indian baby and thankfully she has not heard the derisory term "nigger" yet. She starts school after Christmas so no doubt it will come, but I do not expect to find it in a children's library book!' At the same time, the correspondent showed that she was aware of the number of years that had elapsed since the book had first been published, and that she was obviously an admirer of Wilbert and his books:

> May I add that my son *and* daughter love the stories about the trains – they have increased our interest in steam engines of all kinds and taught me personally, much more about the locomotives *I* can remember. I appreciate the moral attitudes you put forward and like the format and illustrations of 'The Railway Series'.

Wilbert was to reply with a humility that betokened a new appreciation of the argument and he apologised for the fact that the publishers had still not amended the text. Although this exchange closed the file which Wilbert had, originally, entitled 'Nigger Nonsense', it was far from being the last occasion on which his books were to be charged with a lack of 'political correctness'.

The irony of this controversy was that the publicity which Wilbert was receiving was motivated by a book written more than twenty years earlier. There was no sign of there being any new stories. Not that Wilbert had given up writing. In 1973 he had edited *Industrial Archeology of Gloucestershire*; and, although the cover article in the *Observer*, in 1979, was mostly about how Thomas the Tank Engine and his friends 'talk to each other in soothing clickety-clack rhythms as they steam through rolling green countryside', it was intended to publicise a very different book.

Eric Marriott, having left Kaye & Ward in 1973 to become Managing Director of Pelham Books, was looking for a project in which to involve Wilbert Awdry. In conversation with Dr Christopher ('Chris') Cook who was then editing *Pears Cyclopaedia*, Marriott discovered that Cook was a keen railway buff. The result was a collaboration with Wilbert in editing *A Guide to the Steam Railways of Great Britain*, a celebration of 'the new age of steam' that had been brought about by the work of the Railway Preservation Societies. The book listed and described 128 railways and railway museums where people could see 'steam in action'; among them those lines which Wilbert had already immortalised in the Railway Series: the Talyllyn, Bluebell, Ravenglass and Eskdale and Snowdon Mountain Railways.

Although no longer in search of story ideas, Wilbert had lost none of his enthusiasm for the various preservation societies, many of which he is still a life member. How many such groups and organisations does he belong to? 'You name it,' he says, 'I've got it, from the Great Western Society to the Blue Peter Locomotive Society!'

It was through one of these societies, that Wilbert and George embarked on a major expedition. Wilbert's railway trips usually tended to be a leisurely exploration of lines – 'living and defunct' – in the company of either his brother or Teddy Boston; this, however, was to be an altogether more ambitious foray.

The 'Via Festiniog 1980 Canadian Wonderland Tour' was a twenty-day trip by VIA (Canadian Railways) from Toronto through Winnipeg, Edmonton, Jasper, Prince Rupert and Prince George, Vancouver and Banff before returning to Toronto via Calgary. The tour on the famous Canadian Pacific and Canadian National Railways climaxed with a visit to the spectacular Niagara Falls.

Wilbert recorded their travels in photographs and George kept a detailed diary, which material Wilbert later compiled into an extensive illustrated journal: two chunky ring-binders, containing timetables, photographs, postcards and mementoes as well as anecdotes and recollections, all meticulously annotated in true Awdry style and supplemented by Appendices.

There were the usual mishaps and minor disasters: on the outward flight Wilbert's knees came into painful contact with the seat in front when the passenger wanted to recline; George lost the adapter for his shaver and Toronto was unsuccessfully scoured for a replacement; while, on the final leg of their journey, Wilbert and his baggage got separated by several carriage-lengths of train and he found himself having to fight his way back in order to retrieve it and make 'his escape from hell'. Nor was that the end of their problems:

> There on the platform, the handleshackle of G's grip chose just this moment to break loose adding greatly to the general fun and games. We made our way somehow across to the Royal York [Hotel] where G. managed an emergency repair with spares brought along for that purpose. We then dumped it all in a pay locker (25 cents), and went in search of a bar where we awarded ourselves a long gin and lime each.

There were certainly frustrations: 'They do not, as a whole, order train embarkation better in Canada, choosing to make a considerable circus of it . . . ' As for sleeping arrangements, George wrote of one of their compartments: 'The bunk was long enough but the blanket was not, either my shoulders were covered or my feet'; while 'the loos had been designed by and for dwarves'. There were even passengers who complained (as they often do on Sodor) about 'What A Bad Railway It Was'. Canadian hospitality was much appreciated; but whilst the brothers were impressed by the service and friendliness, they were mystified by the immediate provision of coffee at breakfast time and complained: 'Here you can't just have one egg with your bacon, you get two and like it!'

But, whatever the drawbacks – and those, for Wilbert, included not just two eggs but an inexplicable slice of orange on the same plate! – there were plenty of trains, contemporary and vintage, to be inspected, travelled on and generally enjoyed. At Assinboyne Park, Winnipeg, they encountered 'a C.N. 4-8-2 reputed to be the last to have operated in that area, stuffed and caged among the trees'; they visited a local preservation society's line, the Prairie Dog Central, and saw Locomotive No. 3, with its cowcatcher, its Cyclops eye of a headlamp and its huge, black smokestack; its 98 years belied by the shining paint and gleaming brass-work.

In North Vancouver they travelled on a train pulled by Royal Hudson, better known to rail buffs as the 2860, which had been originally built for transcontinental freight across the open prairies, but which now carried rail enthusiasts through the mountains, travelling at a leisurely 30 m.p.h., a speed that prompted George to liken its restrained behaviour to that of 'a caged lion'.

Royal Hudson arrived resplendent in decidedly British regalia, a legacy of the fact that, 'No. 26509 of the same class had been in charge of the Royal Train during King George VI's visit to Canada in 1939, and by his permission the whole class was named Royal Hudson, and embellished with crowns and Royal Arms.' As creator of the talking trains, Wilbert made an appropriate 'find' – a publicity handout about Royal Hudson which reported: 'Every turn of its wheels echoes the same phrase: "Glad to be back. Glad to be back. Glad to be back." '

At Calgary, the Awdrys saw the Selkirk, a two cylinder 2-10-4 with a twelve-wheeled tender, reputed to have been, in its day, the biggest engine in the Commonwealth. Less familiar forms of transportation included the Sky Tram in Jasper which carried them up Whistler's Mountain to an altitude of 7,500 ft ('Whistlers are marmots, so named after their alarm call'); and a 'Snowcoach' which waddled on caterpillar tracks across Columbia's Athabasca Glacier, a relic of the last Ice Age.

There were also striking examples of twentieth century life, such as the Canadian National Railway's building, the C.N. Tower at Toronto:

> Think of a space rocket which has got itself wedged into a transatlantic toroidal doughnut, and you have a general idea of what is reputed to be the tallest structure in the world. Even the 'doughnut' is 1,122 ft up, and there is much more above it, reserved to electronics, the main transmitters for the C.N.R.'s microwave communications.
>
> C.N. appears to have seen the joke, and the lifts taking the public up as far as the 'doughnut' are piloted by girls in aluminised mock space suits. In the 'doughnut' there is a revolving restaurant with prices as exalted as the tower itself.

In contrast, at Lower Fort Garry, they experienced a recreation of life in Winnipeg at the height of the Hudson Bay Company's fur-trading days. 'Costumed animators' interacted with the visitors in the manner of nineteenth-century residents:

> A serving maid stood at the door of the Governor's House, to discover the business with him of each visitor, hinting gently that the less formally dressed were hardly attired well enough to wait upon such an important gentleman; but of course accidents had been known to occur on the river and perhaps they had lost the rest of their baggage. W. and I had been primed by the gatekeeper, and presented ourselves as agents of the Birmingham Small Arms Co. with really good muskets to offer. She fielded

that one neatly, it was Sunday, and we would hardly expect to discuss business. However, if we cared to pay our respects meanwhile . . . The Governor was gravely civil, felt sure his Chief Agent would be most interested, if we could stay till the morning.

The Awdrys' train journey took them through the beauties of the National Parks and they saw the natural wonders of the Lakes and the Rockies: 'Somehow one expects mountains as big as this to be of the hardest stuff, perhaps granite, but surprisingly the Rockies are mostly sedimentary, and the layers are often clearly visible, marked perhaps by snow lodged on them, thus making them stand out, flat or curved as age-old movement has required.'

Finally, there was Niagara Falls, which they viewed from a launch, done up in black, 'rubber monk's habits with pop fasteners for maximum watertightness'. 'To be there,' wrote George, 'even at a navigationally respectful distance; to see and hear those immense quantities of water smashing down; to feel, even through those heavy rubber habits, the impact not of mere spray, but of solid gobs of water splashed up . . . '

The Canadian visit was a great success and a rare enterprise for Wilbert, who was not particularly keen on overseas travel. In contrast, Margaret Awdry loved going abroad; and, as her daughter Veronica puts it, 'while George and Dad wandered up railway lines, she had her own holidays'.

Certainly, railways held a limited fascination for Margaret, whereas for Wilbert, as she confided in an interview in 1979, 'life revolves around them – but, after all these years, one's used to it'. There was, noted the journalist, 'the slightest hint of resignation in her smile'.

Margaret went on holiday with a Christian organisation called Interchurch Travel, and – always making an effort to learn a little of the language of the country she was going to – visited Florence, Cyprus, Switzerland, Austria and Greece, as well as Morocco and South Africa, in both of which countries she had friends. One of the strengths of Wilbert and Margaret's marriage was, perhaps, not just the interests which they had in common, but those that were entirely their own and which gave each of them an independence and topics for conversation.

In 1978, the Awdrys had celebrated their Ruby Wedding anniversary and when, four years later, Wilbert was interviewed for the *Sunday Times Magazine*'s regular back-page column 'A Life in the Day of', he described what might have been the typical domestic routine of any middle-class couple after more than forty years of marriage:

> These days I rarely wake up as early as I used to when I had a parish to attend to. Mrs Awdry is normally out and about long before me, and she brings me a cup of tea at about 8.30. I come to the surface when she loudly pulls back the curtains . . . but if I can get away with it, I snooze for another half-hour. I then come down for breakfast – porridge or cornflakes and coffee – over which I do the *Daily Telegraph* crossword.

Despite his undoubted celebrity, Wilbert lived – as he always had and still does – an ordinary, unpretentious lifestyle. There were his railway interests and his writings, the occasional church duties and a growing family in which to take an interest.

The youngest of the three children, Hilary was the first to wed, marrying her Cornish holiday romance, Alfred Fortnam, in 1966. The following year saw Veronica's marriage to Richard Chambers; and, in 1968, Christopher married Elaine Checkley. Wilbert and Margaret's first grandchild Sara, was born to Hilary and Alfred in 1969, followed by Simon in 1971, and Rachel in 1975. Elaine gave Christopher a daughter, Verity, in 1971; and Veronica and Richard had a son, Mark, in 1972, and a daughter, Claire, in 1975.

For Veronica and Hilary, their careers, families and change of name meant that, whilst they remained close to their parents, they were largely untouched by their father's fame. Christopher, however, carried the family name and, like that other 'Christopher' (Christopher Robin Milne), was widely known to have been involved in the creative process by which the name Awdry first came to public attention: 'My first conscious memory that there were stories being written by my father was in 1949, when I was at prep school and he sent me a copy of *Tank Engine Thomas Again*; the other boys were terribly impressed — "Cor! Awdry's Dad writes books!" '

Two years later, in 1951, Christopher was aware of having the vaguest thoughts about a career in writing. Teddy Boston invited him and his father to Wisbech where they had a footplate trip on one of the tram engines. Christopher remembered how, earlier that year, they had encountered another tram engine in Yarmouth and how his father had created the character of Toby and written a book about him: 'I had the germ of an idea that writing stories was maybe what I'd like to do.' But it was an ambition that didn't crystallise until a few years later when he was at Worksop College. Christopher, who was now coming up for his O Levels and had a lot of essay work to do, found that he was enjoying exercises in creative writing.

Christopher was also working on a non-academic project: 'I wrote a "sensational" detective story about a character called Detective Older (named after the Surrey and England bowler) which filled all of four exercise books with big handwriting, and, when I wasn't working on that, I was writing verse.' Those experiments resulted in another landmark, during the Summer term of 1956: 'I was with a friend, going into prep, and I remember turning to him and saying, "I want to write for a living when I grow up . . . " '

But, as is so often the case with children, there were other possible ambitions. Wilbert remembers Christopher, as a young child, 'always singing around the house' and it was a voice, as his father says, that 'earned him his education' as a Cathedral chorister at St Chad's school in Lichfield. Christopher's love of music and singing was soon being matched by a love of theatre. Every year he went to London to spend a week's holiday with his grandmother. 'To me,' says Christopher, 'she seemed old, but she was remarkably active and, I now believe, was trying to recreate her younger days when she still had two young boys about the house.'

Christopher recalls his grandmother's London house at 14 Franconia Road, Clapham as 'a quiet household'; while his Uncle George went off each day to the National Liberal Club, where he was librarian, and his grandmother's companion, Gertie Whatmore, went to her job at the electrical firm of Phillips, Christopher 'took trips with Granny'. Those trips included a number of theatre visits that were to instil in him a passion for Shakespeare. They went to, among other theatres, the Old Vic, in Waterloo, where Christopher has vivid memories of seeing *A Midsummer Night's Dream*, *The Merchant of Venice* and *Twelfth Night* with Richard Burton as Sir Toby Belch and Michael Hordern as Malvolio.

With a love of singing and a fascination with acting, it is not surprising that when Christopher grew up he should have become involved in amateur dramatics. With his wife, Elaine, he became involved with the Precinct Players, a concert party in Peterborough, for whom he wrote sketches, songs and pantomimes, as well as dramatising Charles Dickens' *A Christmas Carol*. 'It was,' he says, 'good training, even though I didn't realise it at the time.'

Christopher also showed a talent for drawing and staged several art exhibitions of his landscapes and locomotive drawings. In addition to all of which, he had begun keeping a diary and was, once again, writing. He was, however, increasingly aware that all these activities were a form of compensation for feeling unfulfilled: 'It was,' he says, 'simply not enough.'

Despite their shared interests, Christopher and Elaine's marriage was under pressure: 'I felt creative,' says Christopher, 'but stifled. Despite the things we had in common, I was wanting to do something but, as I saw it, was somehow restricted and prevented from doing it.'

At the end of 1976, Christopher and Elaine separated. Christopher's parents were bitterly disappointed at the failure of his marriage, Margaret showing it more than Wilbert. 'Mother,' says Christopher, 'was bewildered; she had had a good marriage herself and found it hard to accept that one of the family had made a marriage that didn't work.'

Christopher and Elaine divorced in 1979, and Christopher married Diana Scott, whom he had met (but taken little real notice of) during a production of *The Magic Flute* in which both he and Elaine had been involved in 1970. Diana was also a keen singer and, along with Christopher and Elaine, was an active member of the Gilbert and Sullivan Society in Peterborough, where she had been born and brought up – near to the railway, as Christopher is quick to point out!

'Although Diana is not a passionate railway buff,' says Christopher, 'she is far more interested in them than Mother ever was. Before we were married, we visited York, home of the National Railway Museum. It takes more than a few hours to do justice to the museum and, by lunch time, we had seen only a fraction of the whole exhibition. We were in the cafeteria, and not wishing to push it, I said: "Well, what are we going to do this afternoon?" To which Diana replied: "What do you mean? We haven't finished *here* yet!" '

The turning point in Christopher's career – what he himself calls 'the breakthrough' – came in 1978. 'Diana and I were driving down through Cambridgeshire and saw the signpost to Elsworth and I started reminiscing about the days when we were there. Suddenly, she said: "Why don't you write all that down and see whether *Cambridgeshire Life* might be interested in it?" Frankly, I didn't expect the magazine to buy it – but they did!'

> Since the road that runs through the heart of Elsworth turns eventually back upon itself, it is, to all intents and purposes, a cul-de-sac. Through traffic expends its fume-laden energies elsewhere, and the row of thatched cottages beside the brook are left to drowse, unobtrusively, yet a good deal more attractive than other over-glamorised ones. So at least they were during the long, hot months of 1947 . . .

'Happy Days at Elsworth Rectory 1946-1949' was Christopher Awdry's first piece of published writing; but it was certainly not going to be his last.

Cambridgeshire, Huntingdon & Peterborough Life invited him to write occasional pieces on Cambridgeshire villages, and this he did for about three years. 'It was,' he says, 'a useful exercise, as it taught me the value of research to the writer.'

Christopher had also written to *Steam Railway* asking why contributors to the magazine only ever wrote about locomotives and not about the preservation of carriages and stock, and whether they might like him to write such an article. *Steam Railway* said that they would and, during the next few years, Christopher contributed a dozen or more 'bits', as he calls them.

It was while Christopher was researching one of these 'bits', that he and Diana became involved with the nearby Nene Valley Railway. And it was on this line that Christopher found the connection with what was to become his future career. 'Diana,' says Christopher, 'was always complaining that whenever we went on one of these trips I was always the one who got to ride on the footplate. So, I rang up the then general manager of the Nene Valley Railway and asked if, while I was doing some research for an article on a van restoration, my wife could have a ride on the footplate.'

It was 1st August, 1982, when they went down to the Nene Valley and Christopher, who was determined to keep the ride a surprise, maintained the suspense right up to the point where they walked down the platform and Diana was handed a footplate pass. 'When we picked her up off the platform,' laughs Christopher, 'Diana was thrilled!' A short time before the train was due to leave, they found themselves having a conversation with the crew:

> The driver said, 'If you're *Mrs* Awdry, then you must be Mr Awdry; are you anything to do with Thomas the Tank Engine?' So, I said, 'Yes, it's my father who wrote the books.' Was he, the driver wanted to know, still writing? I told him that Father had stopped in 1972. 'Then why,' he asked, 'don't *you* carry on?' I replied that he had stopped because he thought he was getting stale and running out of ideas. 'He knows far more about railways than I do,' I said, 'if he felt that he had exhausted all possible ideas, that doesn't really give me a lot of scope.'
> 'No problem,' said the driver, 'I'll give you an idea, happened here only last weekend . . . ' So, he told me a story about how an engine had been sent out to rescue a train, far heavier than such an engine would normally be called upon to pull, and the poor old thing had died for lack of steam about 100 yards short of the platform. As he recounted the incident, I could see that it had possibilities for a Thomas story.

As Diana's train pulled away – and with thoughts of Thomas chugging through his brain – Christopher went off to do his research. The article was written, but *Steam Railway* never used it; however, in view of the events which were to follow, it scarcely mattered.

Several years earlier, Christopher had submitted a number of manuscripts to his father's publisher, Kaye & Ward, for opinion: 'It was adult stuff, and most of it was useless – except for the fact that writing it had taught me a lot.' As for children's books, that was a market that Christopher had deliberately steered clear of: 'At the time of my efforts, Father was still writing the Railway Series and I didn't feel capable of finding something entirely new to write about.'

But now, he began to think again: 'For all my ambition to be a writer, I had never considered that I wanted to write Thomas the Tank Engine. I wanted to make my own way; to write Thomas would simply be horning-in on father's act, and why should I do that? But, on the way home, I thought to myself: "You've got this idea for a Thomas story; you reckon you want to be a writer; you've never written a Thomas story, so damn well try and do one – it will be good practice if nothing else!" '

So, he tried:

> *Gordon was resting in a siding. It was a hot day, and the express had been heavy.*
>
> *'I get out of breath,' he complained, 'but nobody cares – they just say I'll be all right after a rest.'*
>
> *'Get the Fat Controller to give you tanks and a bunker,' suggested Thomas cheekily. 'You'll feel a new engine. We tank engines never get out of breath, you know.'*
>
> *Perhaps it was lucky for Thomas that poor Gordon hadn't the energy to reply . . .*

'I wrote it,' says Christopher, 'and it wasn't bad – I suppose.' There was, of course, the acid test: how would a child react? Usefully, there was already one to hand. Richard Awdry had been born to Diana and Christopher in 1980 and was now two years old. He had had the entire canon of his grandfather's stories read to him by his father. This time there was a *new* story. Just as Wilbert told Christopher the story of 'Edward's Day Out', so Christopher told his story, 'Triple-Header' to Richard. 'He *quite* enjoyed it,' recalls Christopher, with a wry smile, 'but, as it didn't have any *pictures*, he wasn't quite as bowled over as he might have been!'

However, it was sufficiently well received for Christopher to continue the experiment. Over the next six months, he deliberately sought out other ideas for Thomas stories and three more were written: 'At which point I thought, you've done four, that's what there are in a Thomas book. My personal view was that they weren't particularly brilliant or publishable, but they were done! I'd proved to myself that I could make a reasonable fist of doing it; but, as far as I was concerned, when not being used for reading aloud they went, rather like father's, into the back of a drawer.'

Which is where they might have stayed. When, however, in March 1983, Wilbert was invited to open the Centenary Exhibition for the Wisbech and Upwell Tramway, he and Margaret stayed the weekend with Christopher and Diana in Stilton. On the morning when the elder Awdrys were due to leave, they found that they had a little time in hand before setting out for their train, and so were having a final cup of tea with the family:

> I produced these four stories, chucked them across to Father and said, 'Here you are, have a laugh!'
>
> Well, he didn't laugh. Instead, he passed the stories to Margaret who made appreciative comments and said: 'You seem to have caught the character of the engines pretty well.' Father still didn't say anything until they were on the point of leaving, when he turned round and said, 'Do Kaye & Ward know about these stories?' I said, 'No! Good heavens, why should they?' 'Well,' he replied, 'I suggest you send them in and see what they think. I'll write a covering letter.'

Recalling that morning, Margaret Awdry was later to reflect: 'We thought they were very good, but whether Christopher would have done anything about them, without that little prod, I don't know.' The answer is probably not. As with the story of Wilbert's career, chance and happenstance took the upper hand and it was the mothers and wives that provided the pushing and prodding.

'I suspect,' says Christopher, 'that my feelings then were similar to what his had been when Grandmother wrote and said Michael Barsley was going to stay with her and why didn't Wilbert send his stories along; he probably thought, "What the hell, there's nothing to lose." So, just as he did, I tidied up the stories and sent them off to Kaye & Ward.'

Back home in Stroud, Wilbert sent a letter to Rosemary Debnam, Children's Editor at Kaye & Ward: 'You may very well be hearing from Christopher in the near future with some stories that I suggested he sends you. He is not doing anything behind my back. It is all above board.'

The idea was not without precedent: when, in 1937, the French children's writer Jean de Brunhoff died, his hugely successful series of books about Babar the elephant was continued by his son, Laurent. The elder de Brunhoff, however, was not around to object, whereas Wilbert was very much alive. It says much about Wilbert's character that he gave the project his blessing and neither then, nor subsequently, sought to influence how Christopher wrote about those engines that had been, for so many years, such an important part of his life: 'If it had been done by somebody outside, I suppose I would have thought that they were cashing in. But as it is, they are my characters and Christopher is carrying the thing on.'

The *Sunday Express* for 18th September, 1983, takes up the story in suitably storybook style:

> Rosemary the Children's Editor was sitting in her office at Kaye & Ward feeling very sad. It was more than ten years since the Rev. W. Awdry had last written a story about Thomas the Tank Engine and all his friends . . . How she wished he would write some more.
>
> Suddenly, on her desk plopped a whole new collection of stories . . . 'Peep, pip, peep,' she whistled. They were every bit as good and exciting as ever! What's more, they weren't by the Rev. W. Awdry at all, but by his son, Christopher!

At the time Christopher Awdry's stories arrived on Rosemary Debnam's desk, there had been major upheavals at the publishers of the Railway Series. In 1980, World's Work, a publishing house suddenly confronted with serious financial losses, acquired Kaye & Ward which, although a small company, had best-selling series such as the 'Ant and Bee' books and, of course, Wilbert Awdry's railway stories.

However, Kaye & Ward's books were underpriced and its stock insufficiently written down which led to recorded losses of £81,491 in 1980 and £166,006 the following year. Following the take-over, World's Work and Kaye & Ward (who retained their own imprint) both showed profits; but continuing difficulties and corporate disagreements eventually resulted, in 1984, in both companies being absorbed into the publishing house of William Heinemann.

In the autumn of 1983, however, Rosemary Debnam was possibly the only person really interested in the future development of the Kaye & Ward children's list which was then being run alongside that of World's Work from the Windmill Press at Kingswood, in Surrey.

The day on which those stories arrived, happened to be that on which the publishers held their monthly planning meeting. Rosemary Debnam didn't have time to give the manuscript more than a cursory glance before going in to meet her colleagues, but as the meeting (which was rather dull) was drawing to a close, Rosemary announced, 'I may just have Railway Series No. 27 here, tell me what you think . . . '

'Well,' says Christopher, 'they must have quite liked them, because that was a Tuesday and by the following Friday, April 1st, 1983 – I still haven't worked out whether there's any significance in that! – I received an acceptance. Which, if you know anything about the speed at which publishers normally work, was phenomenal!'

The publishers invited Christopher to London in order to discuss the book and to find out whether the four stories they had received were a fluke or if there was any likelihood of the author being able to write some more. Although agreeing to attempt a second book, he had some reservations: 'I was quite uncertain whether I could do another, because I really didn't think the first one was as good as it could have been. Frankly, I had doubts.' Rosemary Debnam, however, appeared to have none, so Christopher tried again.

> I tried to write a book about James but I found it difficult. This time I was starting from scratch, I had father's scrapbook with various incidents and story ideas but I was rather pig-headed and wanted to be independent. First of all, I found it hard to get four stories, then I found it difficult to get into the idiom. That book took longer than any other I have ever written. My one consolation was that the one book my father was dissatisfied with was his third one – *James the Red Engine*!

As for his first book, Christopher had expected Kaye & Ward to wait a year and publish in the autumn of 1984; instead, the publishers began looking for an illustrator and pushing deadlines in order to have the book ready for the coming autumn.

Peter Edwards was still drawing and could easily have picked up the series where he had left off, twelve years earlier. Rosemary Debnam, however, was looking for a different type of artwork: 'Wilbert's stories,' she says, 'had become more sophisticated over the years, maybe because his children were growing up while he was writing them, and Peter Edward's freer, more painterly, pictures were right for them. Of all the illustrations, they were also the ones I personally preferred (John Kenney's were all too neat for my taste!); Christopher, however, had a young child to test his stories on, and was writing in a style that was closer to that of his father's earliest books.'

For this reason, Rosemary Debnam sought an illustrator who could emulate the best qualities of the Railway Series' first artist, C. Reginald Dalby: 'I had watched children selecting books at exhibitions and libraries, and Dalby's style of artwork, which was bold and colourful and *friendly*, was the one that they seemed most to appreciate.'

However, Dalby had been much criticised for inaccuracies in his work, and Rosemary Debnam was aware that she needed to find an artist who could combine the Dalby 'look' with accurate draughtsmanship. 'By this time,' she says, 'I had learnt the importance of the height of wheels, the way in which conrods were attached (very often disguised with steam by those who were unsure), the proportions of the individual boilers, the layout of points and the order of signals. I needed an artist who had an interest in engines and who would wish just as much as the Awdrys to get their proportions and mechanical details right.'

That artist was Clive Spong, who had known the Awdry books since he was a young boy. Never before had the books been illustrated by someone who had first hand memories of having read the stories in childhood and that unique vision resulted in pictures – strongly drawn and boldly coloured – that are closest in style and mood to those made by Reginald Dalby, whilst being, as Wilbert Awdry observes, 'accurate and consistent'.

As Kaye & Ward had doubtless guessed, the resuscitation of what was generally regarded as a national institution, raised considerable interest in the press and the arrival of the twenty-seventh title in the Railway Series was recorded under such headlines as THOMAS THE TANK ENGINE HAS A NEW DRIVER and THOMAS IS BACK ON THE RAILS.

The book opened with the by now familiar feature of the author's letter. The first such letter, in *Thomas the Tank Engine*, had been addressed to 'Dear Christopher'; thirty-six years later it was Christopher who was writing the letter:

> Dear Friends,
> I am happy to say that Thomas and his friends are still at work, trying as hard as ever to prove themselves Really Useful Engines. I am happy to say, too, that my father is still taking a keen interest in the Region's affairs, and it is with grateful thanks that I would like to dedicate this book to him, the person who began it all.
> The Author

The first story, 'Stop Thief!' has Thomas thwarting the work of burglars who have stolen some silver cups and gardening trophies from the house of the Station

Master at Ffarquhar – as well as his new red car in which to make their getaway. At the point where road and rail ran side by side (the very place where, in Wilbert's fourth book, Thomas had raced Bertie the bus) the tank engine spots the thieves in the car and gives chase. When the crooks are apprehended, the Fat Controller (depicted briefly with a luxuriant moustache) congratulates Thomas:

> 'A long time ago . . . Thomas showed how valuable he is to the smooth running of My Railway. I am sure you will all agree that today he has once again proved himself to be a Really Useful Engine.'

The phrase had come easily to mind – it was the Fat Controller's favourite way of praising an engine. Reading the stories over, on his journey to London to meet with the publishers, Christopher had, not surprisingly, hit upon it as a possible title for his first book; by chance, he had chosen the same one which Wilbert himself had planned for the book that he had never got round to writing – *Really Useful Engines*.

'It was,' says Christopher, 'an appropriate title, for it was Really Useful to me!' It was Really Useful for all kinds of reasons. What Kaye & Ward knew at the time of receiving Christopher's stories, was that a television series based on Wilbert's books was currently in production. How useful if the Railway Series was up and running again before the television versions reached the screen.

Although the first attempt at televising the engine stories in 1953 had been an unmitigated disaster, there was no lack of interest in trying again. In 1973, Andrew Lloyd Webber approached Kaye & Ward with a proposal for a musical television series. At the time, Lloyd Webber was very much the rising talent having composed two Biblically-based pop musicals, *Joseph and the Amazing Technicolor Dreamcoat* and *Jesus Christ Superstar*, as well as film scores for *Gumshoe* and *The Odessa File*. He had read the Railway Series as a child and retained such an affection for the books that one of his companies was called The Really Useful Company.

Andrew Lloyd Webber had a number of meetings with Wilbert Awdry and Stanley Pickard, Kaye & Ward's Managing Director. Draft contracts were drawn-up and specimen lyrics submitted:

> Come take a ride with the eight famous engines
> Famous and Faithful and driven by steam
> Each one is run by the branch line Controller
> Each part of his scheme
> The Fat Controller's team . . .

Negotiations, however, became protracted, largely due to a belief on the part of Kaye & Ward's solicitors that the agreement being offered would give Lloyd Webber's company 'control of almost everything – idea, the characters, every one of the twenty-six books, and even anything else not yet written or published'. Lloyd Webber's lawyers argued that such control was necessary in order to 'secure the investment money from America which would be needed to pay for the animation and the film-making'.

The two sets of legal advisers having 'quite fallen out', the project looked decidedly uncertain although, in November 1974, Stanley Pickard advised Wilbert that he was 'maintaining personal contact with Andrew and still had a slight hope that there might be a way out.' Wilbert remained philosophic: 'Once the Americans get hold of it the whole series would be vulgarised and ruined.' Almost a year later, a contract was signed ('not without some misgiving' wrote Pickard) and Wilbert was paid an advance of £500 – of which almost £200 had to go for the payment of legal fees.

Two more years passed, Andrew Lloyd Webber had a huge stage hit with *Evita* but, when the option on the Railway Series came up for renewal, the project was abandoned. In notifying Stanley Pickard of this decision, David Land of the Lloyd Webber company, Superstar Ventures Ltd, wrote:

> You may be interested to know that Andrew Lloyd Webber in association with Granada Television has spent some £10,000 in advancing the original project, but there has been no interest from the American market where an early sale was essential to bring economic viability to the production. Andrew Lloyd Webber has really tried very hard to bring the project to fruition, because he has a high personal regard for the Reverend W. Awdry, and was weaned on his books and was personally entirely committed to the idea.

'Whether all they say here is the exact truth,' Stanley Pickard wrote to Wilbert in May 1977, 'I have no means of knowing, but it is a fact that when he first spoke to us, there was none of this recent insistence on being able to sell in the U. S. A. I feel somewhat let down about the matter and I expect so will you.' Such was their disappointment that probably neither Wilbert nor Kaye & Ward understood the significance of the closing paragraphs of David Land's letter:

> Andrew particularly wants you to know that although the project has had to be abandoned, as a result of being shown in the United States an audio visual recording entitled 'Soul Train' which is the introduction to a nationwide weekly pop programme, he is now going ahead with the

> formulation of a dramatic presentation in both theatrical and television form of a story based on 'Cinderella' using trains as the characters. The first aspect of development is a song which has been recorded and is shortly to be released by M.C.A. Records, and for your information I enclose a copy to show you the general idea being progressed. As you can see, this is very closely orientated to the American market, and is far removed from our dear friend 'the fat controller'.

Andrew Lloyd Webber's stage musical *Starlight Express* opened in 1984 and is still running.

Two years after Lloyd Webber abandoned his interest in the Railway Series, another player entered the game. It was 1979, and British television producer, Britt Allcroft was making a five minute film for the Central Office of Information on the resurgence of interest in steam railways. One of the inspirations for the film had been *A Guide to the Steam Railways of Britain* compiled by Wilbert Awdry and Dr Christopher ('Chris') Cook and published, at Pelham Books, by Eric Marriott, former editor of the Railway Series. The fact that Wilbert was going to take part in the programme, prompted Britt Allcroft to read, for the first time, some of the volumes in the Railway Series. 'Having read them,' she says, 'it really didn't take me long to become intrigued by the characters and the relationships between them and the simplicity of the stories. I was equally intrigued by the illustrations, the landscape in them and the nostalgia they evoked.'

For Allcroft, who had a particular interest in children's television, an idea began to germinate: 'I felt strongly that television had a real role in children's lives and could offer children and their grown-ups an experience that is similar to that which they have when they sit down to read a book together.'

Filming for the steam railways project was taking place, in torrential rain, on the Bluebell line in Sussex. After dinner, one evening, Allcroft told Wilbert that she believed his stories were 'made to be brought to life' and that she would like to be the person to do it. Wilbert, doubtless still smarting from the recent dealings with Lloyd Webber, replied that a number of people had had the same idea, but had failed in the attempt.

Undaunted, Britt Allcroft began pursuing the idea with Wilbert's publishers, Kaye & Ward and, for a reputed sum of £50,000, negotiated a deal for the television rights. Allcroft knew that the financing of such a project would prove expensive – the negative costs were eventually to work out at around £10,000 a minute – and the search for money began. 'There were,' she remembers, 'lots of interested parties but they all wanted control.' Ultimately, the project would be funded by Allcroft's local bank, but it was 1981 before she had sufficient money to put the series into production.

There was also the question of *how* the Railway Series was to be brought to life and Allcroft considered, and costed, different forms of animation from the fiendishly expensive fully-drawn cell animation used by the Walt Disney studio to alternatives such as various types of limited animation employing cut-outs, as used on such B.B.C. children's series as *Captain Pugwash* and *Ivor the Engine*, or the effective, but time-consuming, method of stop-frame animation featured in popular children's programmes like *Trumpton* and *Camberwick Green*.

Allcroft's difficulty was that the central characters were steam engines and she wanted them, and their world, to look *real*. A solution was found when she met David Mitton, a film-maker who had gained some of his earliest experience from working with Gerry Anderson, the creator of *Thunderbirds* and other series, and who was now receiving considerable kudos for his animation work in television advertising.

Discussions with Mitton resulted in a revolutionary process – now referred to as 'live action animation' – whereby, as Angus Wright (Allcroft's husband and business partner) explains, 'You essentially play trains – and film it!' Although, like all electrically-operated model trains, it proved difficult to simulate the movement of the steam engine – the slow start, the building speed, the measured climbing of a gradient – quantities of smoke and steam gave them an air of authenticity.

In constructing the engines, model-maker Peter Eves skilfully captured both the mechanical detailing and the personalities of the various characters. Their faces, such an important feature of the engines of Sodor, were recreated, with a variety of expressions, as a series of interchangeable masks which would enable Thomas and the others to look happy, sad, angry, smug or scared as the situation might require.

Although viewers often describe the engines in the television series as 'speaking', their mouths, in fact, never move. Their eyes, however, *do* move. By the use of radio controls, they look to left or right, are downcast (with gloom), are raised heavenward (with exasperation) or swivel round and round with amazement. These eyes became the centre of animation and personality and Angus Wright observes that when little children come face-to-face with one of the large-scale models used by Britt Allcroft's company for publicity, the first thing they want to do is touch the eyes. Ironically, decisions made for reasons of economy, end up having psychological significance: 'The more you limit a character's means of communication,' says Wright, 'the more likely you are to concentrate what you have to communicate to your target audience.'

From the very beginning, the setting was as important to Britt Allcroft as the stories. Working with Art Director, Bob Gauld Galliers (who came from a background in architectural design), she decided on the look of the series, placing it within the landscapes of the original illustrations and frozen in time in the 1940s and 50s; while lighting cameraman, Terry Permane, working with David Mitton and Assistant Director, Steve Asquith, devised a special periscope lens that created an extraordinary depth of focus. This enabled the camera to film close-ups of the smiling engine faces while the landscape backgrounds remained sharply focused.

One problem beset the team: how to animate the human characters. At first the only option seemed to be to use costly stop-frame animation for sequences featuring the Fat Controller and train crews. After a lot a discussion the team arrived at a radical (and cost-effective) solution: the humans would be represented by static tin toy figures. 'People think,' says Angus Wright, 'that the Fat Controller walks and talks, but what the production team did was enhance the essential animation – which is the engines themselves – by keeping the humans still.' These toytown characters are a far cry from the people of Sodor, but the technique had the curious effect of conferring even greater humanity upon the engines.

As a title for the series, Allcroft chose *Thomas the Tank Engine and Friends*. 'I chose Thomas,' says Allcroft, 'because there has to be a No. 1, there has to be a hero.' It was, in fact, a logical choice, since the books were already being habitually identified by the name of Thomas rather than that of any other character.

Allcroft, who now refers to the kind of programming made by her company as 'storybook television' was determined, from the outset, to use a single narrator for the Railway Series rather than a cast of voices: 'I had always had a belief in the power of the storyteller and had been sure that these stories were to be told as an extension of the way in which they would be told in the home.'

The atmosphere Allcroft was seeking was one of intimacy and, although she listened to recordings by 'a lot of actors', she did not find one with the voice quality she was seeking. This might be thought surprising, since the stories had already been read with considerable style and humour by several readers. In addition to Johnny Morris and Willie Rushton, a most distinguished, if unlikely, performer had assumed the engine personas for the B.B.C. radio programme, *The Noel Edmonds Show*.

Once a week, for six months, from October 1981, the mellifluous tones of Sir John Gielgud could be heard telling stories of Thomas, Edward, Gordon, Henry, James and Percy. Sir John, who remembers the pleasure he had in recording the stories, read with energy and attack and captured all the fun and excitement. Without attempting different vocal characterisations, he recounted the little adventures with a conspiratorial glee – as if sharing a series of rather splendid jokes – which, of course, is exactly what Wilbert Awdry's stories are.

However, along with Morris and Rushton, Sir John was rejected. The story of how Britt Allcroft eventually found the narrator for her series has been told so many times, it has now the status of a myth: 'One Saturday night, the family were in the sitting-room watching *The Michael Parkinson Show* on television. I was not; I was pacing up and down wondering who I was going to find to be my storyteller. I was just passing the sitting-room door when I heard a voice, and I thought, *that* is the voice of Thomas the Tank Engine's storyteller. I put my head round the door and asked who it was – it was Ringo Starr.'

Hearing in the former Beatle's voice what Allcroft describes as 'warmth and originality, "a railway voice" that would transcend all boundaries and be accessible to anyone', she wrote to Ringo and clinched a deal. When the news of Ringo's casting was announced, a journalist speculated on whether 'the purists among Mr Awdry's older fans will approve of the engines speaking in a rich Liverpudlian street drawl'. In the event, however, the public (and even the creator of the Railway Series) accepted Ringo's performance without a quibble.

'Nevertheless,' says Angus Wright, 'the idea that you could take this rather untutored Liverpool voice, which actually has a beautiful dark brown quality, and put it onto this middle-class niche story for little children was an astonishing one.' It was also an example of what Wright calls Britt Allcroft's ability to combine 'creative talent and commercial instinct'.

Defending her choice of Ringo Starr as more than just an unexpected star name guaranteed to generate publicity, Allcroft says: 'When *Thomas the Tank Engine and Friends* was launched, it was a bonus; it intrigued people. After all, Ringo was known to a whole generation who were the parents of the children who first watched the series. That, however, would not have sustained his appeal as Thomas' storyteller, and I believe the reason that Thomas has become the classic that he has is due, in part, to the way in which Ringo tells the stories.'

Ringo Starr himself, credits the success of the series to the original stories: 'Mr Awdry is a charming man and very protective of Thomas – every time I called him "Tommy", he would correct me. I thought the series was terrific. The fruit is in the puffing – the books are still loved by children, worldwide, fifty years on.'

The recording sessions went well, although as Ringo later admitted, he got the character of the Fat Controller wrong to begin with: 'We made him too big and bossy. We had him so mean to the engines that you thought he'd go and pull their wheels off; then we realised he was quite kind, really a sort of father figure.' Although Ringo Starr's storytelling style lacked subtlety, it had a directness and honesty that was well suited to the visual presentation.

Angus Wright maintains, and it is doubtless true, that 'nobody can now think of Thomas the Tank Engine without thinking of that voice' (to the extent that when Ringo gave up the job, he was replaced by fellow Liverpudlian, Michael Angelis); but it is also true that in using so famous a pop icon, Allcroft guaranteed that Thomas' debut would not go unnoticed. 'You've got this extraordinary voice,' says Wright, 'and suddenly a little five minute programme for children is getting full-page coverage in the tabloids.'

That proved especially true when the papers were offered the chance of covering a meeting between Wilbert and Ringo. The magazine of the *Mail on Sunday* described the encounter in extraordinary detail: how Ringo, wearing a blue satin jacket and accompanied by his wife, Barbara Bach, had driven in his bronze Mercedes from his mansion in Berkshire to the town of Stroud – 'its soft Cotswold features scarred and pitted by roadworks' – in order to meet Thomas' progenitor:

> Upstairs, the Rev Wilbert Awdry began to demonstrate the first part of the timetable of the Knapford-Ffarquhar branch line of the North Western Railway for his guest in the blue satin jacket, ex-Beatle, Ringo Starr.
> The creator of the Railway Series, that staple of middle-class nursery bookshelves, with its cast list of cheeky, sad, boastful and troublesome engines wore a cream-lined jacket over his spare, slightly stooping frame. Round his neck hung a small wooden control-box, from which he governed the movements of his engines, Daisy, Thomas and Percy, and their rolling stock. His voice ran through the familiar commentary 'Tell me when you're bored,' he advised. 'Not yet,' said Ringo. Mr Awdry detached a couple of trucks from a line of goods-vans at the touch of an electrode. 'Cool!' said Ringo . . .

There was no end to it: a walk on the back lawn, during which Ringo offered Mr Awdry 'a ciggy' and made that unfortunate *faux pas* of calling Thomas, 'Tommy' – ' "Thomas," corrected Mr Awdry gently, "never Tommy" ' – and some startling revelations: 'Ringo admitted that he had come to the joy of the Railway Series late in life. "We didn't have your books when we were children," he said. "Oh, you were deprived!" exclaimed Mr Awdry.' Eventually, readers were told, the meeting came to an end:

> Mr Awdry was reminiscing for our benefit in that gentle spell-binding way of all good storytellers, when Ringo said he was sorry, but he had to go. His wife roused herself from a state of almost catatonic boredom and they departed with slightly more ceremony than they had arrived. Mr Awdry bade them a courteous, abstracted farewell . . .

Wilbert well remembers Ringo's visit and how impressed his neighbours were on discovering that one of the Beatles had called at Rodborough Avenue. A few months later, the televising of *Thomas the Tank Engine and Friends* began. The title sequence (which would eventually introduce more than 100 films) showed Thomas, Annie and Clarabel, chugging through a country landscape with a blue sky above and a windmill and pond in the foreground. The opening episode featured 'Thomas and Gordon' – the first story which Wilbert wrote about the tank engine.

Having called Gordon a lazybones, Thomas inadvertently remains coupled to the big engine and gets pulled along at high speed until he is quite out of puff. 'He went home very slowly,' wrote Wilbert, ' and was careful afterwards never to be cheeky to Gordon again.' The final shot of Britt Allcroft's television version showed Thomas crossing the viaduct as the sun sinks behind a hill. In a sense, however, Thomas was not so much steaming off into the sunset, as towards the dawn of a new day.

CHAPTER FIFTEEN

Really Useful Engines

THE headline was typical of many: THOMAS THE TV STAR. The accompanying photograph showed the beaming face of Wilbert Awdry flanked by models of Thomas and Gordon from the Britt Allcroft television series. In recent years it has been widely claimed that those television programmes have been almost single-handedly responsible for the place currently held by Thomas in the popular imagination. Such a view, however, denies (or, at best, belittles) the creativity and originality of the books which began it all and which at the time when the television series was first launched had sold more than eight million copies.

The achievement of *Thomas the Tank Engine and Friends* was initially to reinforce existing public affections – to capitalise, in fact, on forty years of work by writer, illustrators and publishers – and then to introduce Thomas to new audiences both at home and, most significantly, overseas. This was represented by a sharp increase in earnings from the books: in the year 1985/86, the Railway Series brought in £71,000; a year later (with spin-off publications resulting from the launch of the television series) that figure had increased to £448,000, and, within five years, would exceed £1 million.

The television series also generated fresh media interest in the creator of the Railway Series, the Thomas the Tank Engine Man, which coincided with a period in Wilbert's life when he and Margaret were scaling down their activities. Margaret, who had developed a heart condition, gave up supply teaching and, after almost two decades' service, her work with the Rodborough Child Health Clinic.

For Wilbert, advancing years and health problems (including spinal troubles, leg ulcers and repeated falls) seemed to be taking their toll. From 1983 onwards he had begun to resign a number of his voluntary and charitable duties: as one of the Chaplains at Gloucester Cathedral; as a committee member of the Stroud Museum Association; and as the Gloucester Diocesan Secretary of the Jerusalem and Middle East Church Association, whose General Secretary wrote: 'You have always shown such wonderful interest in our work and supported us over so many years, I simply can't believe that age and infirmity would ever overtake you, who I know, is so young in heart.'

Not that Wilbert had given up writing. In 1987, he contributed several chapters to *The Birmingham and Gloucester Railway* and shared title-page credit on the book with P. J. Long. A highly detailed study of a pioneering railway, the book is crammed with facts and figures and peppered with abbreviations that might deter any but the specialist reader. Wilbert, of course, demonstrated not only his vast knowledge of railway affairs, but also his love of drama (to be seen in his account of the two-mile-long Lickey Incline which, at 1 in 37 is the steepest mainline gradient in the British Isles) and his eye for a good anecdote:

> The B&G [Birmingham and Gloucester Railway] were a somewhat jimcrack, penny-pinching company, and not above acquiring and laying second-hand rail on their line to save the expense of buying new. Nor was their track building above reproach. The directors and shareholders found this out in an embarrassing manner when their pre-opening Special on 6 July came to a jarring halt on the Millstream curve. One of the locomotives had slidden down between the rails and embedded its wheels in the ballast because a tie-bar (or bars) had been carelessly bolted!
>
> Indignant passengers had to walk some three quarters of a mile over rough ballast to reach their luncheon at the B&G [Birmingham and Gloucester Railway] station. Brunel and General Pasley (Board of Trade Inspector) got no lunch at all. They had to direct the re-railing of the engine and coaches as well as repairs to the track.

A very different volume of railway history appeared in the same year – *The Island of Sodor: Its People, History and Railways* by the Rev. W. Awdry and G. Awdry. The book was the result of all those years of correspondence and conversation between the Awdry brothers, the distillation of a great quantity of material assiduously researched by George and imaginatively chronicled by Wilbert. To publish what is essentially a fictional history may have been seen as a commercially risky enterprise; certainly the authors' 'Foreword' has a note of apology about it:

> *If you are expecting this book to be like those in the Engine Series, we fear you will be disappointed. But though not like the Engine Series, it has nevertheless developed from them. It is written for all readers from eight to eighty who have, very naturally, begun asking important questions about the stories . . . 'Why Sodor?', 'Why did the railways choose the routes they did?' 'Why have the places got such odd names?' (Suddery, Crovan's Gate,*

Haultraugh, Ballahoo), 'What sort of people live in these places?', 'What do they do?', and so on and so on.

The book provides answers to all these and many other questions as well as using the fictional inhabitants of Sodor to point out errors in illustrations – usually by Dalby, but not always his fault:

Dear Mr Awdry,
I am glad to hear that you are at work on a gazetteer of our Island. It has long been needed, and I can think of no-one better qualified than you to undertake it.
I would like to take this opportunity of mentioning several discrepancies in the illustrations to Four Little Engines *which have puzzled visitors to Cros-ny-Cuirn for some time. North of the station an overbridge is shown. There has always been a level crossing here and never a bridge as shown on page 29. Beyond the crossing, (page 27) the scenery should show rock face on the far side and road on the near side, rather than open country. A more faithful picture of the area can be seen in* Gallant Old Engine *pages 19-27.*
With every good wish
Yours sincerely,
Handel Brown.
The Rowans,
Cros-ny-Cuirn, I.O.S.
August 1985

Wilbert had also been commissioned to write his autobiography but, although he was to make several attempts at telling the story of his life, the book never progressed beyond a few autobiographical sketches of his childhood. Wilbert's life was, however, recorded – in admittedly summary form – when he was given an entry in the 1990 edition of *Who's Who*. Although describing him as 'Church of England clergyman and author' the bulk of the entry is given over, not to his church career, but to a listing of all the books in the Railway Series from *The Three Railway Engines* to *Tramway Engines*.

Talking about those books to the present writer, in 1986, Margaret Awdry confessed: 'It is a surprise – a *continual* surprise – that they have lasted so long and still seem to be going full steam ahead!' What she and Wilbert found particularly exciting, she added, was that Christopher was now continuing the series: 'And that,' with unashamed motherly pride, 'is *marvellous*!'

It might, however, easily not have happened. Kaye & Ward had, by this time, been absorbed into the publishing house of William Heinemann Ltd., whose then Children's Book Director loathed the Railway Series and it was solely due to the persistence of Rosemary Debnam that Christopher Awdry continued to be commissioned to write more books for the Railway Series. Following the success of *Really Useful Engines*, came the title which had caused its author so many headaches, *James and the Diesel Engines*, which showed that the old war between steam and diesel power was not quite over on the Island of Sodor, certainly as far as James the Red Engine was concerned: 'Diesels don't use coal and water . . . How can you trust an engine who isn't normal in his habits?' On being told that diesels were mixed traffic engines capable of pulling coaches or trucks, James replied: 'Mixed-up engines, you mean . . . With windows at each end how can they know if they're coming or going?'

In 1985 came Christopher's first book about the Skarloey Railway, *Great Little Engines*; and, the following year, the thirtieth book in the series (and the third to be named after its most famous character), *More About Thomas the Tank Engine*. Although this was the first title to carry the Heinemann imprint, the links with the past were firmly established with the inclusion of cameo appearances by Bertie the Bus and Harold the Helicopter. It was the next volume, *Gordon the High-Speed Engine*, published in 1987, which proved something of a turning-point for the Railway Series and for its new author:

Donald was excited.

'The diesels at yon Wurrks,' he announced, 'say that on the Other Railway there are things called High-Speed Trains. They have a diesel engine at each end, and can go at 125 miles an hour.'

Gordon snorted.

'An engine at each end,' he said scornfully. 'There's only one of me, but I bet I can go as fast as those smelly boxes-on-wheels. Probably faster,' he added.

Diesels were one thing, they had been appearing in the series, with increasing frequency, since 1958; but Christopher Awdry now took his inspiration from a specific locomotive type with which most contemporary children in the United Kingdom were very familiar. As drawn by illustrator, Clive Spong, the train was clearly a British Rail 125 (complete with InterCity livery and logo); in terms of personality, however, it was considerably more endearing:

Philippa (she preferred Pip for short) and Emma were delighted to stand in for Gordon. Pip's cooling system was faulty, making her hot and bothered, but Emma didn't mind doing all the work. They felt honoured to visit the Fat Controller's Railway.

'Children now know that there is an Island of Sodor,' says Christopher, 'but whilst I think it is comforting for them to believe that Thomas has a home in the same way as they have a home – somewhere that can be depended on – there are more mainland connections in my stories. Maybe it is a subconscious attempt to link the steam engines which run on the Island, with the type of engines which children actually know and experience; a way of uniting the strange world of British Rail with the familiar railways of Sodor.'

For Christopher, *Gordon the High-Speed Engine* marked the end of an apprenticeship. 'The name was there,' says Wilbert, 'and the first book came out as a follow-up to my reputation, but from then on Christopher had to rely on his own reputation.' Although scrupulous about avoiding being described as 'the creator of the Tank Engine', Christopher was beginning to feel much more an author in his own right.

This new confidence in what he was doing, prompted Christopher to give up his job of twenty years with the Inland Revenue: 'I had written five books and Thomas was now earning me about same amount as my salary.' In fact, Christopher was receiving a 5% royalty (a rate which was now also being paid to Wilbert), but there was not much financial leeway, if he failed to make a go of it. 'I had a commission to compile an *Encyclopaedia of British Railway Companies*, which was researched but not written, so Diana and I decided that I should buy a word processor, take the risk and go freelance.'

The *Encyclopaedia*, representing some three years' work, was published in 1990, and marked the beginning of a new phase in Christopher Awdry's life, his status as an author of books in the Railway Series enabling him to forge a career as a railway historian: 'I want to make railway history accessible and I get a great thrill from the work. The fact that Thomas provides me with a living and gives me the time to do research, is a step towards that goal.'

Christopher's considerable railway knowledge has, to an extent, influenced the style in which he writes his children's books: 'I would hate people to think I was simply doing a pastiche, which is probably why I haven't worried about the stylistic differences that exist between my father's stories and mine. I think I tend to be a bit more technical and the language tends to be a smidgen more up to date.' Wilbert has few quibbles with Christopher's writing: 'I don't think he has carried on quite the same brand of humour that I used, and he doesn't always end a story with a humorous twist, as I used to do; but his way of writing is necessarily different from mine.'

In one respect, that of their method of composition, father and son have much in common. 'It begins,' says Christopher, 'with the germ of an idea for a story; then I decide who it's going to happen to, and *where*. This has to be decided early on, because I like to develop a link between, if not all four stories, then at least two of them, preferably three, so that whilst they can be read individually they also have a progression.'

Having made those decisions and found a link – 'the link doesn't always come first of all' – Christopher plans each story and writes a draft, usually running to between 650-700 words on 1½ sides of A4. Since he knows that he will eventually have to cut that length by roughly a third, he sets it aside, 'so that it can mature!'

Much as his father used to find, working out the book's pagination is not easy: 'Sometimes I get 80 words and a natural break, but that's rare. Usually it's somewhere between 65 and 100 which gives me a rough idea. At that stage, if I find I've got a chunk with perhaps 120 words, then I know I've either got to gut part out or carry it back or forward to another page – it is only then that you start finding paragraphs that can go!'

Again like Wilbert, Christopher is constantly looking for new illustrative possibilities for each page, ways of avoiding pictorial repetitions by suggesting new viewpoints and angles for Clive Spong's illustrations. 'I am always trying,' he says, 'to think visually and verbally.'

The Railway Series continued with *Toby, Trucks and Trouble* (the first book not to have the word 'Engine' in the title) published in 1988, the year in which Wilbert and Margaret celebrated their Golden Wedding Anniversary with a family party in Stroud. Reflecting on their marriage, Wilbert says: 'We were happy with each other and, over so many years, we grew to depend on one another, each of us wanting to know what the other one thought about anything we planned to do.'

There were, not surprisingly, occasional ups and downs:

> There were times when what can only be described as the cloud of silence settled over the house, or when Margaret would have liked to hit me over the head with a brick and I likewise her! I used to try and explain this to couples

preparing for a wedding; so often they had the idea that it was going to be a bed of roses, that everything was going to be oojy-come-spiff all the time. Of course, it never is. At our marriage service Margaret and I promised to love and cherish one another, for better or for worse. She picked me and I picked her, and we had to make the best of it. And that is exactly what we did, usually resolving any differences between us by laughing about them.

One of the stamps which Wilbert designed for his Junior Church showed a canoe being paddled by a man and a woman; the caption read: 'Partnership: that's marriage.' Wilbert and Margaret's marriage was a strong partnership: they complemented and supported one another; and, importantly, they gave each other room to be an individual within a union. What they did not know as they celebrated fifty years of marriage, was how close they were to its end.

Although Margaret never complained, her health was gradually deteriorating. Growths behind one of her ear-drums, which had been punctured, led to dizzy spells and, finally, an operation to fit an artificial ear-drum. Margaret then began to have problems with her heart and attacks of angina limited many of her activities and forced her to resort to the use of a stair-lift (paid for out of the growing royalties from the Railway Series).

In July 1989, Wilbert had promised to speak at the opening of a railway model shop at Lechlade, in Gloucestershire. Because the nearby Fairford Air Show was going to be taking place that weekend, which would result in heavy traffic, Wilbert decided to travel (by taxi, since he had now given up driving) a day early to ensure that he got there on time. It was arranged that he would stay with a cousin whose husband was the Vicar of Lechlade.

On the morning of July 21st, Wilbert was preparing for the trip, when Margaret's angina gave her a sudden twinge. Wilbert immediately said that he would cancel, but Margaret would not hear of it: 'I remember her saying, "No! you can't! You made the appointment months ago, and you can't drop out at the last minute." I think Margaret's refusal to let me break that engagement shows what sort of a lady she was.'

However, Wilbert was anxious about Margaret's condition and telephoned their doctor, who arranged for her to go into Stroud Hospital for the Friday night. That afternoon, John Forryan, the local Rector, took the Awdrys to the hospital and Wilbert saw Margaret settled in before leaving. It was to be a final parting, for at twelve midnight, Wilbert – asleep in Lechlade Vicarage – was awoken by a telephone call to say that Margaret was dead.

During the evening at the hospital, Margaret had got up, had her supper, and then returned to bed. She was reading a book when she had a sudden and fatal heart attack.

Wilbert cancelled his appearance at the shop's opening and went with Hilary and her husband Alfred to their home, not far away, in Highworth. On the Monday, Wilbert's daughter took him back to Stroud and a house empty, yet full of memories. 'I was,' he now recalls, 'utterly at a loss. I felt as if part of me wasn't there.'

There were also vague feelings of guilt. If Wilbert had cancelled his engagement and Margaret had not gone into hospital, he might have been with her when she died. However, there would have been nothing that he could have done to prevent his wife's death and, since he might not even have been in the same room with her at the time, it would have been as great a shock, if not worse, for him to have found Margaret dead. And what guilt he would have then experienced.

After the funeral, at the local parish church in Rodborough, Wilbert went to stay with Veronica, Richard and family at Kingsteignton in Devon. A month later he was home in Stroud, answering letters of condolence, one of which had come from his old friend and former editor, Eric Marriott. 'Even after nearly a month,' wrote Wilbert, 'I and our children are still in something of a daze at the suddenness of it.'

Wilbert's letter to Eric Marriott, is a testament to his feelings for Margaret:

> Margaret was a wonderful wife for a diffident author to have. It was entirely due to her, when *The Three Railway Engines* existed only in pencil on the backs of old circular letters, that they ever got off the ground at all, and started something which has, amazingly, continued for 40+ years.
>
> She was special to Christopher, Veronica, Hilary and myself, of course, but we never realised till she died, and letters came in from all over the country how special she was to others too.
>
> She had a wonderful gift, not only of making friends wherever she went, but of keeping them too . . . We are now trying to pick up the pieces and live for the Re-Union . . .

For a while it seemed to Wilbert that he wished that Re-Union to come sooner rather than later. 'An epitaph I had once read,' says Wilbert, 'kept going round in my mind: "She first departed; He, for a short while, tried to live without her, liked it not and died." '

A month after returning to Rodborough Avenue, it seemed as if Wilbert's dark hope might be fulfilled as he entered what was undoubtedly the bleakest period in his life. Wilbert was living alone, fiercely independent and (despite Veronica and Richard's willingness to move nearer to Stroud) determined not to impose upon his children.

Wilbert had been having problems with badly ulcerated legs, often being in so much pain that he would sit up all night rather than struggle upstairs to bed. He was due to go into hospital for treatment in September 1989, but found himself there sooner than he had expected. Each week Wilbert had a taxi to take him to Rodborough Church, so that he could put flowers on Margaret's grave; one day, on the return journey, he got out of the car and fell down in the road. With the help of a passer-by, the taxi driver got Wilbert back into the car and took him to the Emergency Department at Stroud Hospital. Wilbert was found to have fractured his hip.

When Hilary first visited him in hospital, she was alarmed to see how sharply her father seemed to have gone into decline: 'I had never seen him so low and depressed.' Wilbert was taken first to Gloucestershire Royal Hospital for the planned ulcer treatment, which involved having a lumbar puncture, and was then transferred to Standish Hospital to be given therapy for the hip. His physical difficulties apart, Wilbert was deeply depressed, telling Veronica: 'I don't want to go back into that house.'

In order that he shouldn't have to return to Rodborough Avenue, Hilary and Alfred had Wilbert to live with them and their family at Highworth. While there, he had another fall and was admitted to the Princess Margaret Hospital, Swindon. To Hilary and Veronica it seemed that their father's depression, combined with the fact that, being in a private ward, there wasn't any particular pressure on him to get up and get out of the hospital, meant that he wasn't making very much attempt to get better.

Hilary found a small residential home in Highworth and the hospital told Wilbert that if he could learn to walk, he could be discharged. Some of Wilbert's old resilience of character returned and, in just one or two days, he was getting around on arm crutches.

Wilbert left hospital and the next few months were spent in care. Apart from the staff, there were only two other residents, both female; Wilbert passed the time watching television, reading books and doing crosswords, but missed conversation and gradually began to wish that he could now return to his home. The solution came with the discovery of Universal Care, an agency in Beaconsfield, who were able to provide live-in carers who could look after clients and provide much needed companionship.

Hilary and Veronica finalised arrangements and some necessary changes were made to the house in Rodborough Avenue: Wilbert and Margaret's bedroom being made into a room for the carers (who were to come on a rota basis for set periods of time) and one of the smaller spare rooms being made into a bedroom for their father.

Wilbert was at home once more, but uncertain, at first, how things were going to work out:

> I had got so used to doing what I was told, to obeying the rules and not having any real preference of my own, that when my first carer, Pamela Smith, asked: 'What time do you want lunch?' I replied: 'When it's convenient.' Pamela looked at me and said: 'It's your house, you make the rules; when do you want your lunch?' In this way, bit by bit, she made me make the decisions; and along the way, we'd 'josh' each other, and I found that I was laughing more than I had done in the last six or seven months.

Pamela Smith was the first of a number of carers, many of whom have become return visitors to 30 Rodborough Avenue. One of these, Melanie White, who did a good many rounds of duty for Wilbert before leaving the service, clearly enjoyed his company as much as he enjoyed hers and confessed that, compared with many clients, working for Wilbert was 'as good as a rest!' Melanie and others who were prepared to show an interest in more than just Wilbert's day-to-day needs and to respond to his interest in them and their lives, found themselves becoming as much friends as professional carers.

There were still hurdles to be overcome – including two cataract operations: one in the spring of 1990, and the other in 1991 – but, after a terrible year, Wilbert embarked on a new lease of life. In October 1990, he was able to attend a service where his daughter, Hilary, was licensed as a lay reader in the Church of England, and, long before that, he had managed to visit several special railway events.

Although, only a few months earlier, it had seemed an impossibility, Wilbert attended a celebration at the Great Western Society in Didcot to mark the forty-fifth anniversary of the Railway Series. The three-day jamboree in June 1990 attracted some 25,000 people and received a phenomenal amount of press coverage.

The following month, Wilbert attended a special birthday party in York at the National Railway Museum's Great Railway Show. The National Railway

Library had chosen the Awdry books to have a permanent place in its collection of historical railway books in recognition of the fact that 'they have played an enormous part in arousing children's interest in railways'.

Such occasions, however, were not applauded by all. In a smugly irate article in the *Evening Standard*, entitled 'All steamed up over Thomas', Charles Jennings denounced the books' literary style as 'at best workmanlike, and at worst, narcotic' and declared that they made 'terrible, repetitive, predictable reading' and were only redeemed by pictures of C. Reginald Dalby, which had set the tone for the whole series :

> At first glance, the illustrations look pretty inept – a fumbled complement to the teak-like prose they accompany. But for all their awkwardness, they manage to convey the sense of a bright, clean, unvandalised world, located somewhere in a mythical 1950s . . . Thomas and Friends only get dirty when they plough into a coal bunker or plunge into the sea. The rest of the time they shine like jewels under the clear, rainwashed sunshine of a welfare state Britain. Meanwhile, lads in shorts jump up and down when Henry flashes by; there are numerous porters and station masters around to deal with passengers' enquires; the roads are empty and clean; the trees are in leaf; ladies wear Swan and Edgar coats and carry parcels.

Charles Jennings' final condemnation was to compare the Railway Series with the 'frankly unreadable' books of Beatrix Potter; both, he maintained, were 'notionally works of literature, in reality made popular by their illustrations'.

A few days later, in an article in the *Independent* – 'On the right lines for a bestseller' – Miles Kington was also examining the illustrations to the Railway Series: 'The first thing I have noticed is that the drawings need not be world-class – in fact, they should if possible be pleasantly amateur . . . You know if a train is going fast when it has white speed lines drawn along it. You know when it is stationary when its smoke is going straight up in the air . . . '

Kington's article – prompted by being on a train 'overrun by hordes of merry children, off to Didcot for Thomas the Tank Engine's birthday party' – was also critical of the texts: 'The plots need not be too inventive – actually, the same plots recur again and again, with minor variations. The chase plot, often between bus and train, the naughty-trucks plot, in which an engine gets knocked about by wicked wagons; the crash plot, the bad-weather plot, the derailment plot . . . Life in Thomas' world is, frankly, a series of disasters, and in the real world there would be a national outcry about a line so badly run.'

All of which led Kington to speculate (as many others have done) on the extraordinary popularity of the series:

> What matters is that the engines are not engines at all. They are all little children. They behave as children do: wilfully, joyfully, stupidly, thoughtlessly, completely selfishly . . . This is not just a child's world – it is a child's view of the world as well. The grown-ups deal out all the punishment and praise, and get none themselves. They seem above any emotion except anger. And no train is ever allowed to do anything by itself. The prevailing feeling of the books swings between the wild exuberance and the abject misery and repentance that only a child knows.

Although, five years later, Miles Kington refers to his article as 'a bad-tempered piece', and admits to having enjoyed the books about Thomas when he was a child – 'Some of the stories are good. The ones before he ran out of puff' – he remains unrepentant of his critique. Baulking at having to read the books to his seven-year-old son ('who likes Thomas and his chums') Kington has invented 'another engine called (more daringly) Oscar the White Engine'!

A public outcry, around this time, about another popular nursery hero, Enid Blyton's Noddy, prompted a satirical letter to the *Guardian* from one of the paper's readers, Jim Prior:

> Having read about plans to bring the Noddy books up to date, my son and I (ages 15 months and 36 years respectively) are concerned that Thomas the Tank Engine may be the next victim.
>
> Like Noddy, Thomas dates back to the 1940s, and some might say that the stories show their age. There is, for example, a distinct class system amongst the rolling stock, from Gordon the Express Engine at the top, to the troublesome (working-class) trucks at the bottom. Where women do make an appearance, they adopt conventional female roles; Annie and Clarabel are carriages, forever being pushed around by Thomas, while Daisy the Diesel is a silly creature, concerned predominantly with her appearance.
>
> Worse still is the attitude to gays. When the fastidious Henry refuses to come out of the tunnel because the rain will spoil his nice red [sic] paint, he is ostracised by all. Is the tunnel here a metaphor for the closet?

The writer concluded by expressing the hope that he and his son would manage to collect all the books before some 'well-meaning but over-zealous editor' introduced 'equal opportunities for all employees (including the trucks)' and had 'the Fat Controller running the crèche'.

As is often the case, satire turned out to be prophetic rather than reactionary. Within a few months, newspapers – from the *Stroud News and Journal* via the *Times Educational Supplement* to *The Advertiser* in Adelaide, Australia – were full of headlines: THOMAS IS SHUNTED OUT OF THE NURSERY; SEXIST TAG FOR THOMAS; END OF THE LINE FOR MACHO THOMAS?

> Thomas the Tank Engine was feeling out of sorts. Gordon and Henry were miserable too. 'I'm not a sexist,' sniffed Gordon, who pulled the express trains. 'Just because we boys have all the adventures.'

It was March 1991 and the headlines were referring to a 40-page report 'on gender equality' drawn up by John Westerby, Chief Education Officer of Dudley in the West Midlands, which questioned the desirability of having the Railway Series books (as well as those about Postman Pat and Spot the Dog) available to children in the council's eighty-five nursery and primary schools. The report, which was intended for consultation and discussion, but which was quickly labelled by the press as being an order for Thomas to be banned, pointed out what had been remarked many times before – that the engines are male, while the female coaches were merely pulled and shunted: 'The message, even if unintentional, conveyed to young minds is clear: men lead, women follow . . . '

Curiously, many of the issues raised by Dudley Council's report had been addressed a year earlier by David Wright of the University of East Anglia. In an article, 'Thomas goes to school', for *Child Education*, Wright suggested ways of capitalising on young children's fascination with – and extraordinary knowledge of – the books in the Railway Series. As well as such suggestions as teaching youngsters about the way in which steam engines operated, there were a number of interesting discussion topics suitable for primary school children:

> The world of Thomas is set in an idealised picture of the 1940s and 1950s. What has changed for the better – and for the worse – since then? In those days, freight travelled by rail, not road. Is that a good idea for today, too? They will also notice the pollution of steam-engine smoke, few family cars, and frequent train breakdown.

David Wright also offered a positive approach to those issues which others would soon be listing as evidence of the Thomas books being 'dubious material':

> All the engines are male and the coaches female. Although this is sexist, it is a fairly accurate picture of the 1950s, when most of the people with power were male. With modernisation comes Daisy the (female) diesel railcar, who is a very welcome innovation, showing that we no longer want the world run entirely by men.
>
> The author is a clergyman, and almost every story raises moral issues. Laziness (Henry), arrogance (Gordon and James) and foolhardiness (Percy) are considered to be bad, while kindness (Edward) and hard work (Thomas – sometimes) are virtues. Most infant teachers and most young children find these values to be part of the key to harmony in the home and the classroom.
>
> In one respect, the engines have a value system which is unacceptable. Their attitude to the trucks is based on discrimination. Yet, without the trucks, much of the purpose and usefulness of the railway would vanish. Can the children suggest ways of creating a positive attitude towards the trucks?

The outcry which came, months later, over the charge of sexism was fierce. Mr Awdry responded in his usual forthright manner, telling the *Gloucester Citizen*: 'I think it is a load of codswallop and you can print that in large print.' Equally strong condemnation was reported in the *Leicester Mercury*, where Mrs Audrey Boston, the widow of the Reverend Teddy Boston (the Fat Clergyman) who had died in 1986, was quoted as saying that the criticisms were 'complete rubbish'.

Eric Marriott wrote to the *Daily Telegraph*, accusing Dudley's chief education officer of being 'thoughtless and prejudicial' and pointing out that when one of Thomas' stories had been translated for a French magazine, 'Thomas became Thomasine, since French railway engines are generally regarded as female.' Marriott added: 'I am not aware that any French educationalist objected to that role reversal; more important I am sure that little French boys relished the story and pictures about Thomasine just as much as little English-speaking girls continue to love the Thomas books.'

Britt Allcroft, in a letter to the *Birmingham Post*, wrote: 'Thomas and his friends are neither "male" nor "female": they are magic'; and a similar view was expressed by *Leicester Mercury* journalist, Joan Stephens, who described Thomas as 'a fantasy figure whose activities make rattling good stories. They're not morality plays, and they're not message bound.'

For some people, however, the stories were seen as having a very clear – if unexpected – message. It is astonishing that, despite being described by some critics as poorly illustrated and shoddily written ('the repetitive plots, the tedious characterisation, the really thin dialogue and the ever-recurring situations of farce and confrontation'), the Railway Series has nevertheless, been the target of much elaborate analysis and exotic interpretation:

> Whether or not you have children, it is sometimes difficult to escape the smug, self-satisfied beaming presence of Thomas the Tank Engine. Thomas resembles one of those preposterous idealised figures of Stalinist propaganda. Face radiant with a dream of heightened productivity. In fact, Stalin would probably have approved of Thomas, who always does what the Fat Controller tells him and strongly disapproves of other engines who step out of line. Whenever one of Thomas' fellow engines shows sign of independent thinking and disobeys instructions, you can be sure that the troublemaker will, literally, go off the rails. The underlying message is simple: conform to society's expectations and you will be rewarded, rebel and you can expect to be punished.

This article, 'Back down the track' by Mike Jarrett, appeared in an occasional column in the *Guardian* entitled 'Reputations'. The author showed a creative flair for polemic: 'women and workers both know their place. The coaches, Annie and Clarabel are content to tag along with Thomas, going wherever he takes them and cooing at his manly feats and superior wisdom. The workers, that grey, grimy mob of troublesome trucks, occasionally stage mindless rebellions until some rough shunting puts them back where they belong.'

However, Jarrett also displayed a singular ignorance of the subject about which he wrote with such fervour. The author of the Railway Series was called 'Rev. W. B. Awdry', the first stories were said to have been written in 1945 when 'an unexpected Labour victory held out a promise of radical social change' (they were written in 1943 and *published* in 1945); and Christopher Awdry was wrongly credited with having introduced 'modern' characters for the television scripts, such as Harold the Helicopter, Daisy ('an eyelid fluttering flirt and a lazy worker') and Diesel ('sly, threatening and black'). 'Stylishly recreated and updated for television,' wrote Jarrett, 'the Thomas the Tank Engine stories remain as unpleasantly narrow, conformist and backward-looking as ever.'

The ever-loyal Eric Marriott entered the fray with a letter to the editor in which he dismissed Mike Jarrett's article as an 'ill-tempered, unjustified and misplaced attack'. The piece, said Marriott, was a 'gallimaufry of extreme silliness and a gratuitous insult to an author whose books, for three generations, can claim to have enchanted millions of children and to have given them their first steps towards literacy and a love of books.'

Writing to thank Eric Marriott for his support, Wilbert wryly observed: 'It seems to be the fashion lately for jumped up critics to try and debunk established authors by reading into them preconceived ideas which are and were never there at all . . . I think after 45 years or so that Thomas and Co are capable of standing on their own for what they really are.'

The *Guardian*'s editor, responding to Marriott's protest against the paper's 'ridiculous attempt at character-assassination', claimed that the article was 'only a personal piece of knock-about opinion designed as much as anything to stimulate debate'. In closing, he observed: 'My daughter certainly likes playing on her (overpriced) Thomas the Tank Engine loco.'

That toy locomotive would have been part of the vast array of character merchandising resulting from the Britt Allcroft television series, *Thomas the Tank Engine and Friends*. It had started in a very simple way, in 1984, with jigsaw puzzles. Allcroft's husband and business partner, Angus Wright, explains: 'We had to find a way of raising the money to put on the screen what Britt wanted to see there. That is how we discovered character licensing.'

The business of selling permission for products to be produced using the copyright images of Thomas and the other engines began at the Harrogate Toy Fair where Allcroft, clutching a handful of the Railway Series books, attempted to interest companies in the idea of buying a license to use Thomas and the others on a variety of toys, games and puzzles. 'Some people,' says Britt, 'remembered the characters, but an awful lot didn't; some of those who remembered thought they might have a go, others said, "You are mad! Today's generation haven't ridden on a train, let alone seen a steam engine!" '

Jigsaw manufacturer, Michael Stanfield, was the first licensee and one of only a handful at the time when the series began being televised. Subsequently, the phenomenal interest shown in the series and its narrator, Ringo Starr, prompted many other manufacturers to sign up to use the Thomas image on a vast range of products.

Although the finance which these licensing activities provided was essential to the success of the Allcroft series, the company imposed and maintained strict standards on the way in which the Railway Series characters were used. In Allcroft's words: 'Anything that lets Thomas down or lets a little child down does not make me happy . . . '

Angus Wright recalls an instance of what he describes as his wife's 'creative unreasonableness': a sample of merchandise was brought for

Allcroft's approval which, for various pressing business reasons, the manufacturer was desperate to get into production. The item featured Thomas the Tank Engine with his characteristic short stumpy funnel and short stumpy boiler, but *sans* his short stumpy dome. When the manufacturer's notice was drawn to the omission, he protested that it didn't matter and that no one would notice. Britt Allcroft, insisting that the standards they had were maintained, refused to approve the product.

Thomas merchandise ranged from children's clothes to nursery china to sweets and comics, but there were also model engines – some powered by clockwork, others by electricity – and, just as Wilbert had based his characters on different classes of real engines, so Hornby Railways began producing models of those very engines, such as an L.N.E.R. class A3 Flying Scotsman or a G.W.R. 0-6-0 pannier tank, suitably transformed – with liveries and printed faces – into their Sodor counterparts, Gordon and Duck.

With *Thomas the Tank Engine and Friends* into its second series in 1990 and the earlier films selling more than a million copies on video, a number of preserved steam railways wanted to make use of the Railway Series characters. After all, Wilbert Awdry had links with virtually all of these railway lines; indeed, the Talyllyn, the Bluebell, the Ravenglass and Eskdale and the Snowdon Mountain Railways had all either been featured in the Railway Series or were known to have inspired one of the railways of Sodor. As a result, in agreement with Britt Allcroft, they were permitted to run fund-raising 'Thomas the Tank Engine Days'.

The railways paid only a token fee of one pound to obtain a licence for such a day, which usually involved real engines being 'dressed up' to look like various engines in the Railway Series. These events – often supervised by a portly gentleman posing as the Fat Controller – were, for many children, their first experience of real steam locomotion, and it was the promise of seeing the characters made popular by the books and television films that drew them there.

There were, however, some members of railway preservation societies who found the notion of attaching a cut-out face to the smokebox of an authentic engine and 'playing Thomas' an anathema: 'It demeans our professional image,' wrote one critic, while another complained that faces on engines 'disfigure fine pieces of railway engineering'. To make matters worse, the opponents of 'Thomas Days' were, nevertheless, forced to admit that these activities succeeded in raising large sums of much-needed money that could not have been earned without the Tank Engine's help. The real problems began, however, in 1991 when Britt Allcroft's company decided to revise their terms. The license fee was increased to £100, and the railways had to agree to pay an additional percentage commission on the 'gate money'. Since some of the events were attended by hundreds of thousands of visitors, this represented not inconsiderable sums.

If the original one pound fee – which was obviously notional and bore no resemblance to any payment required from one of Allcroft's commercial licensees – was an altruistic gesture, then the change came as something of a shock to the railway societies. To make matters worse, there were those who felt that Wilbert's personal dedication to steam – and the fact that the Railway Series had drawn inspiration from some of the preserved railways – gave them proprietorial claims on his characters. The copyright in those characters, however, was not owned by Wilbert Awdry.

Negotiations took place between Britt Allcroft and the Association of Independent Railways, as a result of which new, lower terms were discussed. These, however, were not acceptable to the Association of Railway Preservation Societies, whose then Chairman, solicitor David Morgan, wrote to Wilbert (a Life Member of that organisation) in the strongest terms:

> The long and the short of it is that there is now a huge ground swell of anger and resentment over what many see as a rip-off. Thomas the Tank Engine is fast becoming a dirty word and there is even a move afoot by our members to ban Thomas books – and all your other railway books – from being sold on preserved railways. Having been brought up on your books, sir, I find this all very sad. The view expressed by many is that Thomas and his friends have been tarnished by greed . . .

Wilbert, who was now 80, felt distressed and harassed by an issue that was not of his making and over which he had no personal control. He was particularly aggrieved by the implication that in selling the Railway Series books and *Thomas the Tank Engine and Friends* character merchandise the preserved railways were doing him and the Britt Allcroft 's company a favour:

> In actual fact my engine books have, ever since 1945, been best sellers in their own right and have, through two generations played a considerable part in creating a climate of opinion in favour of steam railway preservation, and the enthusiasm and interest which makes it possible. The sole reason for holding 'Thomas Days' is not to do us a favour, but to be a money spinner for the Preservation Society concerned. In other words appropriating and using our copyright for their own financial benefit.

In June 1991, an angry headline appeared in the magazine, *Steam Railway:* 'Steam lines face showdown over Thomas.' There were, as David Morgan's letter to Wilbert shows, still more points of contention:

> The licence agreement now requires us to make it clear that the engines with faces and any men dressed in top hats are not the real characters or the real Fat Controller respectively. Can you imagine anything more daft? Think of the impact on children a notice in Santa's Grotto would have if it declared that 'this is not the real Father Christmas' . . .

This stipulation was imposed because, in the words of Angus Wright, 'Britt's guiding principle has always been that Thomas' young fans must never be disappointed by him, no matter where they meet him.' In a letter to Wright, Wilbert expressed his own concerns on this subject: 'It distresses me too when pseudo Thomases, not in the least like Thomas in the books, are paraded up and down with blue paint and a No. 1. I comfort myself, however, with the thought that children are not that stupid and that the magic of their imagination can effect the necessary transformation.'

There were more meetings and discussions. 'If parents and children are to be attracted to a Thomas day,' Angus Wright wrote to Wilbert, 'we must try to arrange that those running it are prepared to understand and support certain basic ground rules about how your characters are represented: and that above all, families go away feeling that they've had value for money, having had a Thomas day which was not simply a visit to a railway which has added painted face discs to its locomotives for the day.' As to the special links with some of the railways, Wright added:

> We have made it clear that societies like the Bluebell line, the Talyllyn and now the Eskdale Railway, which actually own locomotives which you and Christopher have written into the Railway Series are perfectly entitled to exhibit them on that basis. Further, we are glad to encourage societies who wish to develop fantasy stories about their own engines without mentioning Thomas to do that; and of course for that they require no licence from us.

A few scheduled Thomas events were cancelled and one or two hostile remarks appeared in print; one railway, announcing a non-Thomas 'Friendly Engines Weekend', said that they were 'sick and tired of hearing of faces upon other engines and singularly unimpressed by the repeated antics of a certain blue tank engine'. A peaceful solution was finally reached in August 1991 with agreed payments of a £100 flat fee, plus 5% of admission receipts up to £10,000 and 10% of sums beyond that. After a tempestuous time, relationships between Britt Allcroft (Thomas) Ltd. and the Association of Railway Preservation Societies have now settled down into a harmonious, and lucrative, partnership.

The Thomas image became an extremely potent symbol. Britt Allcroft (Thomas) Ltd. keep a photograph album, stuffed with pictures of Thomas appearing (mostly without the granting of any permission) in a variety of guises and showing himself to be – in the somewhat affected language adopted by the company – part of the 'Furniture of Life'. These photographs show children in Thomas fancy-dress costume or consuming Thomas birthday cakes, or building Thomas sand castles, or posing in front of ice-sculptures in Japan. There are other pictures of unsightly gas-tanks painted to look like Thomas and Friends and entrants in the London Marathon running inside an improvised cardboard Thomas.

Speaking of the qualities which made the television series such a success, Angus Wright says: 'There was the original unique magic, the stories as told by a father to his son; secondly, you have this extraordinary form of animation which was new and beautifully realised, and the result was popularity.'

That popularity begins at a very early age. 'Children,' says Britt Allcroft, 'start watching films at nine months, drawn to the imagery and sounds; when, they are 1½ to 2 years old, they start taking in the stories and then they maintain their interest until they are six or seven.' As with the original books, the success of the films is, in no small measure, due to the pleasure which they also gave to the parents and grown-ups who not only watch them with children, but – recognising an integrity in the stories – encourage them to do so.

In 1988, Britt Allcroft began plans to launch *Thomas the Tank Engine and Friends* in the U. S. A. Although a quintessentially British creation, the Railway Series had long had admirers in other English-speaking countries including the United States. However, the decision to find a way onto American television was undoubtedly a challenge. As in so many ventures, fortuitous coincidence played a role: it happened that the New York television station 13 W.N.E.T., which had helped develop the highly successful children's series, *Sesame Street*, was seeking a successor for placement in the Public Broadcasting Service schedules. A meeting between Britt Allcroft and Rick Sigglekow of W.N.E.T. resulted in the creation of *Shining Time Station*, a series of thirty-minute programmes, set in an enchanted railway station.

Featuring live characters in an essentially situation comedy format, *Shining Time Station* showcases two stories of *Thomas the Tank Engine and*

Friends in each episode. The stories are introduced and narrated by 'Mr Conductor', a tiny, 18-inch-high railway guard, who magically appears with a Disneyesque scattering of pixie-dust, in order to tell the stories and point the moral. Portrayed first by Ringo Starr, and later by George Carling, Mr Conductor recounts the adventures of Thomas, Edward, Gordon and the rest in much the same way as they are told on British television – with one or two cultural adjustments, such as 'trucks' becoming 'freight-cars' and the description 'Fat Controller' (considered 'size-ist' in politically-correct America) changed to 'Sir Topham Hatt'.

Shining Time Station proved an instant success. Letters flooded in from parents ('The stories involving Thomas and his friends are great teaching, good fun, and get right to the relationship issues that all of us have to deal with') and from children ('I love your show. My brother Eric, loves it, too.'); while the press fuelled what the *Washington Post* called 'a burgeoning cult':

> 'Parents like [Thomas] . . . He's positive, bright, happy, wholesome, clean cut and teaches good lessons. All of us should watch him more . . . '
>
> '*Thomas the Tank Engine and Friends* have introduced the mystique and joy of the railroad to a new generation . . . '
>
> 'Who can resist those wondrously expressive, happy and sad faces and luminous eyes . . . '
>
> 'It's full of self-affirmation techniques and lessons that young children can apply to their own lives . . . '

Although Angus Wright maintains that if you are concerned about messages you need the services of Western Union, the Thomas episodes on *Shining Time Station* clearly had something to say and a writer on the *Village Voice* reached the conclusion that Wilbert Awdry's stories were, in their own way, subversive, since – in the liberal New York of the 1990s – they served to reinforce authoritarianism, order and discipline: concepts which children like and want.

The *New York Times* observed that interest in Thomas had 'raced across the country like a high-speed train'. Within just six weeks of its first broadcast, the series was nominated for two Emmy awards: for Ringo Starr as 'Outstanding Performer in a children's series' and for the series' director, Matthew Diamond who went on to win the award for 'Outstanding Direction'.

The Americanisation of Thomas has been phenomenal: 25,000 people surrounded the New York store, Bloomingdales, to see the famous tank engine at the end of a whistle-stop tour; a sell-out musical stage show, '*Shining Time*

Station – Live! featuring *Thomas the Tank Engines and Friends*'; and an appearance by Thomas at the head of the children's television contingent in President Bill Clinton's Inaugural Parade.

The success in America has subsequently been repeated in other parts of the world: in Canada, Australia and Japan, where numerous special events and exhibitions have been held and where 'Thomas mania' is a serious rival to the long-established popularity of Mickey Mouse.

In 1992, a third series of films – made at cost of £1.3 million – was launched in Britain. For Wilbert, however, the results were a disappointment; as he told a local reporter: 'They have gone off the rails!'

Newspaper headlines announced 'TV wrecked my Thomas' and 'New Thomas series is "on the wrong track" ', and it wasn't difficult to see why Wilbert felt that to be the case, since the stories no longer read like an Awdry text:

> Henry the Green engine has lived on the Island of Sodor for many years. He wouldn't want to be anywhere else. He likes every part of it from the fields filled with flowers to the white, sandy beaches, but there is one place that Henry enjoys visiting more than any other.
>
> His driver knew this too. 'Come on Henry,' he would sometimes say, 'we've made good time today, we'll stop for a while by the forest.'
>
> The forest was full of broad oaks and tall pines. Henry always felt better for being here. He couldn't quite explain why . . .

Not only was the flowery prose a far cry from Wilbert's economic style, but the rules of railway practice were totally ignored: 'What really irritated me,' says Wilbert, 'was a story called "Henry's Forest": Henry goes to look at the forest which is nonsense to start with; the trees grow close up to the track, which would never be allowed, for risk of fire; and to have the driver remark that because they've made good time, they can stop and rest is just rubbish! It couldn't happen – if an engine stopped in the middle of a section, the signal box at either end would have to be alerted.'

The story-lines in earlier film series had remained close to the books, but the 52 films that had been produced had used up a lot of plots. True Wilbert had written 105 stories and Christopher a good few more (some of which had already been used in the previous series), but many featured less well-known engines – such as Skarloey, Sir Handel and others – rather than those on which the television series had originally been founded. The use of such stories would require the making of expensive new models and necessarily limit the number of appearances by the better known engines – especially the series' eponymous hero – Thomas.

At first Thomas was introduced – or, as Wilbert more accurately puts it, 'crane-shunted' – into dramatisations of stories in which he had never originally appeared and onto lines where he would have no reason to be running. Then new stories, featuring Thomas and the other engines considered to be the most popular, began to be written. 'They don't contain any reality at all!' Wilbert complained. 'My stories were based on unusual mishaps which had actually happened to some engine, somewhere, sometime, and so had a proper railwaylike explanation. Some of the new stories that have been dreamed up by Britt Allcroft and David Mitton – like the nonsensical "Henry's Forest" – could not have happened on any railway anywhere and merely reveal their lamentable ignorance of railway matters. That such rubbish should be credited to me is a gross insult!'

As a result of Wilbert's public denouncement of the new series – several national newspapers carried the 'Tale of Thomas and the Very Angry Old Man' – a 'certain coolness' descended on the relationship between the creator of the Railway Series and its re-creator. Defending her decision to devise new stories, Britt Allcroft says: 'My first responsibility was to the audience, to make sure we were making twenty-six films, of the very high standard that we expect, which told stories through the screen.' This suggests a subtle shift in emphasis, that is borne out by a current press release from Britt Allcroft (Thomas) Ltd. A fact-sheet, 'Talkabout Thomas', carries the heading: 'Britt Allcroft's Global Classic "Thomas The Tank Engine & Friends" – *What It's All About*.' And what – or, rather, who – it's all about, is Britt Allcroft:

> Creating an enduring character able to consistently capture the imagination of children around the world is a true feat, and one that is the achievement of *Thomas the Tank Engine & Friends* . . . Britt Allcroft's films (promoted and marketed by Britt Allcroft (Thomas) Ltd.) have won for Thomas the Tank Engine a place amongst the very few true classic characters like Mickey Mouse, or Kermit the Frog, whose appeal transcends race, age or language . . .

There is, however, no mention of the Reverend W. Awdry.

Without doubt, Britt Allcroft brought the Railway Series, in a superbly realised form, to a far wider audience than it had hitherto received; and she masterminded an impressive merchandising programme of a very high standard that, unlike many other television-related 'fads', has maintained its place in the market. But she did not create the Thomas the Tank Engine.

Publicity for Britt Allcroft's company speaks of Allcroft's 'enormous artistic talent'; of the company's relationship with its partners ('a knowing of

one another and a spirit of commitment'); and of its 'mission': 'to entertain, and through entertaining to help nurture, support and enrich the lives of our audience.' Or, to put it another way: 'We make money,' says Angus Wright, 'because we make magic; but we can only make magic if we make money.' According to press reports, in 1994, the value of Britt Allcroft (Thomas) Ltd. was estimated at £50 million.

As a result of these reports, British newspapers were suddenly full of the story that Thomas was also earning his creator substantial sums of money. There were features and articles – some blazoned on the front page – with such headlines as: THOMAS EARNS THE REV AWDRY £7 MILLION (the figures differed in virtually every report), THE CHURCH MOUSE AND HIS MILLIONS and FAT PAY PACKET FOR THOMAS'S CONTROLLER.

Reporters who telephoned Wilbert for comment declared themselves astonished by the fact that he wasn't ex-directory; journalists who travelled to Stroud to interview him, came away surprised by the modest life-style of someone they described as 'one of Britain's richest retired clergymen'; while journalists who wrote their stories without doing their research, described Wilbert as living in a 'tumble-down cottage'.

A year later Wilbert was back on the front pages with a headline in the *Daily Telegraph:* 'Women bring Thomas into line.' The story, arising from the fact that Britt Allcroft was filming a fourth television series, was that Thomas, 'cheery hero of the steam train era' had 'run into the buffers of political correctness'. It was difficult to avoid a sense of *déjà vu*:

> The ultimate male bastion of children's TV is about to be breached by more forceful, female characters. The cosy fraternity of Thomas, Percy, Henry, James and Gordon, under the paternalistic eye of the Fat Controller, is to gain gender balance . . .

The truth about this dramatic innovation was that Britt Allcroft was planning to feature such 'new characters' as the Refreshment Lady, Nancy the guard's daughter, Mavis the diesel engine and Caroline the car, all of whom had been originally created by Wilbert Awdry, at least thirty years earlier. It was simply one more instance of re-writing (or mis-writing) the history of the Railway Series.

In 1989, Ralph Percival, a young student from Staffordshire, wrote a thesis entitled 'Has Success Spoiled Thomas the Tank Engine?' Subtitled: 'An account of the development, and effects of increased exposure of, the "Railway Series" books by the Rev. W. V. Awdry', the thesis examined the history of the series and its subsequent marketing. It concluded that Thomas' huge popularity and his ability to sell had turned him into what Percival described as a 'cheap' product:

> Rather than an established product with origins in the 1940s, he must surely be seen by many as a recent invention, perhaps even owing his very existence to the television series. From this point of view, the generally well designed merchandise, coupled with the successful marketing that it has enjoyed, has in most cases overlooked the fundamental virtues of the original product . . .
>
> Since 1984, Thomas has suffered at the hand of his television twin. At first the two worked together very well, but the twin soon got greedy. Such is his greed that he soon forgot the reason for his existence and such is his power that he might easily destroy Thomas.
>
> Thomas, however, is made of stronger stuff, and will still be with us long after his twin has gone . . . for he is a *really* useful engine.

Whatever eventually becomes of Thomas' television twin, the tank engine himself remains resolutely on the right rails, with Christopher Awdry at the controls. The Railway Series has continued with *Toby, Trucks and Trouble* in 1988 and, the following year, *Thomas and the Twins.* In 1990, Christopher wrote a book about the small engines on the Arlesdale Railway entitled *Jock the New Engine*, although the new character in question (inspired by the Ravenglass and Eskdale Railway's 'Northern Rock') had first been mentioned in *The Island of Sodor*:

> *JOCK (Arlesdale Railway. Livery: Pale yellowish green, lined out in dark red.)*
>
> *A 2-6-2 tender locomotive built at Arlesburgh in 1976 to the designs of Ivan Farrier, the Company's Chief Engineer.*
>
> *As yet there is no illustration of Jock in the books. The shade of green used for his livery is reminiscent of that used for a time on the former Highland Railway, so it is only natural that he should be named Jock.*

Information which, four years later, Christopher incorporated into his book:

> *'He puts me in mind of ma days in Scotland,' Douglas remarked. 'Some o' the engines up in the Highlands were yon colour. Jocks, we used to call them.'*
>
> *'Jocks?' asked the new engine, stopping nearby.*
>
> *'Aye,' agreed Douglas. 'No' a bad name for yoursel' I'm thinking, eh, Jock?'*

Christopher Awdry had ideas for other new characters: 'I once submitted an outline for a new engine named Barry and got the response that children wanted Thomas and the others, but that they didn't want new engines.' Recalling this, Christopher lets out a long, slow breath that sounds like steam coming from an engine. 'But I haven't altogether given up; you could say Barry is dead but not yet buried!'

The clamour for more books that were either about or named after Thomas (another side-effect of the television series) resulted in *Thomas and the Great Railway Show,* published in 1991 and inspired by plans for Thomas celebrations at the National Railway Museum in York. In a delightful series of illustrations (that nevertheless break all Wilbert's rules about engines with faces!) Clive Spong depicts Thomas at the Railway Museum, standing alongside recreations of Stephenson's Rocket (face-less) and the Iron Duke (with heavy, grey eye-brows and a walrus moustache) as well as Green Arrow, Duchess of Hamilton and a snooty-looking Mallard.

After various exploits and mishaps, Thomas is made 'an honorary member of the National Railway Collection', and goes home to Sodor in the 1992 title, *Thomas Comes Home*, in which Daisy gets snowbound (despite her boast: 'A few flimsy flakes can't stop me.') and has her passengers rescued by Harold the Helicopter.

In 1993, Christopher returned to that most troublesome of all the famous engines, as he was to explain in the book's 'Foreword':

> When I went to see Henry recently he was moaning about not having a book to himself for ages.
>
> 'Yes,' I agreed. 'There's the story about patching up your smokebox . . . '
>
> 'And the time my wheel broke,' he interrupted.
>
> 'What about when you came out of the Works before you had been properly painted?' I said.
>
> 'You wouldn't . . . !' he said.
>
> But I would and I have. It might teach Henry not to try and tell me what to do.

That story 'Henry Sees Red', in *Henry and the Express*, tells how the proud engine who had been painted green, then blue and then green once more, was being repaired at the works and was painted all over with a red undercoat – 'like tomato sauce' – only to get called out on an emergency to pull an express before there was time for his green top coat with red stripes to be put on. The incident was one of the first which Christopher had collected for himself from a speaker at The Railway Correspondence and Travel Society, who recounted just such an anecdote about an engine of the Jubilee class.

While Christopher was keeping the engines of Sodor steamed up and running, the Railway Series was also inspiring satirical comment on the way in which the Other Railway was being run. It was in 1993, that *Private Eye* began serialising Incledon Clark's stories of 'Thomas the Privatised Tank Engine'. This witty series, foreseeing the dark days that might follow the privatisation of British Rail, began with the sad story of what happened, one morning, when Gordon was required to pull a non-stop train:

> 'We're going too fast! We're going too fast,' shouted Gordon's carriages. And Gordon rushed through the station . . .
> Thomas's passengers, who caught Gordon's train into the big city every morning, were very angry. They summoned the Fat Controller.
> 'Gordon does not stop here any more,' he explained.
> 'But whyever not,' they cried.
> 'This stop is unremunerative. Cutting it out means Gordon can get to the big city three minutes quicker.'
> 'Then how are we to get there every morning?'
> 'Turn right out of the station and a hundred yards on your left you'll find the Nissan car showroom. Thank you,' he said, and disappeared into his office . . .

No such dire events, however, could ever possibly take place on the Island of Sodor, where life continued happily, in the thirty-eighth title in the Railway Series, with the introduction of a very special engine – *Wilbert the Forest Engine*. It was in 1983 that Wilbert Awdry had become president of the nearby Dean Forest Railway. At the time Wilbert had told reporters that his function would be 'purely decorative', but a few years later, in September 1987, the railway decided that its president's name should decorate the boiler of a 0-6-0 Hunslet saddle-tank engine.

Once Wilbert had become an engine, why not have him appear in the Railway Series? Recalls Christopher:

> I couldn't think of a way of having Thomas meet Wilbert. I didn't want Thomas to visit the Dean Forest Railway – I had done something similar when I had sent him to York. Nor did I want Wilbert simply to be invited to Sodor, because father had done that with Stepney. But suppose Duck and Oliver were getting hard pressed on their little branch line – what kind of engine would the Fat Controller like to have as an addition? There was no reason why he shouldn't choose an 0-6-0 Hunslet, like Wilbert. So I had the Fat Controller borrow Wilbert from Dean Forest Railway, not on a whim

because he wants a holiday or because Thomas wants to meet him, but for the perfectly logical reason that he wants to conduct some trials.

Wilbert the Forest Engine was published in 1994. There was a curious sense of completion: Christopher Awdry writing about an engine, named after his father, meeting Thomas the Tank Engine whom Wilbert had created, almost fifty years before, in order to amuse Christopher.

The end of another era came on 27th October, 1994 when, after a severe deterioration in his health, Wilbert's brother, George Awdry, died at the age of seventy-eight in St Thomas' Hospital, London. Fellow steam and model railway enthusiast, companion on numerous rail holidays, scholar and librarian and fellow historian of Sodor, he was memorialised, during his lifetime, as Albert Regaby (6th Baron and 1st Viscount Harwick) in *The Island of Sodor:*

> *. . . His tastes were literary and he added judiciously to the historical side of the [Cronk] Abbey Library. He also played an important part in encouraging his cousin, the Rev. Nicholas Dreswick, in the preparation of his definitive History of the Island of Sodor, 4 Vols. (Chatter & Windows, Suddery 1899-1912)*

George Awdry's funeral was held on 3rd November, 1994, in Bath, a city for which he and his brother held great affection and which they had visited many time as youngsters. Confined to his bed, Wilbert was unable to join the rest of the family at the service. When, on that day, the present writer visited him in Rodborough Avenue, Stroud, the conversation ran chiefly on George's unique contribution to the creation of the Island of Sodor and on the various railway exploits in which the brothers had shared.

One memory from the Awdry brothers' 1958 visit to Portmadoc in Wales was of Wilbert walking the line, finding and hammering home loose keys, while George 'Spoonered' – a process of locomotion which Wilbert had described in his notes on the trip:

> To 'Spooner' is to walk along the line in the manner which Charles Easton Spooner is said to have used. He would walk along one rail balancing himself with his walking stick on the other. George got quite proficient; W. would come to grief as his aim with walking stick was not so good. W. preferred walking on one of the rails and using walking stick on sleepers between them.

Although ill health had prevented Wilbert and George from meeting for some years, there was a finality about this latest of several partings. The first had been Wilbert's good friend, Teddy Boston, who had shared his calling and his passion for railways, real and model. Then Margaret, who had urged Wilbert to submit his railway stories for publication and had done so much to encourage the continuation of the series, had gone. And now, it was George: the only person in the world, other than Wilbert Awdry, to appreciate fully the complex minutiae of fact and fiction that constitutes the history of the Island of Sodor and makes for an understanding of the ways of its people.

The present writer was looking through some notebooks on the afternoon of George Awdry's funeral when a letter, which he had written to Wilbert many years before, fluttered to the floor. It closed with what might serve as a suitable farewell: 'All apposite salutations to all denizens present or absent.'

Destinations

'THE first thing you will need to do is to go through that red loose leaf binder.' It is a few days after the televising of a B.B.C. television documentary about Wilbert Awdry, in which we had both appeared, and our conversation – until this point – has been largely about the programme's shortcomings. Now it is my turn. During the writing of this book, I haven't once been asked to gloss over controversial issues or to omit any of the negative criticisms that have been voiced about the Railway Series. I have been given complete freedom to report and interpret matters howsoever I choose. But where I have left things out because my researches are at fault, those omissions have quickly been drawn to my attention. 'If you go down to the study, you will find the folder on the bookcase on the long wall . . .'

Once again, I am in the Station Master's office. As I look around, I can't help but notice that whilst the shelves are full of books and journals that are mostly about railways, they are *not* about the railways of Sodor. The large relief map of the Island still hangs over the fireplace and one or two small models of the Railway Series engines stand on the mantelpiece. But very few of Wilbert's own books are in evidence here and none of the recent plethora of entertainments with which the children's shelves in bookshops and libraries are stacked.

There are none of the numerous Thomas Pop-Up Books, Lift-the-Flap Books or Peep-through Books. No titles such as *Thomas and the Hide-and-Seek Animals* illustrated by Owain Bell, in which immaculately air-brushed engines encounter a variety of exotic animals that have escaped from a circus train and turn up in the most surprising places – such as a trio of sealions who invade the ornate 'gingerbread'-style railway-sheds. No sign either of *Thomas and the Dinosaur*, *Henry Goes to Hospital* or any of the other books by Ken Stott, who has taken the classic engine shapes drawn by Dalby, Kenney, Edwards and Spong and rendered them anew as nursery pictures, sharply drawn in bold lines and flat, primary colours; the engines faces no longer grey and round, but white and oval; less like real steam locomotives with faces than toytown trains.

Nor are there any of those charmingly produced early-learning, easy-to-read books for which Thomas has been appropriated and turned into an educator, teaching children how to count: 'One Fat Controller; Two sacks of coal'; how to spell, from 'A for Annie' to 'Z for James's buzzing bees'; or how to tell the time: 'At 7 o'clock Thomas starts out on his first journey of the day with Annie and Clarabel.'

What an extraordinary legacy it is: a literary, publishing, merchandising and financial phenomenon. Some fifty million Thomas books in all shapes and sizes from *Thomas's Big Railway Sticker Book* to the *Thomas Noisy Book* which – at the press of a finger – chuffs, toots, rattles and says 'Really Useful Engine' as many times as a child may like, for as long as the batteries last!

Speculating on this seemingly inexhaustible success, former Managing Director of Reed Children's Books, Ingrid Selberg has remarked: 'Thomas is set in a timeless world apart, and while other phenomena come and go, Thomas seems to be there, solidly without any sign of going away.'

So are Thomas and the other Famous Engines destined to go on and on? When I had asked Britt Allcroft that question, she certainly seemed to think so: 'Can you imagine Thomas not chugging away? My favourite image of Thomas is the big close up of him, where his eyes are looking one way and there is a smile on his face that says "What's happening? What's round the next corner? What's the big adventure?" It's a mischievous face and a friendly face; it's a face full of curiosity and that's what any little child identifies with and draws fun from – and, to a certain extent, inspiration and comfort.'

Christopher Awdry didn't seem to have any doubts either: 'I have no thoughts of giving up. I am doing what I've always wanted to do. I enjoy finding subjects for stories and I enjoy writing – I think I would still write even if I didn't get paid for it!' His thirteenth title (half the total number of books written by his father), *Thomas and the Fat Controller's Engines* commemorates the fiftieth anniversary of the publication of *The Three Railway Engines*, the little book which began it all:

> *'I know what a jubilee is,' announced Henry. 'It's an engine called* Bahamas *–*
> *I met him at Crewe.'*
> *'Isn't it a sort of party?' asked Percy. Thomas and I took some Scouts to one once . . .'*
> *'That was a Jamboree,' put in Thomas with a chuckle.*
> *'Oh, was it?' said Percy. 'Sorry.'*
> *Gordon smiled.*
> *'Actually, it's a train,' he said knowingly. 'Flying Scotsman told me. The Silver*
> *Jubilee used to run from London in the old days.'*
> *'But we're not in London,' objected Henry.*
> *'And if it is a train, why do we need it?' put in James.*

'We don't,' interrupted a well-known voice. 'Our Jubilee is a Golden one, because in 1995 it is fifty years since stories about us began to be in books. I thought it would be a good idea to celebrate.'
'It is *a party!' squeaked Percy excitedly.*
The Fat Controller laughed.
'Sort of, Percy,' he agreed. 'I haven't worked out all the details yet, but you will all know about it in plenty of time.'

The fictional celebrations include a visit to Sodor by a Royal Personage who recalls having heard about the engines from the Queen, and who, perhaps, used to enjoy the books of stories about them and even read them aloud to his brothers . . .

On the mainland, the Golden Jubilee of the Railway Series is marked by a special exhibition at the National Railway Museum in York about Wilbert Awdry's life and work; and, most appropriately, the naming of a real engine (sadly an electric rather than a steam locomotive but, at least, *not* a diesel!) 'The Reverend W. Awdry', an InterCity 225, which will run services on the InterCity East Coast line between London and Glasgow and Edinburgh or London and West Yorkshire.

There was a time when journalists called Wilbert Awdry, 'The Puff-Puff Parson', a phrase which rather annoyed him. Today, he has become an institution and the many epithets used of him are usually affectionate ones, such as 'The Thomas the Tank Engine Man'.

But, however he is referred to, Wilbert knows that, despite a lifetime's service as a Church of England clergyman, it is as the creator of Gordon the Big Engine, Henry the Green Engine and the others that he will be remembered. In 1992, following the death of Graham Greene, the *Daily Telegraph* columnist, 'Peterborough', asked who might succeed to the title 'Grand Old Man of English Letters?' There were, it seemed, various contenders for this unofficial post: William Golding, V. S. Pritchett or Anthony Powell. As far as 'Peterborough' was concerned, however, there was only one runner: 'The Rev. Wilbert Awdry, creator of Thomas the Tank Engine.'

Wilbert, of course takes all such nonsense – flattering or critical – in his stride. He has never been over-bothered about what people say of him; nor need he be – after all, he has earned himself the love of millions of children, from who he still receives scrawly letters:

Dear Rev, I am surprised that Duck hasn't got a book to himself. He is my favourite. Please make one up. *Yours* David M Whitaker

'Dear Mr awdry Mak A Lot Of Train BookS SO they are Plenty in the ShopS . . . LOVe from GeOffrey Searle

If Christopher Awdry wasn't already providing new titles for the Railway Series, there would certainly be plenty of other potential authors ready to take up the pen:

To the Rev. W. Awdry I think that you are a very tallented writer about trains even though there are no steam trains left on british rail but thanks to you you have brought them to life again with the books you have pubblished over the last few years. I was wondering if I could help you with your book writteing I have all ready made a book about Thomas and Pearcy so if you would lick me to help you it would be my deuty to help you . . . If you had finished the books a few years ago could you give me promissen to write at least one book pleses. Thank you very much.
P.S. write back soon
PSS I would love to be a book writer.
Love from Sam

And the same goes for potential illustrators:

Dear Reverand Awdry Since I was a little baby I was fascinated with trains . . . I'm a Rector's Son Too, like CHRISTOPHER . . . I have nearley all your Thomas Books. Thomas is my favourite engine. I think your Thomas Books are marvellous. I have sent you a picTure of a Train comeing down the north Wales coast. Love Deinol Pritchard can you write To me pleas

With such letters as this, come charming, wobbly, colourful drawings of the characters which – largely as a result of the television series – have now come to be known as *Thomas the Tank Engine and Friends.*

At first sight, the description 'and Friends' might seem somewhat inappropriate, considering the rivalries that go on in the stories. The engines call each other names, play tricks on one another and make fun of those who meet with downfalls – especially if such disasters have arisen from unattractive aspects of behaviour such as pride or arrogance. Newcomers to the line are frequently resented and mistrusted; and 'outsiders', such as Bertie the Bus, Terence the Tractor and Harold the Helicopter, are treated with dislike, even contempt – until they have, somehow, proved their worth to the society into which they have so rudely intruded.

The reader is inveigled into identifying with the attitudes and behaviour displayed by, what one of Mr Awdry's young correspondents called, the 'almost human engines'. Grown-ups may even acknowledge that the engine community is right in following the principle that, once confrontations have been sorted out and differences resolved, everyone tries to get on with everybody else.

Analysing the 'magic' of Thomas is a difficult, probably fruitless, undertaking. It is clear, however, that the stories convey a simple philosophy. 'Thomas the Tank Engine's resilient appeal,' writes Mary Cadogan, 'springs from the author's flair for creating what is today referred to as "the feel-good factor". The stories project a mood of expansive optimism and idealism, with Awdry conveying positive social values by niftily coating the pill of moral comment with the jam of joyous adventures.'

Discussing that 'moral comment' in what was probably the first critical analysis of the Railway Series (published, some twenty years ago, in *The Journal of the National Book League*) Denis Butts wrote:

> The main reason for the success of the books surely lies in the peculiarly moral world they capture so vividly . . . a moral world where engines who get bumptious and think they can control themselves end up in ditches; and engines who boast about their skills arrogantly and insult other engines often have to rely on their help when they break down.
>
> And over all this moral universe of Sodor, where laziness and cheekiness are punished, not externally but by bringing their own disasters, and where modesty and perseverance are rewarded, there presides a stern but just Fat Controller. Originally a figure of fun in the early books, where he was liable to have his shiny hat blown off and eaten by goats, he has gradually come to play an increasingly sympathetic part, not unlike a parent, as the series has developed. For it is he who decides not merely what engines shall pull what trains where and when, but is essentially a moralist of the track, strict but fair with the lazy and conceited engines, but quick to forgive and forget the faults of the contrite ones who have learned their lesson. He is a part of the recognisably real and moral world which is profoundly important and satisfying for young children. Knowing the upsets and accidents of their own lives, they see something very like them in these railway stories, and find an order and pattern there which is oddly reassuring, even while it excites and entertains.

Back upstairs, clutching the red, loose-leaf binder, I ask Wilbert how far he feels that his personal philosophy is contained within these stories: 'This world,' he says, 'is God's world. He makes the rules. We have free choice, we can obey him or disobey him; but we cannot choose to disobey him and live happily our way. If we disobey, we bring trouble on ourselves and other people.'

As always, he makes an analogy with his steam-engine characters: 'Like us humans, they go their own way and, inevitably come to a sticky end. Then the offender has to show that he is sorry and accept his punishment.' He pauses thoughtfully. 'But,' he adds with emphasis, 'the point is, they are punished, but they are NEVER scrapped.'

In the world depicted in the Railway Series, there is always redemption and forgiveness, another opportunity to try harder to become a Really Useful Engine. And, in the real world, where humanity is forever claiming (as British Rail advertisements once did) that it is 'getting there' and then demonstrating that it obviously *isn't*, Wilbert's philosophy is deeply reassuring and will no doubt guarantee that, for many years to come, he and his steam engines, will hold a special place in the world's affections.

And how, I venture to ask, would he hope to be remembered? He smiles as if anxious not to seem immodest and replies slowly: 'I would like my epitaph to say, "He helped people to see God in the ordinary things of life, and he made children laugh".'

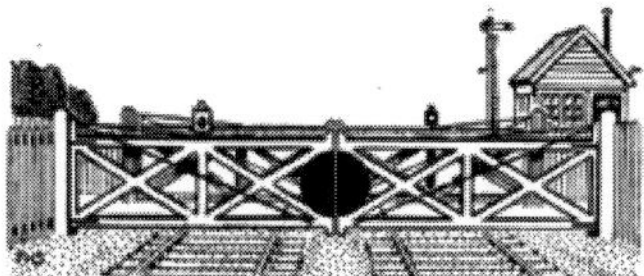

INDEX

Roman numerals refer to Plates
Names in *italics* refer to publications